CONOR CRUISE O'BRIEN

To Katanga
and Back

A UN CASE HISTORY

SIMON AND SCHUSTER

For Máire

Contents

Illustrations

Maps

Katanga and the Copper Belt

Map of the Congo

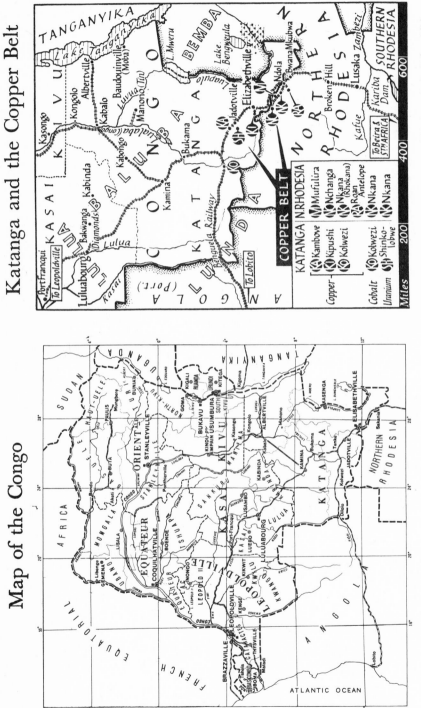

This map is reproduced by courtesy of Methuen & Co Ltd, publishers of *An Atlas of African Affairs* by Andrew Boyd.

'The reader will observe that we were a mixed staff acting under an international syndicate. On the whole I am inclined to pronounce that such enterprises are less likely to succeed than those conducted on more homogeneous lines. Political considerations naturally cause a company thus constituted to adopt a somewhat flabby and vacillating policy.' – JOSEPH A. MOLONEY, *With Captain Stairs to Katanga* (1893).

'In fact our [Belgian] policy reflected both a background of sheer funk (obsession with the Algerian war) and a rather Machiavellian calculation. . . . He [de Schrijver, the responsible Belgian Minister] granted independence immediately, but without carrying out any of the reforms urged by M van Bilsen. The reason for this is that he never intended conferring on the Congolese anything more than a purely fictitious and nominal independence. The financial circles concerned firmly believed – as for our political circles, they were more naïve than anything else – that it would be enough to give a few Congolese leaders titles of 'Minister' or 'Deputy', with decorations, luxury motor-cars, big salaries, and splendid houses in the European quarter, in order to put a definite stop to the emancipation movement which threatened the financial interests.' – M. STAELENS, in *La Relève*, August 27th, 1960.

INTRODUCTION:
STAFF REGULATION 1.5

'All which, Sir, though I most powerfully, and potently beleeve; yet I holde it not Honestie to have it thus set downe.'
Hamlet

Secretary-General

December 15th, 1961

Dear Mr O'Brien,

In view of the press reports of certain statements made by you following your resignation, I wish to call your attention to Staff Regulation 1.5 which is as follows:

'Regulation 1.5: Staff members shall exercise the utmost discretion in regard to all matters of official business. They shall not communicate to any person any information known to them by reason of their official position which has not been made public, except in the course of their duties or by authorization of the Secretary-General. Nor shall they at any time use such information to private advantage. These obligations do not cease upon separation from the Secretariat.'

It will be noted particularly that in accordance with the final sentence of this regulation these applications [*sic*] do not cease upon separation from service, but, on the contrary, continue in effect.

Yours sincerely,

(Sgd.) U THANT

Acting Secretary-General

B

1

When I resigned from the foreign service of my own country,
following my extrusion from the service of the United Nations – in
the circumstances set out in this book – I did so, as I stated at the
time, 'in order to recover my freedom of speech and action'.[1] Staff
Regulation 1.5, were I to consider myself still bound by it, would
deny me that freedom. Under the second sentence of this regulation,
I should have submitted the manuscript of this book to the Secretary-
General and awaited his authorization for the publication of those
lengthy, frequent and important sections which contain information
known to me by reason of my former official position on the
Secretary-General's executive staff and as Representative of the
United Nations in Katanga. It is – to put it mildly – extremely
unlikely that such an authorization would ever have been granted.
By authorizing publication, the Secretary-General – any Secretary-
General – would be taking official responsibility for a personal
account of some critically important events: an account which,
besides being obnoxious to some members of the United Nations,
is different from, and in part inconsistent with, the official UN
version already given of the same events. No Secretary-General is
likely to assume such a responsibility. The observance of the
regulation, therefore, would, in practice, constrain me to silence.

I do not consider myself now still bound by the staff regulations
of an organization which I have no longer the honour of serving,
and I have not submitted the manuscript of any part of this book
to the Acting Secretary-General.

I am conscious that some of my former colleagues – and among
them some of those whom I most respect – are likely to deplore my
decision, and many things in the pages that follow. The publication
of a candid, personal account of the events in which I was involved
as a servant of the United Nations is contrary – in what I gather,
from certain reticences, to be their opinion – not merely to the letter
of the staff regulations but also to the spirit of the organization's
discipline. Furthermore, the actual content of the account will not,
on this view, serve the interests of the United Nations, and part of it
will play into the hands of its enemies.

These observations cannot be dismissed lightly. It is not enough
to reply – adapting a famous phrase of Marshal Juin's[2] – that the
discretion of ex-officials is not the discretion of officials. When I
resigned, in order to tell the story of my strange experience, I
thought that in doing so I was serving the interests of the United

---

[1] The text of my resignation statement is in Appendix III.
[2] 'La discipline des Maréchaux n'est pas celle des sergents.'

Nations. If I did not still think so, if I thought the opinion of these former colleagues well founded, I should not feel justified in having this book published. The impediment would not be Staff Regulation 1.5; it would be the belief that the United Nations, with all its defects, is the most hopeful political institution that human beings have developed.

It is quite true that parts of this book will seem, at first sight, 'to play into the hands' of the enemies of the United Nations; the truth, after all, rather often does seem to 'play into the hands' of undesirable people. If serving the interests of the United Nations were the same as portraying the organization, as it now is, as impeccable and infallible, then most certainly this book does not serve the interests of the United Nations. It contains many passages which suggest that the Security Council, the General Assembly and the Secretariat itself are less than perfect. Some of these passages are likely to be quoted, with unwholesome approbation and with small regard for the wide context, by people whose dislike of the United Nations is inspired, not by any of the organization's imperfections but by the great hopes which it carries and especially by its power of leverage in the cause of freedom. There are people, as François Mauriac has said, whose approval is crushing and the risk of such approval is the most unpleasant of the hazards to which the writer of a narrative like this is exposed. The risk could, of course, be avoided by suppressing all those elements in the narrative which may seem damaging to the United Nations. In that case, however, the narrative would be significantly falsified, partly incomprehensible and entirely unworthy of publication.

Whatever value this story has derives from the attempt which the writer has made to tell the truth. Some of the difficulties inherent in such an attempt are considered later; for the moment the points I want to make are that the attempt is worth making and is in the interests of the United Nations. That the attempt is worth making, in a general sense, will be obvious to anyone with a historical consciousness; that it is in the interests of the United Nations is not so obvious, yet can, I think, be established. The publication of the truth may provide an opening for malevolent criticism, yet, without such publication, constructive outside criticism, of which the organization stands in need, becomes impossible. No organization is very good at telling the truth about itself. The Secretariat of the United Nations is less inclined to the *mensonge officiel* than are most of the member Governments but its reticences are profound, its ambiguities rich. To say this is not necessarily to condemn the

Secretariat, which is obliged, by the complex nature of its multiple
responsibilities to exercise an often tortuous discretion. It is, however,
precisely this servitude of the Secretariat, unavoidable as it may be,
which makes it desirable that one who carried, but no longer carries,
such responsibilities should resume a private citizen's freedom and
habit of relatively unambiguous expression. This outspokenness
may, or may not, be of *immediate* service to the United Nations.
In my own case I believe that my resignation statement – coming,
as it did, at the moment when hostilities broke out for the second
time between the forces of the United Nations and those of Mr
Tshombe – did render service of that kind. The public and true
accusation that Mr Macmillan's Government, as well as that of
Sir Roy Welensky, had encouraged and helped Mr Tshombe to
defy the United Nations in September, must have made it, I think,
a little harder for those concerned to provide such help and encouragement in December. This may not be entirely irrelevant to
the striking fact that, whereas the September operation ended in
Mr Hammarskjold's flight to Ndola, that of December ended in
Mr Tshombe's flight to Kitona, to seek reconciliation with the
Central Government. There were certainly other factors involved –
including the military strengthening of the United Nations following
the September deadlock – but the diminution of Mr Tshombe's
diplomatic support was real and did play its part. Now the interesting point, in the present context, is that whereas all the high
officials of the United Nations knew of, and strongly resented, the
help and encouragement given by Mr Macmillan's Government to
Mr Tshombe, the Secretariat could not possibly have denounced
these activities as plainly and publicly as an ex-official was able to do.
The Acting Secretary-General was obliged, possibly at the request
of a Permanent Member of the Security Council, to remind the
ex-official of Staff Regulation 1.5; but it is possible that the displeasure of the Acting Secretary-General may not have been, on
this occasion, entirely unalloyed.

The truth, however, cannot be relied on always to serve the
immediate interests of the United Nations, or any other immediate
interests. Some loyal servants of the United Nations will probably
consider, for example, that it would be better to allow the official
version[1] of the events of the morning of September 13th to stand –

---

[1] Paragraph 15 of Security Council Document S/4940 dated September 14th,
1961, Report of the Officer-in-Charge of the UN Operation in the Congo to the
Secretary-General, relating to the implementation of paragraph A.2, of the
Security Council Resolution of February 21st, 1961.

historically imperfect though that version is known to be – rather
than to offer, in substitution for it, the fuller and franker account
contained in Chapter XV of this book. Certainly the enemies of the
United Nations are likely to make some use of the account given
here. But the reason why they can make use of it is not that the
events described are inherently discreditable to the United Nations;
it is that the official version, hastily issued and mistakenly allowed
to stand, is in part misleading and in part untrue. The United
Nations is hurt, not by the truths now here published, but by the
elements of falsehood in the version which it itself has maintained
before the world. It is necessary, in the long-term interests of the
United Nations, that these elements should be purged from the
record; it is desirable that this should be done, not by an enemy
but by a supporter of the United Nations.

It is, I know, well to be wary of what exactly one is about, when
one makes this lofty claim: to tell the truth. First of all, I cannot tell
the whole truth about the Katanga events because neither I nor
anyone else knows the whole truth, or is ever likely to know it.
Even to make a reasonably near approach to that goal it would be
necessary to know, in addition to what happened at UN headquarters in Elisabethville – which is what I do know – also relevant
things which must have been happening in Brussels, both in the
Belgian Cabinet and at the Union Minière headquarters; in London,
both at Downing Street and in the City; in Leopoldville, at ONUC
headquarters, in the Central Government, and at the British,
French and American Embassies; in Brazzaville, across the river
Congo, where live Mr Tshombe's friend, the Abbé Fulbert Youlou
and his French advisers; in New York at discussions between the
Secretary-General and the Permanent Representatives of the major
powers; in Washington, at the White House and in the Central
Intelligence Agency; in Rhodesia, both in the entourage of Sir Roy
Welensky and at various private houses in the Copperbelt; in
Kolwezi and Jadotville among the leaders of the dominant European
population; finally in Elisabethville itself, at Union Minière
local headquarters, in the Cabinet Room of Mr Tshombe's
Government in the CSK building, at the homes of Mr Tshombe,
Mr Munongo and others, in the various Consulates, among the
Europeans in the Sûreté and at Gendarmerie Headquarters in
Camp Massart.

I can try to tell the story of ONUC, Elisabethville, during the
time when I was in charge there: about most of the other elements
in the story I can only guess, from what impinged, both verbally

and materially, on ONUC, Elisabethville. Relatively unsatisfactory as this is, I can see no alternative to it. To wait until the relevant records (in so far as they exist) become available (in so far as they ever do) about these other elements, would mean waiting until the whole story had ceased to hold any political relevance or public interest; waiting, in fact, until it had reached that stage, of total detachment from any contemporary preoccupation, which is – in the view of one school of academic thought – the critical symptom of ripeness for the historian's attention. Even if we accept that austere view, there are two cogent reasons why I should not wait to attempt to write a history of that kind about these events. The first reason is that, having been a protagonist in the controversies and clashes to be described, I am among the people least likely to be accepted as possessing the degree of detachment from the subject which this school postulates as necessary in the historian. The second reason is that my own account, the memoir of a protagonist, must be one of the sources – and, for one crucial phase, probably the most important source – on which that detached historian, the Oakeshott of the future, will have to draw.

I can well imagine with what caution, reserve and even suspicion, the historian will use his source. Memoirs occupy – for quite sound reasons – a lowly place in the regard of the professional historian. They are suspect for fallibility of memory, for intent of polemic or self-exculpation and for that extra share of human vanity which must be presumed in people who trouble to write and publish the story of events in which they were personally involved. To any retrospective account the historian prefers, when he can get them, scraps of contemporary evidence, not intended for the public eye, and, above all, not intended for 'posterity'. Only when he has wrung all that he can from such contemporary evidence does he fall back, reluctantly and sceptically, on the memoir material, and even then what he is most likely to take from it will be declarations against interest, if he can find any.

The main element of reassurance I can give this hypothetical historian is – rather paradoxically from his point of view – the fact of early publication. The events I am writing about still arouse fierce passions; there are many people living who know whether this part or that of my story is true; there are also many people who will be anxious, mainly for political reasons, to discredit my story. The historian, by the time he comes to use this source, will know to what degree it has stood the test of controversy. The second element of reassurance is more subjective, and I therefore offer it to him more diffidently. It is that I have undergone, and tried to benefit from, the discipline which is his own. One who has been taught by historians, and has tried to write history, is certainly still liable, when he comes to write of events in which he was personally involved, to all the usual failings of memoir-writers. But he is, at least, conscious of what these failings are and of the need to struggle against them. Even if he is writing a non-scholarly book he will wish to avoid writing a crassly unscholarly one, and even if he is writing for a relatively wide public, the consciousness of the sceptical attention of certain scholars will impose restraint on at least the wilder forms of retrospective self-indulgence.

It is important, at this point, to say a word about sources. The principal source for this narrative – historians will note with regret, and some others perhaps with relief – is my own memory: that memory whose functioning Staff Regulation 1.5 would bid me keep to myself. I possess some copies of contemporary official records, but they are sparse and I have used them sparingly (mainly in Chapter XV). When such records were not available I have checked my own memories, whenever possible, against those of other participants in the same events: in their own interests I refrain from acknowledging their invaluable co-operation. In the dating of events – the field in which memory is least to be relied on – I have found UN official reports and the newspaper dispatches of service. Neither source is wholly to be trusted as to facts but for the exact dates of remembered events they are extremely useful. The fullest newspaper accounts known to me are those of *La Libre Belgique*, and I have drawn on them fairly heavily. The editorial policy of *La Libre Belgique* was generally hostile to the United Nations Congo operation (and extremely hostile to me personally) but this fact renders its files all the more valuable as an aid and corrective to my memory. The great advantage of the running record in *La Libre Belgique*, over that in any English-language newspaper, derives from the fact that Belgian interest in news from Katanga was continuous, not sporadic. The French News Agency, Agence France Presse, gave, mainly for the benefit of its Belgian clients, a very full service and its correspondent, M Jean-Pierre Joullain, became probably the best-informed member of that amiable but curiously fluctuating body, the press corps of Elisabethville. The quality, as well as the quantity, of the news printed must be dictated by the needs of the ultimate consumer, the newspaper-reader. The Belgian reader wanted his newspaper to tell him, as fully and accurately as possible, what was actually happening in

Katanga. He did not want the reporter to tell him what to feel about these happenings; he knew what to feel already.

The only other sources of any significance available to me for the period of my stay in Katanga are the letters – written, mainly for security reasons, in Gaelic sprinkled with Russian – which I sent from Katanga to Máire MacEntee, now my wife. A historian would regard these as among my most valuable sources but in considering their evidence he would make an allowance for what he would assume to be a desire, on the writer's part, to present his own actions in a favourable light. I have no reason to question this assumption; indeed, phrases in the letters bear it out. Yet the letters are, on the whole, a reasonably accurate record of the situation as I conceived it to be at the time of writing: the favourable light was presumed to be more or less constant.

For the background of the Congo operation, as it had developed before my arrival, I have relied mainly – especially in Chapter IV – on the copious collection of documents, and detailed narrative contained in the two volumes and annexes of *Congo 1960* (J. Gérard-Libois and Benoit Verhaegen) and in the volume *Congo 1961* (Benoit Verhaegen) published by the Centre de Recherches et Information Socio-Politiques, Brussels (Dossiers du CRISP). The editorial committee of CRISP is made up, by its own statement, 'of men belonging to different socio-political groups and different scientific disciplines . . . teachers, scientists, jurists and publicists, assisted by trade union, political and other advisers'. Since the following pages contain some reflections on the policies and actions of some Belgians, it gives me particular pleasure to acknowledge here my debt to this collection, and to pay homage to the lucid intelligence and firm integrity which animate it, and honour Belgian scholarship.

To Katanga and Back is not a book about 'the situation in the Congo' or a history of the UN operations there or a treatise on the United Nations itself. The situation in the Congo was still unpredictably evolving, even while this book was being written. A history of the UN operation cannot be written until that operation is concluded – which is not likely to be soon – and it will probably have to be a co-operative effort, necessarily covering a much wider area, both in space and in time, than that with which I became familiar.

One man who had read my *Observer* articles asked me: 'Why have you nothing to say about the Communist set-up in Stanleyville?' The reason is simple: I have never been to Stanleyville and I do not know whether the 'set-up' there was Communist or not. The only Congo set-up I am at all competent to analyse is that in Katanga.

It would be interesting and rewarding to be able to tell the story
of how Mr Gizenga with the aid of volunteers from the Communist
countries defied and fought the United Nations; of how the
Secretary-General flew to Guinea – whither Mr Gizenga had made
his way after a conversation with the Russian Ambassador – to seek
peace; of how the Secretary-General's plane perished in obscure
circumstances near the airport of Conakry; of how the United
Nations then concluded a cease-fire agreement under which
Mr Gizenga returned to Stanleyville and there again raised the
flag of secession in Orientale Province; and of how leading Communist countries then demanded, and eventually obtained, the
removal of the UN Representative in Stanleyville who had, in
their view, 'lost the confidence of Mr Gizenga'. This would make a
magnificent story, which would arouse the just indignation of the
whole Western Press. It is not, however, what happened, and readers
of this book will have to be content with a story which, while in
many ways strikingly similar, has what will widely be regarded as a
fatal defect: the régime concerned is not Gizenga's but Tshombe's,
whose friends are not in Russia or China, but in Belgium, France
and Britain.

As regards the United Nations as an organization, this book has
no pretentions to compete with the many treatises which already
exist – notably Mr Herbert Nicholas's excellent *The United Nations
as a Political Institution*. Anyone who wants a comprehensive account
of, for example, the workings of the General Assembly, will do much
better to turn to Mr Sydney Bailey's lucid and impartial pages[1] than
to Chapter I of the present work. Chapter I, like the rest of the book,
is neither theoretical nor exhaustive: in so far as it deals with the
Assembly it is a participant's account of some aspects of that body's
political workings, as experienced in practice. As the way the
Assembly works in practice is significantly different from what
the records of its proceedings suggest, a participant's account has
its own value, complementary to that of more theoretical works –
much as a real-life equivalent of Fabrice del Dongo's recollection
of the great battle of Waterloo would be complementary to the
more stately and better arranged accounts of the military histories.
Similarly, as regards the main part of the book, dealing with the
Katanga events and their sequel, what you have here is not a detached survey, but the testimony of a participant at the centre of
these events. I have called it, in the sub-title, 'A UN Case History'.
This is not quite as precise as I could wish – case histories, after all,

[1] In *The General Assembly of the U.N.*

are normally written by the doctor, not the case, and here there is
unfortunately no doctor – yet it gives a fairly accurate idea of what
I have tried to do. In so far as I have succeeded, this story should be
of interest to those who want to find out, from study of how the UN
responded to one particular set of severe challenges, how its workings
may be made more secure and effective, to meet the not less severe
challenges which the future will assuredly bring.

In my resignation statement and subsequently, in the Press and
on television, I referred to some of these challenges and said how I
interpreted them politically. That interpretation was based on my
own experience and I in no way disavow it. On the contrary, I here
develop and amplify it. I believe that the bare recital of facts,
without interpretation (but necessarily with a principle of selection,
which must contain an unstated interpretation) would be more
misleading, because less candid, than an account like this, which
combines narrative with explicit interpretation. But in recount-
ing controversial events, I have resisted, to the best of my ability,
the inevitable tendency to allow the interpretation, itself derived
from the experience of the facts, to impose an all too satisfactory
retrospective pattern on the facts themselves. The narrative
section of the book will, I think, quite often puzzle or disappoint,
and may occasionally scandalize, those who agree most warmly
with its political conclusions. Personally, I regret this, being
temperamentally not much inclined to 'letting the Tory dogs
have the best of it', even momentarily. I can only say, to these
political friends of various shades, that this is indeed a case history
and that the doctor, who believes that the history of his case as a
whole points to certain conclusions, is obliged not to suppress
mention of any symptoms which might seem to others to point to
different conclusions, and not to heighten his descriptions of those
symptoms which tend to corroborate his diagnosis. The fact that,
in this instance, it is no doctor but the case himself who is trying
to write the history, does not in the least lessen this obligation; on
the contrary, it increases the need for vigilance in its discharge.

The story which follows is not so uniformly lugubrious as all the
clinical imagery suggests. There was, as the world knows, tragedy
but there was also, among that heterogenous collection of human
beings who made up the UN effort in Katanga, almost everything
else: contrasts in exotism, comradeship and suspicions, luxury
sometimes and occasionally squalor, heroism and prudence, great
talents and impenetrable blankness, hours of gaiety and of horror,
inexplicable arrivals and unforeseen departures, the kindnesses,

bafflements, sacrifices and laughter of Swedes, Indians, Irishmen, Canadians, Englishmen, Ethiopians, Frenchmen, Tunisians, Danes, Malayans (almost everybody except Belgians and Russians), all partly fused, under their blue caps, into something new – 'Onusians'.[1] Nor did Mr Tshombe's Katanga present a face of unrelieved gloom. It certainly had, for us in the United Nations, as well as for many of its own citizens, persistent sinister undertones – I should not like to encounter very often in dreams Godefroid Munongo's dark spectacles or the blood-shot eyes of that grisly refugee, the sorcerer Mantefu. Yet Tshombe's Katanga had also its carefree, even innocent, and sometimes farcical moments. These I like to remember and I have recorded some of them here. 'I am afraid', said a friend somewhat austerely, 'you may be going to write a funny book about the Congo.' I have not tried to write a funny book about the Congo but I have not tried, either, to exclude what seemed to me funny, from this account of events which culminated in tragedy. I take for guidance the opening words of an Irish tinker's story of his own harsh life: 'I was never a sadist', he wrote, 'but always tried to look on the bright side.'

---

[1] In French, especially the French of the Congo, the noun and adjective from ONU, *Onusien*, are in regular use; no parallel formation seems to have taken root in English but 'Onusian' has crept into use among English-speaking UN people.

1

A DELEGATE
AT THE GENERAL ASSEMBLY

'Quid vult concursus ad amnem?'
Virgil

'Who', Mr Macmillan was moved to ask one autumn day in 1961, 'is Conor O'Brien?'[1]

This inquiry was prompted by the news of certain United Nations activities in Katanga. Essentially, what Mr Macmillan seemed to want to know was: What kind of United Nations man is this?

It may be well, at the outset of this story, to answer Mr Macmillan by some account of my political outlook and of the United Nations experience I had, as a delegate at the General Assembly, before going to Katanga. These are relevant to what happened later – and more relevant to what was believed to have happened – and the account of General Assembly experiences should be of interest to those who would know something of the United Nations as it actually works in practice – the functioning political entity, as distinct from the ideal conception and the proceedings officially recorded.

Any attempt at candour in discussing the real workings of a human institution – be it parliament, university, trade union or business – is liable to attract charges of cynicism and of a desire to injure the institution in question. I would suggest, however, that it is often less cynical, and ultimately less damaging to the institution, to bring the realities of its life into public discussion, than to conceal them behind – in Mr Auden's words – 'a set mask of rectitude'. The Assembly, as a forum for mankind, has a most precious function,

---

[1] *The Daily Mail*, September 15th, 1961.

and the world would be in much more danger were it removed. At present, now that no group of powers has a safe majority there, the Assembly is a genuine centre of international bargaining, and a consensus achieved there has a valuable stabilizing effect. Indeed, one important and little-noted phenomenon of recent times has been the partial resuscitation, by the Assembly, of the Security Council, hitherto held to be paralysed by the veto power of the Permanent Members ('The trouble with the United Nations', as a lady remarked to me in Boston, 'is the Veto that the traitor Hiss sold to the Russians at Yalta'). If a consensus is achieved by delegations representing a wide span in the Assembly, and if a draft resolution embodying this is put in in the Security Council, then it becomes very difficult for any Permanent Member, even the Soviet Union, to apply a total veto. This has been shown by the Security Council's Congo decisions. There are considerable dangers in this – as we shall see – but it is undoubtedly an area of growth in United Nations authority. The Assembly then, despite the not always creditable, and sometimes comic, light cast on it in the following pages, has very valuable functions to discharge.

But we are not necessarily helping it to discharge these functions more efficiently if we pretend that mankind's representatives in that forum already behave spectacularly better than the rest of us – mankind at large – are in the habit of doing outside. The Assembly is, in a way, 'the conscience of mankind' – as its speakers so often claim – but the conscience is not necessarily clearer for being on the East River. The importance of what Mr Henry Cabot Lodge liked to call 'the cleansing power of debate' surely lies in the emergence of truth from among the competing 'official versions'. But it is impossible to describe this salutary competition without saying some things which seem unedifying.

My own experience of the Assembly was in and through the Irish delegation, and therefore my examples are taken from that delegation's area of activity and information. I am not seeking to imply that that delegation was central to the Assembly's work; it was central only to this particular writer's experience of that work, central only to the case history here recounted.

Ireland was admitted to the United Nations in 1955, and an Irish delegation took its seat in the Assembly for the first time in 1956. I had been put in charge of a newly-established United Nations section at Iveagh House, Dublin, the Headquarters of the Irish Department of External Affairs. In that capacity

I attended at every session of the General Assembly from 1956 to 1960–61.

Ireland, partly as a result of her neutrality during the Second World War and partly for other reasons, had been isolated from the world for too long and the mental atmosphere in our country had become uncomfortably musty and close. Our Parliamentary delegates to the Assembly of the Council of Europe seemed to devote their time to making speeches about partition: speeches which were designed to be read at home, but which unfortunately had also to be listened to abroad. As such politicians often do, they had underestimated the intelligence of the electorate; I believe that most Irish people read these speeches with a mixture of cynicism and shame. We felt we were involved in an interminable and sterile quarrel: a relationship with our fellow Irishmen which had become sterile because we had allowed it to remain a quarrel.

Like most of my colleagues at the Department of External Affairs, and like many other Irishmen, I hoped that Ireland would do better than this at the United Nations. My colleagues and myself were determined to do what we could – which was not necessarily very much – to see that it did so. For some of us, particularly the younger members of the Department, the ideal of what constituted good international behaviour was exemplified at this time by Sweden. Sweden's action in the international field was, as we saw it, independent, disinterested and honourable. The Swedes in international affairs did not spend much time in proclaiming lofty moral principles but they usually acted as men would do who were in fact animated by such principles. Their voting record was more eloquent than their speeches. It seemed to contain few or no votes against conscience: few or none of those votes which are cast for reasons of convenience or expediency – not to offend a neighbour or an ally who happens to be in the wrong – and are then justified at the podium by an anguished access of legal scruple. Sweden paid its share, and more than its share, for all the humanitarian and peace-making aspects of the UN work and sent out its men, soldiers or civil servants, on various more or less unpleasant or dangerous tasks as the work of the organization required. Sweden's willingness to sacrifice was already symbolized by the death of Bernadotte. But above all, the example of Dag Hammarskjold showed that, even in an organization most of whose members seemed to be guided by standards very different from those of Sweden, a few countries and people could achieve remarkable results. Hammarskjold more than anyone had given the United Nations a focus of moral authority which could attract an international loyalty, and use it in the cause of peace and justice.

We would have been ashamed to use such language (being more given to the elaboration of puns) but these were the common assumptions. We hoped that Ireland would become one of the very small (and mainly Scandinavian) group of delegations at the United Nations whose chief concern it was to safeguard that moral authority; the group which was known to have upheld the Secretary-General against interested pressure from more than one quarter. This group, we later found, was known to its members – rightly, we believed – as 'the decent countries'. The un-English boastfulness of this expression we ascribed to the unfortunate fact that England, under the Governments of Sir Anthony Eden and Mr Macmillan, was not a member of the group.

An independent, 'Swedish', line was what we hoped for. Knowing the unfortunate tendency of many of our countrymen to talk big and act small, what we expected to get was something different. The result, even initially, was considerably better than most of us expected. Mr Cosgrave, who headed our delegation on our entry in 1956, delivered a dignified and felicitous statement which considerably impressed the Assembly. Yet this, though an immeasurable improvement on expected form, was hardly conclusive. Suez and Hungary, as issues at the General Assembly, were 'sitters' from the point of view of Irish public opinion. It was right at that time to demand the withdrawal of the Anglo-French forces from Suez and to condemn the Russian attack on Hungary. But, whatever about France, to criticize England is never entirely unpopular in Ireland and as for Russia, a ringing denunciation was, in the circumstances, absolutely mandatory on any Irish politician who hoped to be re-elected. In short, the right positions were also the popular ones, and when the right and domestically popular courses were also those advocated by the United States, no inward struggle was required in order to know what to do.

It was when, in 1957, Mr Aiken came to head the delegation that we got to know about inward struggles and about pressure as a UN phenomenon. Mr Aiken, an old associate of Mr de Valera's, required little, if any, advice from us, his juniors and subordinates, on the subjects of the virtues of a 'Swedish' position, of resisting pressure, and so on. The views he had long held were along these lines and, being a man of integrity, he proceeded to put them into practice. In his first intervention he urged the advantages of a policy of disengagement in Central Europe; in his second, very soon afterwards, he explained why Ireland would vote for a discussion on the question of the representation of China in the United Nations.[1]

Then the pressure began.

Anyone who has experience of the United Nations, and wishes to discuss the realities of life there, finds it necessary to use, quite often, this word 'pressure'. Yet the oftener one uses it, the more likely one is to encounter scepticism, even a mild version of that polite but strained look which is evoked by tales of personal persecution. I have known discussions with high-minded, and theoretically well-informed, students of the United Nations to take a faintly nightmarish turn in this direction. When I have touched, in passing, on the means by which this or that delegate has been induced to see the force of (say) the State Department's point of view, I have noticed my listeners peering at me warily, as if allowing for the possibility that the next phase of the discourse would concern the ground glass that someone had been putting in my soup, or the tiny radio which had been maliciously screwed into the back of my head. Yet pressure is an objective phenomenon, not a paranoid one. Indeed, if this phenomenon is not taken into account, it is impossible to understand the voting pattern on any important question at the United Nations. This same phenomenon is also of no small importance in relation to the workings of the Secretariat, as I was later to find in and out of Katanga. What, then, is this pressure?

In one sense, it is simply a natural reality, a phenomenon of relative mass. When a large and powerful country expresses a wish to a small country within its politico-economic orbit, the mere expression of that wish necessarily exerts pressure. However great the benevolence of the large country, however fierce the sense of independence of the small one, that pressure remains, real and omnipresent like the pressure of the atmosphere, and as little to be resented by any sane person. But there is a secondary form of political pressure, more active and more variable; this comes into play in those cases – now increasingly numerous, as the number of small States itself increases – where the small decides to resist the 'natural', immanent, pressure of the large, and act in a way contrary to the wish expressed. What happens then depends on the importance of

---

[1] A discussion of the merits of these positions, and the reasons for taking them up, would bring us outside the framework of the present case history. Here the point is that they were new positions and unpopular in Western circles.

the thing wished, on the large country's degree of sensitivity to world opinion, on the small country's unity, prudence and tenacity (or lack of these qualities) and (increasingly) on the presumed posture of the *other* great power group. If the conjuncture of these factors is extremely unfavourable, the small country may have its Government and policy changed for it by external military force, either applied directly, as in the case of Hungary in 1956, or indirectly as in the case of Guatemala in 1954. In other extreme conjunctures, more favourable from the point of view of the small country, States like Egypt, Tunisia, Cuba and (to some extent) Poland have been able to hold on to their Governments and policies, against the threat or the reality of the use of force, direct or indirect, by a great power.

Clearly, extreme consequences of this kind do not flow from a vote at the United Nations – although the speeches and votes at the United Nations of a country like Cuba (or Albania) may do much to bring its relations with a great power to the breaking point. Normally at the United Nations what one might call the *casus pressūs* does not directly involve the vital interests of either the large or the small country, and the penalties for failing to heed the wish of the larger are not dramatic. The *casus pressūs* at the United Nations arises, typically, when a small country votes – less often, when it speaks – in a way contrary to expectations. Such expectations are often very precise. Barring revolutions, it can usually be confidently predicted, for example, that Bulgaria will vote with the Soviet Union, El Salvador with the United States, Cameroun with France, and Australia with the United Kingdom. The reasons for the coincidences of viewpoint are disparate, but the coincidences are highly reliable.

Those who depict the Assembly as an anarchic collection of small countries, constantly voting down, with vindictive glee, the great responsible powers, are wide of the mark. Most of the small countries have to exercise considerable discretion in the way they vote, because of their ties – very often coercive ties – with this or that great power. Great powers get crushing majorities against them – as Britain and France did on Suez – only when they do something very strange indeed. Even then, if the United States had chosen to support the Anglo-French action, it is quite certain that there would not have been a two-thirds majority against Britain and France, and very probable that there would have been a majority in their favour; the majority in favour, however, would have been hard to get, and getting it would have weakened the diplomatic position of the United States. That is one reason why the exercise was not undertaken.

Apart from genuine satellites, like Bulgaria and El Salvador, there are other cases where reasonably safe predictions may be made, but on the basis of a more complex calculus. Thus Pakistan, say, likes, as a member of CENTO, to vote with the West, but is also sensitive to Afro-Asian opinion, particularly sensitive to opinion in Moslem countries and strong on self-determination (Kashmir). A Western canvasser can therefore safely count on Pakistan's vote in a direct East-West controversy (Cuba, Hungary) but must make separate calculations if relevant racial, religious or colonial factors are involved. For example, in a 'colonialist' issue, where the 'Moslem' factor tells on the 'colonialist' side (Cyprus), or where the Kashmir issue comes into play (Goa), the West may reasonably expect Pakistan's support. On the other hand, on a straight racial issue (*apartheid*), or an issue where a Western power is, or has been, in conflict with Moslem populations (Suez, Algeria, Tunisia, Israel), Pakistan will be indistinguishable from the most anti-colonialist Afro-Asians. On issues where both anti-colonialism and the cold war are involved – for example, the Soviet moves on the liquidation of colonialism – accurate prediction of a Pakistan vote becomes impossible. It is in such cases that experienced Western tacticians become fertile in procedural motions designed to get countries like Pakistan 'off the hook' – and safely on to the Western bank – while sparing them the humiliations and dangers which loom when an Asian country casts an obviously 'pro-colonialist' vote.

As long as a given country – Pakistan or another – votes according to such an established and accepted pattern, its delegation leads a comfortable life at the United Nations, on reasonably good terms with all. If, however, a country departs from its pattern in any particular, its delegation will receive some uneasy looks; if the departure is on an important question, pressure will begin immediately. This is what happened when Mr Aiken, having already spoken in favour of a measure of disengagement in Central Europe, announced his intention of voting in favour of a discussion on the question of the representation of China.

Floor-lobbyists of the major powers – 'arm-twisters' as they are regrettably called – carry in their heads sets of assumptions about the delegations they try to influence. These assumptions are seldom made explicit, and they may not even be verbally formulated in the minds of these pragmatic men, but they guide their conduct. If we can suppose the existence of a notebook for such assumptions, in this case as used by a Western delegation, I think the relevant entry in this Manipulator's Manual would have run, when Ireland was admitted to the United Nations, somewhat as follows:

'IRELAND: Refused to join NATO, on grounds of Irish claim to control a part of the United Kingdom (so-called 'Question of Partition'). Is, however, strongly *Roman Catholic* and therefore *anti-Communist*. Political leaders and officials are conscious importance of ties with United Kingdom and other Western European countries, but obliged to take into account *anti-British* and *anti-colonial* elements in electorate.

Conclusions: Absolutely safe on straight East-West issues.

Needs watching on 'colonial' issues and following tactics are suggested: Emphasize pro-Communist character of relevant 'independence movement' (Algeria, Cyprus, etc.); stress absolutely no parallel between historic movement for Irish freedom and Communist-led risings in uncivilized countries; say passage of Afro-Asian (or other undesirable) resolution would damage free world and help Communists; supply details, true if possible, of Communist background of leaders insurrection, sponsors of resolution, etc.; produce *sensible, relevant missionary* (Roman Catholic) if available and if vote of sufficient importance. If delegation already committed to 'independence movement' in question, abstention may sometimes be secured by pointing out that passage of Afro-Asian (or other undesirable) resolution would have adverse effects on progress secret negotiations now being (or soon to be) held between the parties and so would play into the hands of Communists.

Despite all efforts, this delegation is likely to cast some 'anti-colonialist' votes to placate home opinion. In such cases, however, delegation will probably be *helpful on procedural votes*, provided significance of these is not clear to general public. Fortunately, no initiative need be expected this delegation, except possibly on so-called 'question of partition' (claim to annex Northern Ireland). In case of tendency to raise this question, point out that Ireland's case would be supported by the Communist countries.'

In 1956 the Irish delegation, although more creditably active than had been expected of it, did not significantly disappoint these expectations. In 1957 Mr Aiken's speech in the General Debate in favour of disengagement caused some uneasiness but no more than that. It was 'a bad statement' (from the then prevailing Western

point of view) but a bad statement is by no means as bad as a bad
vote. Speeches, indeed, are not taken very seriously at the United
Nations, being used rather often as noble decoration, comforting
to the speaker, reassuring to his home public, and overlaying a
highly realistic and mundane policy of subservience to an outside
power. Thus, the best orator in the Assembly at this period, a Latin-
American lawyer, used to produce masterpieces of towering, far-
ranging eloquence, drawing heavily on history, philosophy, classical
literature and jurisprudence, to show the process of reasoning and
cultural enlightenment which had led him to his decision as to how
to vote on the subject before the Assembly. Curiously, this decision
was absolutely invariably the same as that already reached – on a
more direct method – by the United States delegation. This was
one falcon who could hear the falconer quite distinctly. His remarkable powers, both of speech and of hearing, ensured his election to a
high office. On the occasion of his installation the American delegate
meaning to congratulate him on his distinguished services to the
United Nations, instead referred to him with bleak and uninten-
tional accuracy as *this faithful servant of the United States*. The audience
burst into unseemly laughter; it was a sadly fitting apotheosis of a
United Nations orator.[1]

The distinguished Latin's captive flights were designed to embel-
lish rather than to deceive, and in this they differed from a more
practical type of United Nations oratory; the speech which is
designed to distract attention from the vote (or failure to vote).
Tsetseland – say – is expected by Afro-Asian friends and such home
public opinion as it has, to be 'for Algeria' at the UN. Tsetseland,
however, has been a French colony, is getting a lot of money
from France and has been very clearly told it will get no more
if it votes 'against France'. What is the poor Tsetse delegate to do?
He soon finds out that the answer to his problem is a speech; 'a bad
speech' will be deplored but, unlike a vote, will not have the effect
of cutting off the money. The Tsetse delegate therefore makes a
ringing statement, 'pro-Algerian' in sound, but not very precise.
His statement is carried in full on his home radio, and is quoted with
approval by many Afro-Asian papers. When it comes to a division,

---

[1] In referring to this orator for purposes of illustration I have had to be rather
unkind, since the truth involved here is unpalatable. I should add that he was a
grave, courteous, witty gentleman, who held office with distinction and proved a
capable conciliator. He enjoyed his speeches – as did everyone else – but did not
take himself in. 'The greatest enemy of the freedom of the thought', he used to
say, 'is the freedom of the speech'.

no member of the Tsetse delegation can be found. This is not mentioned on the home radio. The leader of the Tsetse delegation is respected by the public in his own country for his fearless stand, and the French subsidy continues for another blessed year at least.

Against this background, and in the inevitably rather cynical atmosphere of the Delegates Lounge, Mr Aiken's statement did not arouse too much dismay. True, a senior member of the United Kingdom delegation did describe it at a Press conference as 'a straight fellow-travelling speech'; he added that these words were not for attribution. But this remark was not taken very seriously at the time; McCarthyism of the cruder kind, although apparently a pleasing novelty to the speaker, was no longer, in 1957, regarded as attractive in America and in any case some Americans seemed to remember Sir Anthony Eden's once having suggested something rather similar to Mr Aiken's allegedly 'fellow-travelling' proposal. Also, the influence of the British delegation at the United Nations was, in the year after Suez, much less great than it had been and than it later again became.

The trouble really began at 11 a.m. on the morning of September 23rd, 1957, when the Irish delegation, as a matter of courtesy, informed the United States delegation that Ireland, reversing its position of the previous year, would vote in favour of a discussion on the question of the representation of China.

To understand exactly how unwelcome this announcement was, one has to try to enter the Manichean and dramatic mind of the late John Foster Dulles, then Secretary of State. For him, the sessional puppet-show, which preserves a delegation from Formosa as representative of China at the United Nations, had a profound and touching moral significance. It was the annual rebirth of Osiris or, perhaps more accurately, the resurrection of Tinker Bell. The Good Government of China, which was therefore the Real Government, lived again through the faith of the General Assembly. Towards those who manifested doubt about this performance he felt as people who are moved by *Peter Pan* might feel towards a member of the audience who insisted on announcing, at the crucial moment, that he did *not* believe in fairies. Certainly there were also some prosaic calculations involved, but the obviously genuine emotion which pervaded Dulles's utterances on this subject had a Barrie-like quality. Calculation and emotion, indeed, were not altogether independent. Calculation showed that the United States – through its allies in NATO, SEATO and the Baghdad Pact, and its supporters in Latin America – could then still command the necessary two-thirds majority in the Assembly on any subject about which it cared to exert itself, as it certainly did on China. Emotion warmly responded to the annual registration of this vote, as to the verdict of the moral conscience of mankind, stigmatizing Red China as unworthy of membership in the world organization. Unfortunately by this time, the vote, though still sufficient, was beginning to slip.

Since the admission of a number of new members – including Ireland – in 1955 (by the so-called package deal), the 'automatic two-thirds'[1] on which the United States could count in the Assembly was still obtainable, although by the use of somewhat more strenuous means than can have been altogether pleasant either for the United States delegation or for some of its eventual, rather dishevelled, supporters on the floor. Nineteen fifty-seven was probably the last year in which a really safe two-thirds existed. The passage from a position of effectively controlling the Assembly to a position of merely exerting a strong influence over its proceedings was a particularly delicate one for Mr Dulles and Mr Lodge, because of the strong 'conscience of mankind' lighting which they and their friends had projected on the Assembly, during the long period of effective US control. There is nothing so inconvenient as a conscience which does not automatically approve of your actions. From a United Nations point of view, however – that is to say, from the point of view of the real, long-term interests of all concerned – the shift was a most healthy one, because it began the transformation of the Assembly, from being little more than a propaganda organ of the State Department, into a genuine organ of, among other things, negotiations and adjustment.

At this time, then, Mr Dulles's energetic lieutenants at the United Nations were working a little harder than usual on the 'doubtful' votes, like Liberia and Ethiopia, patiently turning projected votes for a discussion on the representation of China[2] into abstentions, and abstentions into votes against. This work was interrupted by the quite unexpected news that Ireland – reckoned as beyond all

---

[1] A two-thirds majority is required in the Assembly for a decision on any questions of importance. The opponents of any proposal seek 'a blocking third'.

[2] The formula, now obsolete, whereby the Assembly annually, after discussion, declined to discuss the representation of China, was of course devised to enable the United Kingdom, which recognizes the Peking Government, to vote together with the United States in effectively, but not formally, upholding the fiction that the Government of China is on Formosa.

question a 'safe' vote – was reversing its previous position, and voting 'for' a discussion. Such a bolt by a non-Communist, non-Afro-Asian country was regarded as a serious blow, both in itself and as an example certain to be noted by waverers. Something had to be done about it. Something was.

At noon on September 23rd, 1957, one hour after notification of the Irish position had been conveyed to the American Delegation, the Irish Consul-General in New York received a telephone message from the Archbishop of New York, Francis Cardinal Spellman. His Eminence wished to know whether it was true that Mr Aiken was 'going to vote for Red China'. The Consul-General did not know, had heard nothing of the kind, was not, in any case, a member of the delegation, and suggested that perhaps His Eminence might consider getting in touch with the delegation itself. His Eminence said he had it on very good authority that Mr Aiken was going to vote for Red China. Miss Irene Dunne had just told him so. She had been sent to tell him so by Mr Cabot Lodge, then leader of the United States delegation. (Miss Dunne, a film-star and, somewhat more relevantly, a Catholic, was a member of the American delegation at this time.) In any case, His Eminence wanted to make his own position clear. 'Tell Aiken', he told the Consul-General, 'that if he votes for Red China we'll raise the Devil.'

Cardinal Spellman was better than his word, for the conjuring feat in question started even before the vote was cast. That afternoon one of the Cardinal's secretaries, Monsignor ——, rang the United Nations, looking for a member of the Irish delegation. Máire MacEntee, as the senior member of the delegation then available, took the call. The Monsignor wanted to know whether Mr Aiken was going to vote for Red China. Máire told him that Mr Aiken had just made a brief statement to the Assembly, explaining that he intended to vote, on the following day, in favour of a discussion on the question of the representation of China. The Monsignor was not interested in 'procedural questions', did not affect to understand them indeed, but thought it would be embarrassing for His Eminence to attend the reception which was being given by the Irish delegation that evening – to which he had accepted an invitation – if his host, on the morrow, were really going to vote for Red China. The conversation then failed to advance for some time, with Máire seeking to establish, and the Monsignor declining to apprehend, the nuance between a vote 'for Red China' and a vote for a discussion of the representation of China. On the social front, also, little progress was made, the Monsignor reiterating his phrases

about the hypothetical embarrassment of the Cardinal on being
entertained by a potential supporter of Red China, while Máire,
speaking as a co-hostess at the coming reception, developed the
themes of the regret which the Irish delegation would feel at the
absence of the Cardinal and the hopes which the delegation
cherished that, when the Cardinal had considered the Chinese
nuance in the parallel passage, he would feel free to attend the reception. This would be embarrassing, said the Monsignor, if Mr Aiken
were really going to vote for Red China. Finally, in an effort to
terminate this complex aria, Máire used the words:

'Of course, His Eminence must do as he thinks right . . .'.

As a move to end the conversation, this was strikingly successful.
The Monsignor immediately hung up. Some hours later Máire had
a call from Boston, on behalf of the organizers of a meeting which
she was due to address on Irish literature. Was it true that, when
Cardinal Spellman had expressed anxiety about a rumour that
Ireland would support Red China, she had replied that she 'didn't
care what the Cardinal thought?' If so. . . .

For an exercise in pressure, Mr Lodge's attempt to raise the Devil,
through the mediation of Cardinal Spellman, seemed original and
rather imaginative. It represented what might be called a theo-
political approach, whereas routine practice in pressure, in Mr
Dulles's day, was bluntly economic. Delegations from countries
receiving aid from the United States would be warned in a friendly
way that 'Congress might find it hard to understand' a given vote.
Such countries rarely allowed to their delegates the luxury of an
incomprehensible, and therefore potentially expensive voting position. Governments of countries in which there were important
American business interests would receive less subtle hints from the
appropriate quarter. Firestone and United Fruit were believed to
be particularly helpful in these matters. Unfortunately neither
technique was then applicable to Ireland – which neither sought
American economic aid nor received any substantial volume of
American investment – and this was no doubt a stimulus to thought
along more spiritual lines. The idea, based perhaps on a reading of
Mr Paul Blanshard's works, perhaps on the utterances of some of the
Irish clergy and laity, was apparently that the Irish, being Catholics
and therefore no doubt essentially a priest-ridden lot, would have
to do what the Cardinal told them. For their superstitious minds the
mere thought of a Cardinal raising the Devil should be enough to
dispel notions about matters which ought not to concern them, like
China.

The Devil, when raised, proved a disappointing imp enough. The diocesan press, in Manhattan and Brooklyn, loudly denounced, and I believe still denounces, 'Ireland's fellow-travelling delegation'; the far right said and says the usual things; an intermittently cultural body in New York called the Oriel Society stencilled, and still stencils, manifestos on the subject; here and there in Ireland a bishop stirred uneasily; the parliamentary opposition gave China a trial as an issue, found it unrewarding and dropped it; in the Dublin and Cork Press began one of those interminable and eventually Byzantine controversies which are among the minor pleasures of life in Ireland – this time under a satisfactorily grandiose title: 'Ireland's China Policy'. But the vote was maintained. Miss Dunne had ridden in vain.

Perhaps, however, not altogether in vain, in the long run. Those of us who thought the whole affair would soon blow over, who spoke of 'a storm in a China teacup', were wrong. It left a mark on our delegation and a mark on some of us personally. Our delegation was, henceforward, listed among those which are known alter-natively – depending on the situation and the outlook of the speaker – as 'the independent countries' or 'the bloody mavericks'. In the politics of the Assembly, these countries have a rather important part. They are more sought after than the 'safe' votes as sponsors of resolutions, and tend to become involved in those compromise efforts which mark the closing stages of the consideration of any important question at the Assembly. They are, in short, in the thick of things, where the other small countries, which are reckoned as 'safe' votes, are not. This position is not due to any special skill or virtue on the part of the mavericks, although it may be used with varying degrees of acumen and responsibility (two qualities which are not always in concord). The involvement of these countries in United Nations politics is an inevitable, indeed almost a mechanical, result of their being recognized as 'independent-minded'; a quality which has to be proved – and continue to be proved – not by speeches but by a pressure-resistant pattern of voting.

On every important question, the major powers strive to influence the outcome by inflecting the wording of the resolution, strengthen-ing it or weakening it. Many competing texts circulate in the cor-ridors as 'working papers'; a few survive, in modified form, to reach the floor of the relevant committee as draft resolutions. Where a tight vote is expected, the interested great powers rarely put

forward their own draft under their own names. Not France but
Peru or (more recently) Senegal will put forward the resolution or
amendment on (say) Algeria which the French delegation needs to
block the Afro-Asian move.[1] But in this game it is important to have
'good sponsorship', that is to say, sponsorship from as far outside
the circle of one's known committed supporters as possible. Thus,
on a hypothetical Latin question, the United States, finding
Mexico or Brazil out of reach, might try to reach agreement on a
text with Argentina and Uruguay; in default of that agreement,
Peru might be asked to take the initiative and if even Peru proved
sluggish, the US specialist in hemispheric solidarity on this committee would turn with a sigh to El Salvador. (Nicaragua, Guatemala, the Dominican Republic and Batista's Cuba might not be
asked to sponsor – being regarded, even in Mr Dulles's day, as
faintly embarrassing – but that might not prevent them from adding
themselves to the list of sponsors as unwelcome volunteers.)
Similarly, the delegation of the Soviet Union, slightly later, in its
efforts to induce Afro-Asian countries to put forward something as
near as possible to Mr Khrushchev's theses on colonialism, might
talk first to the Indian delegation, then to Ghana, then to Morocco,
then to Guinea and only in the last resort – rather often reached –
present a Communist sponsor, which would today be the Mongolian
People's Republic.

In this quest for the least-committed possible sponsors on the
most-committed possible text – the quest which is one of the main
forms which the unceasing competition of the cold war and de-
colonization takes in the Assembly – Ireland's support became,
after the China vote, a desirable prize. The Irish delegate on each
committee and on many questions would be approached by the
stalkers of the Western powers and of the Afro-Asians, and would
quite often find himself a member of the 'fire-brigade' engaged in
drawing up, at the end of the debates, a compromise text or a
rotating device to avoid a clash of candidates. The composition of
the fire-brigade varied according to the fire but at least one
Scandinavian country was almost always on it and there might

---

[1] Curiously enough, considering General de Gaulle's comments on *le machin*,
France, through its influence over the French-speaking African States, can count
on more safe votes in the Assembly than any other country except the United
States. If – as seems likely at the time of writing – the question of Algeria is withdrawn from the Assembly agenda, France's attitude to the United Nations is
likely to become very much more positive.

also be Canada, Mexico or India.[1] Whether to serve or not to serve on a given fire-brigade was often a difficult choice. The decision on such points, as on all important matters, was taken by the Chairman of the delegation – either Mr Aiken, at this time, or the Permanent Representative, Mr F. H. Boland – after a discussion at a delegation meeting. But – and this became important in our lives in the 'post-China' atmosphere – such decisions were necessarily based on the reports from the individual delegate serving on the Committee in question. As these delegates were – by a regrettable necessity which intrudes even into the Civil Service[2] – human beings, their reports were tinged by their personal outlook, temperament and philosophy of life.

For an understanding of the problems involved, it is necessary to say something of the Assembly's method of work. The work of the General Assembly is done in seven main committees (committees comprising the full membership). The First, the Special and the Fourth (Trusteeship) are regarded as the political committees. Countries like Ireland cannot normally afford to be represented by more than one delegate on each committee, with the partial exception of the First, on which it was usual for Mr Aiken to sit for part of the session accompanied by an adviser, usually myself. In Mr Aiken's absence I represented Ireland either on the First Committee or – when, as normally, Mr Boland was available to take the seat on the First – the Special Political. The colleague who represented Ireland on the important Fourth Committee – often known as the African Committee – was Mr Eamonn Kennedy who, at the time of writing, is Ireland's Ambassador to Nigeria. In our delegation, as I believe in most others, there existed, under the cover of the identical, impersonal 'delegation policy', quite a wide span of personal opinions as to what that policy should be; the opposite ends of the span, in our delegation, were represented by Mr Kennedy and myself. Practically, the extent of the difference between us was that I was glad Ireland was neutral and thought

---

[1] Joseph Lash (*Dag Hammarskjold*, p. 174) refers to 'the "fire-brigades" – the groups of middle-sized powers led by Canada, Norway, Ireland, Tunisia, Nigeria, Yugoslavia and Mexico, which worked with the 38th Floor'.

[2] Practice as regards composition of delegations varies widely but Ireland's delegation has always been a team of permanent officials – or perhaps I should now say officials who were intended to be permanent – headed by a politician, the Minister for External Affairs. Other delegations included trade union officials, army officers, film stars, parliamentarians, seamen and so on; there is no restriction.

that it should behave like a neutral, while he was sorry that Ireland
was neutral and thought it should behave as much as possible like
a member of NATO. This radical political difference, of which in
normal conditions at home in Ireland we might scarcely have been
conscious, forced itself insistently on our attention at the United
Nations, through the friction produced by the necessity to vote, and
sometimes to speak, on so many issues where Western and neutral –
mainly Afro-Asian – influences were in deep and often secret
contention. Mr Kennedy and I had been friends but under these
conditions our friendship noticeably wilted. I regretted this. I
believe he did too and I hope that some day, in some more propitious
climate, our friendship may revive.

Some readers, at this point, will certainly say that they care very
little whether it does or not, and that differences of opinion between
Mr Kennedy and Mr O'Brien are not of the slightest importance
to the world in general. In themselves, obviously, they are not; in
their context they have significance, as part of this case history, and
as having a remote but real bearing on events, the importance of
which is not disputed, which took place later, some thousands of
miles away from New York. In any case, it may do even the
refractory reader no harm to be reminded that the United Nations
is made up of people; there are 'Kennedys' and 'O'Briens' on a
great many delegations – I could name, but will not, Polish
'Kennedys' and Canadian 'O'Briens' – and their differences do
affect the proceedings and the decisions of the United Nations.
It is quite true that the effect of such differences is usually marginal;
the basic voting position of a country is laid down by its Government,
very often in direct obedience to stringent economic or military
necessity. But in the case of the few small countries which can permit
themselves the luxury of a relatively independent voting position –
no country is totally independent – the personal outlook of delegates
does become of some importance. It can be argued that delegates,
being there to represent their country, not themselves, ought not to
have personal outlooks, or at least ought not to allow them to
intrude; but this is in practice impossible.

In the case of Ireland, we knew our Government's policy had
been explained as being 'not to vote with any bloc but to consider
each question on its merits'. Although, in actual fact, the delegation
of a country like Ireland will usually – and quite sincerely – see the
merits as being on the Western side, there were, especially in
colonial matters, many border-line cases. In such cases, the assessment of the merits has to be made, in the first instance at least – and

often in the last, also – by the delegate on the spot. I do not know how such an assessment could be made by a delegate who had achieved the total political apathy which some people postulate as desirable in an official representative. In our delegation, assessments of the merits varied widely, because standards differed, in reality if not in words. Mr Kennedy and I each tried to assess merits mainly by reference to the idea of freedom, but our assessments in critical cases almost always produced opposite results. He, like many others, thought of freedom primarily as something already achieved in a given geographical area and to be defended by the defence of that area against the rulers of another given area, who were the enemies of freedom. The free world, for him, existed, although he might have found it hard to draw a map of it; his map certainly included the metropolitan territories of the NATO countries, plus the white Commonwealth and, of course, Ireland; how much else it included I could never be quite sure – I have an idea that for ordinary purposes the frontier ran somewhere between Spain and the Union of South Africa.[1] In certain circumstances, however, the Free World could quite simply be defined as the entire area not controlled by Communist governments. Thus, in the event of a *Communist-led* attempt to overthrow Dr Verwoerd's régime, it will be Dr Verwoerd who will be defending the Free World and therefore freedom itself. As Dr Verwoerd's régime has itself legislatively ruled that *any* attempt to overthrow it is *ipso facto* a Communist attempt, it will be hard, in practice, for the many people who share Mr Kennedy's opinions to disentangle *apartheid* from the institutions of the Free World. They sincerely condemn *apartheid* – Mr Kennedy spoke very well on the subject – but they are conditionally committed to its defence.

For Mr Kennedy, the consensus of the leaders of the Free World – that is, the rulers of the NATO countries – was effectively the voice of freedom. Failing such a consensus, the voice of freedom became articulate through the mouths of the delegation of the United States, the country which was the heart of the Free World. Thus Mr Kennedy seldom had much difficulty in making up his mind, except in the rare cases where, there being no consensus, the United States itself failed to make its position clear.

Not all ideas about freedom are quite so geographical. I valued very highly the freedoms – and especially the freedom of expression

---

[1] If so, Spain was *in* the Free World, South Africa *out*. An English Protestant version of Mr Kennedy might well put it the other way round.

– which the peoples of some advanced Western countries, led by the
English people, had, in their long and relatively happy histories,
won for themselves and transmitted, in various ways and degrees,
to some others. I liked living in a society where wide differences of
opinion were acknowledged and tolerated, even respected. I slept
better for *habeas corpus*, read Macaulay to my daughters, never
doubted that the Glorious Revolution of 1688 was a glorious and
auspicious event indeed, for England.

I was obliged to add the last two words – which an English
liberal would not necessarily have thought of adding – because I
could not help remembering – it was in my bones to remember –
that the event which opened in England such a splendid chapter
of achievement and growing liberty had imposed, in Ireland, a
system of oppression and calculated degradation such as Europe
has seldom seen. The Penal Laws were very similar in conception
to the *apartheid* system, with the distinction that religion and not
colour provided the line between conqueror and helot.[1] The achievement of freedom in the advanced country had involved the negation
of freedom in the backward country.[2] Any Irishman who thinks
about history and about freedom must be conscious of this puzzle
and, unless he suppresses this consciousness, it will eventually affect
his conception of the world around him. He will be a little wary, for
example, when he hears about 'bastions of freedom', for he cannot
help remembering that there was probably never a greater bastion
of freedom than Great Britain in the eighteenth and early nineteenth
centuries, and that his forefathers were prisoners in that bastion.

This is not just a question of 'brooding on the past'[3] – although it
is hard to read history without doing some brooding on the past –
but of a present-day contrast rooted in history. Ireland is still a
relatively backward country, next door to a highly advanced one.
The culture of the advanced country has almost completely destroyed, but only partially replaced, the culture of the backward one.

---

[1] I am aware that there is a school of historiography which regards the Penal
Laws as of small importance because they were never fully applied. The *apartheid*
system, of course, is not fully applied either.

[2] I do not suggest that there was any *moral* difference between the parties.
The Irish fighting for their own freedom would cheerfully, if their side had won,
have helped to impose by force on the English a system which most Englishmen
would have regarded as tyranny.

[3] To those who are going, in any case, to insist that that is just what it is, I
offer – rather handsomely, I think – the following phrase of Evelyn Waugh's
about the Irish in America: 'dragging with them their ancient rancours and the
melancholy of the bogs'.

The replacement can only be partial, for the conquered can never properly assimilate one central element in the conquering culture: the psychological attitudes of racial superiority. True, the *language* of racial superiority has been taboo among enlightened adults since the rise of Hitler, but the thing itself is with us, as not only West Indians or Irish labourers in Birmingham, but any Irish boy at an English school can testify. It is entirely inevitable that this should be so. Of history and its consequences it may be said: 'Those who can, gloat; those who can't, brood.' Englishmen are born gloaters; Irishmen born brooders. There are, it is true, brooders who take to gloating, and they did much to build the Empire. Yet the brooder-gloater, such as the Irishman turned Englishman, is not, as a human type, altogether a success. He is a little too much on his guard, like an excessively assimilated Jew, or a son of Harlem who has decided to 'pass'. The past of the Irishman, the Jew, the Negro is, psychologically, too explosive to be safely buried.

Now, as most of the peoples of the world have unfortunately more reason to brood than to gloat, the status of brooder, if accepted, has a single advantage: it enables one to feel and vibrate with the sense of the great revolutionary movements which shook the world and shake it today, instead of contemplating these movements, as the best-equipped of gloaters must do, from the remote and critical eminence of historical success. A reformed gloater – an English liberal, say, or a Swede – feels, I think, a sense of guilt about South Africa; this is because he still identifies himself, probably without being entirely conscious of the fact, with the master race. The brooder, making the opposite identification, feels no sense of guilt, only a sense of outrage. This is not just an academic distinction, for the man who identifies himself, however guiltily, with the master race, is likely to regard revolution in South Africa as the ultimate horror. The man who makes the opposite identification regards the indefinite continuation of servitude as the ultimate horror, and revolution, if materially possible, as the lesser evil. It is the first view, not the second, which is eccentric, if we take the majority opinion of mankind as the centre.

In all this, I assume that everyone's thinking is profoundly conditioned by the historical experience of the society to which he belongs, and by the way in which he belongs to that society. Each of us sees this well enough in products of other societies, but we necessarily regard our own thinking, while we are thinking, as objective and unconditioned. The dialogue between brooder and gloater – today taking the form of the great dialogue between the

West and the Afro-Asian world – often comes to grief on this. To
the Afro-Asian side, Western language often seems grotesquely
smug and hypocritical; to Westerners the Afro-Asians often sound
as if blinded by irrational prejudice. There are occasions when both
are right: in the United Nations, especially, we have been familiar
over the years with a sufficiency of virtuous attitudinizing of both
sorts. But even when the protagonists on both sides are as sane and
honest as human beings can hope to be, the mutual bafflement is apt
to continue. Each side feels the other is being, at best, illogical; both
may well be reasoning equally logically, but from sets of historical
premises which are far from identical. Thus Americans, Indians,
Englishmen, Irishmen, Russians may be taken as equally sincere in
their attachment to freedom, but the contours of the idea of freedom
have been cut out for them by history into different shapes. Very
rarely indeed does a member of any of these historically-formed
societies make the imaginative effort necessary to translate the
concept of freedom into or out of the cultural language of another
society. Very easily, on the other hand, does he reach the conclusion that members of other societies are cheating, using the
word 'freedom' to delude others, and perhaps also themselves.
Frenchmen, for example, pass easily from cynicism to indignation
when they discuss the concept of freedom which underlies American
anti-colonialism. 'What', they ask, 'happened to the Red Indians?'
The question is pertinent, but the conclusion usually implied – that
American anti-colonialism is necessarily hypocritical – is false.
Not only in America, but also in France and Britain the great
achievements of freedom have cast a dark shadow. The shadows
cast by the French Revolution in Brittany and La Vendée, by the
English Revolution in the Highlands and in Ireland, by the American Revolution across the Alleghenies, are certainly too easily
forgotten by the heirs of these revolutions. Yet these heirs would be
making a still greater mistake were they to adopt that form of
'realism' which regards the shadows, the cruelties and oppressions
against less developed peoples, as being the most important part
of their heritage, and the achievement, the advancement of the
idea of freedom, as being essentially little more than a necessary
reorganization carried out through the incentive value of libertarian
slogans. In short, the American anti-colonialist, even if his memory
plays him a trick or two, is being true to the best part of his own
tradition; his French critic is being true to the worst part of *his*
tradition, if he uses the fate of the Red Indian as an argument to
justify the actions of the French Army in Algeria.

The acceptance of the fact that your own point of view is historically conditioned in a particular way is likely to lead you to attempt to understand the historical conditioning of other people's points of view and of their actions. You look at the world around you – at the United Nations the world is around you in rather a special sense – with, first of all, a curiosity about historical roots and possibilities of growth. The full-grown plant of freedom, in some parts of the advanced societies, will still have all your admiration, but you are likely to notice that it can cast a sometimes blighting shadow. What you are apt to find more interesting, however, are the first improbable-looking spikey shoots, breaking with difficulty through unfavourable ground: the places and times where men become conscious of themselves as men, capable of changing their environment and destiny: the beginnings of freedom. I recognized my own interest in, and feeling for, these shoots as being profoundly affected by the Irish historical background, and seemed to discern, in some Western attitudes towards these beginnings of freedom, in Africa or Asia, important elements of unacknowledged historical formation. Many Westerners talked as if they expected the first shoots of freedom to be miniature models of their own favourite forms of the grown plant. They were shocked, for example, by the violence which occurred in Baghdad on July 14th, 1958; they failed to think of another July 14th, source of far greater bloodshed, and also of so many of our present liberties. The people of Iraq, apparently, were supposed to behave as if they were already the refined and liberal heirs of that earlier July 14th, none of the benefits of which had, in fact, reached them.[1] The particular Bastille which they overthrew, indeed, was precisely one of those 'miniature models' of advanced Western societies which so often serve in underdeveloped countries as façades for feudal or pre-feudal societies.

The immediate reason, of course, why Western opinion was shocked by the violence of the Iraqi revolution, and not by Nuri's terror – just as it was shocked by Castro's firing-squads and not, except in hurried retrospect, by Batista's torture-chambers – was that Westerners were primarily concerned not with Iraqis and Cubans as people, or with any concept of freedom that might be relevant to their needs, but with the effect of the actions of these peoples on the balance of power between the opposing blocs in advanced countries. Even if it were admitted, which it sometimes

---

[1] How the refined and liberal heirs actually do behave is a separate question.

was, that, say, Egyptians seemed to feel a greater sense of purpose and of their own dignity under the revolutionary Government than they had under Farouk, and that they might even feel freer under a dictatorship which they liked than they had felt under a 'constitutional monarchy' which they despised, yet after all – in the eyes of some Western thinkers and many other Westerners – these preferences of the ignorant Egyptian masses were matters of relatively small importance. The real enemy of freedom was international Communism and therefore the real criterion of the interests of freedom, the criterion by which to judge the significance of any political situation, event or decision was: will this help or hurt the Communists? If, on a careful calculation of political profits and losses, it seemed to help the Communists, then it was also inimical to freedom, even if the people immediately concerned thought of it as actually being freedom, for them.

In the conflicting currents of the Assembly every delegate on virtually every vote he cast and every word he said, had to consider exactly how his delegation, and he personally, stood in relation to this proposition. In our delegation, Mr Kennedy seemed to accept it whole-heartedly. I could not accept the ideas of a single world-wide 'enemy of freedom', of a single criterion of freedom by which, from a standpoint of superior wisdom, one could determine what constituted freedom for some other people, irrespective of that people's own opinion. I was well aware of the harsh limitations on personal freedom in the Soviet Union, yet I doubted whether I would feel less free in the Soviet Union than in South Africa, or Portugal, or Spain, or French Algeria, or Guatemala, or Southern Rhodesia or in many other places which are thought of as part of the free world. I was conscious that NATO, which my colleague saw exclusively as a system for defending freedom, appeared in a quite different light to many millions of people: those like Algerians and Angolans, who were oppressed by some NATO members with the aid, or at least the assent, of others.

In Mr Dulles's day, ideas of this sort were decidedly unpopular. They were 'leftist', and 'leftist' was a word of undetermined but menacing content. The prototype, it seemed, was an abominable character in one of the strip-cartoons of the period, who organized spy-rings in cellars, and was known to his friends as 'Fifth' because he had pleaded the Fifth Amendment so often in response to legislative questioning. After that unexpected vote on China, people began to look for 'Fifths' on the Irish delegation. Outside the walls, the 'Fifths' were being identified, by Cardinal Spellman's adherents and some others, as Mr Aiken himself and Mr F. H. Boland, head of Ireland's Permanent Mission to the United Nations. Down by the East River, however, the absurdity of these identifications was manifest. Mr Aiken had been Mr de Valera's closest associate for nearly forty years, and the days when Mr de Valera could be regarded by anyone as a leftist had long gone by. As for Mr Boland, Western delegates, who knew him well and respected him greatly, realized that he would be the last man to counsel 'extremist' courses of any kind. He is a man who could make his own the words of the aged Duke of Newcastle's rebuke to the young Gladstone: 'I confess, young man, I have a great notion of the horrors of enthusiasm.' His favourite tags are in the distinctly unenthusiastic Talleyrand tradition. An indiscreet speech will be likely to elicit: *Il a raté une bonne occasion de se taire*; a refusal of a vote reminds him of the formula, *Nous trouverons une autre occasion de vous manifester notre sympathie*. Both these tags make him happy, and his amusement is infectious, but what makes him happier still is a little music-hall snatch which he will croon when an acquaintance is, in his very shrewd opinion, about to take a foolish risk:

> *It's a wonderful job for somebody –*
> *Somebody else, not me!*

Years later, as I was flying out to Elisabethville, I could almost fancy I heard a well-known and not unfriendly voice softly humming that refrain.

The talents and propensities which were to make Mr Boland the successful Western-sponsored candidate for President of the General Assembly in 1959 – an 'Eastern European' year under the so-called 'gentleman's agreement' of 1946 on rotation of offices – had already made so deep an impression that no one at the United Nations thought of imputing to him any responsibility for Ireland's new 'uncommitted' position. Those who considered Mr Aiken 'badly advised' had to look elsewhere for the bad adviser. They were not long in finding him.

Heads and members of major delegations at the United Nations do not, of course, waste much time in speculating about the political philosophy of secondary members of minor delegations. None the less, for their practical object of influencing votes, the political bird-watchers have become capable of distinguishing the behaviour of individual specimens of a delegation-species. Those species whose voting pattern is apt to waver are, for obvious reasons, the most carefully studied:

> '*Hakim, the Chairman, is a sensible fellow enough, but Ibrahim is a bit of a wild man. If Ibrahim, who has taken the seat on the First Committee for the debate so far, is really going to cast the vote, then it means the instructions from home are wrong, and poor old Hakim wants to keep right out of the whole thing, because it will do him no good. The trouble is, this fellow Ibrahim will certainly make things worse; when his friends realize they're short of the two-thirds, he's quite capable of putting in a "compromise" amendment which will carry, and do just as much damage as the original resolution. The best thing is to press Hakim to take the seat himself. Make it clear to him that we quite understand that his instructions leave him no elbow-room but that, since the whole matter is so delicate, we should feel much happier about it if he handled it himself. He'll like that, and at least with Hakim there'll be no speech and no bloody amendments.*'

Under this system of classification I was definitely an 'Ibrahim'. The bird-watchers were, of course, right – granted their point of view. 'Which are our guys', Eisenhower is said to have asked about Laos, 'and which are the bad guys?' Not being automatically one of theirs, I was one of the bad guys. How such identifications are established, in an Assembly where each delegate votes, and usually speaks, on instructions, is a little hard to say. Partly, it is because the instructions show a slight but significant tendency to vary with the delegate, on whom the delegation (and eventually the Government) relies for its appraisal of the situation on the Committee. Thus our delegation's voting patterns on the Fourth and Special Committees were perceptibly different because the delegates – Mr Kennedy and myself – assessed the political contexts in a radically different way. We both reported as objectively as we could, like the conscientious civil servants we both were, but we could not help *seeing* things differently and therefore giving different pictures of reality. Partly, again, it is a matter of emphasis; no two members of any delegation would explain the same vote in exactly the same way, and an experienced observer can tell whether a delegate casting (say) an anti-colonialist vote has, or has not, his heart in his work. In such matters the vote itself is no sin, 'provided' – in the well-known phrase attributed to an Irish confessor – 'you took no pleasure in it, my child'. A decorous frigidity in the language of a delegate required to cast 'a bad vote' is an index of virtue; warmth of phrase, or – much worse still – the detested aggression of irony, reveals the sin in the heart. And, once the sinner has been identified, the sin actually seeks him out; Hakim is a wily old bird and, despite all blandishments, knows that certain business is best left to Ibrahim.

In the case of this particular Ibrahim, the question of Cyprus was a good example of such business. When this question came before the First Committee of the General Assembly in 1957 and 1958 – 1956 was a rather different matter, for Irish internal reasons of little general interest – it was one on which the Irish delegation was bound, if only because of home public opinion, to cast 'a bad vote' and even make 'a bad speech' from the point of view of the United Kingdom delegation. Call in Ibrahim, then: I spoke for Ireland on this question in these years, although I did not usually lead on the First Committee; my interventions – not just 'bad' but frankly deplorable – completed the identification in the eyes of the United Kingdom delegation. Thus the reputation of the sinner brings about the occasion of sin, and the occasion leads to the further darkening of the reputation.

In our case, however, the original sin was, as I have tried to indicate, the 1957 vote on China, with its assertion of independence and uncommittedness. That had been a delegation decision, taken and defended by Mr Aiken as Chairman. None the less, among the relatively few people who were then interested in the matter, the idea spread that here, too, I had been the bad adviser, the 'Fifth'. How do such ideas spread? I know that none of my colleagues, however different their ideas from mine, would have given any account to outsiders of what took place at a delegation meeting. But at the United Nations, among the like-minded of different delegations, there are modes of silent signalling, comparable to the communications, as we imagine them, between fish or ants. Certain tightenings of the lips, unfocusings of the eye, timings of smiles and cessations of smiles, make up a pattern which says: 'I am too discreet and too loyal to say a word about it, but I deplore, as much as you do, the recent goings on in our delegation, and the man responsible for them is sitting over there.'

At the United Nations, among career diplomats at least, such identifications and reputations are not taken too seriously. Everyone knows that the 'dangerous man' of today is as likely as not to spend the next ten years of his life revising table-plans, seeking import licences for periwinkles, writing unanswered letters about his inadequate representation allowance, re-checking the seniority lists after deaths and retirements, and in general leading the blameless life of the representative of a small country in a minor capital.

Ten years of such a life, experience shows, bring maturity and – normally, though not always – the end of dangerous, and most other, thoughts. Career diplomats, knowing these things, tend to be charitable towards each other, except in the rare cases where unexpected developments or their own immediate interests oblige them to act otherwise.

It was not until the autumn of 1961 that I suddenly realized that chance had made me one of these rare cases, and that a reputation which I had taken rather lightly had acquired retrospectively a weight which was no longer light at all. This epiphany was induced, rather oddly, by a clipping from a Portuguese newspaper which someone – whether wishing me well or ill, I do not know – sent to me in Elisabethville after the September fighting. The four-column headline said:

> *'Um Ezquerdista Exaltado*
> *Levou a Conflagracao a Catanga.'*

The translation kindly supplied by my correspondent said that this meant: 'An Exalted Leftist Carried Conflagration to Katanga.' From other sources I gleaned that 'exalted' was not a tribute to my high rank but meant something like 'crazy', or, more closely, the American 'wild-eyed'. From acknowledgements it appeared that the text had been supplied by the London Express Service to a Portuguese-language newspaper called *O Globo*. The article was based on the thesis, then new to me, that the action in Elisabethville had been started by me on my sole initiative and personal responsibility. The subheading ran: 'Who is Conor Cruise O'Brien, the Man Who Betrayed the Ideals of the UN?' It was the last section which – completing the answer to this question – dealt with my career as an Irish delegate to the Assembly. Headed *'Ambicao'*, it ran as follows:

'Mr O'Brien's lack of political ability is disastrous. He cherishes the ambition of becoming an "international civil servant" in New York. Hammarskjold, before his death, had picked him out as a possible Under-Secretary. But it is clear that we have to do with a man whose discernment does not inspire confidence.

'His policy in Katanga has been a Russian policy. He is not a Communist but [*sic*] in the UN he sought the company of African and Asiatic leaders. Here, as in Dublin, he supports the admission of Communist China to the international organization. He is strongly attached to the policy of 'disengagement' in Europe. He is a great supporter of the non-nuclear club. And politically, if not personally, he hates the English. In this, in my view, lies the explanation of his policy in Katanga.'[1]

Whether derived from Foreign Office sources ('not for attribution, please') or not, the second paragraph is a fair summary of how my 'record' must have appeared to some members of the United Kingdom delegation. It is also entirely accurate, except for the critical and false assertions, which colour all the rest, that 'my' policy in Katanga was 'a Russian policy', motivated by my alleged hatred, whether political or personal, for 'the English'. No evidence at all is produced for the last charge; it rests, I believe, on my share, as seen by the United Kingdom delegation, in the Cyprus debates – which share, perhaps significantly, is *not* included in the list of my UN activities and positions. There are always people, in all countries, who sincerely feel that any foreigner who strongly criticizes a line of action of their Government must be hostile to their country; this point of view was rather well represented in the United Kingdom delegation, and presumably in the Government also. That being so, it ought not to be surprising – although it did surprise me – that this Government and delegation should have sought to eliminate from Katanga, and from UN service, a person whom they may have believed to be motivated, to some extent at least, by 'hatred of the English'. Thus the pattern of my activities as a delegate at the United Nations General Assembly probably did contribute in some degree to the intensity of the pressure which resulted, as will be seen, on my departure not merely from Katanga but from the UN Secretariat.

The same pattern of activities which helped to hasten my departure, the same reasons which deepened the hostility of the United Kingdom delegation, were also, I believe, among the reasons for my being invited by Mr Hammarskjold to join the Secretariat, and selected to represent the United Nations in the key post in Elisabethville.

---

[1] This was a syndicated article and it, and others like it, mainly emanating from London, were published in many Western countries. The original article, by Mr George Gale, appeared, I believe, in the *Daily Express*, London; and the above text may not be identical with it. Whether Mr Gale's prose would be likely to suffer, or actually to benefit, from being translated into Portuguese and then from Portuguese back into English, is a matter of opinion.

2

NEUTRAL MEN?

> '*Talibus ex adyto dictis Cumaea Sibylla*
> *Horrendas canit ambages . . . .*
> *Obscuris vera involvens.*'
>
> Virgil

It was in March 1961 that Mr Hammarskjold first asked the Irish Government to release me for service with the United Nations Secretariat, first as Representative in Elisabethville and later in New York. The date is significant, for the Security Council had just passed – on February 21st – a resolution which transformed the Secretariat's mandate in relation to Katanga.[1] That resolution will be discussed later, in the general context of the political background to the Katanga question. Here it may be enough to say that both the proponents of the February resolution and those who openly opposed it considered it to be aimed principally at Katanga, and to have very drastic implications for the structure of political power in that province, and for the effective maintenance of its claim to independent statehood. Its immediate application – and the resolution used the word 'immediate' in its key paragraph – would, in the Katanga context, be nothing short of revolutionary. The resolution demanded the withdrawal of all foreign officers and mercenaries from the Congo: almost all those remaining, about 500, were in Katanga and were regarded as providing the military basis for the secession of that province.

The Irish Government, perhaps apprehensive about the explosive possibilities of the Katanga situation following the February

---

[1] For text, see Appendix I.

resolution, and feeling in any case sufficiently involved in Congo responsibilities by General McKeown's appointment as Commander of the UN forces there and by the contribution of a battalion of Irish troops, then serving in Katanga, declined to release me at this time. A general election was due in Ireland that year and it was rumoured (incorrectly) that the opposition intended to use the slogan: 'The Best Irish Government the Congo Ever Had.'

Towards the end of May, however, Mr Andrew Cordier, Executive Assistant to the Secretary-General, rang me from New York at my home in Howth, to say that the Secretary-General was renewing the request for my release, but this time without specific mention of the Congo. If I agreed – as I had indicated in March I was ready to do – I would take up duty in New York, on the Secretary-General's executive staff but would leave as soon as possible thereafter for Elisabethville. I could expect to serve as representative in Katanga for about six months; at the end of that time I would return to the executive staff in New York.

As the offer did not mention the Congo, the Irish Government agreed, rather reluctantly, to my secondment to United Nations service for a period of two years. I left for New York on May 27th.

Some seven months later, after the interesting sequence of events which brought about – amid much of far greater significance – my own departure from United Nations service, and from the service of the Irish Government, I found myself speculating on why, in the first place, Mr Hammarskjold had picked me for the post. This question was linked in my mind with another question – inevitable, unanswerable, uncomfortable: whether, if Mr Hammarskjold had made another choice, he might now be alive?

The second question I leave aside for the moment. As regards the first, the answers I made at the time, in an article I wrote for *The Observer*[1], were, first that he needed an Irishman, second, that he happened to have read, and liked, a book of mine, *Maria Cross*. The first answer is entirely correct. Mr Hammarskjold's range of national choice for the Katanga post, after the February resolution, was quite narrow. Obviously he could not pick anyone from the Eastern bloc, which was then vehemently condemning his whole conduct of the Congo operation. Representatives in Elisabethville hitherto had been Westerners[2] – Mr Berendsen of New Zealand, Mr

---

[1] December 10th and 17th, 1961.

[2] I use Westerner here not in a geographical or even a cultural sense but as referring to a citizen of a country which belongs to the system of military alliances of which the United States is the leading member.

Dumontet of France, Mr Brackenbury of the United Kingdom – but, granted the implications of the February resolution and granted the existence of a deep-rooted sympathy in the West with Mr Tshombe's régime, a committed Westerner hardly seemed, at that time, an appropriate choice. There would be strong Western opposition to the choice of an Afro-Asian neutral, since representative Afro-Asians were considered to be by no means neutral as between the Central Government and Katanga. How strong the Western opposition to an Afro-Asian UN Representative could become was just being demonstrated by the ousting of Mr Dayal. The choice seemed to narrow to a European neutral and then – since Austria and Finland are 'neutralized' rather than neutral and Switzerland is not a member of the UN – to Sweden or Ireland. Sweden had already contributed the Acting Special Representative in Leopoldville, Dr Sture Linner. The system of elimination was not (except for Eastern Europe) altogether coercive but it did make an Irishman the best choice, if someone suitable from there could be found.

The reason I gave for his picking this particular Irishman – that he had read a book of mine – was, I admit, inadequate. It was not, I think, quite so far from adequate, so nearly verging on the frivolous, as some of my correspondents thought at the time. A careful reading of a man's book may reasonably, after all, be thought to give a better idea of his character, and therefore suitability for a given task, than can be had from the usual brief meeting combined with the reading of a *curriculum vitae*. Hammarskjold himself might have put the case in more abstract language – he was given to mysticism about literature, as many Swedes are – but, even on the most pragmatical grounds, it is not necessarily foolish to allow one's opinion of a man's book to influence one's opinion of the man. I now realize, however, that the emphasis on the book did an injustice, not to me but to Mr Hammarskjold and his tenure of the Secretary-Generalship. 'This bookish man' – his enemies were enabled to say – 'picked another bookish man, by reason of his sheer bookishness, to fill an extremely important and delicate political post. The result brought unforeseen and avoidable disasters on Katanga, on the United Nations and on Mr Hammarskjold himself.'[1]

---

[1] A good example of the use made of this statement of mine comes from Senator Barry Goldwater's home State, Arizona: 'The former UN "Chief Representative", the virtual ruler of Katanga, Conor O'Brien, was a rather unstable Irish playboy who was chosen for his post by Hammarskjold because Dag had liked one of O'Brien's books on poetry and literary criticism [*sic*]. O'Brien himself boasts about this in his memoirs now published in the British Press.' (*The Arizona Republic*, February 23rd, 1962).

This emphasis also magnified the part – already large enough in reality – of human error and blind chance in the conduct of the United Nations operation in the Congo; it distracted attention from the non-accidental, the clash of fiercely contending national and other interests between whose demands the Secretary-General had, from moment to moment, to choose. The choice of a representative in Katanga, after the February resolution, was an important political choice and a little more needs to be said about it here than I thought necessary earlier.[1] Mr Cordier had, in fact, asked Mr Boland to suggest the names of Irishmen who might be suitable for the post and willing to take it. Mr Boland had suggested my own name and that of my colleague, Mr Kennedy. We were of roughly equal age, rank and standing at the UN. On paper, at least, and perhaps otherwise as well, Mr Kennedy was the more suitable candidate; he was a very well-known and active figure in his Committee, which was generally referred to as the African Committee, and he had represented Ireland more regularly than I had on the Congo Advisory Committee – the Committee of delegates from those member nations which have contributed forces to the Congo operation. Mr Kennedy certainly knew more about African questions generally, and about the Congo, than I did; his UN experience, though no longer than mine, was more continuous. Mr Boland, who knew us both well, gave, I am sure, an objective and penetrating account of each of us; the element in Mr Kennedy's character on which he laid (I understand) stress was reliability, in mine original-ity – an analysis perhaps flattering to me but more apt to commend Mr Kennedy to an ordinary prospective employer. Mr Cordier's report to Mr Hammarskjold, following this discussion, is not likely, I think, to have been weighted in my favour; friendly though Mr Cordier is – and kind as he has been to me personally – there is something about his massive figure, deliberate movements and small, shrewd eyes, which suggests that, confronted with a choice between 'reliability' and 'originality', he will not necessarily plump for 'originality'.

Against this background, Mr Hammarskjold's choice will seem all

[1] The emphasis, in *The Observer* article, on what appeared to be a somewhat eccentric element of Hammarskjold's choice was due, not so much to any real modesty on my part, as to the strategy of self-depreciation which one almost instinctively adopts when writing for a certain kind of English audience. I now realize that it is foolish for a foreigner to attempt this technique. Only a true-born Englishman knows the trick of being self-depreciatory without actually doing himself any damage – I only succeeded in making people as far away as Arizona think I was 'boasting'.

the more surprising, even whimsical. Yet I think the explanation is simple enough. From his assessment of what was needful for the UN in Katanga (and outside Katanga) following the February resolution and from what he knew about me, he decided that I fitted the needs of this particular political situation. If he did not pick the 'safer' man, it is because he wanted the less 'safe' one. We need not assume that he knew, before he had to make his choice, anything of the background given in the previous chapter but, at the time of making the choice, it would have been surprising if he had not made it his business to find out the essential elements – including the fact that I was regarded as the 'radical' member of the Irish delegation, wearing my mandatory anti-colonialism rather more aggressively than was prudent.[1] That book of mine might have given him a hint or two of this, as well as certain reassurances; he may have got a less qualified hint from certain delegates; in any case Mr Cordier's commentaries on the profiles supplied by Mr Boland would not have understated the case. 'He has put the pieces of your personality together', a friend of Hammarskjold's told me; the book was one, but only one, of the pieces.

In choosing between Mr Kennedy and myself for Katanga, he was, and knew himself to be, choosing between people who would use the marginal discretion of a representative somewhat differently. Both would seek to implement the resolutions peacefully, but, if that proved impossible, one would be likely, at need, to prefer the maintenance of the Katangan version of law and order to the full implementation of the February resolution; the other would insist on the implementation of the resolution, even if necessary, at grave risk to that law and order. If Hammarskjold chose the second, it was because by March 1961 he considered, for reasons discussed later, that the policy implied in that choice was the policy which the UN must pursue in Katanga. No one was better placed than he was

---

[1] He may conceivably have had some memory of this himself from the First Committee in Cyprus debates, which he attended regularly. I remember one night debate when Commander Alan Noble, a fine seaman who represented Britain for this question, had made the statement: 'When Her Majesty's Government says "autonomy" it means "autonomy" and not "self-government" or anything else.' This was rendered in French simultaneous translation: '*Quand le Gouvernement de sa Majesté dit "autonomie" il veut dire "autonomie" et non pas "autonomie" ou quoi que ce soit d'autre*'. On a point of clarification I asked what was the exact nature of the distinction which Her Majesty's Government had established between autonomy and self-government. (French translation: *Quelle est la nuance exacte établie par le gouvernement de sa Majesté entre "l'autonomie" et "l'autonomie?"* '). Commander Noble shed no light but Mr Hammarskjold, contrary to his custom, smiled broadly.

to weigh the risks inherent in that policy against the risks of allowing
the February resolution to remain a dead letter, while the 'Independent State of Katanga' continued – as it was then still doing – to
consolidate its position.[1]

I reported for duty at the UN Secretariat in New York on the
morning of Monday, May 29th. When I arrived, Mr Hammarskjold
was giving a Press conference, on the eve of his departure to Oxford
to deliver what became his celebrated lecture on the 'Role of the
International Civil Servant'[2] – the lecture that was in effect a reply
to Mr Khrushchev's thesis that 'there are no neutral men'.

At his Press conference, Mr Hammarskjold radiated serenity and
confidence. I guessed, as most of the Press did, that his air of
confidence was connected not with the Congo news – which was
then no more exhilarating than usual – but with his recent triumph
at the resumed Fifteenth Session of the General Assembly. The
Assembly, including most of the neutrals, had, by clear implication,
voted 83–11 in favour of the proposition that there *were* neutral men
and that he was one of them. The new Democratic United States
administration came much closer than its predecessor had done to
sharing Mr Hammarskjold's conception of the United Nations, and
of his own office. That administration also paid much more heed
than its predecessor to the opinion of the Afro-Asian 'neutral anti-
colonialists', and this brought closer and somewhat more safely
together the two main props on which the Secretary-General,
assailed both by the Communists and by the European Right, was
obliged to rely for support. The international political conjuncture
was therefore more favourable to the particular conception of the
office of Secretary-General, which had become identified with the
personality of Mr Hammarskjold, than it had been at any time
since the Chairman of the Committee of Ministers of the Soviet
Union had summoned the Secretary-General to resign 'in a chival-
rous manner'.

It was no wonder, therefore, that Mr Hammarskjold seemed
confident, that he even allowed himself to show a frosty sparkle of
elation. The idea of the United Nations, and of his own office, which
he had defended so staunchly and so ingeniously, seemed about to
prevail.

It seemed about to prevail; it had not yet prevailed, and there

---

[1] The political background to the Katanga situation, as it was in March–June
1961 is discussed on pp. 58 *sqq.* and in Chapter IV.

[2] A summary of this lecture is given in Mr Joseph Lash's sympathetic and useful
biography, *Dag Hammarskjold* (pp. 288–291).

remained great barriers, not yet fully known, to be surmounted before success would be assured. For that massive vote of confidence[1] had been equivocal; it was, at bottom, a vote of confidence in his capacity and intention *to follow two different and possibly irreconcilable courses of action.* The vote of confidence, like the Soviet assertions of lack of confidence, concerned of course the Congo, and specifically Katanga. It was a vote of confidence that the Secretary-General – whom the Soviet delegation was accusing of collaborating with Mr Tshombe, and of having a share in the responsibility for the murder of Mr Lumumba by Mr Tshombe's régime – would sincerely implement resolutions which were drafted with Katanga especially in mind. For the Afro-Asian supporters of the resolutions – and of the vote of confidence – the resolutions implied that the secessionist régime in Katanga would be brought down by the immediate evacuation of the foreign officers and political advisers on which the régime was generally believed to depend for its continued existence; the vote of confidence, for them, implied their belief that Mr Hammarskjold would see to it that this task was carried out, using, in the words of the resolution, 'force, if necessary, in the last resort'.[2] What the resolutions meant in the mind of Western countries which voted for them, as Great Britain did, is less clear, but the British delegation made it clear what the resolution, in its opinion, did *not* mean: it did not mean what its framers thought it meant – power to use force if necessary against Mr Tshombe's mercenary-led army. The 'confidence' of these Western countries hinged on what they assumed to be his intention never to do what the 'confidence' of the Afro-Asians expected him to do *if necessary.*

As Representative-designate (though then still *in petto*) of the United Nations in Katanga, responsible to Mr Hammarskjold for the implementation of these equivocal resolutions, and for the meriting of all this contradictory confidence, I ought to have been more preoccupied by these considerations, as I listened to Mr Hammarskjold's Press conference, than in fact I was. I was indeed fully conscious, from having served on the Congo Advisory Committee during the Resumed Fifteenth Session, of ambiguities in the

---

[1] Technically, it was not a vote of confidence, but a vote taken at the request of Guinea, on whether the words 'by the Secretary-General' should, or should not, be included in a crucial paragraph of the Congo resolution. The overwhelming majority for inclusion was generally regarded as a vote of confidence, and applauded accordingly, and Mr Lash rightly so describes it (*Dag Hammarskjold*, p. 279).

[2] On 'use of force', see p. 62.

resolutions, and of unresolved conflicts between the different kinds of 'supporters' of the Secretary-General and the United Nations. I knew that the focus of these ambiguities and conflicts was Katanga, and that the task ahead of me was therefore regarded as one of peculiar difficulty. If I felt confident, none the less, that I could handle it successfully, this was not entirely due to conceit. The fact is that Mr Hammarskjold's own confidence was contagious, especially to all those who had, as I had, immense respect for his political acumen. If he felt as cheerful as he obviously did – I half-consciously reasoned – then the remaining unresolved antagonisms could not be irreconcilable. No doubt the *rapprochement*, which was clearly taking place between the United States and the Afro-Asian leaders, so strengthened the United Nations, and the Secretary-General's position, that Mr Hammarskjold's interpretation of the resolutions would prevail without excessive difficulty. If so, my own task, as I supposed, was relatively simple for, in the last analysis, all I had to do – apart from reporting and advising – was to apply the resolutions *as interpreted by the Secretary-General*. I did not, it is true, feel personally very happy about the wide spans of ambiguity, the underlying contradictions, in the resolutions which we were supposed to implement. I knew, however, that to Mr Hammarskjold such ambiguities were the breath of his nostrils, the medium in which he had his being. The greater the ambiguity in a Security Council decision, the wider was the Secretary-General's margin of interpretation. Through ambiguities resolved, through margins skilfully used, the office of Secretary-General had grown in stature and authority far beyond what the framers of the Charter seem to have envisaged at San Francisco. This was quite widely recognized; someone, I know not who, had even jested that the motto of the Secretary-General ought to be *Per Ambigua ad Astra*. To most good 'United Nations people', like myself, this growth seemed entirely healthy. The strengthening of the office was also the strengthening of the international community, the strengthening of the defences of peace. As for Mr Hammarskjold himself, we had complete confidence in him as being – I quote the words used about him, in private, by a Russian member of the Secretariat – 'an integritous man'. We even, I think, found something slightly intoxicating in the paradox of equivocation being used in the service of virtue, the thought of a disinterested Talleyrand, a Machiavelli of peace.

Subsequent experience, and reflection on that experience, were to induce me to modify these opinions significantly, without however entirely abandoning them. Anyone who may be interested in the afterthoughts will find them towards the end of this book. For the moment I had few if any misgivings, and certainly the letter in which, on the following day, I referred to the Secretary-General's press conference, shows little trace of political care:

> '*The same morning the S.-G. gave a Press conference which I attended. Ralph Teatsorth (United Press) asked him what duties were being assigned to C. C. O'B. and whether he was being posted to the Congo. The S.-G. said how glad he was to have been able to secure the services of C. C. O'B., who would be based on New York where he would serve "on my personal staff" (as valet?) However, C. C. O'B. might be sent to the Congo or elsewhere on some special mission, and temporarily.*
>
> '*At the end of the conference I went up and greeted Martin Hill* [a senior member of the Secretariat] *who brought me over to the S.-G. who graciously welcomed me, invited me to lunch but immediately had to cancel the invitation – very Pavlovian. He left that evening for England and is due back on Thursday.*'[1]

The letter goes on to regret the absence of Heinz Wieschhoff – the African expert on whom the Secretary-General most relied, and who was to die with him near Ndola, and of Andrew Cordier, and to describe my induction into the work of the Secretariat:

> '*In the meantime I was taken in hand by C. V. Narasimhan* [Indian Chef de Cabinet to the Secretary-General] *and have a temporary office beside his on the 38th floor, where I sit and read the Congo telegrams. I also sit in when Bunche and himself discuss what to do about the day's telegrams from Leo. – these conferences are normally led by the S.-G. and should be very interesting when he comes back. Narasimhan is polite but unapproachable and uninformative. Bunche is pleasanter personally but a bit vague.*'

When I re-read these lines the 'new-boy' feeling, of being at sea and rather smaller than usual, comes vividly back. It is of some interest that one who, after all, knew the United Nations rather well from the point of view of a delegate at the Assembly, should have experienced quite this feeling on entry into the Secretariat building. This was not really a matter of personalities, although I was not entirely happy in my first mentor. Mr Narasimhan is a Brahmin from South India, one of a regional-social grouping which is, I understand, admired in its native country more for subtlety of

---

[1] Letter to Máire MacEntee dated Tuesday, May 30th. There may be those who find the tone of this unduly flippant, considering the grave responsibilities I was assuming. I can only refer the objectors to the last sentence of the Introduction.

intellect than for openness of character. His manner was a little that of a monk obliged, by his obedience to some holy Abbot, to show a neophyte the fabric of the temple, but determined not to reveal any more of its mysteries than was absolutely necessary. (How right he was, he must now feel!) As, like many people from highly religious countries, I am made uneasy by the clerical manner, Mr Narasimhan and I were not markedly drawn to each other. Such small incompatibilities are, however, part of the ordinary stuff of official life anywhere, and this one troubled me very little. As for Dr Bunche – on whose sensitive and humorous, but increasingly rueful, face the preoccupations of the Congo cast a deeper shadow than ever they did on Hammarskjold – the absent-minded kindness of his manner seemed to say something like: 'What is the good of our trying to tell you anything about the Congo? You'll go there; you'll find something out for yourself; who knows what it will be?' Someone said once that the study of history was like sitting on the cat – meaning, I suppose, that its surprises left their scars. Dr Bunche made no secret of the fact that in his own time in the Congo – which was very recent, according to normal standards, although almost geologically remote by the Congo's peculiar time-scale – he had studied history on this method. He did not try to explain the experience; he no doubt felt there was no point in doing so – in a little while I would understand for myself only too well. He was quite right.

What gave me, on that first day, an ill-defined sense of uneasiness had nothing to do with personalities: it was reading the file of telegrams from Leopoldville. Not that the telegrams contained at this period anything which was in itself particularly startling; the slight shock which they gave me came from the small precisions in the telegrams which, taken together, made a picture quite sharply different from the rounded contours of the one created for us by the official reports, circulated to delegates in the General Assembly and at the Congo Advisory Committee. In itself, this new and sharper picture was in some ways more encouraging than the official version, in which the United Nations was always impeccable and often apparently helpless. The telegrams showed activities which were, quite often, sinful enough from the point of view of this or that group of nations; they also showed that certain representatives in the field, far from being helpless victims, had an almost Elizabethan share of initiative. I shall not give examples simply from my own imprecise memory of this record of events outside my own experience; the rest of this narrative should, in itself, give an adequate impression of the phenomenon which here forced itself on my attention. What produced the sense of shock was the growing impression that neither the General Assembly nor the Security Council had the full materials necessary for an adequately informed discussion, and adequately motivated decisions, on the UN operation in the Congo. The only people who had these materials were the people who saw the actual telegrams – the inner circle of the Secretariat together with those, whoever they might be, to whom these telegrams might from time to time be shown by the Secretary-General or by one of his principal advisers. As for the Congo Advisory Committee, 'advising' the Secretary-General on the basis of the information with which the Secretary-General saw fit to supply it, it seemed, in the light of the telegrams, much less like an advisory body than like a group of innocent outsiders being taken for a guided tour.

I told myself that it was naïve to be surprised at this, and quite wrong, from an international point of view, to have reservations about it. In sovereign States, the Foreign Minister did not take Parliament into his full confidence about the dispatches he received from his Ambassadors, yet Parliaments continued to discuss Foreign Affairs – sometimes, it was said, usefully enough. True, a Foreign Minister normally kept his Cabinet, or at the very least, his Prime Minister, fully informed of all important dispatches. No such relation existed between the Secretary-General and the Security Council, and if there was any 'Cabinet' for the Congo operation it was not the Security Council but the highly informal, and perhaps rather eccentrically composed, 'Congo Club' within the Secretariat itself. In so far as I was conscious at all of this difficulty at this time, my response to it was in the feeling that the Secretariat – rather than the half-paralysed Security Council or the amorphous General Assembly – was the reality of the United Nations, the advancing edge of the sense of international community. If the Secretariat played its cards remarkably close to its chest, as it now seemed that it was in the habit of doing, it was justified in this, because it was tremendously important, for the hopes it represented, that it should win.

Much of this was implicit in my attitude of mind at this time, rather than fully thought out. What I was actually most conscious of was the more primitive feeling of pleasure at now being, as I thought, 'on the inside' of this major international operation, combined with a sense of deflation, on realizing how very much 'on the outside' one had been, as an ordinary delegate in the corridors of the Assembly and at the Advisory Committee. Something of this atmosphere comes through in a letter I wrote towards the end of this brief experience of the 38th Floor:

> *'I've been sitting in on the evening meetings on the Congo, with, at the last one, the Secretary-General, who is now back, in the chair. These are business-like and civilized meetings. We all sit around a big table and go through the day's Congo telegrams, while refreshments are served. This is where the Congo decisions are taken. It's rather like an American cabinet – everyone puts their oar in, but the man in the chair takes the decisions. For a new-comer it is a very educative experience, I need hardly say!'*[1]

From the slightly fatuous tone of these remarks, it would seem that I had then very little idea of how much of my United Nations education still lay ahead of me. The atmosphere, as I now recall it, was much less like 'an American cabinet' than like something more within my knowledge: meetings between a youngish headmaster and a bright sixth form. Not that any one member of the 'Congo Club' was like a schoolboy – and some of them individually were trusted advisers – but that the group at its meetings stood in that sort of relationship to its leader.

The members of the Club at that time, in addition to Mr Narasimhan and Dr Bunche, were Mr Andrew Cordier, Dr Heinz Wieschhoff, Sir Alexander MacFarquhar (United Kingdom), General Rikhye of India and Mr Francis Nwokedi of Nigeria. Mr Cordier, the Executive Assistant, was the senior member of the group; on the scholastic metaphor, he was a housemaster rather than a member of the class. Appropriately, he spoke very little at the Club; one had the impression that anything he had to say would be weighty, and for the Secretary-General's ear alone. Indeed, the only time I remember his intervening – at any of the few meetings of the Club I attended in Mr Hammarskjold's lifetime – was when Dr Bunche, who had the amiable habit of introducing subjects other than the Congo, referred to some interesting article or lecture by a distinguished Jesuit. The rare note of Mr Cordier's deep bass was then heard, pointing out, with good-natured firmness, that for him, as a Methodist, no Jesuit could be distinguished and no article by one could be interesting. One reason why Mr Cordier did not have anything to say at these meetings – except, in this emergency, to hold back Dr Bunche from the edge of the pit – was that he knew he had become – like so many former Congo hands – a controversial

---

[1] Letter to Máire MacEntee, June 3rd, 1961.

figure, as a result of past events touched on later in this book. He was, in any case, on the verge of retirement, and already something of an elder statesman.

Sir Alexander MacFarquhar and General Rikhye are specialists, in economic and military affairs respectively, and Mr Nwokedi, as a relatively new member of the Club, took little part in its proceedings. The remaining member of the Club, Dr Heinz Wieschhoff, was perhaps at this time the most important, though by no means the most senior. He was an anthropologist by training and his interest in the Congo dated back to the twenties – not, as for so many of us, to June 1960. He had been the 'African expert' in the Secretariat for some time: as such, he had served as Secretary of the important Fourth – Trusteeship or 'African' – Committee of the Assembly and he had recently been transferred from that responsible post to the even more responsible one of Secretary to the First (Political) Committee. This transfer had been generally considered as symbolizing the Secretary-General's conviction that African questions were now at the heart of United Nations political concern. Wieschhoff had a hard, lucid mind and a strong, even formidable, personality; there were several other people in that room who were far from being nonentities, but Heinz Wieschhoff was the only one who, when Mr Hammarskjold was there, seemed to continue to radiate on a wave-length of his own. It was a wave-length which produced some crackling, on my set at least, but the emissions were powerful. I can still see quite vividly his odd, striking face, with the heavily corrugated forehead under the almost hairless head; the pale eyes behind slipping spectacles, exactly half-way between the tight, pursed line of the mouth and the deepest crease of the brow. I had sat for many, often weary, hours facing him at the First Committee, and I had thought once that the siting of his features represented the nearest approach I had ever seen, on a real person, to one of those trick drawings of the human face, which still looks like a face even if you turn it upside down. This was an incongruous and idle thought, but it is a measure of the man's personality that an effect which, in a lesser man, would have been merely comic seemed, in his case, positively eerie.

Although – he would have said 'because' – he was an expert on Africans, Wieschhoff was no favourite with the Afro-Asians, and he regarded many members of that group with ill-concealed contempt. I do not know whether he actually coined the term 'Mau-Mau', widely used in private to describe the Afro-Asian group, especially in the Fourth Committee, but certainly those who most used this term tended to be those who most admired him. He had, I believe, an affection for Africans, but it must surely have been an anthropologist's affection, confined to members of 'unspoiled' traditional cultures. Thus, 'detribalized' would have been, for him, a derogatory term – which is strange, since, as an Austrian naturalized American, he could be regarded as 'detribalized' himself. From his Germanic origin he derived, I thought, his almost peremptory manner, and perhaps a certain liking for the authoritarian style. In the Club, when he intervened, as he did briefly and sparingly, he was apt to urge, in cogent words, strong action. I noticed on one occasion that, while he was speaking in this sense, his pencil, held in the clenched fist of his right hand, was stabbing, deeply and repeatedly, into the blotting pad in front of him.

Heinz Wieschhoff died in the service of the United Nations, and his friends, I fear, are likely to resent a picture of him which can have little in common with the side of his character they must have known. To them I can only say that, although I did not, it is true, like this remarkable man, I did – as can be seen – have respect for him, and that a respectful portrait, by an unfriendly hand, is something harder to win than a flattering obituary signed by a friend.

The gentle Bunche, the solid Cordier, the incisive Wieschhoff, had two things in common: they were, all three, Americans and they were at this time the closest advisers of the Secretary-General. Dr Bunche was the second most eminent United Nations personality, the only member of the Secretariat, except Hammarskjold himself, who was known to a wide public. Mr Cordier was regarded, inside the building, as the fly-wheel of the organization; as for Wieschhoff, Hammarskjold had referred to him as his 'grey eminence',[1] and he was generally accepted as being exactly that, at least where African and especially Congo matters were concerned. This 'American monopoly' of the inner circle had been, and was then still being, savagely denounced in the Soviet and Soviet-inspired press, and had caused considerable uneasiness among Afro-Asians. It was, no doubt, in an effort to allay that uneasiness that Mr Narasimhan, General Rikhye, and Mr Nwokedi had recently been introduced into the Club and also Mr Robert Gardiner of Ghana, who was then in Leopoldville, and M Taieb Sahbani of Tunisia, then in Brussels.[2] But old habits of confidence do not automatically expand to match the expansion of a formal group. I have the impression – admittedly a subjective one – that the real advisers remained the same and that

---

[1] Lash, *Dag Hammarskjold*, p. 294.
[2] *Dag Hammarskjold*, p. 259.

the expanded 'Congo Club', at its regular meetings, had become to some extent a practical training school; hence, perhaps, the 'sixth-form' effect I have referred to.[1] At this time the report was current that Cordier, Bunche and Wieschhoff would be leaving very shortly, and that the Congo Club would become almost exclusively 'neutral' – my own appointment was, in its way, a move, or gesture, in this direction. Whatever the intention and the forms may have been, the inner reality – of decision by the Secretary-General, surrounded by a small group of advisers who happened to be Americans – did not, I believe, change during Hammarskjold's life. It is perhaps symbolic that the adviser who was with Hammarskjold on the flight towards Ndola was not one of the 'neutrals' who were supposed to be 'taking over' but one of the old guard, the 'grey eminence' from the American group. The 'Congo Club', at the last, was Hammarskjold and Wieschhoff.

According to one view, which was apparently that of Hammarskjold himself, the nationality of these trusted advisers was a matter of little or no importance – or rather, it derived such importance as it came to have, solely from ill-informed outside criticism. Joseph Lash, an experienced American journalist – and left-of-centre by local reckoning – is firmly of that opinion.:

'Men like Cordier, Bunche, Wieschhoff did not give a damn what Washington said, if they differed from Washington; Hammarskjold knew that, but the outside world says, "We hope so, but . . ."'[2]

Hammarskjold himself asserted a similar doctrine, in more theoretical language, just at this time in his Oxford defence of the 'neutral man' position. He had referred to the 'international civil servant's use of his area of discretion' and to the accusations of lack of neutrality – of being influenced by 'interests which are close to him in a personal capacity' – which will always be made against him when he exercises his discretion. He went on:

'If the international civil servant knows himself to be free

---

[1] The attentive reader will note that this is *not* the way I reported the Congo Club at the time in the letter I have quoted, where I said flatly: 'This is where the Congo decisions are taken.' I am afraid an element of human vanity came into the letter: I wished to think I was where the decisions were taken – and of course some of them actually were taken there. The idea that the really important ones might be taken in consultation, not with the Club, but with one or two members of an inner circle would not have been entirely palatable to me at the time. At the same time, error is also possible in retrospective interpretation. The reader, being warned, must choose for himself.

[2] *Dag Hammarskjold*, p. 284.

from such personal influences in his actions and guided solely by the common aims and rules laid down for, and by, the Organization he serves and by recognized legal principles, then he has done his duty and then he can face the criticism which, even so, will be unavoidable.'

There is no reason to doubt that Hammarskjold sincerely believed that his trusted collaborators, as well as he himself, habitually maintained themselves on this high plateau of intellectual and moral impartiality. Nor is there any reason to doubt that the collaborators believed the same thing and honestly strove to hold these heights. There is, however, surely room for philosophic doubt as to whether any life, intellectual or other, can in fact be maintained on this exalted level. What sort of creature can be guided *solely* by the Charter of the United Nations, the Staff Regulations, the Resolutions of the General Assembly and the Security Council, and textbooks on international law?

Zoologists tell us of tiny mammals who manage to exist in the high Himalayas 'exclusively on a diet of wind-blown debris'. Such a diet should not be expected, however, to keep body and soul together at the altitude of the 38th floor.

I should like to suggest, with due diffidence – granted the example of Hammarskjold's life, and the authority of experience behind his Oxford lecture – that the good international civil servant must necessarily be guided not solely by the factors mentioned at Oxford, but also by what he thinks is right, and that his idea of what is right is historically and culturally formed. The nationality, the social class, the training and the formation, the political background, of an international civil servant, are surely not just 'personal influences' which, by an effort of will, he can entirely dismiss from his mind. They have shaped his will and his mind, and he can no more escape from them than he can escape from his skeleton.

If you accept Hammarskjold's Oxford thesis, and its concrete application by Mr Lash, it is entirely irrelevant that Hammarskjold's closest advisers were all Americans; if you feel that there is any force at all in the critique of that thesis here attempted, then that fact is not entirely irrelevant. You may think it very good, if you think that standards of values generally accepted in America are much better than those prevailing elsewhere; you may think it very bad, if you believe Americans to be wicked or corrupted by obsolete institutions. Or you may think that Americans are at least as good as anyone else, and often better, but that you can have too much of a good thing – specifically that in a world organization

you can have too much of one nation's – or one bloc's – idea of
what is good for everybody.

It is true certainly that these three key people had all a high
concept of international duty – perhaps the same standard, probably
impossibly high, as Hammarskjold had himself. There was no
question of their accepting directives from Washington and it was
common knowledge that at least two of them had, at various times,
resisted pressure from that quarter. It is hard, however, to go all
the way with Mr Lash when he says that they 'did not give a damn
what Washington said, if they differed from Washington'. To begin
with, there was no one in the United Nations, of any nationality,
who 'did not give a damn what Washington said'. Washington
paid most of the bills, was the heaviest contributor to the organization's general budget and by far the heaviest contributor to the
Congo operation, which would be brought to a standstill by a
withdrawal of American support. Washington wielded tremendous
influence in the General Assembly and in the Security Council.
It is almost certainly true to say that any Secretary-General who
lost the confidence of Washington would have to resign. A storm
from the East can be weathered, although with difficulty; a storm
from the West could probably not be weathered at all. To keep a
weather eye on Washington is therefore an elemental, vital necessity
for the Secretary-General and his collaborators. A man like Andrew
Cordier, so far from 'not giving a damn what Washington said', was
an expert at judging the force and probable duration of gusts from
the Potomac, and therein, precisely, lay his main value to the organization. The wisdom of Andrew Cordier did not derive from a reading
of the Charter or of international law, but from the fact that he
remained a down-to-earth American, who knew how his fellow-
countrymen would react, because he continued to react in the same
way. Because of that – not despite it – he had rendered very great
service to the United Nations. But to ask Russians and Afro-Asians
to accept Andrew Cordier as an absolutely detached and impartial
interpreter of a common will, just as indifferent to American
particular interests as to theirs, was to demand the impossible.

The Congo Club, then, consisted at this time of an inner core of
Americans round Mr Hammarskjold, with an outer casing of
neutrals, mainly Afro-Asian. The Western group and the Afro-
Asians are, of course, two out of the three main constituent elements
of the United Nations. The third element – the Communist States –
was not represented in the Club, and care was taken to see that no
member of the Secretariat, who was a citizen of a Communist State,

saw the Congo telegrams. Mr Georgi Arkadev, the official seconded from the service of the Soviet Union who was then Under-Secretary for Political and Security Council affairs, did not have access to the Congo files in the custody of his subordinate 'Director and Deputy to the Under-Secretary for Political and Security Council Affairs', Heinz Wieschhoff. Wieschhoff, in practice, though not in theory, worked direct to Hammarskjold, ignoring his superior officer Mr Arkadev.

This state of affairs was justified on the following grounds:

A Soviet citizen like Arkadev, it was argued, was in an entirely different position from men like Cordier, Bunche and Wieschhoff. They could resist pressure from Washington: he could not resist pressure from Moscow. They were governed by the high, Hammarskjoldian conception of loyalty to the international organization alone; he was ideologically committed – and selected by reason of that commitment – to the political outlook prevailing in one group of countries and he would be obliged, in terms of that outlook, to continue, while serving the United Nations, to give his first loyalty to the cause of Communism. Furthermore, since the Communist countries were at this time bitterly denouncing the Secretary-General's conduct of the Congo operation, how could the Secretary-General, in his conduct of that operation, possibly be expected to confide in, and seek advice from, one who remained a loyal servant of Soviet Russia and of Communism?

The final objection, which seems the most forceful, is in fact the weakest, for it was common knowledge at the United Nations, long before the Congo operation, that the senior Soviet official was being by-passed on all really important political matters. It was generally believed, and seems highly probable, that to by-pass him was a condition of retaining the all-important confidence of the US Government. Certainly it was inevitable, by the time matters had reached the present pass, that people of Mr Arkadev's persuasion should be kept out of the Congo planning, but it could reasonably be argued that one of the reasons why this pass had been reached was that Americans had always been kept in, and Russians always kept out, of the planning in question. It was quite true that the national loyalty expected of, say, Mr Cordier as an American citizen was of a less precise and exigent character than that expected of Mr Arkadev as a Soviet citizen but, from what I have already suggested about Mr Cordier's outlook, it may be conceived that the difference in degree of national loyalty between the 'good American' and the 'good Russian' was less wide in practice than it was in theory. In any case, it is hardly surprising that the Russians, seeing the Secretary-General surrounded by Americans, and withholding his confidence from any Russian, should have come to question his impartiality. If the positions had been reversed, if Mr Hammarskjold had had an inner cabinet composed of Soviet citizens, and had kept the American members of the Secretariat in the dark about what he was doing, it is hardly probable that American public opinion would have accepted this situation with complete equanimity.

Soviet resentment, in itself not incomprehensible or irrational, had by this time reached a pitch where it resulted in violent and unfounded accusations. Hammarskjold was being depicted as a 'tool of Western imperialists' – a charge which must have sounded ironic to genuine imperialists. The Congo Club, presided over by Hammarskjold at this date, was much more determined about applying the resolutions in Katanga – and that was still the crux of the whole matter – than any European conservative, even one disclaiming the imperialist label, would have considered acceptable. The Afro-Asian thesis – that the secession of Katanga would have to be ended, and that the United Nations would have to help actively in ending it – was tacitly accepted round the table, and not less by the Americans than by the others. What mattered most to all of them was that the United Nations should emerge successfully from its Congo ordeal and it was clearly seen that a condition of success was the speedy removal of the props of Mr Tshombe's régime, thereby making possible the restoration of the unity of the Congo. The continued existence of the independent State of Katanga was recognized as a threat to the existence of the United Nations and therefore even those who, from the standpoint of their personal, political opinions, might have been favourably enough disposed to what Mr Tshombe represented, were convinced of the necessity for strong measures. The point that Wieschhoff was emphasizing as he jabbed his pencil deep into the blotting-paper, was the need to expel from Katanga, if necessary by force – '*manu militari*' – the Belgian political advisers Weber and Clémens.[1] Yet Wieschhoff, if he had not been a servant of the United Nations, might well have been a supporter of Tshombe's; this was an example of the victory of an international loyalty over personal predilections. If neutral men are simply men who put the interests of the United Nations first, then Hammarskjold and all around him at that table, were neutral men.

Unfortunately it was hardly as simple as that. Great as was the

---

[1] These cases are referred to in Chapter VII.

loyalty of these men towards the United Nations, and great as was their desire for impartiality, there were important limiting factors on their neutrality. The composition of the group was eloquent of this, expressive of the fact that the Secretariat had become 'neutral between America and Afro-Asia'. True, whether Americans or Afro-Asians, they all put the interests of the United Nations first, but – with due respect to Mr Hammarskjold's Oxford thesis – their conceptions of what constituted the interests of the United Nations were profoundly and involuntarily affected by (among other things) their own national formation. They were also necessarily affected by the wider political context, which had itself helped to shape the composition of the group. Nobody said out loud: 'Keep Communism out of Africa by ending the secession of Katanga', and indeed most people round that table would have been genuinely shocked, and for a moment even puzzled, if such language had been used. Yet, ineluctably, that was the spirit of the unspoken bargain between the United States and the Afro-Asian group: the bargain on which the continuance of the Congo operation had come to depend. 'The first objective of the United Nations in the Congo', since the fall of Lumumba, had become, according to acute Belgian observers, 'the attainment of a political success in Katanga, which would demonstrate the good faith of the UN with regard to the Afro-Asian countries and would remove all grounds for the fear of Soviet bilateral aid'.[1] The vital principle, for the United States, was keeping the Communists out of the Congo; this involved opposing the secession of Katanga which, if condoned, would be a precedent, valid in Afro-Asian eyes, for another secession round Stanleyville, leading to 'a Central African Cuba'. The vital principle for the Afro-Asians was to stop the European-instigated Katanga break-away, with the deadly precedent of disintegration which it represented for so many of the new and vulnerable States. Few Afro-Asian Governments were genuinely preoccupied by the need to keep Communism out of the Congo, and many Americans had considerable misgivings about ending the secession of Katanga; yet neither side could hope to get what it wanted without the help of the other, and so the unspoken bargain came into being.

That was why these particular neutral men were sitting round this particular table, doing their best to cope with one of the most difficult, equivocal and unprecedented tasks which history can ever have set to any group of human beings.

---

[1] *Congo 1960* (Dossiers du CRISP) Vol. II, p. 1085.

In strict theory, of course, the unspoken bargain had nothing to do with these men; their task was to implement a series of resolutions, which provided among other things that the United Nations should not interfere in the internal affairs of the Congo.

Paragraph 4 of the Security Council resolution of August 9th, 1960 (doc. S/4426) reads as follows:

'Reaffirms that the United Nations force in the Congo will not be a party to or in any way intervene in or be used to influence the outcome of any internal conflict, constitutional or otherwise.'

On a strict interpretation of this, it was no business of theirs to keep Communism out of the Congo, and also no business of theirs to end secession in Katanga. Yet, in practice, every day they were taking decisions implying the use of UN forces in ways capable of influencing the internal affairs and the political future of the Congo, nor was it possible for them to do otherwise. Andrew Cordier, rightly or wrongly, had taken a decision[1] which, politically, had broken the back of Lumumba – the Prime Minister who had called in the United Nations – and had been extremely satisfactory from the point of view of those whose main interest was to keep the Communists out of the Congo. From the point of view of the other party – those whose main interest was to end the secession of Katanga – the previous record of the United Nations was much less satisfactory, although there was, it seemed to them, much more legal warrant for firm action about Katanga than there had been for Mr Cordier's anti-Communist *coup*. Why, they asked, did the Secretary-General not implement the General Assembly resolution of September 20th, 1960, paragraph 2 of which requested him to take action: . . . to assist the Central Government of the Congo in the restoration and maintenance of law and order throughout the territory of the Republic of the Congo and to safeguard its unity, territorial integrity and political independence in the interests of international peace and security.'[2]

The new Security Council Resolution – that of February[3] – was seen by Afro-Asians as 'putting teeth in' the earlier Assembly resolution, and was correspondingly disliked by the 'friends of Katanga'.

The United States had supported the February resolution, in the

---

[1] See Chapter IV, pp. 93–4.

[2] A/Res.1474 revision I. This is hard in practice to reconcile with the Security Council resolution of August 9th – which resolution the General Assembly at the same moment, fully supported.

[3] Text in Appendix I.

spirit of the unspoken bargain, because there was a strong danger that, if they did not support it, Afro-Asian opinion might swing over to Mr Khrushchev's side. For each party to the bargain had its 'kibbitzers'. The Communists were assuring the Afro-Asians that 'the Americans who run the Secretariat' were only interested in fighting Communism and would do no more than make empty gestures in the direction of restoring the unity of the Congo. The British, French and Belgians were letting Americans know of their fears lest any undue concession to the Afro-Asian view, any 'unwise' pressure on Mr Tshombe, might result, not in keeping the Communists out, but in letting them in. And more than one American official privately – or semi-privately – felt that the British, French and Belgians might well be right.

The men around the table could not ignore, and did not ignore, this political context in their day-to-day interpretation of their mandate. The contradictions and equivocations in that mandate allowed them a good deal of leeway, and this, as I have mentioned, Hammarskjold was adept at using. Sometimes, as I heard some feat of interpretation, some especially refined harmonization of S/4426 paragraph 4 with A/Res.1474 paragraph 2, and noted how neatly it fitted the political needs of the moment, I was reminded of an excellent formula invented by a Central American Chairman of the First Committee, when he found it desirable to stretch the rules a little for the benefit of Mr Cabot Lodge: 'Under the rule', he said, 'it would seem that the Delegate is not permitted to speak at this stage. I shall, however, interpret the rule in the spirit of the principles of philosophical jurisprudence. I give the floor to the Representative of the United States.'

The men round the table on the 38th floor were often inspired by the spirit of philosophical jurisprudence, and indeed the Congo operation, if it were to be carried on at all, demanded such a spirit. Yet the necessity to justify present action in terms of the earlier resolutions – which had been passed for precise though unstated political reasons in political contexts which had now changed beyond recognition – put the Secretariat permanently, and a little deviously, on the defensive. Clearly this difficulty would become greater when it came to the point of seriously implementing the February resolution. Those who secretly disliked the drastic implications of that resolution would seek to nullify it in practice by invoking the 'non-intervention' doctrine of August 1960.

Sir Patrick Dean, the United Kingdom delegate, had made this fairly clear in explaining his vote 'in favour' of the resolution:

Specifically as regards paragraph 1 of part A he said: 'I must explain that the interpretation which my delegation puts upon the words at the end of that paragraph, namely, "and the use of force, if necessary, in the last resort" is that force will only be used to prevent a clash between hostile Congolese troops. There can be no question of empowering the United Nations to use its forces to impose a political settlement.'[1] (S/PV.942 pp. 9–10). The Soviet representative, Mr Valerian Zorin, on the other hand, used the British and other interpretations in justifying his own abstention: 'Some of the points in this resolution were not drawn in a very clear manner so that the colonizers and those who serve them could use these provisions at the time of the implementation of this resolution. This was brought out by the explanations made by many representatives of countries which voted in favour of the resolution and who interpreted, each according to his own way, the various paragraphs of that resolution.' (S/PV.942, p. 121). Hammarskjold in rebutting the charge implied by Mr Zorin's reference to 'the colonizers and those who serve them' indicated clearly that he would lean to an 'Afro-Asian' rather than an 'Anglo-French' interpretation of what the resolution meant. 'I shall urgently avail myself', he said, 'of the valuable assistance of the Advisory Committee. It is from its members, fifteen of which are from African and Asian countries, that I will seek guidance in its implementation.' (SPV.942, pp. 133–135). These three statements should be carefully borne in mind. Taken together, they provide a central clue to the main course of subsequent events.

The fact was that if the Secretary-General really held to 'non-intervention', the new February resolution would become a dead letter and the 'unspoken bargain' would break down, thereby shattering the foundations of the United Nations operation. If that

---

[1] Sir P. Dean earlier, drawing attention to Part A, paragraphs 1 and 4, and part B, paragraph 2, said that 'each of these paragraphs if taken in isolation could, it seems to me, mean that the United Nations would take action in the Congo by force without appropriate consultation with the representatives of the Congolese people. This interpretation would be, in the opinion of my delegation, extremely dangerous'. He did not refer to paragraph A2 (mercenaries): the paragraph actually invoked by the UN in relation to the operations of August 28th, 1961, and September 13th, 1961. Paragraph A2 does not specifically authorize force but the Secretary-General interpreted it – not without 'appropriate consultation with the representatives of the Congolese people' – as warranting, in the context of the resolutions as a whole, the use of force for the apprehension of the mercenaries (see Chapters XII to XV). The use of force for this purpose was later specifically authorized in the Security Council's Resolution of November 24th, 1961, Sir P. Dean abstaining. As regards the action of September 13th, see Chapter XV.

happened, there would be a serious danger not exactly of a Korea but of a 'Spanish Civil War' situation in the Congo. The risks of other similar situations elsewhere, and even the risks of general war, would also be greatly increased, for the United Nations would have received a mortal blow by the failure of the greatest operation it had ever undertaken.

By any reckoning there were storms ahead. The captain's problem in setting his course was to decide which storm-centre presented on the whole the lesser risk. In deciding, as he did, on the 'Afro-Asian interpretation' – the vigorous implementation of the February resolution – Mr Hammarskjold decided to head for the storm centring on the English Channel – that is to say, to risk the hostility of England, France and Belgium. He may have underestimated the dangers of this course; he was surely right in considering it less dangerous – to the United Nations, to the Congo and to general peace – than was the alternative of drifting towards collapse.

At the time I was aware of these storm signals, but that does not mean that I had much idea of what the fury of the storm, when actually experienced, would be like. On the face of the situation, as I interpreted it intellectually – without, however, being emotionally convinced of it – there was a strong possibility that I should become, administratively at least, a casualty. There were some whitened bones around, on the 38th floor itself, which should have brought the thing home to me:

'*I had half an hour with Dayal before his depature*' – I wrote in the letter from which I have already quoted – '*and he spoke very openly indeed, but what he said is not meet to be here set down.*'

Mr Dayal was just leaving that day to rejoin the Indian Foreign Service. He was leaving at his own request, following his 'controversial' term of office as UN Special Representative in the Congo and was thereby terminating a long period of 'consultations' for which he had been summoned to New York. On the morning of this brief meeting he was, as usual, dignified and calm. He explained without rancour, but as things important for me to know, the basic reasons for his departure. Every great power, he explained, wished to turn the United Nations into an instrument of its own policy, but some powers were in a better position than others to do so. In his time in Leopoldville (he had taken up duty on September 8th, just after the fall of Lumumba) the powers in the best position to make this use of the United Nations were the United States and, secondarily, Britain. Ambassadors of these powers, and of France, effectively – although not always in unison – controlled President Kasavubu

and General Mobutu, and they were therefore most anxious that
the United Nations should accept these gentlemen's nominees as
being the Government of the Congo. As the legality of all this was
highly questionable, and as it represented the viewpoint of only one
group of powers within the United Nations, Mr Dayal had held out
against it and in favour of the convening of parliament and the
election of a government of unquestioned legality. In this stand he
was supported by the Secretary-General. The Western powers,
who were at that time opposed to this course – because they feared
that a Congolese Parliament would be Lumumbist – became
severely critical of Mr Dayal, and an inspired campaign began
against him in the Western Press. He was 'arrogant', he did not
know 'how to get along with Africans', he had 'lost the confidence of
President Kasavubu', above all, he was pursuing 'an Indian policy'
not a 'United Nations policy'. Hammarskjold refused to disavow
Mr Dayal, and even explicitly refuted the charges against him.
But it had become clear that, since the Western countries were now
publicly committed to their 'anti-Dayal' position, his continuance
in office would add to the already heavy burdens of the Secretary-
General, and would even endanger the maintenance and success of
the principles for which he, Mr Dayal, had stood. He had therefore
asked to be released and to return to his own Service, and his
request had been reluctantly granted.

The above is a paraphrase of what Mr Dayal had to say. The only
actual words of his which I recall – because he spoke them with
particular earnestness – came at the end of our interview. 'The
essential thing', he said, 'is to safeguard the office of Secretary-
General.' He put a slight stress on the word 'office'. I understood
him as meaning that everything else, all personalities, his own and
even Hammarskjold's, were secondary to the main theme of preserving the independence of the Secretary-General's office, as a focus
of supranational loyalty.

Coming from a man who had, in effect, been ousted by *Western*
pressure, and at a time when it was *Eastern* policy which demanded
the recasting of the office of Secretary-General, these were impressive
words. Mr Dayal's whole bearing, indeed, was extremely impressive;
I found in it no trace of the 'arrogance' so persistently ascribed to
him, but on the contrary an unusual degree of considerate courtesy
towards his interlocutor and a dispassionate attitude, altogether
worthy of a stoic, towards his own personal fate.

Some months later, at a similar crisis in my own career, I thought
back to Mr Dayal. I admired his conduct although by reason of

some important differences, partly in the objective situation, partly in judgement, and partly no doubt in temperament, I could not emulate his example of silent departure.

At this time, just before leaving for the Congo, I also met two old Congo hands in the Secretariat, who were not in the Congo Club. To quote from the same letter:

'*Another man I saw was Ian Berendsen, who was in Katanga during the worst of the trouble there (so far!).*'

For the benefit of certain people who might wish to seize on this text, I must specify that the 'so far' does not imply preconceived intent to carry fire and sword to Katanga, but simply the apprehension that trouble did lie ahead. After referring to some criticisms of Mr Berendsen's tenure, the letter went on:

'*This is all rather sad because he seems in fact to be an honest and reasonably intelligent man who did about all that anyone could have done in quite appalling circumstances.*'

The rest of the letter sets out how much better I would have done, in my own opinion, in the same circumstances. It would have been wiser of me to listen more carefully to Mr Berendsen who, in his rather sad, matter-of-fact way, across a table at Ferdi's Sidewalk Café, opposite the UN building, went straight to the heart of the matter. I told him of my fears lest the drastic implications of the February resolution might not have been fully understood. Might not there be a mass exodus of the European population, a breakdown of economic life in Katanga, if the mercenaries, who were there essentially to protect the Europeans and their property, including the mines, were removed, as they must be, unless the resolution was left a dead letter? Mr Berendsen said yes, he thought there would be some kind of exodus, some kind of breakdown. He used, he explained mildly, to consider that this was the disaster which must be avoided at all costs, but he was no longer of that opinion. The troubles of the Congo were interrelated; the Europeans of Katanga had provoked many of these troubles and it was foolish to believe that they could escape their share of them – certainly unless they adapted their policies more rapidly than they were at all likely to do. Things would be worse before they were better, in Katanga as in the rest of the Congo. But he was not, in the long run, a pessimist. In Katanga life would, eventually, return to normal. The copper was the permanent fact and it would always pay anyone who was in charge there to have it worked. Technicians would be needed, and would be found somewhere, and economic life would go on. But in the short run, there would be trouble. To imagine that life would

continue normally in Elisabethville while the February resolution
was actually being put into effect was to delude oneself.

He wished me luck.

There was nothing much for my comfort, either, in the discourse
of the other Congo hand, Mr Gustavo Duran, who had been one of
Mr Dayal's aides. Unlike Mr Berendsen, who carries modestly an
air of cosmic sadness, Mr Duran's temperament, despite his storm-
tossed career – he was a General on the Republican side in the
Spanish Civil War – remains ebullient, gay and witty. This did not
make his picture of the Congo any more cheerful.

'The Congolese? You will hate them all – all without exception.
Mobutu, Gizenga, Munongo, left, right, blacks, whites – all horrible.
But don't judge Africa by the Congo. There are wonderful people in
Africa. Not in the Congo. You will not like them, no. But it will
be an experience. There is nothing like the Congo. You will thank
God for that.'

As Mr Duran had spent much time in Stanleyville, I asked him
whether Gizenga was a Communist. He smiled at me compas-
sionately. 'A Communist? No. Gizenga is a constipated sacristan.'

The wise words of Mr Berendsen and Mr Duran added touches of
disconcerting life to what I had learned in the more abstract
atmosphere of the Congo Club. But whatever I had learned, or had
not learned, in this crowded ten days – all the time the now pressing
rhythm of the UN necessities would permit – the hour had struck
for me to go to my post. Mr Hammarskjold gave a luncheon for me,
with the Congo Club, on the day of my departure. He was, on that
day – the last time I ever saw him – cheerful and confident, as I
had seen him at his Press conference. But nearer at hand he did
show more trace of the tremendous strains he had undergone, and
knew he still had to face. When he was talking of the tests ahead,
and still more when – as I most dreaded – he engaged in his grim,
Nordic rite of literary discussion, his manner was grave and even
regal. But when he relaxed, one was startled as if by the snap of a
spring, tightly compressed and suddenly released.

Both at such times – as when he discussed a picture of Mrs
Kennedy in the *New York Times* – and in his graver moods, I was
struck on this occasion by a somewhat febrile undertone in his
manner and in his conversation. I attributed this at the time
entirely to external pressures, but, in retrospect, I would associate
it also with the inner strain imposed on him by his concept of his
office and of himself. By the very high, and at the same time
strangely empty, concept of his role which he had propounded at

Oxford, he was demanding of himself to be both more and less than a human being, to be a kind of supranational angel. So high and unreal a concept, so tense and exigent a conscience, must have made the realities of flesh and blood and history – and the making of practical political calculations which could not afford to be always so very lofty – something of a torture.

If there was a perceptible trace of such strains in his manner, it was an undertone only. Close up, he seemed only a little less confident, less radiant, than he had seemed at his public appearance ten days before. He wished me luck, more cheerfully than the clairvoyant Mr Berendsen had done, and I left for the Congo.

3

THE JACARANDAS
OF ELISABETHVILLE

> *''Twas a land transfigured, 'twas a new creation,*
> *Oh, a singing wind swept the negro nation.'*
> Vachel Lindsay

I left New York on June 8th, 1961, and travelled to my post by way of Paris, Brussels and Leopoldville.

In Paris, I met by arrangement my immediate predecessor in Katanga (who, later, very nearly became also my successor) M Georges Dumontet. M Dumontet, a stolid amiable Frenchman, gave me a more hopeful general account of the Katanga situation than Mr Berendsen had done. I shall return later to some of the details of what he said, but the essence of it was that there was no need to be in any great hurry and that – except for a few 'ultras' – the people in charge in Katanga were good fellows enough who understood the need 'to co-operate with the United Nations'. The implications of the resolutions did not weigh heavily on him. I would find life in Elisabethville pleasant enough, he thought, though not very interesting. 'It's a provincial hole, you know', were his last words.

In Brussels, Mr Sahbani, the taciturn Tunisian who was Hammarskjold's unofficial 'Ambassador' to the Belgian Government, struck a less cheerful note, and so did Brussels itself. In the cold, cavernous, ornate dining-room of the hotel in which I dined with Mr Sahbani one felt something of what Conrad meant when in *Heart of Darkness* he called Brussels 'the sepulchral city'. What Mr Sahbani had to say was also rather sepulchral in its implications. In New York, the degree of confidence which Hammarskjold and his collaborators felt rested in no small part on an assumption that the resolutions could be implemented in Katanga through the co-operation, however reluctantly given, of the new Belgian Government (in which M Spaak was Foreign Minister) and that in this way the head-on clash which seemed implicit in the conflict between the resolutions and the actual situation in Katanga, could be averted. Mr Sahbani, the man on the spot, radiated no such confidence. The atmosphere of Belgium, he intimated, in a voice choked by a heavy cold, would not permit M Spaak, or anyone else, to give active co-operation to the extent which New York expected. There might be some token gestures of co-operation but no Belgian Government was going to risk assuming the responsibility for really serious actions, like the repatriation of foreign troops, which might endanger Belgian lives and property in Katanga. If the thing was to be done, it must, in the last analysis, be done in Elisabethville. Whether it could be done there peacefully or not would be for me to judge.

I had long realized, intellectually, the dangers ahead but it was only in the Hotel Metropole as I listened to the husky voice of Mr Sahbani that I had, for the first time, any emotional intuition of what this meant: the first faint smell of violence and death. The ormolu clock on the great marble mantlepiece struck, and it was time to leave for Leopoldville.

At Leopoldville airport in the early morning there was an air, not of chaos, but of lethargy; workers stood around in the baggage area looking out at the passengers, until the passengers themselves climbed the barrier and carried out their baggage; the airport employees, silent and inscrutable, neither helped nor interfered: perhaps it was too early in the morning. Yet, on the long road into the city, hundreds of people were already up and walking, often with heavy loads, to their work. One of them crossed the road; our driver did not slacken speed, and missed the pedestrian by about a foot; neither driver nor pedestrian showed any emotion. As we approached the centre, the tall concrete buildings whose pictures I had seen so often in Belgian brochures – Congo: Land of Contrasts – did indeed look like skyscrapers, almost touching the sullen mass of cloud that hung low over the city. But – to eyes lifted towards them from the road, with its barefoot, long-distance pedestrians – the buildings looked subtly different from their image in those glossy pages. They seemed somehow irrelevant, and even a little silly, as if waiting to have more pictures taken, long after those flattering cameramen had gone home to Belgium.

It was oppressively close in the little room they had found for me, in a half-deserted apartment building near the Hotel Royal – where ONUC[1] had its headquarters – and I was glad there was an air-conditioner. I switched it on and it immediately projected into the room a dense column of yellow dust, like ambiguities coming out of a resolution.

I stayed just long enough in Leopoldville to make the acquaintance of those colleagues at UN headquarters, who were going to be important for me in the months ahead. Dr Sture Linner, the Officer-in-Charge, with his eager manner and pale Swedish eyes, skin and hair, gave me a very friendly reception. He had a strong sense of loyalty, even a devotion, to Hammarskjold and the fact that I had been personally selected by Hammarskjold sufficed for him. Dr Linner, who had done outstanding administrative and social work as head of UN Civilian Operations in the Congo, had at this time little political experience and had even a certain understandable distaste for politics. Perhaps partly for this reason, he had a tendency to delegate highly important political tasks to his collaborators and he had taken on the role, effectively, of Chairman of a Committee and *rapporteur* to Hammarskjold. He may have felt that this was appropriate as he was not Special Representative – no official successor to Mr Dayal having been appointed. This conferred on his collaborators on the 6th floor – the equivalent in the Royal of the 38th floor in New York – a quasi-autonomous importance such as they had not, I believe, possessed in Mr Dayal's time. His closest collaborator and assistant was a large Swiss citizen, M Poujoulat, generally known as 'le Maréchal' because of his masterful bearing, Mussolinian chin, and unhesitating willingness to accept responsibility. M Poujoulat was at this time on first-name terms with several of the Congolese leaders, notably Bomboko – 'mon cher Justin' – although some of them were said to be a little frightened of him. M Adoula, then Minister for the Interior, not yet Prime Minister, had been offered – so the story went – the services of a certain Swiss technician under UN Technical Aid. 'A Swiss!' he cried in alarm, 'No thanks. I know one already'.

Another important figure on the 6th floor at this time was Vladimir Fabry, an American citizen of Croat origin and ONUC's legal adviser ('Special Counsellor'). Fabry was a thin-faced young man with a frequent but unamused smile and a stoop brought on by unremitting work. Even in an organization where all the key people worked excessively hard (surrounded, for no apparent reason, by

---

[1] ONUC – 'Organization des Nations Unies au Congo'.

and actions would transform the whole future course of my life, but I was hardly conscious of him at all, or only as one would be conscious of a man who came to read the gas-meter. I took in a vague impression of a person accustomed to work with his hands, and must have drawn the subconscious, mandarin-like conclusion that this was not a person who needed to be reckoned with intellectually. When he withdrew, without any comment on the important telegram he had read, I dismissed him from my mind, labelled 'E.G.D.' This was a contemptuous UN term, applied to those rather numerous officials who appear to have been recruited, not so much for any personal merit, as in deference to the Charter principle of 'equitable geographical distribution' – 'we have nobody from Patagonia'. I was, of course, profoundly misinterpreting the situation. The silence was not caused by absence of ideas – very far from it – but by mistrust. He had not come into the room to read a telegram – which he had read already – but to take a look at the man who was going to Elisabethville. This I learned later. Of my impressions at the time, faint and peripheral as they were, I remember no more. I do not even remember, strange as the thought now appears, whether anyone at any time bothered to introduce me to Mahmoud Khiary.

I left for Elisabethville on the morning of June 14th aboard the Force Commander's D.C.6., the *Anne-Marie*. General McKeown was attending a briefing conference at Kamina (the great former Belgian and NATO base, or rather bases, in western Katanga) which the Belgians had continued to hold under their Treaty of Friendship with the Independent Republic of the Congo, which they had used, in violation of Article 6 of the same Treaty, as the springboard for their intervention in Elisabethville on July 10th and which they later abandoned under United Nations, and probably United States, pressure. It had been intended 'for the defence of Central Africa against international Communism' and was laid out on an appropriate scale, over an area equivalent to that of a Belgian province. With its gigantic hangars and miles of runway, its great maintenance shops and powerful radio transmitter, its long, well-paved roads of handsome and comfortable 'American suburban' bungalows, its churches, cinemas, clubs and swimming-pools, it seemed exactly like one of the major bases in the south-eastern United States. All this grandeur now hung loosely and rather forlornly round a few companies of United Nations troops – Irish at this time, later Indians. They were there partly to symbolize the departure of the Belgians and verify their non-return, partly to maintain the airfield as a staging area for UN replacements, reinforcements and supplies *en route* to Elisabethville, one hour's flight away. If – as American officials devoutly hoped, and partly believed – the Kamina base was still helping to 'defend Central Africa against international Communism', it was doing so by means considerably more strange and subtle than those originally envisaged.

To the outsider, there was something almost sinister about this great base, constructed with such a huge expenditure of labour, materials and skill – for an end held to be vital for the existence of the Free World – and then suddenly, almost casually, abandoned. The tiny UN force seemed a little like a salvage-crew taking a derelict liner into port – but only a little, for there was no conceivable port, no function proportionate to its importance, for this preposterous immovable Central African fact. You could not help asking yourself whether the disarmer's favourite question – 'Why not spend the money on schools?' – was after all so very naïve, at least in this context. Central Africa, it was painfully obvious, had great need of schools, especially secondary schools; it was also painfully obvious that it had no need of this kind of base – and presumably never had any need of it, since nobody claimed that the 'Communist threat to Central Africa' was any less now than before. There were, it is true, those who regarded the use made of the base on July 10th, and the consequent secession of Katanga, as part of the effort to keep Communism out of Central Africa; but this had become by now a minority view, even in the West.

The United Nations garrison, rightly from its point of view, did not worry about all this. Kamina was a popular posting, with comfortable quarters, splendid amenities and an excellent supply-line and most of the soldiers would have thought it perfectly right and proper that bases on this scale should have been spread thickly all over the Congo. No doubt they would have been, if time and the pressures of African nationalism had permitted.

The briefing conference, with General McKeown in the chair, was about problems of integrating the command, rotations of troops, pleas for reinforcements, reports on local situations and the like routine matters.

I had not known General McKeown very well before in Ireland, but I knew the high and steady reputation which he had in a country which is no great respecter of persons, especially of those who – like Generals – need, in the opinion of their countrymen, to be saved from the dread disease of a 'swelled head'. Certainly Sean McKeown has been entirely spared that affliction. He is the kind of soldier Tolstoy liked: modest, shrewd, tough and realistic. He had at his

THE JACARANDAS OF ELISABETHVILLE

disposal a force constantly fluctuating in numbers and composition but never rising very much above the 15,000 mark. That is to say he had, for discharging the multifarious and ill-defined tasks laid down by the Security Council and Assembly, in a turbulent country over four times as large as France, a mixed force about one-third the size of the homogeneous force with which the British Government had attempted, unsuccessfully, to 'maintain order' in the tiny island of Cyprus.

In this situation, General McKeown permitted himself neither illusion nor alarm. Having accepted in advance that this situation implied plenty of trouble, and a good score for the inevitable chorus of criticism, he took the trouble and the criticism as they came, in his slow, stubborn and unexpectedly formidable style. There were certain officers under his command who may well have considered themselves better equipped than he, whether by reason of combat or staff experience or, in their view, sheer intellectual ability. He had no difficulty in accepting this as a fact of life, without resentment – and also no difficulty in handling it. At this conference he consulted his officers as one consults people from whom one is likely to learn, and the decisions which he finally took emerged from the discussion with what may have been to some an almost disappointingly indisputable air of common sense.[1]

At this conference I first met, and seriously misjudged, the Swedish officer in command in South Katanga, Colonel Jonas Waern. When you meet someone who is much taller, handsomer, richer and more socially exalted than yourself, you are quite liable to assume, on insufficient evidence, that he is less intelligent. Colonel Waern – who has been aide-de-camp to the King of Sweden, and looks the part of a military courtier – possessed all these superior attributes and I fell into this trap. I was to come to know him, before long, as an officer of great courage and capacity, with a peculiar sense of humour. It was the latter quality that he was demonstrating on this occasion, although I did not recognize it. In his report on the situation in Elisabethville he referred to several items of information as having been gleaned from 'my spies'. Now this touches a sensitive point, where the United Nations operation in the Congo is concerned. Individual powers supporting the UN

---

[1] There will be those who feel that this portrait, more favourable than some others in this volume, is influenced by the fact that General McKeown and I are both Irish. I would remind these critics of Dr Johnson's well-known, and not ill-founded saying: 'The Irish are a fair people; – they never speak well of one another'.

operation did maintain intelligence networks, but the UN itself did not. Hammarskjold had referred to this once at a meeting of the Congo Advisory Committee, had admitted that it was a serious handicap, and had justified the lack on the grounds that the UN 'must have clean hands', and therefore could not do the sort of thing that intelligence services habitually do – lying, bribery, blackmail, theft and so on. More pragmatically, an international organization, drawing its agents from many countries, with many points of view, could not ensure anything like the degree of security needed in serious intelligence work, and would be peculiarly liable to infiltration by agents of national services.

This lack, inevitable as it was, was just as inevitably resented by UN representatives, and especially officers, in the field. 'The trouble with us in the United Nations', one officer used often and ambiguously to say, 'is that we have no intelligence.' Even in the sense intended, this was no longer altogether true. We did not have an internationally-run 'answer' to the CIA or the MVD, but we infringed the 'clean hands' doctrine to the extent of employing in Elisabethville one Greek ex-policeman with an imperfect knowledge of French, who was already – as we later found from captured documents – known at the headquarters of Tshombe's Gendarmerie by the proud title of 'Chief of the United Nations Intelligence Services in Katanga'. The rest of the said services consisted of a few Baluba houseboys who, sometimes for money but more often out of sheer political zeal, would bring scraps of information, usually alarmist gossip, from time to time. This was what Colonel Waern meant when he referred to 'my spies'. He took, I think, a certain mischievous pleasure in reminding the company that the organization had so far fallen from grace as to employ, at all, people who could, without much stretching the facts, be referred to as 'spies', and also in hinting that, within the limits dictated to us by the nature of our task and backing, the attempt to use 'spies' was bound to become a little comic.

From Kamina to Elisabethville I flew with Lieut-Col Bjorn Egge, of Norway, with whom I was to work very closely and happily in the months ahead. Colonel Egge was himself a highly-trained intelligence officer, who had spent some time at the Ecole de Guerre in Paris and at NATO headquarters. He was not, however, bound for Elisabethville in order to organize 'spies' but on a special mission of which I shall have more to say later. Despite some severe experiences as a prisoner in World War II, he was astonishingly young-looking – he was, like myself, in his early forties, but he looked about thirty; with his bright blue eyes under the blue beret, he could well have posed for a UN recruiting poster. As we flew towards Elisabethville he talked, not without sympathy, of the Belgian Regular Officers in Tshombe's forces, and of the then Commander of that force, the famous Colonel Crèvecoeur. 'He is a boy-scout', said Egge, 'and I understand him, because I have been a boy-scout too.' Whatever about Crèvecoeur, whom I was soon to meet, there was certainly something pleasantly boyish about Egge himself, and something of the scout's idealism. He liked – and did not affect not to like – the cloak-and-dagger side of his profession, but, despite a certain natural romanticism, he was a highly serious and competent professional. Though an extremely cheerful man, he was essentially an earnest one and he neither shared nor appreciated Colonel Waern's vein of irony. Indeed the mutual disapproval of these two able, handsome Scandinavians was to provide one of the most reliable elements of light relief in the sometimes heavy atmosphere of Elisabethville.

Politically, Egge thought of himself both as a 'good UN man' and a 'good NATO man', and he had some trouble in persuading either people like myself or people like Colonel Crèvecoeur that it was possible to be both at the same time under one blue beret. It was the 'neutral man' puzzle in an acute form, for Egge wore, with the 'neutral' beret, the 'committed' uniform of a member State of NATO. A few years earlier he might conceivably have attended, wearing no blue beret, another kind of conference at that same base in Kamina, dedicated to other means of defending Central Africa. He felt no contradiction and no conflict of loyalty, and if it is indeed possible for anyone to be simultaneously 'a good UN man' and 'a good NATO man', then Lieut-Col Egge was that man.

On the airfield of Elisabethville was an Irish Guard of Honour – the UN force there consisted at that time of two battalions, one Swedish and one Irish. I was greeted by the acting Representative whom I was relieving, Mr Charles Brackenbury, a distinguished-looking, genial Englishman, by Lieut-Col Eugene O'Neill, the shrewd and thoughtful officer commanding the Irish battalion, and by Michel Tombelaine, the Frenchman who was Deputy Representative. The first two were to leave very shortly, and only Michel Tombelaine, of whom more later, was to be present for what we called 'the events'. From the airfield we drove to the Villa des Roches, the residence of the UN Representative in Katanga. The Villa des Roches – leased from a local Belgian with the magnificently Conradian name of Sepulchre – was a large and very agreeable bungalow, built round a swimming pool, with grounds sloping down towards the rapids of a little river. The sky was as blue as a beret and already – it was getting on towards six o'clock and sunset – there was a cool breeze, gently shaking the tall flame-tree by the verandah. The Villa des Roches once, by a fortunate misprint, appeared in the local paper as the Villa des Riches and – although it was not the most luxurious villa in this prosperous little town – it deserved the title well enough. 'These Onusians live like kings' – *ces Onusiens qui mènent une vie de prince* – was the opinion of many local people who lived in very much the same way themselves. In fact, though certainly pleasant, this life was rather less than princely, for the Villa des Roches functioned as a sort of hotel. There were living in it at this time, besides Mr Brackenbury and myself, Colonel Egge and General Iyassu of Ethiopia, and later Colonel Waern and his Chief of Staff, Major Rosen, were to join us. Frequent, and sometimes mysterious, teams of officials from Leopoldville used also to come to stay, and indeed the place was almost always bursting at the seams: this, however, simply added to its picturesqueness without detracting from its charm. As for the swimming pool, the most obviously 'princely' feature, this was almost always occupied by the military – officers at lunch-time, private soldiers after three o'clock. However, our neighbours, from their similar and very much less populous bungalows, resented the Villa des Roches, with the large blue flag which floated from a tall flag-staff high above it, and they easily convinced themselves that what in them was sober, bourgeois decency, was, in the UN Representative, an insolent luxury worthy of Heliogabalus.

As the Heliogabalus-elect, I liked the Villa des Roches, the climate of the high plateau (about 4,000 feet) and the pleasing prospects of Elisabethville. Things that, later, I was to find irritating and 'symptomatic' – like the huge and utterly unnecessary fire-place with its massive, hideous copper chimney – I now found simply quaint. I was pleased to be far from Leopoldville with its preoccupied bureaucracy, its lowering skies and dust-bowl air-conditioners. In fact I was, though I hardly realized it, experiencing some of the basic emotions of the local settlers: their pleasure in their 'European' climate and high standard of living, as well as their dislike and distrust of the distant Congolese capital. Elisabethville – as the settlers often reminded each other – is as distant from Leopoldville as Athens from Brussels. Therefore . . .

Whatever about the political 'therefore', which was shaky enough, it was not hard to understand the settlers' affection for their city of

Elisabethville. True, it was no longer 'theirs' – in the sense that it had become, very much with their approval, the capital of the independent African state of Katanga – but this made little difference to daily life. The elegant residential parts of Elisabethville remained overwhelmingly European, and the Africans, with the exception of the new Ministers, remained where they had 'always' been, in the 'native city', generally known, to the confusion of the new-comer, simply as *la cité*. The European sections, *la ville*, were laid out on a matter-of-fact gridiron plan, appropriate to the company town which this was, and were made attractive only by the profusion of flowering trees, notably the great, blue jacarandas lining the central avenues. The local Belgians had a strong affection for these trees. Those who spoke or wrote with emotion about 'nos chers jacarandas' were, I felt, moved not solely by aesthetic feeling but by the fact that these beautiful trees are *both* peculiar to the tropics *and* capable of taking root and flourishing in a suburban environment. This may have set at rest certain half-conscious but growing doubts.

In these sections everyone had a comfortable house and garden and everyone had a car. They had to, for there was no public transport in the normal sense: just the buses which moved the African labourers from 'the city' to mine or factory and back again. There was a fine theatre but it rarely seemed to put on a play. There was a golf-course, to reach which there was a tarred road past the Villa des Roches from the city centre, and there were several flourishing night-clubs and restaurants. There was no educational segregation but there were schools 'on the European system' and schools 'on the Katangese system' and that gave, in practice, on the whole the desired effect. There were 32,000 Europeans in Katanga at the start of 1960, making 2 per cent of the total Katanga population (1,654,000): this was the largest proportion of any province of the Congo. These Europeans were not, however, really settlers in the normal sense. Hardly any of them owned land – except on the fringes of Elisabethville as a speculation – and few of them had their own businesses. They either worked for one of the great companies of the Union Minière group – Sogelec, Metalkat, Minsudkat, etc. – or for economically ancillary enterprises like the BCK railway or the Simba Brewery – or they were professional men, making their money indirectly out of these companies. Or again, they were soldiers and technicians whose pay came at one remove from these same companies when it did not come from the Belgian Government itself. The most vocal members of the European community had a strong tendency at this time to say proudly that

they were 'not Belgians - Katangese!' and a few of them seem to
have felt, towards Belgium, rather as French Algerians feel towards
France.

But the community as a whole had an equally strong tendency to
spend Sunday at the airport, and also to crowd the airport on those
weekday evenings when the Boeing arrived from Brussels. Some
Onusians, who liked to stress the 'materialism' of the local Europeans (the Katabelgians as they were sometimes called), claimed
that the extraordinary predilection of these people for flocking to
the airport was due solely to their need to verify the arrival of fresh
oysters, lobsters and crayfish, which they then – it was believed –
rushed off to devour at the Sabena Guest House. There was a little
truth in this – the new, white 'Katangese' seemed to retain the
hearty appetites of the Flemings or Walloons that they had been a
few months before – but the real source of their airport fixation was,
I think, deeper and less material. These 'Katangese' went to the
airport by instinct, because the airport was the nearest thing to
home. Elisabethville was status and standard of living and 'home'
for purposes of rhetoric; real home was nine hours away by Boeing.

I cannot claim to be a detached and well-informed reporter about
the Europeans of Katanga. I did not get to know them well, or in
favourable circumstances. When I arrived, their attitude towards the
United Nations and, therefore towards me, was one of cold hostility,
tinged with a mixture of fear and contempt, sometimes covered
over with a thin and displeasing layer of effusiveness; there were a
few, very few, exceptions. When I left, their attitude had become
one of hate, bordering on hysteria; there were probably still some
exceptions, but they, quite understandably, did not make themselves known. In their situation I should probably have felt and
behaved in much the same way (see below, page 101). As it was,
being in my situation, I liked them, as a community, more but not
very much more, than they liked me.

Rather than attempt, myself, therefore, to sum up their situation
about this time, I prefer to quote from an article which appeared,
a few weeks later in a Belgian paper, very sympathetic with their
point of view.[1] The writer's thesis is that 'a national consciousness
has been born in Katanga'.

'For the first time white and black feel a sense of solidarity, feel
plunged together in a great wave of Katangese patriotism. That

---

[1] Article 'La Nouvelle Chance du Katanga' signed J. K. in *La Libre Belgique*,
July 8th to 9th, 1961. J. K. – M. Vanderdussens de Kestargat – is a leading
Belgian conservative expert on the Congo.

is a fact and a very important fact. The blacks have discovered that Katangese faith, a little hesitant up to now, and the whites, many whites, have become conscious of a change of heart. A European woman, more than one hundred per cent Katangese said to me:

'"When the President arrived I was caught in a crowd of blacks. A fat 'mammy' put her arm around my shoulders, pulled me forward into the front row and shouted: 'Look, Madame, look at the President'. I was astonished because, I admit, a year ago, I should have considered such familiarity intolerable. And a year ago she would not have dared."

'I do not claim that all the problems of Katanga are solved because a black woman embraced a European woman. But anyone who knew Katanga as it was will understand. I do not claim, either, that this solidarity between blacks and whites is very deep. It is perhaps deep but it is at the same time fragile. If there is no longer any racial problem, properly speaking, it remains true that there are in this country too many whites who are, not exactly hostile, but indifferent to the social advancement of the Africans.

'There are also some who are hostile to such advancement and who see, in Katangese independence, nothing but a means of saving their prosperous personal positions, relying on the prudence and moderation of the Katangese leaders. A European, an old Elisabethville hand, told me, and I quote his words:

'"Listen, Mr Journalist: we are living exactly as we lived four years ago. Nothing has changed. Yes, there are a few, more or less ridiculous parades and manifestations, but that does not trouble us."

'One must not exaggerate the significance of such words. I must have happened upon the last European who believes that Katanga has any hope of a future if people persist [sic] in considering it as a second Kuwait [sic].

Feathering their nests.

'I do not say there are "too many whites" in an absolute sense: ten thousand whites is not too many for Elisabethville provided they are useful whites – useful in the sense that they work for the Country and help to develop trade. But at present some whites are not useful enough. They work, of course, they supply services, but the essential service which the blacks should receive from them, education, the preparation of the Africans who will be able

to take over responsibility, is neglected by many. I keep on thinking of those officials who reason: "It will last as long as it lasts – as
long as possible". They can feather their nests, for they are quite
handsomely paid, and Katanga is extremely generous in respect
of financial transfers to Belgium. If it is true that the ideal rule of
technical assistance is to make yourself unnecessary as soon as
possible, we are still rather far from this ideal here. People are
trying, on the contrary, to remain necessary as long as possible.
This is human, and no doubt Belgium is to blame, for not having
been able to provide minimum guarantees for her officials lent
to the Congo. It would be surprising if, some day, a price did
not have to be paid for the old policy of packing off as many
Belgians as possible in bulk to the Congo. Uncertainty about the
future has led many to "hang on" and accumulate savings. Personal
currency transfers total one hundred million Belgian francs a
month, and those of the companies two and a half thousand
million a year. That makes a total of more than three and a half
thousand million a year leaving Katanga without – in the still
uncertain circumstances of today – being balanced in any way
by investments from outside. From whatever point of view one
considers this situation it would be difficult to affirm that it is a
very healthy one.'
The writer concludes this revealing account of the Birth of a
Nation with the words, which gain their full weight from what has
gone before:
    'People told me here:
      ' "Katanga is going well because it has had its crisis. The
    other regions of the Congo have not had theirs."
    'I must confess I found this hard to understand because it
seems obvious to me that it is the other way round. The Congo is
in the middle of its crisis. Katanga has not had its crisis. So much
the better, if it can pursue its evolution without a jolt.'

4

THE INDEPENDENT STATE
OF KATANGA

'The same arts that did gain
A power, must it maintain.'
Marvell

It is necessary at this point, if what follows is to be understood, to say a word about the very recent history of Katanga, which these Europeans and their employers in Brussels had done so much to shape.

The Independent State of Katanga at the time of my arrival was not quite a year old. It had been proclaimed by Tshombe's Government on July 11th, 1960. This was the day after the Belgian para-commandos had arrived in Elisabethville, nominally to protect the local Europeans from the violences which had been occurring for days in other parts of the Republic of the Congo and had now begun in Katanga itself. Five Europeans were killed in Elisabethville on July 9th to 10th.[1]

The interventions in Katanga were the first Belgian interventions after Congolese independence, although the first violence against Belgians had occurred a thousand miles away, in the Bas-Congo several days before.

---

[1] Five according to the Dossiers du CRISP; seven according to M Davister (*Katanga*, p. 90). One of them was the Italian Consul. It has been universally assumed that the deaths were the result of a spontaneous outbreak of mutiny by 'Lumumbist soldiery'. If so it was singularly ill-timed from a Lumumbist point of view and singularly well-timed from the point of view of Tshombe, Munongo and the Belgian interventionists. For an eye-witness account of another spontaneous, but curiously discriminating, mutiny involving violence to Europeans see Chapter XVII. The initial mutinies in other parts of the Congo may or may not have been spontaneous, but they were certainly not Lumumbist since they were directed against Lumumba, then Prime Minister and Minister for Defence.

The idea of an independent Katanga had been canvassed before this date, and Tshombe's party, the Conakat, had for some time been strongly secessionist in tendency – it had made an attempt at secession in June which was checked by the Belgian Government. In the elections which preceded the independence of the Congo, however, it had not run on a proclaimed secessionist policy but on federalism. This party had come to represent an alliance of the local Europeans – grouped in such bodies as Ucol and Upak, as well as in the association Assekat of the major companies – with a federation of chiefs' nominees of various tribes, notably the Lunda tribe, of which Mr Tshombe's father-in-law is paramount chief, and the Bayeke tribe of which Mr Godefroid Munongo's brother Antoine is paramount chief.[1] The elections of May 1960 gave the Conakat twenty-five seats out of sixty in the Provincial Assembly. The anti-secessionist Cartel Katangais – of which the largest component was M Jason Sendwe's Balubakat party – had twenty-three seats. The Cartel, which claimed that the election had been unfairly conducted by the Belgian administration, decided – unwisely as it seems – to boycott the Assembly, in the belief that – since a two-thirds majority was legally required to elect a Government – their abstention would render it impossible for the Conakat to form a Government and use its power – as it was already feared it might do – to secede from the nascent Republic of the Congo. After considerable agitation by the Conakat – Tshombe threatened to appeal to Rhodesia or, oddly enough, to the United Nations – the Belgian Parliament amended the relevant legal provision, and, on June 16th, the Provincial Assembly, sitting without a quorum, elected a Government consisting entirely of the Conakat and its allies.[2]

---

[1] A sympathetic Belgian observer, M Pierre Davister, makes it quite clear that this African party was formed by Europeans. 'Who cemented this Union (Conakat)? We do not hesitate to say it: the European.' (*Katanga Enjeu du Monde*, p. 53). Elsewhere (p. 67) he refers to it as being 'clearly manipulated from the wings by the Europeans.'

[2] *Dossiers du CRISP. Congo 1960*, I, pp. 243–254: cited hereafter as '*Dossiers*'. This decision of the Belgian Parliament is of great significance. The point about the *Loi Fondamentale* is that it was worked out at a Round Table with the political leaders of the Congo as a whole. Now it was amended in a critically important way by the Belgian Parliament, without consulting any Africans except those of the 'European-cemented' Conakat. These last, of course, had not waited to be consulted. 'If the Conakat did not obtain satisfaction', said Mr Munongo to the Provincial Assembly, 'a *coup d'état* would be envisaged'. He also envisaged sending, and presumably sent, what he called 'an urgent and virulent telegram' to the Minister for the Congo in Brussels. (Belgian papers cited in Chomé, *Crise Congolaise*, p. 48.)

Mr Tshombe became Provincial President, and Mr Godefroid Munongo, Minister of the Interior.

It was this Government which on July 11th, 1960, without any popular consultation, proclaimed the independence of Katanga. Its Declaration of Independence, issued on that day stated:

'This *Independence* is *Total*. None the less, conscious of the imperious necessity of an economic collaboration with Belgium, the Government of Katanga, to which Belgium, in order to protect human lives, has just granted the assistance of its own troops, asks Belgium to join with Katanga in a close economic community.

'It asks Belgium to continue its technical, financial and military aid.

'It asks Belgium to re-establish public order and security.'[1]

The Belgian response to this singularly accommodating Declaration of Independence was of a dual character: positive inside Katanga, and negative on the international plane.

Inside Katanga, the Commander of the invading Belgian troops, on the very day of the Declaration, told the Press that political affairs were entirely within the competence of the Katangese Government, under whose orders he was working to maintain order and security, setting up to that end, five departments: Military Affairs, Propaganda, Supplies, Refugees, and Public Health.[2] A Belgian 'technical aid mission' arrived headed by the Comte d'Aspremont-Lynden, later Minister for African Affairs in the Belgian Government.

On the international plane, however, the Belgian Government, still on the same day, declared itself opposed to the setting up of the State of Katanga. M Wigny, Foreign Minister in the Eyskens Government so informed the diplomatic representatives of five friendly States: France, Britain, Western Germany, Netherlands and the United States. 'Intrigues', cabled M Wigny, 'are going on in Katanga, aimed at setting up the province as an independent State and having it recognized by foreign powers. Belgium is opposed for many reasons. Short-term reactions in the rest of the Congo would endanger lives and property of Europeans falsely accused of having participated in the plot. Middle term Congo is equipped with constitutional law and is still to work out definitive structure; it will be possible and even necessary to review in a calmer atmosphere the relation of Katanga to the rest of the country. Long-term

---

[1] *Dossiers*, II, p. 719.

[2] *Dossiers*, II, p. 720. The administrative apparatus set up included 'Belgian technicians who knew all there was to know about State security' (Davister, *Katanga*, p. 103.)

secession would compromise the economic vitality of the rest of the Congo which would fall a prey to Communism. It is doubtful whether Katanga could resist ulterior [sic] subversion or aggression. Belgian Government stresses need for prudence and at least temporization [sic] on the part of friendly powers and also Tshombe. Must be noted that Belgian metropolitan troops are at Elisabethville arriving from Kamina. Troops ensure order and efficiency, will remain on spot as long as necessary. Any interventions would be unnecessary and would risk increasing the confusion.'[1]

It is not unfair to conclude from these texts that Belgium encouraged, in practice, the secession of Katanga, while opposing the recognition of that secession by other powers. It is clear also that Belgium feared intervention in the area by another power or powers. The reference to the need for 'prudence and temporization' on *Tshombe's* part shows in the context that the Belgian Government attributed, to some at least of the powers addressed, some degree of political influence over the President of Katanga. The Belgian action may reasonably be interpreted as designed, not only to protect Belgian lives and property in themselves but also to protect the said lives and property from being protected by someone else. The Belgian Press was speculating about the possibility of Rhodesian intervention and Tshombe, on the previous day, had threatened to seek the aid of Sir Roy Welensky.[2]

A meeting of the Provincial Assembly, apparently without a quorum and certainly without an opposition, approved the Declaration of Independence on July 17th,[3] and the Assembly subsequently became the 'National Assembly' under the 'Constitution of the State of Katanga', drafted by Professor Clémens of the University of Liège, and promulgated on August 8th.[4]

All taxes formerly paid to the central treasury of the Belgian Congo had now to be paid to the State of Katanga. The principal taxpayers were, of course, the European interests – notably the great mining consortium, *Union Minière du Haut Katanga*. It is worth while to quote the brief summary of this company's activity as given in *Congo, 1960*:

'The UMHK, third world producer of copper after the American firms of Kennecott and Anaconda, produced in 1959,

---

[1] *Dossiers*, II, p. 721. Cable (July 12th, 1960) summarizing Notes of July 11th, 1960.

[2] *Dossiers*, II, p. 540. On Rhodesia, see also Ch. XIV.

[3] *Dossiers*, II, p. 728.

[4] *Dossiers*, II, p. 754.

280,403 tons of copper and, in 1960, 300,704. The last figure constitutes its own record.

'The UMHK is the chief world producer of cobalt and produced 8,431 tons of this metal in 1959. Also a producer of zinc, germanium, cadmium and precious metals and uranium-radium ore. Employed 21,146 wage-earners in 1959.

'Profits in 1959, 3,535,599,030 Belgian Francs.'

These accepted the authority of the State of Katanga to levy these taxes. A Belgian authority, Professor F. Herman, calculated that in 1957, the contribution of Katanga to 'the total resources of the Congo' was almost 50 per cent; Mr Colin Legum, writing late in 1960, put the figure at 60 per cent.[1] The export duty on copper, which was to have gone to the Central Government in Leopoldville, now was paid to Mr Tshombe's Government. The export duties paid by Union Minière alone had amounted to half the export revenue of the former Belgian Congo. The copper, which, under the law of the Belgian Congo, had had to be sent out by way of Leopoldville, now went out through Angola, on the Benguela Railroad, owned by Tanganyika Concessions, associated with the Union Minière combine. 'The whole economy of the Congo', declared the semi-official Belgian *Agence Economique et Financière* in June 1960, 'finds a solid foundation in the existence of the Union Minière.' The same source had estimated that the Congo exchequer was receiving 3,000 million Belgian Francs (three milliards) – *the indispensable basis of the Congolese economy*' – as 'a product of the activity of the Union Minière'.[2] The total ordinary budget of the Congo was seven milliards. The economy of the Congo was now to be deprived of its 'solid' and 'indispensable basis', and the revenues in question were actually to be used *against* the Republic of the Congo.

These revenues, highly satisfactory for a 'country' with a population of under two million, provided a basis, with at first considerable direct Belgian aid, for the formation, training and equipment of large armed forces for the defence and internal security of the new State. The Gendarmerie of Katanga – quite distinct from the large forces of armed police which were also maintained – was now to be trained as an army, ready to take the place of the regular Belgian forces when these would have to withdraw.

---

[1] *Dossiers*, I, p. 223: *Congo Disaster*, p. 121: An even higher figure, 66 per cent, was given by Mr Kibwe, Katanga's Minister for Finance, in a lecture cited by M Jules Chomé (*La Crise Congolaise*, p. 36).

[2] A.E.C., June 4th, 5th and 6th, 1960: cited in J. Chomé, *La Crise Congolaise*, p. 36.

From the point of view of the Central Government, and of its friends abroad, these revolutionary proceedings amounted to annexation, for the benefit of foreign interests, of most of the resources, and a large part of the territory, of the newly independent Republic of the Congo. Indeed Western observers, not at all unfriendly to the forces behind the State of Katanga, saw the matter at this time in much the same way. 'Tshombe's régime', wrote the correspondent of the London *Daily Telegraph*, 'depends entirely on Belgium for arms, men and money. Without this, his Government would, in all probability, be quickly pulled down from within and without.'[1] But the Central Government, paralysed by the mutiny of a large part of its military forces, and by the consequent invasion of its territory by Belgian troops, was in no position to deal with this secession. The day after Mr Tshombe had proclaimed the independence of Katanga, the President of the Congo, Joseph Kasavubu and the Prime Minister, Patrice Lumumba, appealed for UN 'military aid'. They made it clear that what they sought was aid in putting all Belgian and other foreign troops out of the whole of the Congo, including Katanga. On the same day, July 12th, Kasavubu and Lumumba flew to Elisabethville, but the Katanga Government refused to allow their plane to land at Elisabethville Airport, which was then held by Belgian troops. The Security Council, on July 14th, called on the Government of Belgium to withdraw its troops from the Congo, and authorized the Secretary-General to provide 'such military assistance as may be necessary until . . . the national security forces may be able, in the opinion of the Government, to meet their task'.[2] The Security Council did not specify what the Government of the Congo was going to be 'militarily assisted' to do. This was, in effect, left to Hammarskjold. UN troops began arriving in the Congo on July 15th, and Tshombe stated that they would not be allowed to enter Katanga. On July 20th, Hammarskjold made a critically important statement to the Security Council affirming that Belgium's obligation to withdraw from the Congo included Katanga, but affirming also that the UN force could not become a party to an internal conflict and that its presence in Katanga would not be used to settle the constitutional issue. This definition and limitation of what UN 'military assistance' meant seems, when it was understood, to have come as a painful surprise to a Central Government which had supposed that the assistance in question would be entirely at its disposition; the Central

---

[1] Eric Downton in *The Daily Telegraph*, July 27th, 1960.
[2] UN document S/4387.

Government does not appear at first, however, to have understood the full purport of Hammarskjold's statement.

Hammarskjold announced on August 2nd that Dr Bunche would go to Elisabethville on August 5th, and that a first UN contingent would arrive there on August 6th. Dr Bunche went to Elisabethville where Tshombe informed him that general mobilization had been decreed and that Katanga would resist the entry of UN troops by force. Dr Bunche recommended to Hammarskjold that the troop movement should be halted in view of the 'stubborn and unreserved opposition of Mr Tshombe, his Ministers and the Paramount Chiefs', of their warning that UN entry would be resisted by force; of the tangible proofs of opposition to such entry in the Press, in 'mobilization' calls, in long columns of new recruits in the streets; of the possibility of an ambush and of the 'fanatical opposition' encountered by Dr Bunche himself at the airport. On receiving this report, Hammarskjold informed the Congolese Government that he had countermanded the dispatch of troops to Katanga for the date envisaged and that he was asking the Security Council to clarify his mandate.

On August 9th, the Council for the first time reached specific conclusions on Katanga. It called (paragraph 2 of the Resolution voted) for the withdrawal of Belgian forces from that province and declared (paragraph 3) the entry of UN troops necessary, but it also 'reaffirmed' (paragraph 4) the Secretary-General's doctrine that the UN force would not become a party to 'an internal conflict' or influence 'a constitutional issue'.[1] In retrospect it seems rather surprising that this restrictive interpretation of 'military assistance' should have won – as it did – Soviet and Afro-Asian[2] as well as Western support. The countries which were anxious to preserve the unity of the Congo may have optimistically assumed that the withdrawal of the Belgian Government's forces would automatically entail the collapse of Tshombe's régime; if so, they underestimated the strength and resourcefulness of the forces behind the 'State of Katanga'. Paragraph 4 was to prove one of the sturdiest of the diplo-

---

[1] S/4426: relevant article, 4, quoted and discussed, p. 60.

[2] I am indebted to Mr Andrew Boyd, of *The Economist*, an acute observer of the UN scene, for the following pertinent comment as regards Afro-Asian support for paragraph 4: 'Many Afro-Asians were, I think, cautious about creating precedents for UN action in domestic conflict cases. In the various UN discussions about UN forces there had always been a marked Afro-Asian caution arising, one supposes, basically from fear of "neo-imperialist" use of the UN in weak newly-independent States'. The Communist countries share, and even foster, this attitude of caution.'

matic bulwarks of that State, and one of the gravest barriers to the success of the United Nations operation in the Congo.

'Mr Tshombe', according to his Belgian admirer, Pierre Davister, 'understood immediately the possibilities which paragraph 4 opened out for him. He agreed to the entry of UN forces but on conditions.'[1] Hammarskjold told him that he could not accept 'conditions' or an agreement, but that he proposed 'to enter into *pourparlers*, myself personally with you, on the modalities of deployment of UN troops in Katanga'.

On August 12th, 1960, Hammarskjold flew to Elisabethville with the first UN troops, five plane-loads of Swedish soldiers. The joint communiqué, after the Tshombe-Hammarskjold conversations, announced that 'the participants' took note of 'the principle of non-intervention in internal affairs which applies to UN forces as the Security Council has explicitly stated in its resolution of August 9th'. Tshombe, for his part, also announced that the Secretary-General had accepted his ten conditions which were, in brief:

(1) UN troops in Katanga not to include troops from Communist or Communist-line countries.

(2) UN not to interfere in internal political or administrative affairs of Katanga.

(3) Joint UN–Katanga control of ways of entry (*voies d'accès*) to Katanga.

(4) UN not to permit the use of its means of transport to carry into Katanga persons sent by the Central Government.

(5) UN not to hinder police operations of Katanga Government.

(6) UN not to intervene in administration, finance or customs.

(7) UN not to hinder the organization and training of Katangese forces of order.

(8) Katanga reserves the right to find its own military and other technicians.

(9) Constitutional *status quo* until such time as Katanga may agree to change it.

(10) UN to oppose paramilitary party formations throughout the Congo.

To what extent, and in what way, these conditions might be said to have been accepted is by no means clear. CertainlyTshombe's unqualified statement that Hammarskjold accepted them all may

---

[1] *Katanga Enjeu du Monde*, p. 146. The conditions are summarized above; Davister gives them in detail.

be rejected; not only must we allow for the unusual degree of historical license which Tshombe – as I found myself – permitted
himself in publishing his version of negotiations; we must also allow
for the fact that the Hammarskjoldian language, with its delicacy
of emphasis and reservation, was something novel in Katanga. Yet,
whatever Hammarskjold intended to convey, there is no doubt of
the impression he left on his auditors: that is to say not only Tshombe
but Tshombe's very much more experienced Belgian advisers. The
best witness on this point is M Pierre Davister, a Belgian journalist
who was present in Elisabethville at the time and enjoyed easy
access to the people principally concerned. M Davister refers to the
effect produced by Hammarskjold's interpretation of the August
resolution, as given in the 'addendum',[1] on the implementation of
that resolution which he produced for Tshombe at this meeting:

'. . . the Katangese Government found in it a *barely disguised*
agreement to the ten conditions which it had formulated earlier
and which it had already given up as lost. This is not very widely
known because people are amazingly discreet about it (is the UN
perhaps afraid of being accused of weakness with regard to
Katanga?) but *semi-officially* eight[2] of Tshombe's ten conditions
are tacitly accepted and effectively block off the ambitions of
Lumumba's Central Government, should it try to come in in the
wake of the UN in order to wreak its vengeance.

'Eight conditions out of ten accepted in practice, including
that implying that the UN will not disarm the Katangese forces,
will not oppose the organization and training of these forces!

'It was beyond anything one could have hoped for. The ruling
team[3] (*équipe-reine*) of d'Aspremont-Lynden and Rothschild could
not believe its eyes! Little Ambassador Rothschild especially was
literally bursting with joy and one had only to see his little eyes
sparkling with delight, to hear his bursts of piping laughter, to
know that he had had some say in drawing up the Table of the
Ten Commandments of Moses (*Moïse*)!

'Certainly, the whole of the "Katanga solution" had consisted
up to this moment of a terrific bluff which had now brought off a

---

[1] *S/4417/Add. 6. Second Report by the Secretary-General on the implementation of
the Security Council Resolutions.* . . . There is no reason to believe that Hammarskjold
went much beyond this document (which does little more than underline paragraph 4) with Tshombe. But the language of the addendum conveyed a different
meaning in Elisabethville to what it did in New York.

[2] Presumably the exceptions were 5 and 8.

[3] The reference is to the official Belgian Technical Aid Mission.

sensational novelty in the history of the world. It had come to
this: that the Secretary-General of the United Nations had
accepted to enter *officially* into *pourparlers* with an *unrecognized*
State.

'. . . Yesterday's bluff could none the less soon become *a solid
reality*. If the internal structures of Katanga can be solidly but-
tressed, if the "blue helmets" confine themselves strictly to their
police role, if the security apparatus of Mr Tshombe becomes
something more than a myth, then Lumumba can go boil
himself an egg; the game will be up.'[1]

It is not surprising that a mission which appeared in this light to
the masters of Elisabethville should have been considered unsatisfactory by the Prime Minister of the Congo. Lumumba, who had not
been consulted in advance about this visit – although members of
his Government were aware of it – refused to see Hammarskjold on
the latter's return journey from Elisabethville through Leopoldville.
He also – belatedly – began to contest Hammarskjold's restrictive
interpretation of 'military assistance'.[2]

That interpretation had, however, in its most important and
controversial aspect, now received the endorsement of the Security
Council – an endorsement asked for by, among other people,
Lumumba's own Foreign Minister, Mr Justin Bomboko. Lumumba
then began a campaign of incitement and insult against the United
Nations and against the Western countries. His Government did not,
however, do what it could have done – simply to declare that in its
opinion the national security forces of the Congo were now able to
meet fully their tasks. Had the Government made such a declaration, the United Nations operation ought automatically to have
come to an end, under paragraph 2 of the original Security Council
resolution of July 14th. The Government may not have adverted to
this or may have adverted to it and been unable to agree. In any
case the UN forces stayed on, a target for denunciation by the Prime
Minister who had invited them in.

The evacuation of Belgian troops was carried out – 'without
excessive haste' according to *La Libre Belgique* – throughout August,
but did not include the regular Belgian officers, and Belgian
volunteers, now in the service of the State of Katanga. The 'State of
Katanga' was consolidating its authority, in the southern mining

---

[1] *Katanga Enjeu du Monde*, pp. 154–156. All the italics in the passage quoted are
M Davister's; he has a right to them. M Davister was writing immediately after
Hammarskjold's visit and before the fall of Lumumba.

[2] Above, pp. 88–9.

area of the former province, although a large part of North and Central Katanga was 'in rebellion' – while the Central Government, through its obvious inability either to deal with this situation itself or to get the required 'military assistance' from the United Nations, was rapidly losing whatever coherence and authority remained to it. Its attempts to bring under its rule South Kasai, which – also with foreign encouragement, and help from Katanga itself – had followed the example of Katangese secession, rapidly degenerated into a savage tribal war, and this situation was, in turn, used as an argument in defence of the secession of Katanga.

Lumumba had already turned for aid to almost every conceivable quarter including the United States and now, disappointed in the United Nations, he received some aid from the Soviet Union. 'The Russians', states Mr Colin Legum, 'delivered one hundred military trucks and twenty-nine Ilyushin transport planes, together with 200 technicians.'[1] This aid was intended for action against Katanga as well as against South Kasai. On September 5th, 1960, President Kasavubu with, it was generally believed, at least the approbation of United States Ambassador Timberlake (whose country's policies were being denounced on Radio Leopoldville, that same day) declared on Radio Leopoldville, that Lumumba was dismissed and that he, President Kasavubu, had charged Joseph Ileo with the formation of a new Government.[2] On the same evening, Lumumba, on the same radio, declared Kasavubu dismissed. On the following day, at 1.30 p.m. Mr Andrew Cordier used UN forces (Ghanaians) to close Radio Leopoldville. Kasavubu could still be heard throughout the Congo and was, on September 6th, on the powerful, and to him friendly, Brazzaville radio; and Tshombe, on the not less powerful Radio Elisabethville, appealed, also on September 6th, for an anti-Lumumba front. Lumumba, however, by Mr Cordier's decision, could not address the people whose uncontested Prime Minister he had been the day before. Mr Cordier also, by closing the airports to non-UN traffic, rendered it impossible for Lumumba to obtain outside aid whether Soviet or African, and very difficult for him to rally aid inside the Congo.

Had it not been for Mr Cordier's vigorous action, there is little doubt that the support Lumumba could have rallied at this crucial moment would have been most formidable. US Ambassador Timberlake himself, no admirer of the Prime Minister, is reported

---

[1] *Congo Disaster*, p. 141. This was late August and early September 1960 (*Dossiers* II, 635).

[2] *Dossiers*, II, 815 seq.

to have said that if Lumumba had walked into any gathering of
Congolese politicians as a waiter with a tray on his head he would
have come out as Prime Minister. As it was, however, Lumumba's
authority never recovered from the blows dealt him, not only by
Kasavubu and his diplomatic backers, but also by the United
Nations force. Parliament, it is true, rescinded on September 7th
the dismissals of both Mr Kasavubu and Mr Lumumba and on
September 13th, in more doubtful circumstances, a meeting of
Parliament voted full powers to Lumumba. On the following day
Colonel Mobutu, with similar diplomatic support to that of
Kasavubu, seized power and effectively dissolved the Parliament.
The Security Council refused to receive the delegation of the
Lumumba Government. More than two months later (November
23rd), the Assembly, under pressure from the US delegation, seated a
Kasavubu delegation, over a strong protest by Afro-Asian neutrals. At
the same time, Colonel Mobutu expelled the Ghanaian diplomats
from Leopoldville; the Soviet and Czechoslovak representatives had
been expelled immediately after Mobutu's *coup*, on September 17th.

Mr Cordier's actions – taken apparently without consulting
Hammarskjold, but approved by him[1] – had played a decisive part
in this crucial series of events, as a result of which the Congo no
longer possessed a universally recognized Government, and the
United Nations no longer possessed a consensus in the Security
Council. Mr Cordier had certainly acted courageously, and no doubt
solely in the interests of the Congo and the United Nations, as he
then saw them. Yet it would be difficult to argue, without sophistry,
that his actions did not involve the use of the UN force to 'influence
the outcome of any internal conflict, constitutional or otherwise'.
The famous paragraph 4 had been invoked to protect Tshombe's
régime, but it seemed to have been of no avail to protect Lumumba.
Dr Bunche's scruples and Mr Cordier's toughness had contributed
to the same political results: the fall of Lumumba and the strengthening of Tshombe. On UN action up to this point, Mr Colin Legum
has accurately commented: 'The total effect of UN policy in
Katanga had been to freeze the position in Tshombe's favour.'[2]

These events naturally caused jubilation among the dominant
groups in Elisabethville. Ambassador Rothschild, who had just
succeeded d'Aspremont-Lynden as head of the Belgian Govern-

---

[1] Lash, *Dag Hammarskjold*, p. 247. It was generally believed in the UN .at
the time that Hammarskjold was dismayed by Cordier's action, but felt he had no
alternative but to cover it.

[2] *Congo Disaster*, p. 170. For 'paragraph 4', see pp. 60, 89.

ment's 'Technical Aid Mission' in Katanga, cabled as follows to his
Government, on the day (September 6th) following Lumumba's
dismissal:

'The recent developments in Leopoldville have caused great
relief in E'ville. Although it is too early to draw any general
conclusion, the following reflections can be made:

(1) At the level of Katanga: it is clear that the example given by
the order and economic activity reigning in *Katanga* has
strongly contributed to encouraging other Congolese separa-
tisms (*particularismes*) to rebel against a contested authority.
The dismissal of Lumumba has also strengthened in a high
degree the leadership which Tshombe possesses as defender
of the political reconstruction of the former Belgian Congo
on a confederal basis.

(2) On a general level: success of the Katangese experiment will
probably bring about the political reconstruction of the Congo,
on an Elisabethville line (*à partir d'Elisabethville*). One may
well imagine that in this way a reunited Congo might adopt a
favourable attitude to the West, which would have a particular
importance, granted the geographical position of the Congo
in the heart of Africa, and considering the communist
offensive which Mr Khrushchev will no doubt launch
spectacularly at the coming UN Assembly.

(3) It is essential that Tshombe's action be encouraged in such a
way as to make it possible for him to remain a Congolese
leader, so that he can participate at least on an equal footing
with other Congolese leaders in the rebuilding of the Congo.
Similarly it is necessary, through the diplomatic help which
can be given, not to his régime but to the thesis which he
defends, that Tshombe should be able to appear as a competent
party (*interlocuteur valable*) in the eyes of other African leaders.

(4) Seen from Elisabethville, it would be extremely unfortunate
for the Government to be too early in declaring an offer of
aid to the rest of the Congo. It is necessary to give priority,
at least for the moment, to action in Katanga. . . .'[1]

The Belgian Government either were impressed by the arguments
of their 'Technical Aid Mission' or were thinking simultaneously
along the same lines, for on the day following this report, the Reuter
Agency announced the arrival in Elisabethville of nine tons of arms
from Belgium. They were arriving, according to a spokesman of

---

[1] *Dossiers*, II, p. 963.

the Katangese Ministry of the Interior, as part of a continuous airlift from Brussels.[1]

The Soviet Union, incensed by these events, and especially by the expulsion of its diplomats on September 17th, let loose the full force of its propaganda against Hammarskjold, and began to campaign for the 'troika'. This was hardly surprising, for the Soviet Union had seen resolutions, for which it had voted, used in such a way – even stretched in such a way – as to bring about the closing of its own Embassy. I am not a supporter of the international policies of the Soviet Union, but I cannot say that I find its reaction on this occasion so 'irrational', 'incomprehensible', or 'blindly destructive' as many Western commentators found it, or affected to find it. Granted that the Soviet Union was 'interfering in the internal affairs of the Congo', so also were the United States, Great Britain and almost everybody with an Embassy in Leopoldville – not to mention Belgium. The difference was that the Western powers 'won' – with considerable help from at least one United Nations representative who happened also to be a United States citizen. Any great power similarly treated would have reacted similarly.

The most significant reaction, for the future, was that of the Afro-Asian neutrals. Although they strongly disapproved of what had been done – and several of them, including Guinea, Indonesia and Morocco, withdrew their troops from the United Nations force – they did not as a group support the Soviet attack. Their attitude was indicative of the degree of credit which Hammarskjold had previously acquired among these countries, and also of the importance which they attached to the United Nations. But their confidence was severely shaken, and Hammarskjold had to make a serious effort to recover it. This, and the wide breach opened by Mr Cordier in paragraph 4 had important, though long-term, implications for Katanga.

The Security Council remained deadlocked from September 1960 to February 1961. During this time, Hammarskjold and Dayal, his representative in Leopoldville from September 8th on, resisted Western pressure to recognize the Kasavubu-Mobutu-Ileo-Bomboko group as the Government of the Congo. They also resisted Mobutu's demand that Lumumba, who had sought UN protection on September 15th, should be handed over. As a result of this Dayal – though not, directly, Hammarskjold – came under heavy fire in the Western Press. Lumumba left Leopoldville, and UN protection, on November 28th, in an attempt to reach Stanleyville, where his partisans had

---

[1] *Dossiers*, II, p. 770.

the upper hand. He was captured, held for a time at Thysville in the Bas-Congo and then, on January 17th, handed over to Mr Tshombe in Elisabethville. On February 13th, Godefroid Munongo, Tshombe's Minister of the Interior, announced that Lumumba and his companions, Okito and Mpolo, had escaped from custody and had been killed by some villagers.

This announcement, which hardly anyone pretended to believe, came at an unfortunate time for the 'State of Katanga'. Not only did it provoke a great wave of indignation in Afro-Asian countries – it would have done that at any time – but it provoked that wave at the very moment when a new American administration, very much more sensitive than its predecessor to Afro-Asian opinion, was framing its Congo policy. It also temporarily discouraged Mr Tshombe's many friends in Western countries. The man who had been presented as, above all, an upholder of law and order, now looked uncomfortably like a murderer. His admirers pointed out – quite rightly – that he was not the only murderer in the Congo, but even this did not altogether recommend him to the wider public in the West.

Mr Tshombe's official relations with the Belgian Government were also now much cooler than they had been during the months of July to September when the State of Katanga had been established and consolidated. This was because he – and even more Munongo and the local ultras – resented the *rapprochement* between Brussels and the Leopoldville authorities who had taken over after the fall of Lumumba. As early as October the governmental 'Technical Aid Mission' headed by Rothschild had been replaced by a private 'Service of Technical Co-operation' headed by Professor Clémens of Liège, author of the Katangese Constitution.[1] All in all, Katanga's diplomatic position was considerably weaker than it had been in September. The Katangese Government was disappointed and disconcerted by the fact, that while the Belgian Government had helped it domestically, it had actually opposed, diplomatically, the recognition of the State of Katanga. Partly as a result of this, that State, despite the feelings of friendship towards it which were prevalent in many Western countries, still lacked any diplomatic recognition.

It was in this climate that the United States was able to agree with the Afro-Asian countries on a policy for the UN in Katanga, which went considerably beyond anything hitherto sanctioned. In this climate, too, neither the Soviet Union – despite its radical hostility

---

[1] *Dossiers*, II, p. 969.

to Hammarskjold and the UN Congo operation as a whole – nor the United Kingdom and France – despite their Governments' sympathies with Katanga – felt able to veto measures agreed on by the United States and the Afro-Asian countries. In those circumstances, the fateful resolution of February 21st, 1961, came into being.[1] It was to ensure that that resolution was applied, that I had been sent to Katanga. I shall have to say more later about the problems of applying it. It is enough to say here that both its supporters and its opponents – open or concealed – believed that if it were fully applied – by the removal of *all* foreign officers and *all* political advisers – the secession of Katanga would be at an end. Many, both of its supporters and opponents, however, doubted whether it would in fact be applied. Soviet propaganda asserted that Hammarskjold would never carry it out. Hammarskjold and his collaborators were, as we have seen,[2] determined that it must be carried out, if the whole operation, and even the UN itself, were not to founder through the loss of the all-important, neutral Afro-Asian support. And Hammarskjold could rely on a degree of backing from the new American administration which he had not received from the old. The Democratic administration has in fact steadily supported the United Nations effort in the Congo; the United States, under that administration, has been the only major power to give such support.

The implications of all this do not seem to have been immediately apprehended in Katanga, or in the rest of the Congo for that matter. Tshombe, Ileo and Kasavubu, and others mostly of similar outlook including the Mulopwe Albert Kalonji, met at Tananarive on March 8th to 12th – perhaps as a result of French mediation – and there agreed on a 'confederation' which would, if put into practice, have meant the break-up of the Congo into a number of separate States with Kasavubu as their nominal President. This 'settlement' was denounced by the Lumumbists, nominally headed by Antoine Gizenga, from their stronghold at Stanleyville. It was unacceptable to Afro-Asian opinion and had, from an American point of view also, distinct disadvantages, since it would make it hard to prevent the survival, within this vague confederation, of a substantially independent Lumumbist state in Orientale province: a State which might well, it was thought, become a 'Congolese Cuba'.

Whether for this or other reasons the 'Tananarive Confederation' was still-born. Kasavubu – who had attended the Tananarive

---

[1] Text in appendix I. See pp. 40, 60–63.
[2] Chapter II, pp. 58–63.

Conference only after considerable hesitation, and against the opposition of Bomboko – signed an agreement with the United Nations (April 17th), under which he accepted the Resolution of February 21st, and the UN, in turn, agreed to assist him in ensuring the departure of the foreign officers, political advisers, etc. This implied Kasavubu's backing for a stronger UN line in Katanga, and Mobutu discontinued the rather theoretical hostilities which he had been waging against Stanleyville. When Tshombe went to Coquilhatville on April 23rd 'to discuss the implementation of the Tananarive agreement', he was, not unnaturally, displeased at this trend, and when he called on Kasavubu to repudiate the agreement with the United Nations and then tried to leave the conference he was arrested (April 26th). On May 7th, Bomboko announced that Tshombe would be tried for high treason.

It is, at first sight, mysterious that Kasavubu, Ileo and Bomboko[1] who in March were able to agree with Tshombe on a programme which in effect would have ratified the *de facto* secession of Katanga, should in April hold him imprisoned for trying to maintain this policy. The only clue I can see to this change of front is that the consistent element in the policy of these gentlemen has been its tendency to conform to the policies of the United States. United States policy had moved towards an 'Afro-Asian line' ('unity of the Congo') and away from an 'Anglo-French-Belgian line' ('order in Katanga'). Kasavubu and his friends, after some discussion and with variations of pace, moved in the same direction. This does not explain all their actions – the other Western powers have also to be taken into account – but it would account for the general trend.[2]

Tshombe, when I arrived in Elisabethville, was still a prisoner in Leopoldville. The Government of the 'State of Katanga', regarded by the United Nations as the Provincial Government of Katanga, was being carried on in his absence by a 'Collège' consisting of the Vice-President Jean-Baptiste Kibwe, the Minister for the Interior, Godefroid Munongo, and the Minister for Education, Joseph Kiwele.

My first official duty was to call on the Collège and invite their co-operation in carrying out the Security Council Resolution of February 21st.

[1] Bomboko did not attend at Tananarive, but he continued to serve as Foreign Minister in Ileo's Government. Ileo's signature as 'Prime Minister of the Republic of the Congo' appears under the Resolutions of the Tananarive Conference *below* that of Tshombe, 'President of the State of Katanga'. Mobutu was not at Tananarive either, but he continued to support the Ileo Government. The texts of the Tananarive Resolutions are in *Congo, 1961* (CRISP), p. 35 seq.

[2] For developments in North Katanga during this period see Chapter VIII.

5

WAITING FOR TSHOMBE

*'Videant Consules ne quid Respublica
detrimenti capiat.'*
Cicero

'He is Suffering for Us', ran the words above Mr Tshombe's portrait
on the posters on all the available walls of Elisabethville at this time.
Below, the legend was: 'Let us be Worthy of Him.' The face in
between, flexible as any worn by Mr Kingsley Amis's heroes, did
indeed portray a noble pathos. Fortunately, the conditions of
Mr Tshombe's confinement were, by this time at least, considerably
less rigorous than those of Lumumba's had been, either in Thysville
or on the journey to his death in Elisabethville. 'How is President
Tshombe?' a Belgian correspondent had asked General Mobutu a
week before. 'He is well,' replied the General, 'I brought him some
bottles of whisky this morning, because the soldiers had been giving
him nothing to drink but beer. He has everything he needs – I often
drop in for a man-to-man chat with him. But, by the way, I would
like you to write that it is completely false to say, as people are saying
in Elisabethville, that Tshombe gave me money to pay my soldiers.
. . . It is true that Katanga has presented the Army with a million
francs which were handed over to Major Pwatu. We did not touch
that money, and the notes are in a special safe.'[1]

Experienced observers augured correctly, from these words and
some other indications that Tshombe would soon be at liberty.
The moment of my arrival, therefore, coincided with a period of
expectation, since it was clear that all major political decisions

---

[1] *La Libre Belgique*, 6.6.61. Mobutu became a General in January 1961.

must await Tshombe's return – or, failing that, his trial, so often announced as imminent by Mr Bomboko and others. As for the resolutions, and notably that of February 21st, the Collège had just agreed to 'study ways and means of applying them'.[1] Pending Mr Tshombe's return – hardly anyone believed that he would be tried – the Collège could hardly be asked to do more.

When, therefore, I drove up to the CSK[2] building – the house of the parastatal trust which had formerly ruled Katanga directly, and whose premises now accommodated the State Government – my call was mainly one of protocol, rather than serious business. It is appropriate, in view of later events, and comments thereon, that I should say something of my frame of mind at this point. Naturally, I did not come to Katanga entirely without preconceived ideas, with my mind an ideal blank. From the character and arguments of Mr Tshombe's friends abroad, I thought it likely that his régime was indeed – as its critics said – a device for preserving local European, and outside financial, control of this very profitable territory. From what I have said, in Chapter I, about my general views, it will be understood that I did not find this system particularly congenial. But it would be wrong – and in one sense too flattering to myself – to assume that I came in any crusading spirit. I thought it quite natural that the local Europeans, the Union Minière and other large interests, should try to hold on to what they had, and not at all surprising that they should have been able to find some local Africans to co-operate with them. The Europeans of Elisabethville, in the circumstances of July 1960, had reacted very much as any community placed in their position would have done and I knew that if I had been born and brought up among them I should have been likely to react in the same way (just as if I had been born a Kikuyu, and poor, I might have joined the Mau Mau). Historical relativism is not a point of view conducive to keeping

---

[1] *La Libre Belgique*, June 10th to 11th, 1961.

[2] The *Comité Spécial du Katanga*, set up in 1900, was a mixed State and capitalist board for the exploitation of the mineral resources of the territory, and for its administration. The CSK had, in theory, very wide powers – including that of nominating the President of the Union Minière. The State nominated four of the six members of the Board of the CSK. If this state of affairs had been maintained up to Congolese independence (June 30th, 1960) the Republic of the Congo would have had a very important say in the economy of its province of Katanga. The CSK was, accordingly, dissolved, with the assent of the Belgian Government, on June 27th, 1960, and the Government of the State of Katanga inherited, not inappropriately, its mansion. See Joye et Lewin, *Les Trusts au Congo*, pp. 280–281, 290–292.

up a high level of moral indignation. At the same time – now that the temporary and realistic qualm I had experienced in Brussels had passed – I felt that it should be possible, rationally, to convince those concerned that what had perhaps served their interests once – the secession of Katanga – could no longer serve them in the new 'American-Afro-Asian' political conjuncture, and could only, if persisted in, bring upon them the very disasters they most feared. I knew that the great resources of American diplomacy would now be seriously exerted in this direction and I believed that the resources of British diplomacy – no less great in this area – would also be brought to bear, even if somewhat reluctantly. Against this background – and despite what I knew of the nature and tenacity of the forces supporting 'Independent Katanga' – I thought it should be possible for a combined effort, pivoting on Hammarskjold and using the lever of the resolutions, to bring back Katanga into the Republic of the Congo without violence. Not only did I not desire or expect violence but at this moment I did not even take the prospect of violence very seriously, inclining – too schematically – to the belief that people behind Tshombe had too much at stake to risk disorder.

The first meeting with the Collège on the morning of June 15th was, naturally enough, civil and not unfriendly. Colonel Egge and Mr Brackenbury accompanied me; sitting opposite us in Victorian leather arm-chairs were the members of the Collège.

Mr Kibwe and Mr Kiwele both belonged to the Batabwa tribe of Eastern Katanga. The local Europeans, who like to attach immutable characteristics to each ethnic grouping, ascribed cunning and evasiveness to the Batabwa and, at least as regards these two tribesmen, they were not altogether wrong. Mr Kiwele (like many educated Congolese, including Mr Munongo) had studied for the priesthood, Mr Kibwe had attended the Institut St Boniface, and the vocabulary of the Collège bore a distinctly ecclesiastical imprint. The combination of a slightly furtive bearing with highly spiritual language does not make an agreeable first impression and I thought Mr Kibwe, in particular, distinctly unprepossessing. As Minister for Finance, he had a reputation, among both Europeans and Africans, for extreme corruption and his manner did nothing to make this reputation implausible. He had a habit of crouching forward in his chair, almost bent double, and then still further lowering his chin, so that if he wanted to see whoever he was talking to – which was not always the case – he had to twist his neck and cock one eye, looking a little like a tortoise, and a little like a shark. From this

stance he ejected remarks which were usually cryptic, often surly
and sometimes had a smack of Tartuffe. Later I was to find that
Jean-Baptiste Kibwe had some surprisingly good qualities – including courage and good humour in adversity – but on this occasion
I did not feel we were destined to be friends. Joseph Kiwele made a
somewhat pleasanter impact. For one thing he sat up straight and
looked one in the eye – attitudes which in Mr Kibwe's presence
seemed extravagantly virtuous. He had been a music teacher – had
indeed composed the Katanga National Anthem – and although
his little bullet-head and bright, beady eyes had no obvious aesthetic
associations, there was something of the classroom, something
paternal and didactic about him which, after a while, made one
begin to take to him. He was getting on in years and inclined to
ramble a little, sometimes even in the direction of truth. The reason
he was in the Collège at all was to serve as a buffer between the two
strong characters, Kibwe and the third member – Godefroid
Munongo.

Of the three – and, as I was to find, of all the Katanga politicians,
not excluding Tshombe – Munongo was the most impressive
personality. He had features such as one sees on certain African
wood-carvings, with long, almost flat cheeks and a heavy pouting
under-lip. You could not tell what his eyes were like – because of the
famous dark glasses which he invariably wore – and this increased
the rather uncanny sculptural effect. Tall and well-built, he carried
his head high, with the bearing of one who was conscious of being
an aristocrat. He spoke good French in a low, deep voice which
came in rapid surges and as he spoke he had the habit of turning
his head slowly from side to side, making the light flash from his
spectacles. When things went normally, as on this occasion, he used
to sit well back in his chair, immobile save for the restlessness of his
head and long, well-manicured hands. If warmed by argument,
however, he was liable to violent, convulsive movements. Once, a
few weeks later, I happened to mention the name of Lumumba in
his presence. He raised his right arm with a jerk and then sharply
slapped the back of his neck. At first I thought he had been bitten
by an insect: then I realized that his instinctive reaction, which he
had barely, at the last moment, brought under control, was to
strike the man who mentioned Lumumba's name.

When I walked into that room that morning I had felt a considerable degree of confidence in the power of rational persuasion: that
these men, and those around them, could be induced to see that it
was no longer in their interests to preserve a State of Katanga

which had no open friends and many implacable enemies. Neither the meeting, nor subsequent events, entirely destroyed this faith in the power of rational persuasion, but one became more conscious of the limits of that power the more one talked with Godefroid Munongo (and I talked with him often in the next few weeks). Most of the people who talked about 'the Katangese nation' had their tongues in their cheeks; this was unpleasantly obvious in the case of the many 'white Katangese' who affected to feel a sense of common nationality with Africans, whom – as they made abundantly clear in other contexts – they both despised and feared. But for Munongo 'Katanga' had clearly a deep, emotional significance: it meant the power of the chiefs, the hope of preserving, or restoring, a traditional Central African society, like the Katanga ruled over by his ferocious grandfather, the Bayeke paramount chief, M'Siri, after whom he had named his little son. The element of the absurd in this archaic dream did not lessen its power. His voice used to shake with pride as he spoke of Bunkeya, the capital of his slave-trading ancestors; with pathos when he spoke of this or that traditional chief, done to death by 'Lumumbists'. For him, 'the unity of the Congo' meant Lumumbism, and Lumumbism meant the destruction of his cherished dream. It was generally believed in Elisabethville that he had killed Lumumba with his own hands.[1]

This reputation may well have given some of his colleagues and even his leader, when they considered compromise, cause to hesitate.

Mr Kibwe began, this morning, by asking me whether I had come to bring order or disorder?

Was it to sow, Mr Kiwele inquired, the good wheat or the chaff?

Mr Munongo asked whether I was a Communist.

I told them I was not a Communist and had come for one purpose only: to see that the resolutions of the Security Council and the Assembly were applied. These resolutions included the

---

[1] According to a witness before the UN Commission on the death of Lumumba, 'M Munongo, who was awaiting his arrival [on January 17th, in a villa near Elisabethville airport], came towards M Lumumba and, after making some remarks, took a bayonet from the rifle of one of the soldiers and drove it into Lumumba's chest'. A Belgian mercenary, one Ruys, then, mercifully, dispatched Lumumba with a bullet through the head. After being preserved for some time in a refrigerator belonging to the Union Minière, the body was dissolved in phenol. The Commission neither endorses nor rejects this witness's testimony. It concludes that Lumumba and his companions are most likely to have been killed, on January 17th, 'before the eyes of certain members of the Government of Katanga, notably MM Tshombe, Munongo and Kibwe.' (S/4976 Conclusion 2).

maintenance of public order. They also included the unity of the Congo. Of greatest immediate importance, however, was the resolution passed in February, for the withdrawal of foreign officers and political advisers. That was obviously a dead letter in Katanga – for example, foreign officers in Katangese uniform were everywhere to be seen in Elisabethville. This situation was completely unacceptable. I had been glad to learn that they accepted the resolution in principle, and I would be glad to co-operate with them in its swift and orderly application.

It was being applied, said Mr Munongo, there was no problem.

Mr Kiwele said that, in his opinion, it would be at least twenty-five years before Katanga could do without foreign officers. Mr Munongo turned his dark glasses in Mr Kiwele's direction and Mr Kiwele subsided.

Mr Kibwe was glad I had used the word 'orderly'. This showed, he thought, that I was probably not a Communist. Communists were the enemies of order.

I pointed out that I had also used the word 'swift'; the resolution, passed four months ago, had used the word 'immediate', yet today there were just as many foreign officers in Katanga as ever – more than five hundred of them; as for political advisers –

The letter killeth, said Mr Kibwe.

But the spirit giveth life, said Mr Kiwele.

Mr Munongo said that outsiders were completely wrong in imagining that Katanga was run by Belgians. He personally hated the Belgians. Belgians had murdered his grandfather; his father had died in a Belgian jail.

Mr Kibwe said that many Belgians were Communists.

Spaak, for example, said Mr Kiwele.

Mr Munongo said Belgian socialists had caused the whole trouble, by teaching the Congolese not to respect the authority of their traditional leaders. He wanted to get rid of all the Belgians as soon as they could be replaced by others. He would rather rely on France than on Belgium.

France, said Mr Kiwele, was the Eldest Daughter of the Church.

I said it was illegal – under a resolution mandatory on all nations – to recruit, for any part of the Congo, any foreign officers not assigned for the purpose by the United Nations. This applied to the French officers whom Katanga had recruited after the resolution, and in defiance of it.

Mr Munongo said that no decisions could be taken while President Tshombe was still a prisoner. If he were released and if the people in Leopoldville returned to 'the spirit of Tananarive' everything was possible. The Leopoldville people were, however, flighty and unstable, especially Bomboko. Some of them were descended from slaves. Katanga accepted the resolutions, but must be the sole judge of when and how to apply them. He warned me against the dangers of being 'administrative'. Legal texts were very good, but Africa was an old continent, and must not be hurried.

The letter killeth, said Mr Kibwe.

But the spirit giveth life, said Mr Kiwele.

The next fortnight was a pleasant one in which there was little to be done except meet people and wait for Mr Tshombe's return – in the half belief that he would bring with him, and carry out, a settlement with Leopoldville. I made the acquaintance at this time of the Consular Corps in Elisabethville. an interesting and rather anomalous body of foreign representatives. Since no Government recognized the State of Katanga, these representatives were all, in theory, purely consular officials, whose main task was to protect the interests of their countries' citizens in the Elisabethville consular area. Elisabethville was recognized by the powers concerned merely as one of a number of Congolese provincial towns. Mr Tshombe was a provincial president. These officials were, therefore, generally under the orders of their countries' Ambassadors in what was, in the official view of the people with whom they had to deal, a foreign capital – Leopoldville. Their own citizens in Katanga were, virtually without exception, strong supporters of Mr Tshombe and of secession and they themselves – with the single exception of the American Consul – were discreetly but stubbornly inclined in the same direction. From a strictly consular point of view this was not unnatural, for it was evident that any change in the *status quo* would be likely to affect adversely, in some degree at least, and perhaps very drastically, the interests of the Belgian, French and other foreign residents of Katanga. The State of Katanga had been set up, after all, in their interests, and few if any of them could see that, in present circumstances, it was already becoming a liability. The Consular Corps in Elisabethville had also, as a body, a reason to support the *status quo*. One of their number had been murdered in the July mutiny. 'The Consular Corps on the spot', state the compilers of *Congo 1960*, 'shocked by the incidents of the night on which the Italian Consul had perished, seemed favourable to a political autonomy in Katanga'.[1] Perhaps partly for this reason the

---

[1] II, 717.

Consular Corps was treated by the Government as if it were a
Diplomatic Corps, and was often – and usually, to its annoyance, at
week-ends – summoned to the Palace or the CSK building to hear
important political pronouncements. Some of its members – notably
the British and French Consuls – were also often called on for
advice or help, in private audience.

The doyen of the Corps was M Henri Créner, the Belgian
Consul-General. M Créner was, even for a member of the Elisabethville Consular Corps, in an odd position, for there was no Ambassador to whom he could report, the Belgian Embassy in Leopoldville
having been closed. According to normal rules, the Consulate in
Elisabethville should also have been closed – since Belgium did not
claim that Katanga was an independent State – but normal rules
had ceased to apply in the Congo. M Créner stayed, and reported
direct to Brussels. M Créner was a portly and affable man and,
like many such people, he hated almost everything and almost
everybody. Suppressed fury, covered over with ceremonious
effusiveness, was his attitude towards the United Nations, the
Republic of the Congo, the Independent State of Katanga, the
Continent of Africa and especially, most especially, the Belgian
residents of the city of Elisabethville. His state of mind was that
which Gustavo Duran had predicted for me and which I did not
stay long enough to attain. M Créner was unpopular with the
Katangan authorities and with the local Belgians – it was, for most
practical purposes, much the same thing – because he was thought
to be 'in league with Spaak', and also because the local Belgians,
now calling themselves Katangese, made it a point of honour to
show their poor opinion of 'official Belgium', for its failure to give
open diplomatic support to the State of Katanga. The person who
suffered from this was not M Créner – the more people there were
who refused to talk to him the better he liked it – but his subordinate
M Jules Herckens. M Herckens was the statutory Fleming, who
must be Consul if the Consul-General is a Walloon. His ponderous
movements and unhurried thought-processes made him a butt of
the favourite Walloon joke, the riddle:

Savez-vous le comble du pléonasme? Un primitif flamand![1]

M Herckens suffered much from the ostracism of his compatriots and strove, quite unsuccessfully, to recover their good
opinion by cautious little displays of 'pro-Katanga' and 'anti-UN'

---

[1] 'The most tautological possible expression is the phrase, "A Flemish primitive".' The joke is more pointed in French.

sentiment. He and M Créner had only one thing in common: they both made it clear from the outset that no active co-operation in carrying out the resolutions could be looked for from them.

The French Consul, M Lambroschini, a little Corsican, with that degree of self-esteem which we associate with little Corsicans, made the same point in his own way. He knew there were Frenchmen in the Katanga Gendarmerie, but he could do nothing about it. As far as he was concerned, these Frenchmen did not exist. 'You can do what you like with them – when you catch them.' The little pause in the middle of this sentence and a flicker in M Lambroschini's narrow cat-like eyes told you, more plainly than any explicit language, exactly where M Lambroschini stood. They told you not merely that he would be a dangerous adversary, but that he already was one.

Mr Denzil Dunnett, the British Consul, was quite a different case. I have found, to my regret, that, because I have had occasion to criticize publicly certain of this gentlemen's official acts, I have been taken as attacking him personally. This was far from my intention; what I wished to criticize was the policy of the Government which he represented and whose instructions and interests, so far as I know, he did no more than follow loyally. In all personal relations, Mr Dunnett was civil to the verge of friendliness. He was what Quakers call 'non-verbal', his virtues being of a solider kind than those associated with ready repartee, but he retained – even in difficult times – his sense of humour and his courtesy. He took his responsibilities very seriously – I remember him best with shoulders bowed, eyes fixed on the ground and massive jaw doggedly set – but he was not hostile either, like M Créner, to the world in general, or, like M Lambroschini, to the UN in particular. He was in favour of the United Nations – he had once worked for it indeed – but he liked it best in a state of total immobility. 'Let well enough alone' was the advice which he habitually implied and he considered that, on the whole, things in Elisabethville *were* well enough. Mrs Dunnett, unlike most of the ladies of the Consular Corps, was a personality in her own right. She had a pair of blazing blue eyes, and decided opinions, which she expressed forcefully and readily. She believed, and stated, that Africans were not, and would never be, able to govern themselves. Joyce Cary's *Mr Johnson*, told you, in her view, all you needed to know.

The Belgian and French Consuls could fairly be described as 'anti-UN' and (exception made for M Créner's general misanthropy) 'pro-Katanga'; the British Consul was 'pro-UN', with the ominous reservations of his Government. The only Consul of a major interested power who was on the United Nations side without reservations was the American Consul, at this time Mr William Canup. Mr Canup was not deceived by the surface calm of this period. He realized, no doubt from the briefing he had been given, that the 'Independent State of Katanga' could not, as some of its rulers imagined, talk itself into untroubled perpetuity by references to 'the spirit of Tananarive'. Knowing Mr Tshombe, as I then did not, he did not imagine that Mr Tshombe's return would make any important difference to the situation. Mr Canup, unlike M Créner, had a happy, rather youthful temperament but Katanga and the air of impending doom, which he was almost alone there at that time in sensing, had come to oppress a normally buoyant spirit. He must have felt all the time what I had felt for a moment in the dining-room of the Hotel Metropole in Brussels – the approach of violence and death. At this time, my colleagues and myself used to be rather amused by what we regarded as his 'alarmism'; we did not realize, as we should have done, that this was a situation in which an alarmist was likely to be right.

Apart from premonitions, there was another cause for Mr Canup's despondency. All the other Consuls in Elisabethville represented Western European countries and the general feeling among them – expressed, as usual, most clearly by the wives – was one of resentment at the American Government's 'pro-Congolese' and 'pro-UN' attitude. The American Consul was *ex officio* somewhat unpopular – and became more so – not only among his consular colleagues, but with the Government with which he had to deal and with the society of the city in which he had to live. It is no wonder that, when Mr Canup, later, learned that he was to be posted elsewhere, his joy was extravagant, even to whoops of laughter and clapping of hands. His joy was so unrestrained indeed that I warned him to be careful, lest the wrong reason be imputed to it, for the post to which he had been nominated was Moscow. This thought quickly sobered him.

Although – or perhaps because – the United Nations was pledged to the removal of foreign officers and political advisers, the local Europeans who were on the closest terms with UN personnel at this time were the leading foreign officer, Colonel Crèvecoeur, and the most important political adviser, M Victor Tignée. The view of my predecessor, M Dumontet, had been that, through their co-operation, the objectives of the United Nations (which included the 'immediate withdrawal and evacuation' of the people in question) could eventually be achieved. That this was a logical absurdity does not seem to have troubled M Dumontet but it irritated the more Cartesian mind of his compatriot, now my deputy, Michel Tombelaine. Michel thought that the 'co-operation' furnished by these people was entirely in the interests of the Independent State of Katanga, and was clearly intended to gain time – by token gestures – during which that State would consolidate itself domestically and diplomatically, and the support for the United Nations, essentially a shaky coalition, would crumble. Michel's attitude to 'co-operation' was sensed by the 'white Katangese', who detested him more than any other UN person, more even than myself at the pinnacle of my subsequent unpopularity. The rest of us Onusians, mainly Scandinavians and Irish at this stage, were thought of more or less as beings from outer space, a scourge certainly but an impersonal scourge. Michel, being a Frenchman, was thought of as a human being and hated accordingly. He, with the inner confidence which comes from being a Parisian, an intellectual and the son of a rich banker, was coolly amused by these uncouth provincial rumblings – the thought of Elisabethville as a 'provincial hole' was one of the very few ideas which he shared with M Dumontet. The little smile which used to play around the corners of his lips when, at a cocktail party, he listened to some excited Flemish doctor or mining engineer, was not the least of the 'atrocities of the United Nations'.

The Sunday morning after my arrival I went, with Colonel Egge, for cocktails at Colonel Crèvecoeur's house. Colonel Crèvecoeur, contrary to his dramatic name and reputation, was a shy, gentle-mannered, rather lymphatic officer, with a belief that he was misunderstood. He and his collaborators, especially the able and reserved Major Mathys, stressed the difference between themselves – regular Belgian officers seconded by the Belgian Government – and the mercenaries, the Frenchmen, South Africans and others who had volunteered for Katanga service, for money in most cases, out of fanaticism in some. Colonel Crèvecoeur and his friends did not conceal their distaste for, in particular, the French officers – mainly men of an 'OAS' type implicated in the recent Algerian putsch – of whom Munongo thought so highly. By contrast, Colonel Crèvecoeur and his colleagues underlined their own respectability, conversing in diffident undertones as they passed around, after the cocktails, the poisoned arrows and long trade muskets (*pou-pous*) which they had captured from the 'rebel' Baluba in North Katanga in their successful spring offensive. Here in this room, they seemed to mur-

mur, was our common civilization – which included, yes indeed, also *white* UN people – and out there were the forces of darkness. Could we not, even now, try to make a fresh start, sensible people on both sides, deprecating all our fanatics, French, 'Hindus' or Baluba?

Again, it was the women who gave the show away. I remember Madame Crèvecoeur, a stout, motherly woman, sitting grim and unsmiling in the middle of the room, with radical distrust of the United Nations in every fold of her honest face. 'It may be your duty as an officer to give these people fair words' – she seemed to say – 'but I have done *my* duty in letting them into this house, and beyond that I will not go.'

She was quite right. What these people represented and what the United Nations represented were fundamentally irreconcilable and there are few things more depressingly distasteful than ceremonies of feigned reconciliation. I never met the Crèvecoeurs again; they left Katanga shortly afterwards at the request of the United Nations.

M Victor Tignée, as befitted a political adviser, was more subtle than the Commander of the Gendarmerie. M Tignée, *Chef de Cabinet* to the Minister of the Interior, Godefroid Munongo, used in those days to visit me at Les Roches in the evenings. He would drive into the compound, accompanied by his young and attractive wife, who, however, remained in the car while M Tignée came into the drawing-room for a whisky and soda and an hour or more of political conversation. His wife, he explained, was not interested in politics. This, if true, made her a very unusual person in Elisabethville; the result in any case was to deprive me of such guidance on M Tignée's real outlook as might have been obtained from his wife's expression while he 'talked politics'. Talk he did, fluently and interestingly. He had been in the Congo for many years, as a District Officer, and he spoke with much expertise, combining a genuine love of his subject with the pleasure of conveying to the new-comer how much – impossibly much – he had to learn. Tribal peculiarities were his main theme, always with the implication that the disparities and hostilities were so great as to make the idea of a Congolese State altogether unworkable. As far as Katanga was concerned, he was strong for the principle of 'co-operation with the United Nations', but a little vague about how this would work in practice. Munongo, he said, was fundamentally reasonable and wished to co-operate; local 'ultras', however, were trying to 'poison his mind' and it was important not to 'play into their hands'. With patience, and a little ingenuity, everything would come out all right.

M Tignée was a small, grey-haired, pipe-smoking man, rather like the actor Claude Rains. His conversation was entertaining and instructive and at first I found him to some extent persuasive. Here, I thought, was an intelligent man who had realized that the Independent State of Katanga had become a liability as far as long-term European interests were concerned; a man who would use his considerable persuasive power, with enlightened self-interest, to secure the obviously vital settlement with Leopoldville, getting guarantees of 'respect for order in the province' in exchange for dropping the 'Independent State' and the foreigners recruited to defend it.

If this were really so – and it was not an unreasonable conception – then we could work together, and make progress towards a peaceful and stable settlement. Unfortunately, the more I worked with him, the more my faith in this hypothesis wavered.

In general, when working with Belgian officials in the Katanga Government, I found that their manner developed disquieting undertones of a sort of racial complicity. 'We have to pretend', their inflections seemed to convey, 'that we are working for Munongo and his friends who, you and we know, are simply savages. You have to pretend to work for a United Nations which is run by Africans, Asians and simple-minded Americans. The reality here is European rule; you and we are Europeans; surely it is not beyond our ability to rig up some façade which will satisfy both these sets of ignorant people while preserving the reality – the only possible reality?'

To return to M Tignée; even discarding the more hopeful hypothesis, I thought my contact with him still useful as a source of information. Here, too, I was destined to be disillusioned.

At three o'clock on the afternoon of June 21st, Tignée rang me, apparently in some excitement, to say that his Minister, Munongo, had had a heart attack and would not be able to keep an appointment with me that evening. I cabled this important piece of news to Leopoldville. Later that afternoon Tignée gave a useful Press contact – Jean-Pierre Joullain, the AFP correspondent – a tip: keep an eye on the airports. The same evening, the radio carried the accurate report that Munongo had arrived in Brazzaville. He had come to negotiate Tshombe's release, which was announced by Mobutu the next day.

6

A TURN FOR THE BETTER

'There was a beginning but you cannot see it.
There will be an end but you cannot see it.'
Robert Penn Warren

Monday, June 26th,
Public Holiday in Katanga'[1]

'. . . We are having every kind of sport and pastime here since our President came back on Saturday. We went to the airport; the flower of Katanga was there, both black and white – about 500 of them.[2] Some of the women wore flour on their faces; everyone had a Katanga flag in his hand; the President's Special Guard were in very special uniforms – an imitation of those worn by the Garde Républicaine at the Elysée Palace, but several sizes too big. Evelyn Waugh would have been delighted with them, curse him. When the plane landed, the politicians started a race to be first to shake His hand. The gendarmerie tried to keep the crowd back and one of them drove the butt of his gun sharply into the stomach of that affable man, the Belgian Consul-General, doyen of the Diplomatic Corps [sic]. This spectacle gave no little satisfaction to the United Nations representatives there present.

'The local Belgians are not so much in love with Tshombe as they used to be, on account of his coming back with black officers from the "foreign" Congo, having signed a treaty (*it seems*[3] . . .)

---

[1] Extract from letter of mine to Máire MacEntee: translation from Gaelic.

[2] *La Libre Belgique* (June 26th, 1961), says 5,000. Both computations are certainly influenced by the observer's political outlook.

[3] These words, in different ink, were clearly added later.

113

to amalgamate the gendarmerie with the Congo army. Heart-break instead of Crèvecoeur!

'We called on the President today to congratulate him. He's an educated man, quite clever and amusing, not a bit like the gloomy, arrogant Munongo. I think it should be possible to make progress with him more easily than with the others There are difficulties to be overcome, because we have to speed up the question of the political advisers – there are about ten of them who must go quickly. But on the whole the situation looks much better than it did. It seems now that the Central Parliament will meet, with the participation of the Tshombe people, as well as those of Gizenga and Ileo. What with that and the treaty about the Army and Finance, it is certain that the situation in the Congo has taken a turn for the better.'

I had been less than a fortnight in the Congo when I wrote this letter. I think it is the last time the word 'certain' appears in my correspondence from there, in relation to any future event or trend.

Tshombe had, indeed, signed an agreement in Leopoldville after his release from prison, but while he was still in some danger of re-arrest. The text of this agreement had been made known in Leopold-ville on the previous day; it provided for, among other things, the abolition of customs barriers between Katanga and 'the rest of the Congo', the payment into the Central Treasury of all import and export duties, the progressive amalgamation of Katanga currency with Congo currency, a single diplomatic representation for the whole of the Congo, the immediate liberation of all political prisoners in Katanga and the placing of the Katanga Gendarmerie under the authority of the Congo Commander-in-Chief.

This agreement, if genuinely applied, should have meant the peaceful liquidation of the secession of Katanga. In fact, none of the above arrangements was ever applied at all except for the military part, and that was applied only formally and briefly. Some of Mobutu's officers accompanied Tshombe on his return and one of them, Colonel Ndjoku, was placed in nominal command of the Katanga Gendarmerie. Tshombe, however, somewhat weakened the new commander's authority from the start by declaring publicly that he would be kept on only 'if he proved himself fit to carry out his duties'. The real command of the gendarmerie remained, as always, in European hands, and Colonel Ndjoku and his colleagues were sent home, after a few weeks, on the ground that they were 'subverting discipline' – that is to say, trying to take over effective command from the Europeans.

'Sign anything you like', Munongo, from across the river in
Brazzaville, was reported to have told the President, 'since your
signature will have been extorted from you.'[1] The President signed,
went home, and refrained from doing what he had pledged himself
to do. Characteristically he personally did not, in so many words,
denounce the agreement. He simply ignored it. Addressing the
'National Assembly' of Katanga on June 28th, he declared that
Katanga would remain independent; 'We shall see to it that the
Katangese Nation shall endure. Let the enemies of Katanga know
that they have to deal with a people.'

The argument that the broken treaty was signed 'under duress'
was never used, to me, by Tshombe himself. I have heard it used
by Munongo, with some emphasis, in Tshombe's presence, and
had the impression that Tshombe neither liked the argument nor
was intended to like it. I also began to have the impression that it
might not be only in Leopoldville that Tshombe was under duress.[2]
However that may be, the arguments he did use were ingenious.
Katanga being, he asserted, a democracy, any agreement would
have to be ratified by the 'National Assembly'. He, Tshombe,
was not a dictator. Furthermore, he had scruples about the credentials of the other signatory. Ileo had signed as 'Prime Minister of the
Congo'. But was Ileo Prime Minister of the Congo? Had he ever
been invested by Parliament under the *Loi Fondamentale*? Had not
the last really legal Government of the Congo, that of Patrice
Lumumba, fallen on September 5th, 1960?

This last argument was particularly ingenious, since the United
Nations had been resisting heavy Western pressure to accept Ileo
(or someone of his stamp) as Prime Minister of the Congo and had
refused to recognize any 'Prime Minister' not invested by Parliament. Tshombe was making use, for his own ends, of an argument
which a United Nations representative had to concede to be impeccable. (I suspected the inspiration of that eminent cardiologist,
Victor Tignée.) These, however, were mere legal loopholes. The
basic fact was that Tshombe found it convenient to repudiate (by
ignoring) in Elisabethville, an agreement which, in Leopoldville,
he had found it convenient to sign.

Two questions, of more or less lasting political interest, are
suggested by these transactions:

Why was he released?

Why did he repudiate the agreement?

---

[1] *La Libre Belgique*, June 27th, 1961 – Report of a Special Correspondent.

[2] See footnote at end of chapter (p. 125).

The simple answer to the first question, and the one current in Elisabethville, is a financial one. Certain numbered accounts in Swiss banks were alleged to have suddenly swollen in the last week of June. There is nothing inherently improbable about this, but it hardly by itself fully explains what happened. The persons directly responsible for Tshombe's release – Mobutu, Bomboko and perhaps Ileo – have always worked closely with Western Embassies, notably the American Embassy, and it is a reasonable assumption that had that Embassy disapproved of this transaction it would not have happened. There were strong reasons for approving it. By this stage, the UN had succeeded in bringing about a *rapprochement* between the Leopoldville politicians and the followers of Antoine Gizenga in Stanleyville. Both groups had agreed to take part in a session of the Central Parliament to take place in early or mid-July. The United States Administration, which, throughout the period when I was in the Congo, was backing the UN effort, certainly welcomed this *rapprochement*, but was also preoccupied by the possibility that the new Parliament might be dominated by Gizengists.

It was true that Antoine Gizenga might not really be a Communist. Indeed, in the early troubles of the Congo, on July 12th, 1960, he had signed the letter to the US Ambassador asking for American troops:[1] a fact which suggested that his Communism, if it existed, was neither fanatical nor doctrinaire. But Gizenga was regarded by a large public in the United States as a particularly dangerous Communist, and the election of a Gizengist Government in the Congo would be considered as a serious reverse for United States policy. The presence of conservative, 'federalist' representatives from Katanga would offset the feared Gizengist preponderance. This lent urgency to the general reasons for desiring Katangese participation. The dangers involved, at this stage, in Katangese abstention were now recognized even in Belgium.

'Supposing such a Government (Leopoldville-Stanleyville) is formed and recognized by the UN as "legal",' wrote *La Libre Belgique*, 'then there can be no doubt what the fate of the State of Katanga would be. Inevitably the new Government would demand the intervention of the international forces to oblige Elisabethville to return to legality.'[2]

From any point of view, but at this stage most especially from an

---

[1] *Dossiers*, II, pp. 542–543.

[2] June 26th, 1961. This clairvoyance did not prevent the same paper from being extremely surprised and angry, when, in August and September, what it predicted actually took place.

American or 'moderate Western' point of view, it was highly desirable to 'bring Katanga in'. Since he was prepared to sign a very satisfactory agreement, Tshombe had to be given liberty to carry it out. This was a justifiable experiment; what is unfortunate is that its negative results do not seem to have been as clearly remarked in the West as they might have been. 'Agreement under duress', followed by implicit or explicit repudiation, is a technique which Tshombe was to use again, and may even now not have used for the last time.

Why did he, at this time, repudiate an agreement which most reasonable, conservative opinion would rightly have thought it prudent to respect? Neither the 'National Assembly' nor scruples about Mr Ileo's political legitimacy provide the answer nor, I think, is Tshombe a naturally intransigent man. The answer, I believe, is symbolized by Munongo's trip to Brazzaville. Munongo, as he made clear himself,[1] preferred to rely on French rather than Belgian support. While some of his advisers liked to represent him as 'really a moderate', it must be said that if so he was the kind of 'moderate' who liked and relied on French officers from Algiers who regarded General de Gaulle as a traitor. Brazzaville, capital of the former French Congo, was regarded by many Belgians as a centre for the intrigues of 'certain French circles in Katanga',[2] and the ruler of Brazzaville, President Fulbert Youlou, is an enthusiast for the disintegration of the former Belgian Congo. Munongo made it clear, both before and after Tshombe's release, that beyond 'the spirit of Tananarive' (secession labelled 'confederation') he would not go. He had reasons for this, since, as Lumumba's putative murderer, he might well not have long to live in a united Congo.[3] Faced with the decided opposition of Munongo and his French circle and the suspicion of many local 'white Katangese', and perhaps also depressed by the financial implications of the agreement he had signed, Tshombe shelved the agreement, whether he had ever had any serious intention of executing it or not.

On this and subsequent similar occasions, it was something of a puzzle why those who controlled the Union Minière and the other great industrial and commercial concerns of Katanga did not act,

---

[1] See p. 105.

[2] *La Libre Belgique*, June 26th, 1961.

[3] Long before Lumumba's death, Munongo believed that the failure of secession would mean his own violent death. '*Si on échoue,*' he told Pierre Davister, '*je suis zigouillé.*' (*Katanga*, p. 102). *Zigouiller* is a slang word meaning, according to Harrap's French-English dictionary, 'to kill, murder, knife; to bayonet'. It is an interesting word, in the light of the evidence later given before the UN Commission on Lumumba's death (Chapter V, p. 104 n.l.).

effectively and with foresight, to safeguard their great investments. It was common knowledge, openly discussed in the Press, that the coming meeting of the Central Parliament, and the emergence of a legal Government, spelled great danger for Katanga if the secession attempt was maintained. One would have thought – I thought myself – that those with most to lose would have seen to it that Tshombe did not burn his boats and theirs. Yet events did not take a shape such as rich and cautious Conservatives might be thought of as wishing; they took a shape which seemed to be dictated to a great extent by a desperate feudal chieftain, surrounded by a little band of émigré fanatics. We shall encounter this riddle in various contexts.

From this time on I saw Tshombe almost every day, sometimes at the CSK building with his Ministers, more often in his Palace, formerly the Governor's Palace – a large suburban villa in front of which groups of his supporters, Lunda tribesmen or white-robed members of the revivalist sect of Apostles, would gather to beat drums, dance and sing. I suspect that this continuous spectacle was organized, like other spontaneous manifestations of African feeling in Elisabethville, by the Minister for Information, Lucas Samalenghe, with the help of French specialists who were used to organizing similar demonstrations of Moslems in Algiers. (A pleasing and not untypical item in the *Echo du Katanga* at this time told of a patriotic Katangese woman who had given birth to triplets which she had christened Tshombe, Moise; Munongo, Godefroid and – Samalenghe, Lucas.) We used to sit in a little, rather over-furnished salon with a French window giving on the lawn: a French window through which Munongo used often to arrive 'accidentally' and rather out of breath, when I had been twenty minutes or more with the President. He had, apparently, his sources of information in the Palace.

Tshombe was always hospitable and friendly in manner. He often wore an attractive, rueful but consciously winning smile, like a spoiled boy caught with the jam, but knowing that he is not likely to be punished. He had a pleasantly reminiscent vein of conversation: about the shop at Sandoa; about the Belgians – how they had always hated him, because he, a black, was successful in business – how they had worked against him and caused his three bankruptcies; about his brother who now owned a chain of shops and had nothing to do with politics and how he, Tshombe, envied his brother; about the Leopoldville politicians and what a worthless lot they were, with the exception of Mobutu; about his sufferings and apprehensions in Coquilhatville and Leopoldville – the sufferings seem to have come to not much more than the refusal of writing material, but the apprehensions must have been real enough; above all about his health, which he believed to be very bad. While he was talking, a maidservant would come in carrying on a silver tray glasses of champagne and beer; both of us took beer; I don't know what happened to all the champagne. Tshombe, unlike Munongo, was reasonably abstemious and, like the moderately good Methodist he was, very censorious of the night-club existence of several of the Leopoldville Ministers. Indeed the only political theme which he ever discussed voluntarily was the incompetence and irresponsibility of these ministers. Unlike Munongo, he never showed any outward sign of 'Katangese patriotism' – or indeed of any other political feeling. Politics, he conveyed, was the business he happened to be 'in' at present – unlike his more fortunate brother – and its ups and downs were distinctly trying. He made no pretence of being master of the situation in Elisabethville. 'Munongo is a very loyal man', he said, 'but if I tell him to do something he doesn't like, he simply refuses. He tells me, "You are just a President. You are not Dictator. This is a democracy and as Minister of the Interior I do what I wish".'

It would be wrong, I think, to regard Tshombe either as simply a tool, or as an independent agent. It is certain that he would not have reached the eminence of a 'Head of State' without the support – including at a crucial stage, military support – of local and other Europeans, but it was by no means certain that the same interests which had made him President – in preference to the more eminent and impressive Munongo – now had direct control of him. In a sense it might be said that the more moderate Europeans were prisoners of their own fiction; once it had been proclaimed that there was a Katangese Nation, of which the hero, the symbol and the spokesman was Tshombe, then it became considerably more difficult for local European residents to control Tshombe than it had been when he was a moderately successful grocer. This, in a rather unpredictable way, gave remarkable scope to Munongo and his friends. Tshombe knew he did not have to fear the moderate, or the faint-hearted, Europeans; they could not publicly attack him – or if they did he, and especially Munongo, would have a splendid time defying 'Belgian dictation'. Moderate industrialists could try discreet financial pressure – since the 'State of Katanga' was entirely dependent financially on the great European enterprises – but that too had its risks. One of Munongo's favourite themes, both in public and in private, was the 'scorched earth' policy which Katanga would pursue if it were ever 'betrayed to the Lumumbists'; this programme included blowing up the great hydro-electric station at Le Marinel, and doing such other damage to the highly valuable technological network of the mining area as would take many years to repair. His French friends backed him in this and also dropped hints about what the 'counter-terrorists of the Main Rouge' had done to industrialists of Milan and the Ruhr who had helped the FLN. In the Katanga situation, remarks of this kind had their impact and the 'moderates' – and also, I believe, Tshombe himself – were distinctly impressed. Tshombe had nothing to fear, he believed, from the moderates and little from the UN; he might have much to fear, politically and even physically, from his own right wing (which included, of course, many Belgian civilian advisers as well as Munongo and the French). The more I got to know Tshombe, the more I regarded him as, above all, a sensitive indicator of the actual balance of political forces in Katanga. Personally, he might well have preferred a safe and dignified place, as Provincial President, to the glorious and dangerous hazards of leading a secessionist State; if he made no serious move to end the secession, it may be that he felt the process of ending the secession likely to be even more dangerous than the secession itself. The obscurity of private life often tempted him, as he confessed; his opponents, like his schoolmate Jason Sendwe, believed that he clung to office so tenaciously because he could not make anything like so much money doing anything else. Certainly glory and patriotic emotion – powerful motives with Munongo – seemed to have little sway over his – Tshombe's – astute though limited intelligence. If Munongo resembled a nobleman of the Wars of the Roses, Tshombe brought to mind the more realistic politicians of a somewhat later age. 'Crooked as this man's course was' – wrote Macaulay of the Restoration statesman, Sunderland – 'the law which determined it was simple. His conduct is to be ascribed to the alternate influence of cupidity and fear on a mind highly susceptible of both those passions, and quick-sighted rather than far-sighted.'

The last four words are particularly to the point. All the proposals, suggestions and requests which, as UN representative, I was required to put to Mr Tshombe, would have been taken very seriously by a far-sighted man; to a merely 'quick-sighted' man it seemed possible to evade them, or offer only a token compliance. A characteristic, though minor, example of Mr Tshombe's 'quick-sighted' technique concerned the political prisoners. Not only did the Security Council resolutions – which Mr Tshombe 'accepted' –

demand the liberation of these prisoners, but he himself had just
undertaken, in the Leopoldville agreement, to liberate them. The
following is what took place:

On our first meeting (June 26th) he said there were no political
prisoners; they had all been liberated long before.

Some days later he telephoned me to say that he had just liberated
all the political prisoners. Out of gratitude they had all volunteered
to take part in Katanga Independence Day parade (July 11th). In
fact a group – headed by Ismael Kanza, who later fled to Leopoldville – did march in that parade carrying a banner: '*Vive le Katanga
Indépendant*'. Bystanders observed that several of these men had no
teeth.

On August 30th, more than 400 prisoners broke out of the
Kasapa prison in Elisabethville and took refuge with the United
Nations. Tshombe asked that eighty-two of these should be handed
back as 'common law offenders'. He admitted that all the other
prisoners were political. He now agreed to liberate them, and asked
me to tell them that they had 'his word' that they could return in
safety to their homes. Every one of them chose to remain, in very
uncomfortable conditions, under UN protection.

What Mr Tshombe demonstrated, in this and many similar
contexts, was, according to his European supporters, simply 'the
Bantu mentality'. Tshombe was, relatively, a decent fellow, but he
was, after all, one of 'them'. It did not matter that (for example) the
whole apparatus of law-officers, political police and prison officials
was in the hands of the Belgians; they were never held to have any
responsibility for the excesses and the breaches of faith, all of which
sprang from 'the Bantu mentality'. Whether the mentality was
Bantu or Katabelgian, or a turbid synthesis of the two, it made
'negotiations' in any ordinary sense difficult to conduct. Neither
statements of fact nor written engagements could be relied on; no
contradiction, no detected lie, caused Mr Tshombe the slightest
embarrassment. If caught out in some piece of duplicity – on political
prisoners, refugees, mercenaries or anything else – he would show
absent-mindedness, tinged, I sometimes imagined, with a paternal
compassion for the *naiveté* of anyone who supposed he would tell
the truth, if he could derive the slightest advantage from telling
anything else. In all negotiations there is an element of, at best,
suppressio veri, and the United Nations itself, both in the wording of
the resolutions of the Security Council and General Assembly, and
in the Secretary-General's interpretations of these resolutions,
reconciled contradictions and exploited ambiguities to, at least, the

outer verge of the permissible. When I confronted Mr Tshombe, therefore, I could not feel exactly like the Champion of Truth versus the Champion of Falsehood. Poor Tshombe, mendacious as he was, had something to complain of, too. I never told him a lie, but I had to talk to him in the murky language of the resolutions, which made it very hard to bring the truth home to him. There was only one real issue as we both knew – the secession of Katanga and what, if anything, the United Nations was going to do about it. But, at this stage, we were not able to press this question in the only way which would have carried conviction to Mr Tshombe's force-balancing mind. Francis Nwokedi of Nigeria – sent to Elisabethville specifically for the purpose – with myself, urged Tshombe to take part, under UN safe conduct, in a 'triple summit' with the other Congo leaders, in the capital, Leopoldville, to prepare the way for a parliament in which Leopoldville, Stanleyville and Elisabethville would all be represented. At this point (June 26th) Tshombe had not yet buried the agreement he had signed in Leopoldville, and he did not tell us he was going to do so. Our discussion therefore was based on the assumption that he would respect his signature. He solemnly agreed to participate in a 'summit' but not in Leopoldville – his recollections of that city were too near and too unpleasant. Yes, he agreed that he had had no UN safe conduct when he was arrested before; he agreed that such a safe conduct would ensure his security, but he could not go to Leopoldville: it was something 'psychological'. Why not, he suggested, Brazzaville, or Tananarive? We explained that there was little chance of persuading either the Leopoldville leaders or those in Stanleyville to meet outside the Congo. It was already much that those in Stanleyville had agreed to go to Leopoldville. We expatiated on the inestimable advantages for all concerned – including Katanga – which an agreed solution would bring. We hinted at the dangers, from his point of view, of allowing a recognized legal Government, based *only* on Leopoldville and Stanleyville, to come into existence. He agreed with all this, but not Leopoldville. Perhaps Kamina? Kamina had some advantages: it was a 'neutral' site under complete UN control. It had the obvious disadvantage that, Leopoldville having been already agreed on by the other two parties, it would be difficult to persuade them to make the concession to Tshombe which would be implied by meeting even in a neutral zone within the borders of 'the Independent State of Katanga'. In view of the Leopoldville agreement, however, which seemed to have virtually signed away that independent State, it might just be possible to bring about the meeting at Kamina. The attempt seemed worth making, in view of the supreme desirability of holding the tripartite meeting anywhere at all in the Congo where the rival blocs would agree to meet. We agreed to recommend consideration of Kamina.

Two days later, in the 'National Assembly', Tshombe, without waiting for any reply on his Kamina 'proposal', ignored what he had signed in Leopoldville, and unfurled, with fanfare from Mr Samalenghe, the flag of the 'Katangese Nation'. The Leopoldville agreement was formally and unanimously repudiated, in all its articles by the National Assembly (with twenty-two out of the seventy-two deputies sitting) on July 4th. The Assembly also decided not to send Katanga's elected representatives in the Central Parliament to the coming meeting of that Parliament.

Tshombe's refusal – for such it now effectively was – to participate in a summit gave more urgency, for various reasons, to the two questions on which the UN mandate in Katanga was clearest: those of the foreign officers and mercenaries and of the political advisers.

The more important of the two questions, both in numbers and in nature, was the military one. If Tshombe and Munongo were singularly unimpressed – as they were – by the thought of a 'Leopoldville-Stanleyville' legal government in Leopoldville, which would have the unquestioned right to take military action against secession, the reason for their confidence was that they knew their large and well-armed force, trained and led by its 500 foreign officers, would be likely to be more than a match for anything the Central Government, at the end of a year of turbulence and indiscipline, could send across tremendous distances against it. But the Central Government, if faced by such a foreign-led force, could justly reproach the UN with culpable failure to apply its own resolution of February. More than that, the original reason why the Government of the Congo had invited in the United Nations was to give 'military assistance' in getting rid of foreign soldiers. Clearly the United Nations could not indifferently look on while foreign soldiers – whose illegal presence in the Congo it was required by the Security Council to bring to an end – prepared to resist by force an undisputed legal Government of the Congo, now about to come into being.

Under United Nations pressure – and with the aid of some luck – some of the mercenaries, about forty, had already gone, and the Katanga authorities had dropped, for the time, the idea of 'White Companies'. But the core of the problem, 500 foreign officers, remained. This was the problem Colonel Egge had been studying with Colonel Crèvecoeur. Colonel Crèvecoeur and his staff were quite willing to go – as soon as the United Nations could supply replacements for them. It seemed unlikely, they mildly pointed out, that the UN could find, immediately, sufficient officers, speaking both French and Swahili, to fill all the posts that would be vacated by a departure of all the foreign officers, and some of these would clearly have to stay. But there would be no objection to filling, eventually, some of the higher command posts, at least, with UN sponsored officers.

Colonel Egge thought that a reorganization along these lines would be worth studying, and he was at this moment working out, on the basis of information furnished by Colonel Crèvecoeur, how something of the kind could be put into practice, if it were approved in principle by the UN. His report was later sent to the Belgian Government, which, however, made no comment on it until the more vigorous methods of 'reorganization' subsequently applied had given the so-called 'Egge plan' a retrospective attraction.

The fundamental reason why a reorganization on these lines was not feasible was inadvertently made clear to me, some weeks later, by Tshombe himself. I was pressing him to remove the French-Algerian officers and in fact he did remove some of them, although they may well have come back later under other names. ('We have no intelligence'.) The most fanatical officer of all, however – Commandant Faulques – Tshombe could not part with immediately:

Tshombe: He does essential work. We cannot part with him.

Self:　　We have been studying together the possibilities of the UN supplying replacements. Perhaps we could help you here?

Tshombe: That's a very good idea. He is in charge of the School for Paracommandos. If you can let us have a competent officer to take over from him there, we shall get rid of him.

The idea of the UN training Katangan Paracommandos likely to be used to fight against the Central Government was only an extreme example of the difficulties inherent in the whole scheme. The Gendarmerie was not a police force – Katanga also had an armed police, also with European officers – it was an army. It had three objectives. The first and most important was to defend Katanga's borders. The second was to hold down by force the vast Baluba territory in North and Central Katanga, which was hostile to Tshombe and loyal to the Central Government.[1] The third was to

---

[1] See Chapters VIII and IX.

guard against a possible pro-Central-Government rising in South
Katanga. All these ends would be condemned by the Central
Government. Unless the Katangese Government solved its differences with the Central Government by dropping its claim to secede,
it was apparent that the United Nations could not possibly 're-
organize' the Gendarmerie in this way. In short, this 'reorganization'
only made sense in a political context which had not yet come into
being and which Tshombe's volte-face had made more remote than
ever.

Yet, for the moment, the military field was covered by the Egge
Study – and by the briefly feigned 'integration' of the Gendarmerie
into the Congolese Army – and it was not yet generally accepted
that no *technical* study, however competent, could produce a scheme
which – in the absence of a *political* agreement – could be both
accepted by the Katanga authorities and approved by the Central
Government.

The only area in which the UN could make any significant advance at this critical point was that of foreign political advisers,
whose 'immediate withdrawal' was also demanded by the February
resolution. The next phase, therefore, once the 'turn for the better'
had led into a blind alley, was an effort to trace and remove some
at least of the foreign advisers: those who were known to be committed to the independence of Katanga and who, it was believed,
had helped, at the crucial moment of Tshombe's return, to dash
what then seemed the bright hope of reconciliation.[1]

---

[1] On the repudiation of the Leopoldville agreement a passage in *Congo, 1961*
(p. 284), which came to my attention after this chapter went to press tends to
confirm the hypothesis suggested above (p. 117): 'At a Press conference on June
29th, Mr Tshombe declared: "These agreements were *not signed under duress* and I
am not the kind of man who signs agreements lightly" (Belga dispatch, *La Libre
Belgique*, 30.6.61). On the same day, in an interview with *La Libre Belgique's*
special correspondent, Messrs Tshombe *and Munongo* [my italics] stated: 'The
agreements signed *under duress* at Leopoldville will not be honoured" (*L.B.*
30.6.61).

7

MR SPAAK
AND THE OCCULT COUNSELLORS

'In the multitude of counsellors there is safety.'
Proverbs, XI, 14

'The Colonel (Weber) left at 13.20 today[1] – the first of the two who must leave immediately. The second – the Professor (Clémens) – will not leave voluntarily and we shall be obliged to arrest him tomorrow and put him on the plane on Monday – if the Swedes can catch him. There will be a great outcry (I think); the Rector of the University was prepared to tell him to leave if we would agree to allow him back for a few days next month to finish his students' examinations. That was reasonable enough and we recommended it to New York, but we have no answer – they probably think it preferable to expel him unconditionally. Perhaps they are right – glad to hear an outcry from this place – and for other people to hear it too. In world politics that is sensible enough, but here, where we are trying to get the confidence of the people in authority – and succeeding – it would be better not to break any windows. That's my opinion on the politics; personally, I should have no objection to expelling him, and a couple of hundred more like him. The Colonel went quietly and decently and no one on the Government side gave any sign that the UN had anything to do with the matter. That's a big change here. Three hundred people at the airport – not a large crowd, considering the Colonel was a great hero and, in the opinion of all the Belgians, saved "Elisabethville" (that is, the whites) last

---

[1] Letter of mine, to Máire MacEntee dated June 17th (translation).

126

July. When you think of that, you say to yourself that perhaps there will be no stir about the Professor either. But there is a difference – the Professor will be the first Belgian to be forcibly expelled. Every Belgian will think that the same thing may happen to him. Therefore, they will make a great stir, if they think the UN can be frightened into drawing back. But if they think the UN is going to win, they will be quiet enough. We shall see.'

Up to that date, three political advisers had left Katanga under the authority of the February resolution; one of these, a White Russian named Belina, had been forcibly expelled. The authority for these removals was double: the resolution itself and the agreement of April 17th between the United Nations and the President of the Congo, under which President Kasavubu agreed to apply the resolution. Almost all national Governments have the power to deport undesirable aliens, at short notice or none, and without judicial proceedings. Essentially, under the April agreement Kasavubu classified all persons in the categories named in the resolution as being undesirable aliens; in the removal of such aliens the United Nations Force acted in a dual role: from a Security Council point of view it was applying the resolution, while, from the point of view of Congolese sovereignty, it was acting at the request of the Republic of the Congo. And virtually everyone – including Britain, France and Belgium – agreed that, in theory at least, Katanga was part of the Congo. By the April agreement, therefore, Kasavubu agreed, *inter alia*, to give the UN his blessing in removing foreign military personnel and political advisers from Katanga. Tshombe regarded this agreement as such a betrayal that he broke off the Coquilhatville Conference and consequently became a prisoner. From his point of view, he was undoubtedly right in resenting the April agreement which inserted a legal wedge into 'independent Katanga'. The deportations of certain political advisers were the first taps on that wedge; the August action against the foreign officers was to be the first real blow.

In itself, the removal of a handful of political advisers had little significance. To begin with, the United Nations – having 'no intelligence' – could not know with certainty who all the advisers were or what advice they were giving. Second, almost all the Europeans in Elisabethville were capable of giving 'political advice' to anyone who would listen to them, including Ministers, and anyone who was removed was, therefore, easily replaced. Third, the classes whose political advice carried most weight were the most difficult

to touch. The French and British Consuls and – to a lesser extent
now – the Belgian Consul certainly gave political advice to the
Government; their right to give such advice was doubtful; the
nature of the advice, as far as the UN was apprised of it, had been
usually unexceptionable: whether the UN was apprised of everything may be doubted. But the expulsion of the Consuls was not
within the bounds of possibility. The underground opposition – the
Balubakat – sent us, shortly after this, *their* list of political advisers;
they included the heads of all the major industrial concerns in
Katanga – including the Union Minière – and also the Catholic
Archbishop of Elisabethville. Such a list might well have been more
realistic than the UN list, but the UN, without clear and damning
evidence – which, for the usual reason, it was unlikely to get – could
hardly remove such pillars of the region's economic and spiritual
life.

In any case, Tshombe, Munongo and Kibwe were not fools and
they had had more than a year's political experience in an exceptionally hard school. 'Political advice' had made them, and guided
their early steps, but by now, after all, the basic advice had been
taken. They could get along without political advice about the
Congo situation, which they knew well; the field in which
they did need political advice was that of general international
politics – whether, in the present international conjuncture they
could securely maintain their 'independent State'. There was hardly
anyone in Elisabethville, outside the Consular Corps, who was
capable of advising them on that. The UN representatives and the
American Consul gave them some good advice on it, which they
did not take. Their advice from other sources was, it appeared, that
the State of Katanga was safe: the UN had not the authority to use
force against it itself; the Central Government was too weak, and
the Western Powers, through the UN or – if necessary – otherwise,
would see to it that the Central Government did not bring in external aid for the purpose. In its plainest and most extreme forms, this
advice came from people like the French officers and some Belgian
civilians. I believe, from my own conversations with Mr Dunnett,
that he is not likely, in his conversations with Mr Tshombe, to have
done very much to remove the impression created by such advice.
I am quite certain that he conscientiously advised Mr Tshombe to
reach a reasonable agreement with Leopoldville. What Mr Tshombe
wanted to know, however, was whether, if he did not reach such an
agreement, anything would happen to him. The impression he
derived was that nothing would; the UN was either bluffing or

overreaching itself; the State of Katanga could be maintained.

In this general situation, the expulsion of a few political advisers of an obvious kind – and therefore of usually secondary importance – would normally have no more than a marginal significance. Yet at this particular stage it had the value of serving notice, both to Tshombe's Government and to the Europeans of Elisabethville, that the United Nations was in earnest about applying the February resolution and that – in the interests of the form of order which Tshombe and his friends supported – it would be wise not to obstruct the restoration of the unity of the Congo. It was, I think, mainly for this reason that the Secretary-General now cabled in respect of political advisers: 'breakthrough must be made by our representative in Elisabethville'.

The scruples I had myself in the first days – and which the letter quoted shows – about removing political advisers were founded on optimistic illusions about the 'turn for the better'; they and the illusions were dissipated together when the 'National Assembly' swept aside the Leopoldville agreement. Many people, including some Onusians, were touched by the passionate and pathetic arguments of the 'Katabelges' to the effect that it was immoral to evict people who had lived most of their lives in Katanga. The local Press, run by these same Katabelges, had much to say, on this score, about Human Rights, a subject in which it had previously shown no interest, although this was a city in which hundreds of political prisoners were confined in unknown conditions, a city in which the Minister of the Interior had met a charge of murdering prisoners – the murder of Lumumba and his companions – with a simple and laconic 'Prove it'. The political advisers – whether *ex officio* advisers like Tignée or the so-called *conseillers occultes*, secret advisers or private individuals active in secessionist politics – had their share in the responsibility for these things; they were playing revolutionary politics, and many who have played that game have suffered a worse fate than being handed a ticket to Brussels.

I experienced no moral difficulties about expelling these politicians; I soon found, however, that I was going to experience technical difficulties. The retired Greek policeman who incarnated our intelligence reported to me that Professor Clémens and his wife had taken the plane to Brussels. Professor Clémens, however, is not married and the people who had left turned out to be a M and Mme Clément. The author of the Katangese Constitution had 'disappeared into the geography' and was perhaps in Rhodesia – no one had a photograph of him. A young Swedish officer who spoke

Swahili thought the Professor might (but perhaps might not) be
staying with a certain Belgian family; Baluba houseboys reported
his presence simultaneously in eleven different places; Greek
intelligence found the reports hard to reconcile. Finally, the problem
was solved; New York agreed the Professor might conduct his
examinations: the Rector of the University, M Frenkiel – a highly
intelligent and courteous man who is himself a political adviser
of the more discreet and less deportable kind – agreed to send
Clémens away after the examinations, and actually gave a dinner
for Clémens and myself. Clémens then left, and sent me a polite
farewell letter. Like so many things in the Congo, the removal of
political advisers was having an unexpectedly propitious first
phase, soon to be followed by storms.

'The temperature', reported the Agence France Presse very truly,
'began to rise in the Katangese capital with the arrival, at the
beginning of July, of M Charles Muller, one of the principal private
secretaries of M Henri Fayat, Under-secretary of State for Foreign
Affairs of Belgium. According to members of the Consulate,
M Muller's mission consisted essentially in making known to his
compatriots M Spaak's aims: unification of the Congo, end of the
secession of Katanga, which, if it continued, would tend to bring
about the secession of Orientale Province, and the installation of
the Soviet bloc in that part of the country. M Muller was also to
facilitate the task of the representatives of the UN in the application
of the resolutions of February 21st.'[1]

I do not know whether M Muller ever addressed his compatriots
along these lines, or whether M Spaak imagined that arguments
about the hypothetical fate of Stanleyville, 800 miles away, were
likely to make much impression in Elisabethville. Almost all the
Belgians ('not Belgians–Katangese!') of Elisabethville denounced
M Spaak, and the odd variety of 'socialism' which he represents,
more loudly and more often than they did Gizenga and his not less
odd variety of 'communism'. M Muller's mission to his compatriots, or ex-compatriots, was therefore an ungrateful one. His
mission, in so far as it concerned the application of the resolution
of February 21st, was, however, of a more practical character. He
was the bearer of M Spaak's list of Belgian political advisers, suitable
to be expelled by the United Nations from Katanga.

M Muller was a large, phlegmatic, Belgian Socialist, with chestnut
hair and moustache and prominent, pale eyes. He clearly did not
much like his mission; he had not been very cordially received at

---

[1] *La Libre Belgique*, July 10th, 1961.

his own Consulate, he knew that he was being watched and that his comings and goings over the few hundred yards between the Consulate building and the UN offices in the Avenue Fulbert Youlou were noted with suspicion. He was not at ease and he had little small talk; we 'talked list' and that was all. The 'Spaak list' was a short one; it contained eleven names of which I remember four: Thyssens, Onckelinckx, de Vos, Michel. It soon became clear that not all the people on the list were political advisers in any real sense. De Vos and Michel, for example, were assistants of Clémens at the University and were quite obscure figures. I asked M Muller why they were there and he said they were 'ultras'. On inquiry I found that this term had here a special significance. The University of Elisabethville was a 'lay foundation', intended to balance the 'clerical' Lovanium at Leopoldville, according to that apparently schizoid official Belgian system whereby everything comes in opposing pairs; every Fleming must be paired with a Walloon, every Christian with an atheist. 'Socialism' did not thrive among the Katanga Europeans, however, and after 'independence' the anti-clericals were removed from the University and replaced by Catholics like de Vos and Michel, regarded as more reliable. M Spaak, in naming these men, was inviting the United Nations to purge the 'lay' University of its Catholics by classifying them as political advisers. I asked a colleague what he thought. I knew that this colleague had been brought up in much the same *laïque* tradition as M Spaak and that his advice would not be biased in favour of the people on M Spaak's list. My colleague indicated that he yielded to no one in his enthusiasm for forcibly removing Catholics from Universities, but that the resolution had said 'political advisers' not 'Catholics'. People like M de Vos and M Michel would undoubtedly give bad political advice if they were asked, but no one would dream of asking them; they were, therefore, not political advisers. If M Spaak wished to remove them, he could perhaps do so by using the Belgian soldiers whom – in defiance of the very resolutions he was asking us to apply to these superstitious but harmless pedagogues – his Government still maintained on the soil of the independent Republic of the Congo, province of Katanga.

I reported to New York that some of the names on M Spaak's list quite clearly did not fall under the resolution at all; some probably did, but were marginal cases which could await further study. There was, however, one name on the list which was unquestionably that of an important political adviser, close to Tshombe, and a fanatical adherent, almost the inventor indeed, of the Independent State of

Katanga. This man, a *conseiller occulte* if ever there was one, was Georges Thyssens. He ought, under the resolution, to have left long ago. Spaak's request was timely. Thyssens should go now.

'Thyssens' – I wrote in a letter shortly after this – 'is the man who founded Conakat and thought up independent Katanga – *Pater Patriae*, you might say. A great enemy of Spaak and also of the United Nations. He was working with the French officers and with Kibwe to prevent any *rapprochement* with Leopoldville. In order to try to check these activities and discourage Belgians of his type, we asked New York for authority to expel him. We got this authority.'[1]

On July 4th, the 'National Assembly' proclaimed the Leopoldville agreement invalid and declared that the Katanga deputies should not go to Leopoldville for the meeting of the Central Parliament. On the same evening we sent Major Rosen with two military police to invite M Thyssens to depart. This created some preliminary stir. The Katanga Ministers and myself were at the Independence Day party in the grounds of the American Consulate. M Kimba, the Katanga 'Foreign Minister', spoke to me very earnestly, but unfortunately I could not hear a word he said, because the Irish pipe-band was in full eruption at our elbow. Fortunately, he could not hear my reply either. Whether as a result of this well-orchestrated diplomacy or not, things passed off without immediate incident – except that Colonel Egge, as he was only too apt to do in moments of excitement, reminded Major Rosen that Sweden had not been at war for 150 years. Major Rosen, a stout and kindly, but perhaps rather pedantic officer, seemed inclined to brood over this.

In order to avoid a clash with the Katangese police – an armed contingent of which went on Munongo's orders to M Thyssens's apartment – we had agreed to accord M Thyssens some days' grace.

'He used this delay' – my letter continues – 'to incite Munongo against the new Belgian Consul [*sic*], Muller, who is here, on Spaak's orders, to co-operate with the United Nations in applying the resolutions. He (Thyssens) succeeded so well that Munongo arrested and imprisoned Muller yesterday. He did not allow the Consul-General or anyone else to see him. When the Consul-General told me of this I decided to have Thyssens expelled immediately, to make it clear to everyone and the local ultras in particular that they could not go on defying the UN and resolutions of the Security Council. The Swedes went off, three of them, and then – Donnybrook! The two

---

[1] Letter of July 8th to Máire MacEntee (translation).

Thyssens sons (22 and 25, one of them in the gendarmerie) started hitting the Swedes; the two Thyssens Alsatians attacked the Swedes too; the Swedes hit the two young men on the head; they shot a dog and killed it (it seems: the story is not quite clear[1]) and off with poor Thyssens to the plane. Then I went off to see the Speaker and the President to try to get Muller released.'

The Speaker of the 'Katanga National Assembly', M Charles Mutaka-wa-Dilomba, was a cousin of Godefroid Munongo's, but normally an amiable young man, though rather hare-brained. He had presided over the deliberations of the Provincial Assembly during the historic days when it was ratifying the secession of Katanga and transforming itself into a 'National Assembly'. He had been in touch with me earlier that afternoon to announce that if M Thyssens were not immediately set free, the Government of Katanga would 'send the Fougas'. These were the little jet aircraft of which Katanga possessed, at this time, three; the Katangese overestimated their military importance and the UN Command was perhaps rather inclined to underestimate it. I told M Mutaka that the Secretary-General had ruled, and President Kasavubu had agreed, that M Thyssens fell under paragraph A.2 of the Security Council Resolution of February 21st and must leave Katanga. I had no power to release him, even if I wished to do so. I on my side wanted to see M Muller and make sure he was safe. If the Provincial Government wished to make war on the United Nations, that was its affair, but I suggested it would be a mistaken policy. It was obvious that, in the long run, 'Katanga' could not win, but, even in the short run, the consequences of such action would be disastrous for Katanga. M Mutaka said that the UN forces in Katanga consisted only of a 'few hundred Swedish and Irish tourists'; the Fougas. . . . I mentioned that larger United Nations forces were within reach in Northern Katanga, the Gurkhas. . . . The two words *Fouga* and *Gurkha* – both of which were to grow more familiar in the months to come – occurred rather often in the subsequent exchange. M Mutaka, indicating that he could no longer prevent the take-off of the Fougas on their bombing mission against the Avenue Fulbert Youlou, hung up.

There was a visitor from Leopoldville in my office at that time, who listened to this conversation with interest.

---

[1] No dog was in fact killed. A Swedish M.P. fired a shot on being attacked by the dogs, at which the dogs seem to have taken fright. Apparently the bullet hit a telephone directory.

'Is that', asked Mahmoud Khiary, 'the way you talk to the Speaker of the Assembly? "You send me the Fougas, I send you the Gurkhas!" Is that the language you usually employ around here? In Leopoldville we are used to a quieter kind of diplomacy.'

His face is not exactly expressionless, but its expression is not easy to read. His brown eyes, more opaque than most people's, were turned inquiringly in my direction. This was something, as I was to find, unusual with him; he is more apt to look into space, or at the ground, and his method of obtaining information is seldom the straight question. He had then only just arrived in Elisabethville; I had already had time to note that he was not at all the gas-meter-mender of my Leopoldville imaginings, but a formidable personality. What his political outlook was, I had no idea and his Tunisian nationality gave no clear clue. Some Tunisians were, in their own peculiar way, very 'moderate'. I remembered one prominent Tunisian diplomat whom I met in New York the previous autumn at the time of Lumumba's arrest. 'Why wasn't he "killed trying to escape"?', asked the Tunisian. 'After all, chaos has its own logic. . . .' In what direction logic might be taking Mr Khiary I could not know, but his question annoyed me.

It was necessary, I explained stiffly, to react with great firmness. The people who ran Katanga had got the idea that the UN would do no more than make a pretence of applying the resolutions: it was time to convince them that things had changed and that the UN could neither be intimidated nor cajoled into leaving the Katangan *status quo* intact.

Mr Khiary smiled. 'Don't let me get in your way,' he said, 'you have work to do.'

M Mutaka rang again. War might be averted, he thought, if I would come and see him immediately.

M Mutaka's drawing-room was festooned with rifles and sten-guns. M Mutaka's servants, who were also, it seemed, his tribal henchmen, kept going and coming in groups, into and out of the drawing-room, like a *corps de ballet*, portraying fear and resentment. M Mutaka himself was fairly drunk and a little tearful. He had, he explained, got 89 per cent in his law exams. He removed some lethal weapons from a chair and offered me a glass of beer. I could, he said, trample him to death if I wished. I declined the offer and said that I wanted to see M Muller. M Mutaka said he would not be treated like a child. I was, in his opinion, just like a Belgian. This went home; I winced. M Mutaka picked up a rifle, not with war-like mien, but simply to emphasize his point, which was that people who got 89 per cent in their law exams should not be treated like children. The reason he was talking to me at all was that I, too, was a cultivated man, a Doctor of Philosophy. Philosophy was a beautiful subject. His cousin Godefroid did not understand philosophy and had just seized the Belgian Consulate. The soldiers had burned all the papers and had pushed M Créner and M Herckens down the Consulate steps, prodding them with their bayonets. M Mutaka made the gesture, with his rifle, of one who prods a Consul-General down a flight of steps; it brought the scene to life wonderfully. 'If they hesitate' – Godefroid had said – 'if they hesitate, shoot!' That was just like Godefroid – a heart of gold but impulsive. Fortunately M Créner and M Herckens had not hesitated otherwise they would be quite, quite dead. Did I know whether they were Catholics? Well, that was all right. A lot of people were afraid of Godefroid, but that was because they did not know him. He was the soul of kindness but not – M Mutaka's voice sank confidentially – not really a cultivated man. He – Mutaka-wa-Dilomba – had always got better marks than Godefroid. This was not generally known outside Katanga. As for me and my Gurkhas, we could tear out his heart and eat it. It was all, he concluded, the fault of the Socialists.

The part about the Consulate rang true, and was. I thanked M Mutaka for his valuable mediation and suggested that we should go together and see M Munongo and President Tshombe. I was, by now, beginning to be seriously worried for M Muller's life.

M Mutaka did not know whether Godefroid would see me. Godefroid had said I was a lackey of Spaak. He, Mutaka-wa-Dilomba, had pointed out that I was not a lackey of Spaak but a Doctor of Philosophy.

M Munongo's large and beautiful villa was only a few doors away. M Mutaka stopped his car outside the gate and shouted: 'Godefroid! It's Charles!' A tall figure came swaying down the dark path. Munongo greeted Charles with a grunt. Then he saw me, spoke a few words in Swahili to me, in a low, guttural voice, turned and walked unsteadily back to his house, ignoring a plaintive call from M Mutaka.

'He doesn't want to see you,' explained M Mutaka, 'he is not in a good humour. We had better see the President.'

The President was sober, and harassed; even frightened. It was not, I thought, entirely of the UN that he was frightened. He told me immediately that I could not see M Muller unless I could get permission from Munongo himself. Munongo regarded the whole matter as one within the competence of his own department. But M Muller was all right; he could guarantee me that. The President did not say in so many words, but he managed to convey that it was useless for him to talk to Munongo in the evening. As far as M Muller was concerned, I had to content myself with the President's promise that I could see him in the morning at 9 o'clock in the Palace.

Tshombe and I agreed that it had been a trying day with 'too many emotions'. He said we should not remove political advisers without the agreement of the Katanga Government. I indicated that, having the agreement of the Central Government, we did not absolutely require the agreement of the provincial authorities, but we should be very glad to work with them if they were really prepared to get rid of the advisers. So far, we had had nothing but months of procrastination and we should have to go ahead on our own if they continued to protect political advisers while paying lip-service to the resolutions. Mr Tshombe said that, rather than go through another such day, he would get rid of any political advisers we wished. He agreed to set up a joint UN-Katangese committee on political advisers; he promised that it would give quick results. It was in Katanga's own interests that it should. He could not see why we attached so much importance to political advisers, but if we felt so strongly about it we could have them. They were Belgians anyway. He became more cheerful as he launched on his favourite 'anti-Belgian' anecdotes. As for M Muller – at the Palace, 9 a.m. tomorrow. We shook hands and woke up M Mutaka. The Speaker and I left.

In the car, M Mutaka said that I took him for a child but he was going to surprise me: he had taken a tape-recording of our conversation at his house and was going to play it for the Consular Corps. I advised him to play it on Radio Katanga also.

At 8.30 the following morning, July 8th, Tshombe's secretary, a rather leonine Belgian lady, rang up to say the appointment with the President was cancelled: he had forgotten he had to go to the Elisabethville International Fair, which opened its doors that morning. As for M Muller, I had better contact Mr Munongo.

A few minutes later visitors were announced. Two Belgians, of more imposing appearance and agreeable manners than the local variety, came into the room. They were the Prince Albert-Edouard de Ligne, and M Georges Velter. The Prince de Ligne was carrying *L'Essor du Katanga* and M Velter *L'Echo du Katanga*. Both of these local sheets are firmly under the control of the Ministry of

Information and this morning's issues were certainly a credit to M Samalenghe. The front pages were devoted to the Thyssens case, with pictures of the Thyssens youths, looking as people are liable to look after they have assaulted military policemen, and of the Thyssens telephone directory pierced by a bullet which, according to the caption, had been aimed by a Swede at Madame Thyssens, and similar exhibits. The Muller side of the story was played down to half a column on a back page, headed *Expulsion d'un Valet de Spaak*.

The Prince de Ligne has a handsome, aristocratic face, with the watchful eyes and tight lips of a nobleman who has no archaic prejudices against engaging in business. M Velter is small, dark and spectacled with a clever, humorous face. Both he and the Prince, however, wore this morning politely anxious expressions. The Prince explained, in the English of upper-class England, that he and his friend had just arrived from Brussels to open one of the metallurgical stands at the International Fair. They were both, he indicated, not without importance in the economic and financial life of Belgium. M Velter's position could hardly be explained in English terms – I gathered that it was partly governmental and partly business, as if in British terms he was an important functionary of the Board of Trade and also an executive of the Federation of British Industries. M Velter chuckled modestly. 'I 'ave two 'ats', he said. Both gentlemen were anxious for the success of the Fair. The morning's news worried them. They had no intention at all of criticizing my action; they knew I was only doing my duty and in any case they were not concerned with politics. 'It is too 'ard for us', said M Velter, looking remarkably non-retarded. The trouble was, said the Prince de Ligne, that they simply did not know what would become of the Fair if there were any more arrests.

I told them there should be no need of further such arrests, as Mr Tshombe had now agreed – I thought this time sincerely – to work with us on the political advisers question. But what concerned us at the moment was the safety of their compatriot, M Muller. I was going to the Fair to try to get hold of either Tshombe or Munongo. I should be grateful if they would help me on this. I appealed to them also to use their influence with their friends in control of local business to start working for a political settlement, dropping the secession claim. Otherwise, things were moving towards clashes and disorders of which the Thyssens/Muller affair was but a first faint foretaste.

The Prince de Ligne and M Velter listened to this attentively and

the Prince replied in his business-like way. They would see Munongo
and try to ensure Muller's safe departure. They would see Tshombe
and try to get an apology for the invasion of the Consulate-General.
As for the larger question – which, he agreed, was of fundamental
importance – they thought there was little they could do themselves
– knowing little of the political background – but they could see that
I met all the people concerned, under the best possible conditions,
and they would support my efforts of persuasion.

On all points, they were as good as their word. M Muller, who had
passed the night on a bare, stone floor, but had not been otherwise
maltreated, was put on the Boeing that morning, Tshombe apologized to M Créner, and M Créner consented – also at the Prince
de Ligne's earnest request – to open the Belgian stand at the
Fair. As for the 'people concerned', the Prince and M Velter did
– as will be seen in a later chapter – all that could be reasonably
expected of them.

All in all, the issue of these two days seemed favourable from a
United Nations point of view.

The fracas in the Thyssens's apartment was regrettable in itself,
but not all the effects were regrettable. It ended the rather unhealthy
phase of fraternization between UN officers and the foreign officers
they were supposed to be getting rid of. Major Rosen who, on his
first visit to the Thyssens's apartment, had almost broken down and
had kissed Madame Thyssens's hand repeatedly, wore, after his
second visit, the sterner and more martial air of a man whom people
were calling names like 'Goering' and 'the Butcher of Elisabethville'.
He looked as if he were defying Colonel Egge, *now*, to introduce the
subject of Swedish military history since the death of Charles XII.
As for Colonel Waern, he sent me a memorandum:

Subject: Dog-ghost-haunted men.

The main point achieved was that the required 'break-through'
on political advisers had been made – for Tshombe did now get rid
of a number of these people from the administration. Of greater
importance, we felt, was what was implied by our two latest visitors:
the recognition by some business circles at least that the UN
presence in Katanga was a factor to be taken into account, and that
the political position was ripe for review.

M Spaak's list of 'occult counsellors' had its defects, and its
unforeseen consequences, but on the whole it seemed to have helped.

That certainly seems to have been the view in New York. 'As
Charpentier (French Ambassador in Leopoldville) said of another

Onusian', Hammarskjold cabled, '*il a du cran*'. (He has pluck).[1]

My pleasure at this compliment would not have been greatly diminished but might have been tinged by a sense of historic irony, if I had realized then, as I do now, that the 'other Onusian' whose nerve M Charpentier had applauded must surely have been Andrew Cordier, and the occasion almost certainly the fateful act of closing Leopoldville radio and the airports.

---

[1] In my *Observer* article (December 17th) I quoted this in connection with *Rumpunch* (August 28th). I did not then have copies of telegrams, and my memory misled me. The point is of no material importance as the Rumpunch message was similar in tenor (Ch. XIII).

8

THE PROVINCE OF LUALABA

'This is a hell of a way to run a railroad!'
Anon.

The Elisabethville International Fair, for which my visitors from Brussels had come, was designed to coincide with the celebration of Katangan Independence Day, on July 11th. It was hoped, apparently, to draw foreign exhibitors into some sort of implicit recognition of the State of Katanga; perhaps for this reason, the only official foreign exhibitors were Portugal, Angola and the Rhodesian Federation.

A solemn *Te Deum* was scheduled for July 11th; another *Te Deum*, oddly enough, had been sung in Elisabethville Cathedral less than a fortnight before, on June 30th, in honour of the Independence of the Congo. The two *Te Deums* were planned, I suppose, on the principle: 'The Lord hath given and the Lord hath taken away'. I had attended the first *Te Deum* and did not propose to attend the second; on my instigation, the Consular Corps was dissuaded, not without difficulty, from celebrating Katangan Independence, and most of them were leaving town for the day. I decided to follow their example, and take advantage of the occasion to visit the United Nations garrisons in North Katanga. I planned to leave on Monday, July 10th.

On the morning before, I got word that the President wanted to see me urgently. As it was Sunday, as I had an appointment to go rowing on a nearby lake with Mr Ray Maloney, the distinguished and far-sighted correspondent of United Press International, and as I knew what the President wanted to talk to me about, I left word

that I would not be available until early the following morning.
An appointment was made, accordingly, for 6 a.m.

Mr Tshombe's features, as I remember them in the light of that
short dawn, were tinged with violet; the two creases between his
batrachian eyes were deep sunken; his voice was husky and low-
pitched. Why, he wanted to know, was I going to see Sendwe? And
why had Sendwe been flown into Katanga in a United Nations
aircraft?

I told him, correctly, that my visit to North Katanga had been
planned before I had heard the news of Mr Jason Sendwe's arrival
at Kabalo, in north-west Katanga. I was not going there in order to
see him. Kabalo was part of my itinerary and when I was there, if
Sendwe wanted to see me, I should certainly not refuse. As regards
Mr Sendwe's mission, I was not fully informed but my understanding
was that he was coming to explain to his supporters why the
Balubakat party, of which he was leader, had agreed to participate
in the coming meeting of the Parliament at Leopoldville, and had
agreed to uphold any Government which would issue from that
Parliament as the legal Government of the Congo, including
Katanga. He would also, I understood, advise his supporters to
await the outcome of that Parliament and to refrain from violence.
As all this was in accordance with the principles and purposes of the
United Nations, it was natural that an aircraft should have been put
at Mr Sendwe's disposal – just as such an aircraft would be supplied
for him, Mr Tshombe, if he agreed to travel to Leopoldville for a
'Congolese summit', or for the Conakat parliamentarians if they
should decide to disregard the recent unfortunate decision made for
them by the provincial Assembly and agree to attend the Central
Parliament. I took the occasion to urge on Mr Tshombe once more
the importance of attending the Parliament and of accepting – even
with temporary reservations as regards army and police – the
authority of the Government which would issue from it.

Mr Tshombe said he was still willing to attend a summit, but he
had had no reply to his proposal of a meeting at Kamina or outside
the Congo. I regretted that, but said it was clear that the Leopoldville leaders considered the capital to be the most suitable place for
such a meeting; I knew that they considered that a meeting outside
the Congo – in Brazzaville or Tananarive or any of the other French
African centres which Mr Tshombe had suggested, or even elsewhere – would be tantamount to accepting outside arbitration in
Congolese affairs. As regards Kamina, no doubt they considered
that, while Katanga maintained its claim to independent statehood,

they could not meet Mr Tshombe on Katangese soil without implicitly accepting that claim. I reminded Mr Tshombe that by laying down conditions as to where he would meet the other leaders, he was simply making things easier for those who – like the Stanleyville leaders – did not want him to be able to exert any influence at all on the proceedings of the coming Parliament or on the choice of a Government. They would, therefore, urge the rejection of any precondition he would try to lay down and – as they had put themselves in a strong position by dropping the claim that Stanleyville was the seat of Government, and the Western powers were very anxious that that claim should not be revived – they were likely to get their way. I pressed Mr Tshombe strongly, not for the first or the last time, to go to Leopoldville, and to defend the interests he represented – as the Stanleyville people were defending theirs – by means appropriate to the changed conditions. Both Gizenga and his friends, and Ileo and *his* friends had wisely, though tacitly, dropped their untenable and conflicting claims to be the 'Government of the Congo'. Mr Tshombe and his friends would be equally wise to drop *their* claim to statehood. At this conjuncture, when all the others concerned were revising positions to which they had adhered with such vehemence, Katanga could radically modify its own stand without loss of dignity. Their watchword now, if they were wise, would be, not 'independence of Katanga', but 'preservation of order in the province'. They did not need to apologize for having seceded: they could claim that their secession, in its time, had served the purpose of sparing Katanga the torments which had afflicted other parts of the Congo; but, to serve the same purpose now, they should accept the unity of the Congo.

Mr Tshombe did not, and never did, seriously contest this line of argument. He simply wore the worried but closed expression of a man who knew of cogent arguments, which he could not state, for not taking advice which, in itself, he considered sound and serious enough. He reverted to Sendwe. He feared that the UN, in bringing Sendwe to Katanga, wished to 'sow disorder' so as to put pressure on him, Tshombe, to attend the Parliament. I pointed out that UN forces a few days before had repelled Gizengist troops which had tried to enter Katanga from the direction of Sentery in North Kasai. If the UN's policy had been what Mr Tshombe feared, these troops would have been allowed, even encouraged, to enter Katanga. As it was, not merely had the UN kept them out, but it also intended to continue to repel such bands. The UN could do this, because the various 'armies' which infested the country were – in the UN view – no more than armed factions, or brigands. But, once a legal Government had come into being, then the United Nations could not oppose the entry into Katanga of forces loyal to that Government. That situation undoubtedly presented grave potential dangers to the security of lives and property in Katanga; the time to cope with these dangers was now, through exerting an influence on the composition and policies of the new Government.

Once more a veil seemed to come over Mr Tshombe's features. He muttered something about 'the party' and 'the Assembly' reaching their own decisions. Then he gave the smile of a man who realizes he is putting too much strain on human credulity, and wished me a pleasant journey.

A pleasant journey indeed in some ways, it was. My son, Donal, an undergraduate at Cambridge, had come to join me for the holidays and he came with me on this trip, as did Michel Tombelaine and his attractive American wife, Verdalee. As we got into the plane, Michel gave me the latest telegram from Leopoldville, which was to tell me not to go to Kabalo, as Sendwe was there and Tshombe might misinterpret the motive of my visit. Having already had this out with Tshombe, I decided to disregard the telegram as there was greater danger of Tshombe 'misinterpreting' a change of plan. Tshombe, I felt, though not the mere catspaw that many of his enemies claimed him to be, was a man who registered the balance of forces, as he understood it. He was not 'anti-UN', but he had to be convinced that what the United Nations represented was not less resolute, and not less formidable, than whatever force it was which made him persist in a line of policy which could only bring disaster on all concerned.

The United Nations garrisons in North Katanga at this time were strung out along the line of the CFL railroad – from Albertville on Lake Tanganyika in the east to Kabalo, near the Kasai border on the west, with another garrison to the south of that, in Manono. Under the resolutions, their duties included the maintenance of order and the prevention of civil war; they constituted, in principle, a 'neutral zone'.[1] In practice, North and Central Katanga as a

---

[1] The 'neutral zone' agreement was concluded between Tshombe and General Rikhye on October 17th, 1960. It was declared void by the Katangese authorities on January 12th, 1961, after the UN had not opposed the entry into Manono of troops from Stanleyville who were welcomed by the local population. The UN local command, however, seems to have regarded itself as stopped by the agreement from preventing the reconquest of the town by Tshombe's mercenaries, against the will of the inhabitants, in March. But Kabalo showed that attitudes of the local UN commanders varied (see page 149).

whole was a shadowy and anarchic region. In the immediate vicinity of UN garrisons, life was fairly safe; in the areas controlled by the Baluba 'rebels' – who were, in fact, in insurrection against the rebel authorities of Elisabethville – life was safe only for Balubakat and Cartel supporters; in areas controlled by the gendarmerie, life was not safe for Baluba.

The area in question was a vast one. *The Times*, which is liable, editorially, to be a little vague about Katanga questions, seemed to think of it as a thin strip on the top or round the edges. 'Except in certain border areas', it wrote on July 31st, 'the (Tshombe) Government enjoys popular support'. The exact opposite would be nearer the truth. The main non-European support for Tshombe is in the Lunda region of the western border areas, while even the Katanga Government's own propaganda shows that the 'rebel' region goes deep into the heart of the province. The White Book of the Katanga Government about 'the outlaw activities in some Baluba areas' contains a map 'Situation in Katanga on June 30th, 1961' showing, in its own words:

'*In green*, areas whose populations are pro-governmental,

In white, what is left of area where pacification is taking place.'

In fact, the green area includes, as well as regions which are considered tribally pro-governmental, like the western and mideastern regions, also huge areas which were simply held down by force, like Manono in north-central Katanga, which became 'pro-governmental' when Major Mathys took it by storm the previous March, or Nyunzu in north Katanga whose buildings were 'pro-governmental' but most of whose population had unfortunately fled to the bush. Even so, the white area, where it may reasonably be assumed the 'popular support' for Tshombe was but tepid, pending pacification, extends on this map from Kabalo in the north to a point south-east of Bukama, at the dead centre of the province of Katanga.

Should the editor of *The Times* contest this point of view, I am prepared, in a sporting spirit, to make him an experimental offer. I am willing, and can arrange, to travel, without any other escort than, say, Mr Prosper Mwamba Ilunga and two unarmed members of the local Cartel Jeunesse, through any region of Central Katanga where there are not gendarmerie posts – let us say from Malemba-Nkulu to the neighbourhood of Bukama. I shall carry with me a large portrait of Jason Sendwe; I shall wear the leopard-skin insignia of the Cartel Jeunesse and travel under the flag of the Central Government. The editor of *The Times* will traverse the same region,

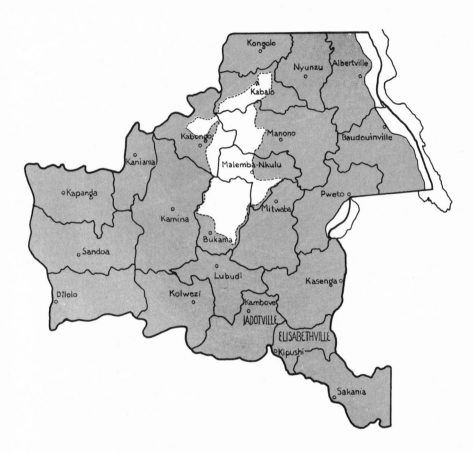

This map, dated June 1961, is referred to on page 144 and is taken from the White
book of the Katanga Government on *Outlaw Activities in some Baluba Areas*. The
tinted portion represents areas whose population, according to the Katanga
Government, 'is pro-Governmental'. The white portion represents 'what is left of
the area where pacification is taking place'.

also without armed escort, carrying a large portrait of Mr Tshombe and flying the flag of the Independent State of Katanga. He may, and I hope will, be accompanied on his journey by three members of the Katangese Government, one of whom should be – since this is very much the interior of Katanga – the Minister of the Interior, M Godefroid Munongo.

The competitor who finishes the course is the winner. The executors of the loser will undertake, in my case, to publish a posthumous recantation of the whole of this chapter, and, in the case of the editor of *The Times*, to publish a posthumous qualification, or footnote, to the editorial statement of July 31st: 'Except in certain border areas, the Government enjoys popular support'. The admission that 'enjoys' was not the *mot juste* would suffice.

Not only were the UN forces thin on the ground in the contested area of North and Central Katanga, but there was often division of opinion as to what they were supposed to do. There were those who felt that the UN should leave the gendarmerie a free hand to restore order, by the only methods which gave practical results, among a population which, left to itself, was dominated by its most ferocious elements, addicted to degrading superstition and bestial cruelty. And there were those who felt that the UN should use force to stop the gendarmerie from committing wholesale arson and murder against a population which, in its overwhelming majority, rejected the régime which sent the gendarmerie.[1]

The holders of both these conflicting views were passionately sincere, and both had some reason for their passion. Both Baluba and gendarmerie had committed, and were continuing to commit, criminal excesses on a large scale.

The Katanga Government's White Book contains revolting pictures of atrocities stated to have been committed by Baluba, and, while that Government has less hesitation even than other Governments in inventing atrocities for propaganda purposes, it is unfortunately true that Baluba, in some cases, saved it the trouble of having to invent. Irish and other officers in the area reported ferocious treatment meted out to Tshombe supporters, or suspected supporters. One officer wrote of 'men with broken spines stretched out on crosses in the sun'. (*Irish Times*, October 4th, 1961.) Torture, murder and mutilation moved in the path of the Baluba rebellion, as they have in the path of other rebellions.

---

[1] This division of opinion had an important practical bearing on events. The attitude of UN forces at Kabalo in early April was quite different from that of UN forces at Manono in late March.

As regards the repression, the activities of the gendarmerie, it is best to quote a Belgian source, sympathetic to Mr Tshombe's régime:

'In December, 1960', writes Pierre Davister, 'the number of rebels killed since the beginning of "reprisal" operations by the Katangese Army in North Katanga was reckoned at 7,000. We know what that kind of figure means in Africa. Generally they must be multiplied by two, by three, by ten, and you can still not be sure that your figure does not fall short of the truth.

'In Elisabethville, no one denies that the gendarmerie has used "strong-arm methods" in dealing with certain nests of rebels. Whole villages have been razed to the ground and automatic weapons have mowed down whole ranks of "Cartel youth" who – it must be admitted – marched stupidly to death.' (*Katanga Enjeu du Monde*, p. 254.)

M Davister wrote at a time when Mr Tshombe's power over North and Central Katanga was at its lowest ebb. Subsequently, in February-April 1961, the gendarmerie, brilliantly led by a Belgian regular officer, Major Mathys, recaptured and 'pacified' much of the area, including Manono. UN forces had, on the whole, not resisted this development,[1] except at Kabalo, and the pacification was still proceeding. A Belgian observer even noted with approval, in an article which appeared when I was still in North Katanga, the 'co-operation' between UN and gendarmerie:

'The Katangese gendarmerie', wrote this reporter, 'is carrying out, with the help of French and Belgian specialists, a campaign of pacification which seems to be bearing fruit. It is estimated that 50 per cent [*sic*] of the population has been coaxed into going back to the towns and villages and to work. Even the "terrible Gurkhas" show a co-operative spirit.' (*La Libre Belgique*, July 12th, 1961.)

The officer commanding the UN forces – Indians and Ethiopians – in North Katanga at this time, Brigadier K. A. S. Raja, was hardly as full of 'co-operative spirit' towards this pacification as the Belgian journalist and most of his readers would have wished. I was, in fact, coming north, at his invitation, mainly to clear up a disputed point about the pacification. Brigadier Raja had reported that the gendarmerie was still, at this moment, terrorizing the population

---

[1] 'In view of the resolution of the Security Council of February 21st,' states the relevant UN report (S/4791 of April 15th), 'the force commander instructed the UN commander in North Katanga to oppose and resist any further aggressive moves by the Katanga gendarmerie.' At Kabalo this directive was carried out; at Manono, as the same report makes clear, it was not.

and burning villages. Mr Tshombe and Mr Munongo denied that
the gendarmerie had ever burned villages; any burned villages seen
must have been destroyed in inter-tribal war (Mr Tshombe) or
burned down by their own inhabitants (Mr Munongo). Our Belgian
acquaintances, notably M Tignée, had a more sophisticated story.
They admitted that villages *had* been burned down, during the
February-April 'repression of the rebellion'; that was very sad,
but it was war. That phase, however, was now over and the gendarmerie was now, with the aid of Captain Labourdonnais, a
French expert on psychological warfare, engaged solely in reassuring
the population. Any 'burned villages' now reported were old ones,
dating from April or earlier. In any case, reports from 'les Hindous'
should be treated with reserve. They were carrying out, not a UN
policy, but a 'Nehru policy'. Also, being polytheists, they did not
have the same attitude to the truth as we, who were products of
Western Christian civilization.

Albertville, where the UN force in North Katanga had its headquarters, is an attractive little harbour-town among the sand-dunes
by Lake Tanganyika. The Indian forces there got their supplies
direct from India, via Dar-es-Salaam and the lake. The food
at the mess was exactly what it would have been in India and,
for anyone who likes curry and Kipling, as I do, an evening
in the officers' mess at Albertville was a most agreeable experience. Brigadier Raja is a handsome and generally taciturn
officer with a fierce smile and flashing eyes. He and his officers had,
and were conscious of having, a more martial mien than most of our
European officers in Elisabethville: they had all seen much active
service. They were punctilious about, I should imagine, everything,
but especially about refraining from any political comment: they well
knew they were accused of 'pursuing a Nehru policy' and they
never failed to make clear, both in word and in practice, that they
had only one instruction from Mr Nehru, and that was to carry out
the directives given by the UN Command. You might, if you were
very attentive, deduce – from, say, the degree of military swagger
in Colonel Hazari's burly shoulders, or from a fleeting expression
over the delicate and deceptively mild-looking Kashmiri features of
Brigade Major Dhar – that some orders were pleasanter to carry
out than other orders, but, pleasant or not, they were carried out.

From Albertville, we toured the area – as I was often to do afterwards – in a light aircraft, a Beaver. Major Dhar accompanied me,
and told the pilot to fly low over the long stretch of the CFL railway
from Kabongo, north-east towards Kabalo. This area is represented

on the White Book map by a tongue of green stretching into the white area; that is to say, it is an 'area whose population is pro-governmental'. On each side of the track, over a distance of perhaps thirty or forty miles, no village contained any house with a roof. I was already losing count of the number of burnt-out villages – there were at least fifteen of them of, I should say, twenty to fifty huts each, sometimes more – when we flew over a group of five jeeps full of Katangese soldiers, parked beside the line. In one of the jeeps a white officer in uniform stood up and waved to us with his broad-brimmed bush-hat. Beyond the jeeps, in the direction in which they were pointing, the villages were intact but empty.

The place where the jeeps are parked is the movable border between 'white' and 'green': between 'areas whose populations are pro-governmental' and 'what is left of areas where pacification is taking place'.[1]

At Nyunzu, beyond UN-held Kabalo, I met the local adviser-to-the-administrator and the commander of the gendarmerie, both Belgians. I told them what I had seen and that it would have to stop. I must have told them this with some emphasis, for I remember the gendarmerie officer rising from his seat with a strange wordless cry and running off down the wooden steps from the porch of the Indian mess and away along the path to his jeep. The administrator, a pasty and obsequious person, said he had no knowledge of any villages being burned and no responsibility for the behaviour of the gendarmerie, some of whom were perhaps a little unstable, as I could see.

In retrospect, I am not at all proud of this little scene in Nyunzu. It takes no great courage to be beastly to a Belgian officer in an Indian mess; it would be different if I had gone to Camp Massart, or the depot at Shinkolobwe, to tell the gendarmerie what I thought of their 'pacification'. But, however much, and rightly, you may distrust the emotion of moral indignation, there will be times when it hits you. It hit me, not immediately at the sight of the roofless villages, for which I had been more or less prepared, but at the friendly wave of the white officer in charge of these operations. What came into my mind was the face of a political adviser in Elisabethville, and his persistent, clinging insinuations about 'them' and 'us': anything 'we' did to 'them' was perhaps regrettable, if detected; anything 'they' did to 'us' was an atrocity. The hand

---

[1] 'By August 1961', according to Mr Ian Colvin, 'Mr Tshombe could tour the whole State undiminished in size'. (*The Daily Telegraph*, September 8th 1961.) No doubt a whistle-stop tour from Kabongo to Kabalo was included.

waving the hat said the same thing, in the complicity of jeep and
aeroplane against the huts and the trampled patches of manioc.

I left Nyunzu – under, for the first time in my life, armed escort –
for the river and rail junction of Kabalo, where a different state of
affairs prevailed. Pacification had stopped short at Kabalo, because
the UN Ethiopian forces had blown up a gendarmerie steamer on
the Lualaba river, and had also captured and expelled a sizeable
contingent of European officers and soldiers. The commander of
this Ethiopian force was Colonel Alemu, a handsome and dashing
young officer who spoke excellent English, French and Spanish in
addition to his native Amharic. The Colonel's authority over his
men was, to say the least of it, impressive: not merely did they
seem to carry out all orders at the double but while the order was
actually being given, they used to twitch or shudder in a mixture of
awe and propitiation; I do not know what penalties the Ethiopian
military code prescribes, but I suspect there is nothing mawkish
about it. When, at a later stage, Colonel Alemu and I became friends
I found his disposition was exceptionally sunny, with a slightly
madcap Brigadier Gerard touch. At this point, however, his
attitude was solemn, even forbidding. He informed me, not without relish, that if I were so much as to step out into the street,
I would be instantly 'lynched': the mere sight of my white, or pink,
face would, it seemed, be enough. I could not see at the time why
he took so much pleasure in conveying this rather depressing piece
of information. I found out later that he had spent some time on a
training course at a military base in an American southern State –
North Carolina, I think – and had found his movements severely
limited by his pigmentation. It was natural enough for him to enjoy
letting me know that my particular type of skin was not always and
everywhere a passport to universal esteem and mobility.

The flag, at Kabalo, was not the green and red, with crosslets, of
Katanga, but the seven stars of the Republic of the Congo. Kabalo,
being the only important Katangese centre then not occupied by
the gendarmerie, had been constituted after the fall of Manono the
'provisional capital' of the 'Province of Lualaba' – the province
which the Balubakat and other Cartel elements wished to form out
of the vast area of North and Central Katanga where the predomi-
nantly Baluba population was hostile to Tshombe's régime. The
Balubakat leader, Jason Sendwe – who had become a deputy
for Elisabethville at the last elections – was now in Kabalo, to
Mr Tshombe's chagrin, and we discussed the pacification.

Mr Sendwe is a solid, gentle, slow person, with the manner of a

conscientious, non-intellectual school-teacher. He was at the same
Methodist school as Tshombe, and he reads the Bible every day.
He spoke of Tshombe without resentment. Tshombe was not really
a bad man but – he rubbed thumb and index-finger together over
an invisible bank-note. He and his deputy, Prosper Mwamba
Ilunga – a younger man, of exceptional intelligence and, as I found
later, courage – spoke quietly but firmly about the situation. As
they saw it, Tshombe's army, which was really the army of the
Europeans of Elisabethville, was burning their villages and killing
their people almost under the eyes of the United Nations forces,
which remained passive. Questioned, they agreed that while a UN
force was actually on a given spot, the gendarmerie did not commit
excesses against the population there. But working from bases where
there were UN forces, the gendarmerie carried out terror expeditions
into the bush, not merely burning villages but – they claimed – mas-
sacring the population. Any man, woman or child found in a village
which came within a 'rebellious' area selected for pacification was,
they said, automatically shot.

It is right to say here that this last statement was not proved, and
that it was vehemently denied in Elisabethville by Colonel
Crèvecoeur and Major Mathys. I am inclined to believe that, as
with most things in the Congo, practice varied according to the man
in charge on the spot. I cannot imagine either of these officers
murdering women and children, but some of their colleagues were
certainly less squeamish. Some of the mercenaries – *les affreux*, as
they liked to be called – boasted of such exploits and one of the
French officers, Captain Lasimone,[1] told me that he wanted to leave
the gendarmerie because he was sickened by the things that his
superior, Commandant Faulques, had ordered him to do to Baluba
prisoners. Captain Lasimone was not necessarily a reliable witness
but nothing in Commandant Faulques's past record, as a pacifier
of Algeria, makes Lasimone's evidence inherently unlikely. In any
case, the empty villages in the path of the gendarmerie jeeps on the
line from Kabongo were eloquent as to what treatment the population *expected* at the hands of the forces of order.

I asked Mr Sendwe and Mr Mwamba Ilunga about the other
side of the case. If Baluba flogged people to death with bicycle
chains, as they had done in some places, they put themselves outside
the law and beyond the protection of the UN. The discussion at this
point became a little confused as Colonel Alemu's little sitting-room
had filled up with silent people wearing the leopard- or cat-skin

---

[1] For Captain Lasimone, see Chapter XV.

insignia of the Jeunesse Balubakat, and the presence of these people
clearly exercised an inhibiting effect on the conversation of Mr
Sendwe and Mr Mwamba Ilunga. Their answer, however, as they
hinted then and as Prosper Mwamba Ilunga developed it to me
subsequently, was substantially as follows:

Murders, tortures, mutilations and other brutalities had unquestionably been committed by some of their supporters in the
Cartel Jeunesse, though some of the worst crimes attributed to the
Jeunesse were, in fact, the work of a religious sect, the Watchtower.
They, the leaders, were doing everything in their power to discourage such acts – that this was true at least as regards Prosper
himself I can testify from my own subsequent experience – but
their power at present, was limited. The population was crazed
with fear and hate, and the sorcerers and drug-peddlers found easy
markets. The gendarmerie 'pacification', far from curing the disease,
was intensifying it. If the people now had a blind hatred of whites,
this was because whites had directed and led the burning of their
villages and the killing of their brothers. The idea of the pacification
was to make North Katanga safe and profitable for whites, but it
was bound to have the contrary effect. It was not possible, not even
for Tshombe's well-equipped gendarmerie, to hold down by terror
the whole population of this vast area. The only way to 'pacify' it in
a real and lasting sense was to restrain the gendarmerie, and allow
the people to live under the flag of their own country – the Congo –
and the authority of their own elected leaders. Even then it would
take some time to calm the population, and lives, especially European lives, would continue to be in danger for a time. But that quiet
and confidence could be restored, in areas where there had been
violence and anarchy, had been shown in other parts of the Congo
and would quite soon be shown in the whole Congo, Prosper
believed, if the provocation of the European-engineered secession
of Katanga were ended. Nobody, he pointed out, had asked the
population of North Katanga whether they wanted to secede from
the Congo – everyone knew they did not – but now they were
being treated as if they had seceded, and being massacred for
'rebelling' against the 'State of Katanga'.

I went with Sendwe and his friends to the airport, where Sendwe
was to address a meeting. I was interested in this, because of what I
had heard in Elisabethville about Sendwe's standing in Kabalo. It
was said generally that his popularity had waned. Munongo said
that if Sendwe came to Kabalo, the people would cut his throat.
Victor Tignée, as always more moderate than his master, said that

Sendwe would be well received in Kabalo – but only if he came 'in the baggage waggons of the UN – because the UN represents, to their minds, power. They respect power, nothing but power.'[1]

As representing power, I trudged along the airport road in clouds of red dust raised by the cheering crowd in front of me, which was carrying Jason Sendwe shoulder-high on a leopard-skin chair. They neither lynched me, as Colonel Alemu had predicted, nor fawned on me, in accordance with Tignée's law. They simply ignored me, and roared for Sendwe with such enthusiasm as neither my son nor myself had ever heard from a crowd before. All Kabalo, I believe, was there, cheering and singing and making that oddly didactic motion with the index-finger which is the sign of the Cartel, and which an African could not publicly make in Elisabethville without risking his life. After Sendwe had spoken, a group of solemn school-girls in veils presented me with an address, distinctly inspired with the principles of the Cartel. I made a brief and guarded reply in French, saying merely that I would send the address to the Secretary-General. It took Prosper about ten minutes to translate these few words into Kiluba and his speech was punctuated by thunderous cheers from the crowd.

Manono, where we next touched down, is a tin-mining centre, and was under the control of Tshombe's gendarmerie. As soon as we landed, a jeep drove out at full speed on to the airstrip. The driver, a European, was beside our aircraft as we climbed down. He was the 'adviser-to-the-administrator' and he wanted to know whether we had Sendwe aboard. He beamed with joy and satisfaction when he found we had not. I asked him why he was so worried about Sendwe. Was Sendwe then so very popular in Manono? Of course he was, said the adviser, and in the whole region: his arrival could be the signal for a general uprising. This man, was, for a Belgian 'adviser' in Katanga, astonishingly frank; he agreed that the whole Baluba territory of North Katanga was simply being held down by force, and that this situation could not last long. He surprised me also by expressing a hope that the UN forces would stay in the area, and save as many lives as possible when the change-over came. 'It's not the whites I'm worried about,' he said, 'They'll clear

---

[1] 'It must be pointed out', wrote Tshombe to the UN on April 10th, 'that Kabalo is in the hands of the Katangese forces, that the population has remained there and shows itself entirely favourable to the legitimate authority.' (*Congo, 1961*, p. 225). Kabalo was not at that date in the hands of the Katangese, the mercenaries' attack having failed. The population, when I saw it, was entirely favourable to the legitimate authority, but not in Mr Tshombe's sense.

out anyway. It's any Baluba that haven't worked with the Jeunesse. There aren't all that many of them but they'll *all* be butchered if the UN isn't there; some of them are bound to be butchered in any case.' He spoke in the rather exaggeratedly unemotional tone of a man concerned with preventing atrocities, not in that other tone to which some of his colleagues had accustomed me: hysterical anger, dwelling on details of atrocities in order to exclude a given set of people from the human race, and thereby justify atrocities against them. This was a brave man – he had remained in Manono when almost all the other Europeans had fled. If it was not the positive side of the Belgian presence in the Congo that was most in evidence that July in North Katanga, that was not the fault of men like this.

That night, back at Albertville, took place perhaps the most unsuccessful social function I have ever attended. The host, in principle, was M Béraud, then the UN civilian officer in Albertville. M Béraud was a gentle, dreamy man who smoked a pipe, read Dante aboard UN aircraft, collected pictures and admired the directors of the CFL railroad. The dinner was at the house of the general manager of this line. The other guests, besides myself, were Brigadier Raja and some of his senior officers. The main course was beef, which the Indian officers, all being Hindus, naturally declined; they also declined, politely but firmly, any substitute. Poor M Béraud, being a sensitive man, was much distressed by the result of his absent-mindedness. The railway magnate, through a mouthful of beef, was heard to inquire why Hindus considered the cow to be an unclean animal. An Indian officer, with as much lack of warmth as was consistent with courtesy, explained that Hindus did not consider the cow to be an unclean animal; they regarded it as a sacred animal.

Three Europeans went on eating, two of them without much appetite; six Indian officers looked fixedly in front of them.

The railwayman, in the voice of a man accustomed to wielding authority, asked when the UN was going to get the railway line open.[1] Shaken by the sights of a crowded day and unduly irritated by the beef incident, I answered this question rather too elaborately.

---

[1] Under the Rikhye-Tshombe agreement of October 1960, the UN had undertaken to 'work for the complete pacification of the regions in question while keeping open the means of communication whose security the UN would ensure'. (*Congo, 1961*, page 214.) The attempt to honour this surprising agreement, in the context described in this chapter, led to the death of nine Irish soldiers, at the hands of Baluba, in the following month. Fortunately the agreement was denounced by Tshombe in January 1961.

I told him of the method of keeping his line open which we had been studying near Kabongo.

His face showed no surprise; just a trace of sober satisfaction.

I understood, I said, that this was the traditional method and no doubt – in a region where the population was fighting against the authorities which controlled the railroad – the only method that worked. I did not wish to condemn it; it was a method not invented by Katanga, or even by Belgium, and it was widely practised by many nation-states against minorities.

The Indian officers stared into space. The CFL railroad took a second helping. I was, in its opinion, talking sense. There was too much sentimentality about these savages. Force was the only thing they understood. I heard my own voice going on:

Fortunately or unfortunately, Katanga was neither a nation nor State but legally a part of the Republic of the Congo. If Belgium had so wished, it could, no doubt, have set Katanga up as one of a number of successor-States within the territory of the former Belgian Congo – much as France had dealt with her former African possessions. Katanga would then, like Senegal, or the Cameroons, be generally recognized and admitted to the United Nations. As an independent and sovereign State, it could have had whatever treaty relations it wished with the former colonizing country and it could also have dealt precisely as it wished with its minorities or even with a rebellious majority if, as was often the case, the former ruling power had handed over the reins of government to a dominant minority.

The CFL railroad said it was afraid it was not interested in politics, which were above its head. *La politique nous dépasse. . . .*

I said I would try to show a connection between politics and business. Belgium had made decisions about the Congo, decisions which, having received international ratification, could not now be withdrawn or modified by Belgium alone, still less by a group of Belgian business men. As a result of these decisions, and of later attempts to change them, there were United Nations forces in this and other provinces of the Congo. Not only could these forces not help the provincial authorities in putting down the so-called rebellion, or help – as he suggested – to crush the population in the neighbourhood of the railway line, but they would now be obliged to stop the gendarmerie from doing these things.

M Béraud's depression deepened. One Indian officer was smiling faintly: the nearest thing to a note of hilarity which the evening achieved. The CFL railroad looked a little congested.

If the UN acted in that way, said the railway manager carefully, the line would go bankrupt. He reminded me, quite truly, that the CFL was the economic lifeline of the area.

I suggested that the line should use its influence with the provincial Government and its backers to get a settlement acceptable to the majority in the area. Force was one way of dealing with that majority; if force was ruled out, the only other way was negotiation.

The CFL railroad said something in a low, thick voice to M Béraud. Soon afterwards M Béraud said he thought perhaps it was time for us to go. The Indian officers agreed, and we left together. M Béraud apologized to the CFL, to the Indians and to me. I apologized to M Béraud for having incensed his friend. It happened to be an unfortunate day to talk to us about clearing the CFL railroad line. Things, he observed sadly and accurately, seemed to go like that in this country.

The following day we flew back, over the great tracts of tawny earth and stunted trees, apparently as empty as the moon, to Elisabethville; a city which we would now see through eyes which had also seen a hat waving beside a railway line, north-east from Kabongo.

9

MISSIONARIES AND MERCENARIES

'Christ's lily and beast of the waste wood:
From life's dawn it is drawn down,
Abel is Cain's brother and breasts they have sucked the same.'
Gerard Manley Hopkins

'I have three Belgian friends here', I wrote home about this time.
I was exaggerating, I found a little later. Major Geurtz turned out
to be Dutch and his wife German. That left only one, Père Martin
de Wilde, who thus has the curious distinction – I hope it will not
embarrass him, if a copy of this book ever reaches Elisabethville – of
being the only Belgian in Katanga whom I remember with affection.

Père Martin was a big, tall man, a most impressive figure striding
along in his white Benedictine habit. His face was a little like
François Premier, a little like an elephant: he had an aristocratic
nose and unusually small grey eyes which often twinkled with a
kind of saintly *astuce*. What he enjoyed most in the world, I think,
was being cunning in the service of God: rather like Hammarskjold
in a way. He was, in many things, the right-hand man of the Archbishop of Elisabethville, Cornélis. Archbishop Cornélis was a
wizened little man with an inability to suffer fools gladly – an inability of which, to my no small surprise, I had once found myself
at the wrong end. This was at a party on the roof-garden of
Munongo's house. Outside on the lawn a number of Africans – I
took them, almost certainly wrongly, for Bayeke – were dancing
and beating drums. When Munongo introduced me to the Archbishop, I thought it appropriate, in the absence of any other topic of
conversation, to say something about how interesting, or how
agreeable, this spectacle was. 'I have been twenty years in Africa',

157

said the Archbishop, contemptuously wagging his little grey goatee, 'and that makes me sick. *Cela me donne la nausée.*'

The Archbishop had, I think, delegated Père Martin to show this raw Onusian something of 'the real Katanga'. Père Martin, accordingly, took me to see the principal schools and missions in the neighbourhood of Elisabethville – using 'neighbourhood' in the spacious, African sense. Both Père Martin and I, and also my son, enjoyed these excursions very much. What Père Martin enjoyed most, I think, was appearing unexpectedly at the door of some convent in the bush, and introducing – always throwing the line away a little – *M le Représentant de l'ONU.* The effect was somewhat as if one had said casually to Christians of an earlier time, 'May I introduce the Emperor Nero?' I became used to the tiny intake of the breath which announced the following struggle in the mind of a Reverend Mother: 'This man is working for the Communists, but Père Martin would not have brought him here if it had not been the Archbishop's wish. It is therefore my duty to overcome my personal revulsion and, yes, to shake his hand.'

Père Martin always watched this little scene with something like the satisfaction – based on superior knowledge and daring – which a snake-charmer must experience, hearing the gasps which result when he introduces one of his repulsive pets into a drawing-room.

I like and admire missionaries as a class. Wherever I have met them, they have seemed, morally, far above the level of most people, including most religious people, and they also have many other engaging characteristics, including love of adventure and a certain boyishness. Ireland is a great producer of missionaries and I have long thought it one of my country's misfortunes (though good fortune for other lands) that so much that is best in the Irish Church departs for the mission field, while among those who remain at home there will always be some whose favourite music is the anthem, *Ecce Sacerdos Magnus.*

I was, therefore, disposed in advance to like the men and women whom Père Martin took me to see in the bush but, as so often in the Congo-ex (?)-Belge, something went wrong. It was not just their suspicion of the UN, the little intake of breath and the rest; that, I expected, and it could have been got over. It was whatever may be symbolized by the following encounters:

Quite in the bush, *en pleine brousse*, is one of the most lavishly constructed schools certainly in Africa and probably in the world. It is a secondary school for girls, built with a bequest of a director of the Union Minière as, in a sense, a monument to his wife, who had pre-deceased him. It is laid out in accordance with Bob Hope's favourite scheme of interior decoration – 'all done over in contrasting shades of money'. I should guess that the expenditure on the magnificent buildings of cut stone, the delightful lawns and grounds – there was even a zoo – would have paid for about ten quite satisfactory schools on a more utilitarian plan. It seemed wasteful, for everyone now admitted that there were far too few secondary schools in Katanga, as elsewhere in the Congo, and that the Belgian authorities' failure to provide such schools was one of the basic causes of the Congo's troubles. The schoolgirls, in any case, looked neat and well; their material welfare was efficiently looked after. We could not tell the quality of the instruction – school was just breaking up at the end of term – but in the Congo context, it was much that children, especially girls, should be receiving any form of secondary education at all. The Reverend Mother, who showed us around, gave no sign of affection for these African girls, but then I should not have expected her to do so: headmistresses, more particularly Reverend Mothers, are not, as a class, effusive people. But there was a little more to it than this. Her manner of referring to her charges was not quite that of the superintendent of an institution for mental defectives, and not quite that of the head-keeper in an aquarium; it was more distant and more impersonal than either – more like a factory-manager, satisfied with the emergence of a standard product out of recalcitrant raw material. 'It doesn't', she said, as she showed us over a spacious, airy dormitory, 'smell of blacks at all'. (*Cela ne sent pas du tout le Noir.*)

In the Benedictine school for boys at K——, as in all the other schools we saw, there were pictures of President Tshombe on the walls. One of the pupils, the Rector told us, had recently been reported as having spoken disrespectfully of Tshombe to some of his friends. For this, he had been, said the Rector, instantly expelled. The Rector also said that he, the Rector, took no interest in politics. This, like all the other schools we saw, had African pupils and no others. Months later, back in New York, I did see on television a 'school in Katanga' with white and black children playing happily together. The impression created was that of a multi-racial Paradise. These things may happen in Katanga. I can only say that I have not seen them except on television.

The third mission we visited was near a lake where we had seen people fishing in dug-out canoes and living, as people do generally throughout Katanga, outside the mining and communication

centres, a stone-age existence. We had afternoon tea with the
Mission fathers; four Belgians and one Congolese. The conversation
ran on African superstitions: how even the Catholics kept fetishes
in their houses, how they turned to the sorcerers in times of illness,
how fortune-tellers and other 'occultists' in Brussels were now 'cash-
ing in', by mail-order, on local gullibility, thus taking business away
from the native witch-doctors. I had no reason to doubt the truth of
any of this, and much of it – especially the witch-doctors of Brussels –
was interesting. But what was also interesting was that the Belgian
priests took no pains at all to spare the feelings of their Congolese
colleague, the weaknesses of whose brothers they were discussing.
They did all the talking; he just smiled, and handed round the
biscuits. One of the Belgian priests insisted that backwardness and
superstition were *ineradicable* elements of the native mind.

'It doesn't matter what diplomas you give them', he said. 'A
native can get good marks in his exams, complete his courses,
become a teacher, even a lawyer or a doctor. Underneath, he's still a
savage.'

The Congolese priest smiled.

On the way back, my son and I tried to find out what Père Martin
felt about this scene. We had both noticed that Père Martin had
refrained – with the instinctive good feeling which was characteristic
of him – from joining in the chorus about African barbarism, but we
could not help noticing, also, that this good and gentle man seemed
to find nothing abnormal about the behaviour of his colleagues:
behaviour which seemed to us to be the intellectual and psychological equivalent of a Dixie mob on one of its bad days.

I never really found out what Père Martin thought. He was not
much given to speech except for occasional curious anecdotes – as
of how embarrassed the Belgian Government had been by having to
prosecute Munongo's aged father when he ate a three-year-old
child in order to restore his virility – and the conditions of our
journey were not propitious for delicate inquiry in the manner of
Henry James. The roads of Katanga, except for those which link
the Union Minière centres, Elisabethville-Jadotville-Kolwezi, are
simply ribbons of dusty earth, rutted and hollowed by the rains to
varying and unpredictable extents. Along these roads it was Père
Martin's habit to hurtle as fast as his Volkswagen – or, on one
terrifying day, my Buick – would carry him. The larger holes –
three feet deep or more – he would skid around, without slackening
speed, in clouds of red dust; the smaller ones, a foot or less, he just
ignored: it was the medium ones, where his behaviour was unpredic-

table, which used to worry his passengers most. Certainly the most dangerous experience I had in Katanga was driving in the country with this precipitate missionary. My son felt that there was something unfair about the hair-raising risks Père Martin took. The priest, after all, could be sure that, if the car hit a tree, he would go to heaven; we, for our part, could not feel so sure.

'Paternalism' is the name generally given to the sort of phenomenon we had noticed among the missionaries. I am not sure that the word is not, in most cases, too favourable; affection and a sense of kinship, two important elements in a really paternal attitude, were both lacking, as far as I could see, in Belgian feeling towards the Congolese. The people we saw on these excursions were 'the best Belgians', among the few who had come to the Congo for another motive than that of enriching themselves. These missionary priests and nuns had dedicated themselves to the good of the Congolese and they led, without complaint, a hard and dangerous life for the sake of these Africans. They would do anything for them, short of actually liking them. I am sure there were exceptions to this, but they did not come my way; even Père Martin was more apt to talk about Africans as a distinct species, than about any African as an individual – in the manner in which he would have discussed Belgians. And what someone has called the 'pejorative singular' – 'the African' does, thinks, or feels, this or that – was much in evidence.

If the attitude of the Belgian administration and the industrialists and missionaries had been genuinely paternal – as that of some British administrators in some other parts of Africa had been – there would have been much to be said for it. A good parent, after all, wants his children to grow up. He does not want to stunt their intellectual growth; he encourages them to take on responsibilities progressively; he steps aside, and stays aside, as soon as he reasonably can. There is little evidence that Belgians in the Congo generally were paternalist in this good sense. The priest who, in the presence of a Congolese colleague, emphasized not only the gravity but also the ineradicable nature of Congolese defects, was 'paternalist' in the manner of a father who enjoys sneering at a son's awkwardness, and keeps impressing on him that he is congenitally and incurably defective. I found this form to be, on the whole, the prevalent type of paternalism in Katanga.[1]

---

[1] 'Is there a finer relationship', asked M Wigny – defending as Foreign Minister of Belgium his country's paternalism – 'than that between father and child?' The contrast between this kind of rhetoric and the realities of the Congo is nothing short of macabre.

Months afterwards, after my resignation, I was asked to give a German television team, bound for the Congo, some briefing on the UN operation in Katanga. I told them that our main difficulty had been the mercenaries. I talked about the technical problems of apprehending and expelling mercenaries, how hard it was to track them down, how often they had come back through Rhodesia and had to be caught and expelled again, and so on. I noticed that my listeners were first startled, then increasingly horrified. I was puzzled by this apparently excessive reaction until I found that when I said 'mercenaries' they thought I was saying 'missionaries'.

It is probable that, to some missionaries, especially in Baluba territory, the confusion would not have seemed altogether ludicrous. For the missionaries had identified themselves to such an extent with the régime of which the mercenaries are the main prop, that in many regions of Katanga the missionaries cannot live in safety unless the mercenaries are at hand. In a very real sense, therefore, the UN *was* expelling the missionaries, at least from some areas and for a time, because it expelled the people who protected them. It is a hard fact for the UN to face, and its implications are also hard for the missionaries themselves. Before Belgian rule had been established in the Congo, Christian missionaries had lived unmolested at the court of the terrible M'Siri. Now – seventy years after the destruction of M'Siri's empire by the Compagnie du Katanga – Christian missionaries could not survive in much, perhaps most, of Katanga without the protection of European gunmen.[1]

Whatever the reason for this unhappy state of affairs, the fact itself is unfortunately proved. It was Père Martin himself who came to me – after the UN had forbidden military movements by the gendarmerie in North Katanga, in mid-July, shortly after my return from there – to tell me of the anxiety of the Bishop of Kongolo in North-west Katanga. Archbishop Cornélis of Elisabethville wanted to know what measures the UN proposed to take to protect the lives of missionaries in the diocese of Kongolo. I told them the UN forces, wherever they were actually present, would intervene to protect the lives of missionaries. Of course, there were a great many places where the UN was *not* present, and it could not disperse its forces in small

---

[1] The form in which this problem struck the earliest missionaries was the flight, from Léopold's forces, of the natives among whom they had been working in M'Siri's time. '*Actually* we know they have fled from the Congo Free State Officers', wrote the Reverend Daniel Crawford, 'but alas *practically* they have fled from us too. We therefore see how very advisable it is for us to be located a good distance from these heralds of "civilization" '. (Crawford's notes, in F. S. Arnot, *Bihé and Garanganze*, p. 115).

groups all over Katanga. Brigadier Raja, who had then taken command of all Katanga, was absent from Elisabethville at that moment and I suggested that, on his return, the Brigadier and I could, if the Archbishop wished, discuss the matter with him. This was not taken up, probably because all concerned knew the answers all too well. The gendarmerie could effectively protect the missionaries, and other Europeans, as the UN could not do. The reason for this was not, as was sometimes alleged at the time, that the gendarmerie was a more efficient force; the gendarmerie in those regions of North Katanga where both forces were present, was decisively worsted by the UN in September, and it did not win, except the propaganda war, in South Katanga. The reason why the gendarmerie, unlike the UN, could furnish effective protection was that the UN could not, and the gendarmerie could and did – as we saw in the last chapter – employ *la manière forte* of collective punishment. If, in a given region, large elements of the local population, enjoying widespread sympathy, hate Europeans enough – for whatever reason – to want to kill them on sight, there is only one way in which a relatively small but well-equipped force can protect Europeans, and that is by terror. The Bishop of Kongolo must have known, and known better than I did, that the 'freedom of movement of the gendarmerie' meant freedom to burn villages, and to do certain other things of which some ex-gendarmerie officers have since boasted. He must have known also that these actions had a double effect: on the short term, they made the lives of missionaries and other Europeans more secure; in the longer run they were adding fuel to the flames of deadly hatred which similar actions in the past had kindled. The Bishop of Kongolo had, therefore, only too good reason for the anxiety which he felt on learning that the UN had, in effect, given a negative answer to a question which had hitherto, with his acquiescence, been answered positively. That question was: 'Is it permissible to burn villages in order to protect the lives of missionaries?'

That his anxiety was well-founded was tragically demonstrated when, in January 1962, nine priests of the diocese of Kongolo, who had bravely remained at their posts, were reported to have been brutally murdered. Whether they were murdered – as Tshombe claimed – by elements of the Congolese National Army or, as seems rather more likely, by local adherents of the Jeunesse or the Watchtower, it is clear that the immediately predisposing cause of their death was the breakdown of the protection system under which they had lived, the terror inspired by the European-led gendarmerie.

It is obvious that, without the United Nations, that system could have continued in effect for some time longer. Many Evillois will tell you, with burning sincerity, that the blood of these victims is on the hands of the United Nations, especially of myself and my colleagues in Elisabethville who started the 'interference' with the gendarmerie. They will not tell you that, by continuing to decline to interfere with gendarmerie reprisals, the UN would have had other, and certainly not less, 'blood on its hands'. The cost, in African lives, of protecting European lives, was not a matter which weighed heavily with the Europeans of Elisabethville.

It is, of course, true that the Baluba and other supporters of Congolese unity did kill, also, some Congolese (as the FLN killed many Moslems and the IRA some Catholic Irishmen). That does not alter the central fact that the State apparatus of Katanga was designed mainly for the protection of European lives and property, and that the actions committed by its agents, including murder and arson, are directed to the same ends. The real tragedy of the missionaries of Katanga is not the martyrdom of some of them; it is that all have allowed themselves to be caught up in, and even to depend for their physical existence on, a system which cannot be justified in terms of what they represent. It is not so very far from the tragedy of Kurz in *Heart of Darkness* – Kurz, who, towards the end, scrawled across his careful, high-minded thesis on the eradication of barbaric customs, the three words: 'Exterminate the brutes'.[1]

A few, a very few, missionaries were troubled by these aspects of the situation. Père Martin never discussed politics directly with me but I think I detected – I hope I did – some reserve in his attitude towards the 'State of Katanga', what it represented and how it was upheld. But among the other, simpler missionaries whom we met in the bush, the atmosphere was most definitely one of 'loyalty to Katanga' – that Katanga, misleadingly referred to as 'Tshombe's', which preserved so much of what they regarded as the sane realities of the old Belgian Congo. They detested Congolese nationalism – the spirit of Lumumba. They regarded it as anti-Catholic, anti-Christian, and so it had to a great extent apparently become, at least in part of

---

[1] 'Repression', wrote Father J. Roussel of the Scheut Fathers' Mission – one of the most 'enlightened' in the Congo – 'must be effective. It will be so, if it is infrequent and appears accidental. Let it be moderate, prudent, carried out with calm and dignity, but always with energy. He who punishes must be respected and, up to a point, loved. . . . The Black must tell himself, they [*sic*] must tell each other: "The White Man himself obeys a higher law which tells him: Thou shalt punish".' (Roussel, *Déontologie coloniale* (1949), p. 29; quoted in M Merlier *Le Congo de la colonisation belge a l'indépendance*, p. 221).

Katanga. It genuinely did not occur to them that the bitter hostility
to priests and nuns which existed among some Congolese – and
found vent sometimes in acts of hideous brutality – was often not
connected with the religious, or social, or medical activities of the
missionaries, but with their political activities. They did not think
of themselves as having any political activities even when they
preached, as many if not all of them did with fervour, the duty of
obedience to the constituted authorities of the State of Katanga.[1]

By this time, it must be admitted, it had become difficult for any
missionary, even for the hypothetical one who might have been
against the secession of Katanga, to disentangle himself from the
embrace – in the long run, I believe, the deadly embrace – of the
Katangese State. There was, for example, an American missionary,
a Seventh Day Adventist, who wished to distribute food to the
starving population of North Katanga. Reverend Robinson thought,
I believe, that the Tshombe régime was about the best that the
Katangese were likely to get, but, not being a Belgian, he did not
have what was called 'the Katangese faith' in anything like the
same fanatical form as most of the Catholic missionaries. He wanted
to help people who were in need, and that was all: he proved this
amply later by the help he gave to the refugees under UN protection
in Elisabethville. But at this time he could not go into the worst-
affected parts of North Katanga without the co-operation of the
gendarmerie: if he had tried, he would probably have been killed
by the Baluba, in what had become their almost blind hostility
to Europeans and especially missionaries. The result was that the
aid was distributed under gendarmerie auspices, and within the
framework, effectively, of Captain Labourdonnais's 'psychological
warfare'. It is true, even so, that it is better that the people were fed
than that they should have starved: 'warfare' by feeding people is
better than 'warfare' by killing and burning. Yet the two kinds of
warfare were systematically interconnected: the stick for those who
refused to submit to the authority of the secessionist State, the carrot
for those who submitted because they did not wish to starve. The

---

[1] This attitude was, of course, the logical continuation of that adopted by most
missionaries throughout the Congo before independence. 'Natives', wrote Father
Roussel, 'have duties: the duty of acknowledgement and gratitude. Respect,
docility, genuine and sincere collaboration are the great virtues which any
colonialist in love with an ideal must teach to his Black brothers. Let the population
see, feel, understand and appreciate the immense debt which is theirs towards the
mother-countries. Let them realize fully that this debt must be paid off, at least
in part, by a proper respect and by returns in the economic and political fields.'
(*Déontologie coloniale*, p. 45, quoted in Merlier, *op. cit.*, p. 221.)

distribution of aid was carried out with great fanfare of publicity, and speeches by Tshombe announcing the *ralliement* of North Katanga. I thought of the 'mass conversions' to Protestantism in parts of the West of Ireland during the famine years of the 1840s: those 'conversions' did not last long, but what did last was the legacy of hate, springing from humiliation, which they left behind. I fear the fruit of these 'political conversions' in Katanga is the same.

For the life of me, I cannot see that the Reverend Robinson could have acted otherwise than he did. What he did was 'the best possible in the circumstances' but, as often in the circumstances of Katanga, the 'best possible' came out as a sinister farce.

A picture which haunted my mind in Katanga came back to me just now as I wrote about charity and the gendarmerie. My son and I were walking in the bush, somewhere off the road to Kasenga. We were feeling very cheerful and a shade intrepid, with the word 'safari' somewhere in our minds. We came to a glade in which there were a number of colossal, gleaming gourds scattered about, dappled by the sunlight through the trees. My son caught one up, laughing, and instantly a stream of foul, yellow ichor ran out over his clothes, from the rotten inside of the beautiful gourd.

Above left, '. . . *the complicity of jeep and aeroplane against the huts and the trampled patches of manioc*' (p. 149). This village, just burned out by Tshombe's forces, was photographed from the air in the author's presence in July 1961.

Above right, '. . . *people who from the 6th floor of a Leopoldville hotel were directing, with varying success and unrelenting hope, the most novel international operation in man's history*' (p. 72). Robert Gardiner of Ghana (left), U.N. Officer-in-Charge in the Congo, with his predecessor Sture Linner (Sweden).

Below, '. . . *the cheering crowd in front of me, which was carrying Jason Sendwe shoulder-high in a leopard-skin chair*' (p. 152). Sendwe, representing the Central Government of the Congo, being welcomed at Kabalo, N. Katanga, in July 1961.

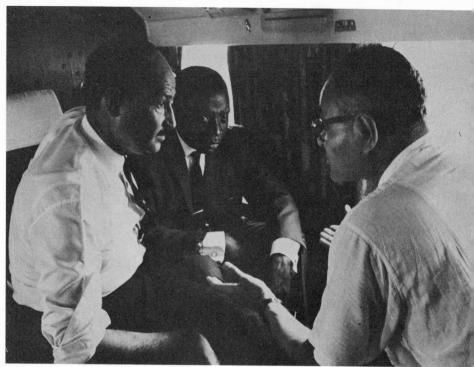

'. . . his closed watchful face in conference, looking like some impenetrable and resourceful envoy of Genghiz Khan . . .' (p. 189). Mahmoud Khiary (left) with Premier Cyrille Adoula (centre) and Dr. Ralph Bunche.

' "We are the Jews of Katanga," one of them said' (p. 241). The author meets representatives of the 45,000 inhabitants of Elisabethville who sought U.N. protection from Tshombe's forces in the period before the September conflict.

10

DON BENITO'S MASTERS

'Wrought, till he crept from a gutted mine
Master of half a servile shire.'
Tennyson

Immediately on my return from North Katanga, the Prince de Ligne and M Velter got in touch with me to arrange a series of dinners, at a villa they had rented, to meet members of the industrial oligarchy of Elisabethville, the people who were running the Union Minière and its associate companies.

These people kept aloof from United Nations circles and I had had, hitherto, only fleeting contacts with them at official receptions, where they were apt to stress the dangers of a native revolt. One of them, a M F——, was particularly strong on the subject. I can still see his bulging eyes, the veins standing out on his forehead, the upper lip slightly flecked with foam as he thrust his face into mine and shouted: 'You have never seen the native city when it breaks loose!' (*Vous n'avez jamais vu la cité indigène déchaînée!*) I could see what he meant. M F——'s excitability, however, was an exception. Most of his colleagues were grave, reserved men and I had not come to know them at all.

I was counting a good deal on the intervention of the Prince de Ligne and M Velter, and this for several reasons.

It was already clear to me, first of all, that such progress as I could make with Mr Tshombe and his colleagues was limited by various barriers which were (because of what we had not got) outside my field of vision. In Melville's great story, *Benito Cereno*, the central figure is a sea captain, the master of a slave ship, who acts

167

in a most mysterious way; the solution of the mysteries is that he only *appears* to be the master of the ship; the real masters are the slaves themselves, who have revolted; the captain, who is, in fact, their prisoner, is serving to conceal the reality. It seemed to me that Tshombe was in a sense an inverted Benito Cereno: the slave who *appears* to have been made master of the ship, while the real masters are still the old slave-owners, now pretending to be simple passengers.

I still believe that to be, essentially and profoundly, the truth, but there are qualifications to the picture, which were now to be brought to my notice.

Who exactly were the masters of the ship? Surely not the local officials of the companies, for these were servants of organizations whose headquarters were in Brussels. It was in Brussels, I believed – and it does seem fairly clear from the sequence of events – that the button had been pushed, or the string pulled, for the secession of Katanga. True, the Belgian Government had simultaneously, or almost simultaneously, urged 'friendly Governments' *not* to recognize the secession of Katanga but that, I reasoned – and would still reason – was because they did not wish these Governments, and private interests in these States, to become altogether too 'friendly' with Katanga and its resources. A *de facto* secession, the maintenance, more or less intact, of a lucrative *de facto* piece of Belgian Congo suited Belgian interests; *de jure* recognition of that secession might take Katanga and its mines right out of Belgium's orbit. So M Wigny sent his diplomatic Notes of July 11th, 1960.[1]

The Belgian Government had, of course, changed since then and it was plain that whoever the masters of Katanga might be, they were not M Spaak and his colleagues in the current Cabinet. M Muller had been put in a position to report that to M Spaak personally. The masters of Katanga surely must be – as they had been ever since Captain Stairs, the servant of the Compagnie du Katanga, left Katanga in February 1892, bringing with him M'Siri's 'curiously-shaped' head in a petroleum tin[2] – financiers of Brussels, now the directors of that complex structure of companies of which the Union Minière was the

---

[1] See Chapter IV, pp. 85–6.

[2] D. Crawford, *Thinking Black*, p. 309. Crawford was a British missionary, present in Bunkeya at the time. 'When a balance was struck, the accountants established that M'Siri's head had cost the Compagnie du Katanga 327,300 Belgian francs in the currency of the day.' (René J. Cornet, *Katanga*, p. 207).

centre.[1] These people were indeed the *pravyashchiye krugi*, the 'ruling circles', on whose activities Mr Zorin, in the Security Council, laid such embarrassing stress.

Now if ever men looked like members of the *pravyashchiye krugi* these were the Prince de Ligne and M Georges Velter. It was characteristic of them that they drove around Elisabethville in a Volkswagen, something which none of the local bourgeois would have dared to do; a gesture of people whose arrival at the top no longer needs to be announced. They were not perhaps the very top of the very top – there were no doubt inner summits which could not be discerned from the valley – but they were the highest thing in sight at the moment. They had also given signs of being able to exert authority; it was the Prince de Ligne who, on the day after the sack of the Belgian Consulate, had induced Tshombe to apologize to M Créner; an action which cost Tshombe a certain loss of face, and must have caused tension with the Minister of the Interior. I thought, furthermore, that their presence in Elisabethville was probably not entirely due to the need to open a stand at the International Fair. They also might have come to report back on the situation for the benefit of the other members of the 'ruling circles'. And they might – and this is where the dinners came in – have come to give guidance to the local management-level of the companies. Both the reporting back and the guidance ought, I believed, to be extremely helpful towards the accomplishment of my mission.

I realize as I look back on it that, although this reasoning was not altogether unsound and although the power and influence of the visitors from Brussels was by no means imaginary, I was somewhat inclined to overshoot the reasoning and magnify the influence. I have examined my conscience as to why this should have been so and I find, I fear, the following:

Like most people who read history – however progressive their opinions – I was not insensitive, at a sub-rational level, to the penumbra of a historic name. (Reader: 'A pompous way of admitting he is a snob'.) Proust's narrator was not able, until nearly the

---

[1] M Jules Chomé in *La Crise Congolaise*, dealing with the Belgian Cabinet meeting of July 9th on Katanga, at which the intervention seems to have been decided, quotes an interesting reference from *La Libre Belgique*: 'At 10.05 a.m.' – the Cabinet meeting opened at 9 a.m. – 'we caught a glimpse of M Gillet, governor of the Société Générale, who had a brief interview with a Cabinet official.' M Chomé points out that 'despite the discreet silence of *La Libre Belgique*, M Gillet is not only the Governor of the Société Générale but also President of the Union Minière du Haut Katanga – Moise Tshombe's sleeping partners'. (*La Crise Congolaise*, p. 172.)

end of his life, entirely to separate the name of Guermantes from the Patriarchs and Judges on the portal of the Cathedral of Laon, and I was in similar trouble with the Prince de Ligne. I was liable to accord to his utterances a respect, and to ascribe to his influence a cogency, which I should not have been likely to accord or ascribe if his name had been, say, Winterbottom.

As regards M Georges Velter, a different kind of romanticism came into play; there must be a part of my mind which has no resistance at all to *any* of the varieties of romanticism. This particular variety is the one about the Very Rich, and it is exemplified in the famous Scott Fitzgerald/Hemingway exchange:

Scott Fitzgerald: 'The very rich are different from us.'

Hemingway: 'Yes, Scotty, they are richer.'

The world is divided between people who feel that Hemingway scores in this anecdote, and those who feel that he merely demonstrates insensitivity. I belonged, at least some of the time, to the second class. Although I did not consciously admire the very rich at all, I subconsciously attributed to them a subtly different quality of being, and also a profound and mysterious influence, tending towards omnipotence. I therefore exaggerated, in my mind, the quite real significance of M Georges Velter.

It is a little painful to have to admit that my subconscious mind believed that the two gentlemen who had walked into my office in the Avenue Fulbert Youlou, and who had now invited me to dinner, were the Duc de Guermantes and the Great Gatsby. That, however, is how it was.

Some of my less amiable readers will undoubtedly pounce on this admission as evidence of my fevered brain, to which they will then ascribe subsequent events. I would advise these people not to examine their own thought processes too closely, if they do not want to spoil their fun.

This lurking delusion did not influence my actions to any significant extent but it encouraged a naturally sanguine temperament to form an over-optimistic picture of the lines on which the talks with these business men would go. The local officials would, I felt sure, treat the Brussels visitors with considerable deference, and would hear their opinions with respect. Under their influence, these officials would consider carefully what I had to say on behalf of the United Nations. At a frank talk, at which both the Brussels and Elisabethville levels of the financial structure were represented, it should surely be possible to 'get across' to those concerned the fact that the State of Katanga, which had been invented to protect their interests, was now the greatest danger to these investments. Since – to use the language of *The Times* – they had been 'forced by economic reasons' to 'recognize' the State of Katanga, it should be possible to show them economic reasons which now pointed in a different direction. I thought that I could demonstrate this to them, from my knowledge of the New York background. Once these hard-headed industrialists became convinced of this, they would take effective action; wheels would begin to move, both in Brussels and Elisabethville, Mr Tshombe would become more *compréhensif*, and Katanga would begin to be reabsorbed peacefully into the Republic of the Congo. What had been started from Brussels could also be ended from Brussels.

It did not, of course, go quite like that. The dinners were not very successful, except from a culinary point of view. From a culinary point of view they were superb and in every way a credit to Belgian civilization. My son got rather sour about this when I told him the menus, because at this time in Les Roches we were living exclusively on veal and spinach. This was because there had been a change in the UN Command. General Iyassu, of Ethiopia, the previous Commander, had been a dignified and portly gentleman, who devoted much thought, very rightly, to the question of food. His critics called him a *général de salon* but he might – more aptly and more honourably – have been described as a *général de salle à manger*. His first action, when he moved into Les Roches – which he did very shortly after I arrived – was to hire a first-class cook With this cook, Ngoye – a tall, handsome Muluba, whose front teeth were filed to sharp points – the General used to spend much time, planning the day's menus, with the care he would have devoted, I am sure, to planning a military campaign, had that been required of him. Under General Iyassu's beneficent sway, therefore, we lived extremely well. Unfortunately General Iyassu took a dislike to Katanga and decided to go back to Leopoldville with its greater gastronomic resources. His successor, Brigadier Raja, a soldier of a more modern stamp, ate his curries in the Indian mess. The cook, Ngoye, deprived of the General's guidance, showed himself to have one defect: total inability to plan a menu. Unless someone told him what to buy, what he bought was veal and spinach, and, as no one seemed to have any time to tell him what to buy, what we ate was veal and spinach – perfectly cooked, but veal and spinach. Even today, *le veau aux épinards* is an item I pass over on a restaurant menu.

For the change of diet they provided, therefore, the Ligne-Velter dinners were altogether satisfactory. Politically, little progress was made. Among the guests, I remember M van Waeyenbergh of the Union Minière, M Wénès of the Bas-Congo-Katanga railroad, and the director of the Brassekat breweries (*Simba La Bière du Lion*) : these three companies, and virtually all the industry and commerce of Katanga, formed part of the vast ramification which includes the Compagnie du Katanga, the Société Générale and Tanganyika Concessions. It is strange that I have no individual recollection of the other guests – about a half-dozen of them, all from the same industrial complex. My memory is a collective one, as if these people were not individuals at all, but part of one biological organism. It is a memory of many dusty, peering, red-rimmed eyes, of short necks and folds of yellow flesh, of indefatigable voracity and a congested, almost speechless, but formidable and proliferant vitality. The feeling was not quite that of sitting down to dine with a group of one's fellow-men; it was almost that of beginning to be oneself ingurgitated by some diffuse, repetitive, tentacular form of life. I had always taken the word 'octopus', applied to great industrial combines, to be a dead metaphor; now I felt the metaphor, coming alive, all around me.

I am sure that any one of these gentlemen would have made a jolly and reassuring figure on the beach at Ostend. The uniform and chilling impression which they made on these occasions was due not to their personal character but to the rooted hostility of the Union Minière group to the presence of the United Nations in Katanga. I knew, of course, all about the existence of that hostility, in theory, long before I came to Katanga but the abstract awareness – as one is aware of the rivalry of François Premier and Charles V – is quite a different thing from being in the same room with the interests concerned, incarnated in fleshy masses of cautious hate. The impression was chilling, not merely because it is not particularly heart-warming to sit there and be hated – in the middle of a room full of pictures of the Belgian Royal Family – but much more because one felt, for the first time, the full force of what one was really up against. Most of these people felt so strongly, and in such unison, because they were defending something solid which they had and which they intended to hold. The complex coalition which I represented had no motivation of equivalent clarity and power. I was in Katanga, rather than in Dublin or New York, because of ambiguous resolutions and an unspoken bargain which, though far-reaching, might, after all, break down. They were in Katanga, rather than in Ostend or the Borinage, because of the following figures:

'Average profits of firms principally active in Belgium and firms principally active in the Congo.'[1]

Year	Belgium Per cent	Congo Per cent
Average 1936–39	7	10·10
Average 1947–50	6·88	15·07
Average 1951–54	8·20	21·48
1955	8·19	18·47
1956	9·40	20·16
1957	9·49	21·00
1958	7·85	15·10

The Congo is a more profitable field of investment than Belgium; Katanga is the most profitable field of investment in the Congo. The total net profits of Union Minière alone from 1950 to 1959 are estimated at 31 thousand million Belgian francs.[2]

Léopold II addressed congresses about the civilizing mission of Belgium in the Congo; in private, the words which he wrote to a friend were: 'What a splendid piece of cake!' These gentlemen had a large slice of this splendid cake and, in their opinion, I was trying to take it off them. True, what I was trying to do in reality was to explain to them the imperative need – if they wanted to be sure of holding on to most of their slice – of letting go of what one might call the icing – the State structure of Katanga. I had felt, as I have said, that they, as hard-headed industrialists, ought to be capable of understanding this. I now began, not so much to detect, as somehow to apprehend physically, what was wrong with this argument. Industrialists are not 'hard-headed' in the sense of being unemotional. They are accessible – some of them even more accessible than the rest of us – to certain emotions such as that of greed, which, like any other emotion, may blind a man to his long-term interests.

To these audiences, then, I rehearsed certain themes, most of which were already well-worn in my conversations with Tshombe. I spoke of the imminence of the election of a recognized Central Government; the certainty that that Government would have to use or call in force if the secession of Katanga continued: the probability that it would call on the UN forces for aid in this and the possibility at least, that the Secretary-General, or the Security Council might agree; the certainty, finally, that, if the UN did not

---

[1] 'Net profits in relation to own resources (capital and reserves), from the balance sheets published by the firms.' Table in *Joye et Lewin, Les Trusts au Congo*, p. 57.
[2] *Ibid.*, p. 218.

itself agree to help, it could not now prevent the Government from calling in help from other African countries, and perhaps even from the Eastern bloc. If the companies wished, in their own interests, to prevent a catastrophe for Katanga, the time for them to use their influence was now.

These remarks were always heard with considerable stolidity. Only M van Waeyenbergh, of Union Minière, deigned to make any substantial reply. He said that people were quite wrong in imagining that he and his company had a dominating influence over Tshombe. He had seen Tshombe only once since his return, and that was at a public reception. Tshombe no doubt had his advisers, but the Union Minière was not interfering in politics. If things were drifting in the direction I indicated, that was very regrettable, but there was little the Union Minière could do about it.

That this was not entirely candid appears from a well-informed article, published about this time:

'For some reasons', wrote a Special Correspondent of *The Times*, 'the Union Minière has been forced to recognize the Tshombe Government. The shareholding in the company of the former Government of the Belgian Congo, amounting to 16·95 per cent and giving a voting power of 23·82 per cent is frozen pending a decision to which of the Congo Governments it shall be allotted. The dividend, however, is paid to Katanga in the form of an advance. The company also pays well over 2,000 million francs a year in miscellaneous duties and taxes (accounting for) at least 60 per cent of the national [sic] income. The figure does not show the true extent to which the company is the milch cow for Katanga, for it ignores house-building and a myriad "voluntary" activities. It happens that the Government supports free enterprise, not surprisingly, for the system not only keeps the treasury healthy but provides ministers and other senior advisers with salaries, cars, villas and other fringe benefits to a standard which would be impossible if the taxes were paid by ordinary citizens instead of foreign business men.'[1]

It was, therefore, apparent that the Union Minière's spokesmen

---

[1] *The Times*, July 24th, 1961. The '60 per cent' is, I think, an understatement. The 'forced to recognize' is a euphemism. The Conakat party, which is the Government of the single-party State of Katanga, was built up, financed and supported by the Union Minière. M Davister, who makes no bones about the European origin of this party, mentions among its supporters, 'especially the local managers of the big firms, known as "the colonels of the Union Minière".' (*Katanga, Enjeu du Monde*, p. 87.)

had a certain right to be heard when they addressed themselves to what *The Times* exactly one week later described editorially as 'that phenomenon of African nationalism, Mr Tshombe's Government'.[1]

Yet, within certain limits, what M van Waeyenbergh said was literally true. Tshombe was likely to be aware, through intermediaries, if not directly, of Union Minière thinking but, if he chose to disregard their opinions, or one of their opinions, while leaving their interests intact, there was probably indeed little enough, in normal circumstances, that the Union Minière as a company could, or at least would, do about it. Mr Munongo's repeated threats to sabotage Union Minière installations, were Katanga to be 'let down', were taken very seriously, in appearance at least, by the local management of Union Minière, and no doubt gave pause even to those in Brussels who may have had doubts about whether, in the changed circumstances, secession still remained the best way of protecting European business interests. Effectively these threats, and 'Munongoism' generally, were the weapon of the local ultras (Europeans plus Munongo) against any tendency to retreat on the part of the Brussels financiers.

Companies like the Union Minière may perhaps engineer a *coup d'état* against a Government which directly threatens their interests. They are not likely to use any sanctions against a Government which, on the whole, defends these interests even if it is doing so by means which may be in the long run dangerous and unwise. The short run, is, of course, a different matter; if the Union Minière, through effective external pressure, became convinced that the State of Katanga really was collapsing, it might be expected to act energetically.

It is possible, therefore, to accept the statement that the Union Minière as such was not actively and directly promoting secessionist politics in Katanga at this time. But of course such 'non-intervention' in the affairs of a State whose foundation the company had encouraged, if not instigated, a State which lived on duties paid to it by the company in defiance of the law of the Congo, and which was known to be defended on the international plane by the company's agents and money – was non-intervention of a rather special kind.

All in all, I concluded, as a result of these dinners, that the men on the spot, the local representatives of the companies, were determined to hang on, as long as possible, to the State of Katanga. There was, no doubt, a mixture of motives involved: it was not just sheer greed, there was also a certain kind of patriotism – not the dubious

[1] *The Times*, July 31st, 1961.

'Katangese nationalism' but the kind of patriotism which the Belgians of Elisabethville have in common with the Afrikaners and Algérie Française. The 'men on the spot', animated by this spirit, seemed to have more influence over affairs than their nominal positions as agents of the companies might lead one to suppose.

What had happened to my picture of the *dei ex machina* from Brussels? Alas, neither the Prince nor M Velter appeared to exercise the slightest charisma over these massive Evillois. Rather, to my surprise and chagrin, it seemed to be the other way around; the gentlemen from Brussels almost fawned on the old African hands. M Velter seemed to drink in the wisdom of M van Waeyenbergh when he said something like:

'I have been thirty-seven years in Africa and I am *not even beginning* to understand them.'

'Them', without antecedent, always referred to the African part of the 'multiracial Katangese nation'.

As for the Prince, he flung all political care to the winds and hooted with helpless laughter when the brewer, an enormously fat man – and more relaxed than the rest of the company – told the story of how, when waiting on a station platform, he had been approached by a harassed woman, holding a child by the hand, 'Excuse me, sir, but are you by any chance expecting a child?' 'Of course, Madame; can't you see that I am?

'Est-ce que vous attendez un enfant?'
'Vous voyez bien!'

But the social success of the series was undoubtedly M Wénès who, over the brandy, waxed sentimental over 'the African' – in this case, the 'unspoiled African', living in his traditional world, *le milieu coutumier*. He was, M Wénès ruminated at some length, really happier, in his simplicity and child-like nature than we, harassed sons of civilization.

It was a sort of Belgian Congo version of *The Scholar Gypsy*, with the difference that Arnold did not make any money out of the gypsies. In any case, the best thing that could be said for M Wénès and his friends was precisely that, in the service of the profit-motive, they had made inroads on the old *milieu coutumier*, with its disease and ignorance, and provided some decent housing, wages which were high by African standards, medical services in the mining towns, and schools which though inadequate in number, limited in curriculum and heavily 'paternalist' in the character of instruction were still better than no schools at all. It was true that the companies

were not the losers by the existence, throughout most of the Congo
and of Katanga in particular, of primitive and poverty-stricken
populations. 'It is said', wrote the Special Correspondent of *The
Times*, 'that there is poverty in some of the remote villages.'[1] Some
of these remote villages could be reached comfortably in the course
of any Sunday afternoon's drive along the Elisabethville-Jadotville
road, the central axis of Katangese prosperity. The villages, remote
and near, furnished a reserve of docile labour, easily attracted, often
aboard M Wénès's trains, into the quite relative paradise of the
mining towns.[2]

I heard M Wénès's hymn to the simple life, therefore, without any
great gush of responding sentiment. It was otherwise, I saw – somewhat to my disillusionment – with Gatsby and Guermantes. When
the railway magnate had stopped talking and gone, M Velter
turned to me, clasping his hands, and said:

'The old Wénès 'as shown this evening a side of 'is character
I never, never 'ave before suspected. 'E is poet!'

This· was not, I felt, a way in which the very rich should be
encouraged to be different from us. I looked M Velter coldly in the
eye and what I saw there were tears. I was sorry, because I liked
M Georges Velter, whereas M Wénès's discourse only made me
think of the words of that astringent man, the Archbishop of
Elisabethville:

Cela me donne la nausée!

The qualifications which I introduced into the *Benito Cereno*
picture, as a result of these encounters were roughly these:

The old slave-owners are still in control of the ship, and of the
slaves, as far as anyone is. But the slave-owners are divided. Some of
them fear the ship may be headed for shoals or rocks. Others think
she should stick to her course. As the second group are the tougher
and more resolute element, and nearer to the bridge, and as some
of them threaten to scuttle the ship if a new course is set, the black
helmsman holds the course unchanged into uncharted waters.

---

[1] *The Times*, July 15th, 1961.

[2] 'No mining company', declared Governor-General Pierre Ryckmans in 1935,
'can claim the right to be surrounded by a dead zone in which destitution does its
recruiting for it.' (Ryckmans, *Etapes et Jalons*, (1935), p. 22.) I cannot say whether
the Union Minière had 'claimed' such a right or not, but Katanga, outside the
mining centres, is exactly as it would have been had that right been claimed and
granted. The Governor-General, in the same speech, made the proud and relevant
claim that 'as an element in the cost of production our natives can stand competition from any quarter'. (*Etapes et Jalons*, p. 26.)

11

PHENOMENA OF
AFRICAN NATIONALISM

'D'Affrike i ad un Affrican venut.'
The Song of Roland

'Because most Belgians do not want to involve themselves in the politics of Katanga', wrote the Special Correspondent of *The Times*, 'they bitterly resent the presence of the United Nations. The fear of being on the black list as a *conseiller occulte* is another thing that makes life nerve-racking for them.'

The correspondent goes on to describe some of the forms taken by this detachment from politics: 'From only one quarter', he writes, 'do they draw any comfort and that is from the Katanga Government. Mr Tshombe is their only protection. Isolated, misunderstood, fearful, they take refuge in supporting, at all costs, the system that provides them with a niche. The result is an obsequiousness towards Ministers that would be despicable if it were not pathetic. Cries of *vive le Président* come more ecstatically from European than African throats.'[1]

The behaviour here accurately described was not hypocritical, and its inconsequence is only apparent. Like most people in possession, the Belgians of Elisabethville genuinely failed to see that by 'supporting at all costs the system that provided them with a niche' they were automatically 'involving themselves in politics'. 'Politics', for them, referred exclusively to political activities which were likely to lead to social change, and in that sense, it is absolutely true that they did not wish to involve themselves in politics. For them, 'the

---

[1] *The Times*, July 24th, 1961.

independence of the Congo' was politics; 'the independence of
Katanga' was simply a fact which one accepted. In cheering
Mr Tshombe they felt, I think, a rush of emotions which they
regarded as 'non-political' – patriotism, loyalty, even a kind of
broadmindedness, of generosity and daring, the sense of doing
something just a little 'fast':

> *'Look at me! Cheering a black man!'*

They felt, I think, for the moment, better and more advanced than
those old segregationist fuddy-duddies over in Rhodesia; keeping, for
the moment, well at the back of their minds the fact that the reason
why they were cheering this particular black man was that he
represented, for them, the best chance of maintaining essentially
the same system as that which their more fortunate neighbours in
Rhodesia could still permit themselves the luxury of maintaining
without having to cheer any black man. (Although, even in
Rhodesia, some were beginning to discern a potential, conditional
cheer-worthiness in people like Mr Harry Nkumbula.) It would
not be unfair to say that this feeling was somewhat evanescent,
restricted and superficial. Towards Africans generally their feeling
was what it had always been, a mixture of fear and contempt;
their remarks about *la mentalité bantoue* showed little trace of what
they sometimes regarded as their new-found liberalism. But for
Tshombe personally their affection was genuine; unlike any of his
colleagues, even Munongo, he had crossed the line and was – for
most purposes – no longer really thought of quite as 'one of them'.
Tshombe knew this and felt in the same way. He had even his own
manner of referring to *la mentalité bantoue*. 'I know my brothers', he
would say. The words *je connais mes frères* were invariably the prelude
to the same catalogue of weaknesses as a European would introduce
under the heading of *la mentalité bantoue*.[1] He had ceased to be one
of 'them'; he had become, not Belgian, of course, but Katangese.

---

[1] The *mentalité bantoue*, as far as it existed, was largely a product of Belgian education. The conclusions of the Congrès Scientifique d'Elisabethville (1950) on how
to teach Africans have been summarized as follows: 'For the Congolese pupil there
is no such thing as demonstration. One must proceed by aphorisms and the conclusion must be extracted from a parable, an anecdote, a fable: abstract ideas and
pure science cannot be understood. . . . For the Black, experimental proof does not
exist and would not be acceptable: one must invoke superior authority.' (Merlier,
Le Congo etc., p. 224). Thus the Belgian authorities defined *a priori* what 'the
African mind' was capable of understanding, and then taught it in a way designed
to keep it within these limits. Tshombe himself was rather better taught, by
American missionaries.

The Katangese Nation consisted, for most practical purposes, of the Belgians of the South Katanga towns, plus Tshombe.

The European fear of being 'on the black list' must, in many cases, indeed have been 'nerve-racking'. When M Thyssens was expelled and later one or two other *conseillers occultes* – a lawyer, M Herman; a journalist, M Decoster – the Europeans generally seem to have felt that, since they sincerely did not regard these people as having been engaged in what they regarded as politics, the ways of the United Nations were inscrutable and arbitrary, as well as being foolish and wicked, and any European might be arrested and hurled out of the country - his own country – at any moment. It was the white-hunt, *la chasse aux blancs*, of which Spaak – even Spaak – complained.

In the vast majority of cases, of course, the fears were groundless. A *conseiller occulte* had to cease to be *occulte*, had to become a vocal, even clamorous politician, before he ran any risk of being classified as an *adeuxien* – the· word, loathly opposite of *onusien*, by which we designated persons falling under paragraph A.2 of the resolution of February 21st. There was no *chasse aux blancs*, and the European population as a whole – if it refrained from working for the Ministry of Information, or otherwise becoming conspicuously political – had nothing to fear from paragraph.A.2. Yet, as is often the case with fears which seem inadequately motivated, these fears had deep foundations in reality. The resolution in question was the product of the Americo-Afro-Asian 'unspoken bargain' and it was aimed at securing, by indirect means, the end of the secession of Katanga. That end did imply a *chasse aux blancs* for it was the *blancs* who had made and supported the secession. If the UN could have been ruthless and determined, in the use of paragraph A.2 as a lever for the purpose for which it was intended, it *would* have engaged in a *chasse aux blancs*; the use it did make of A.2 – a few token repatriations – was intended mainly, I believe (apart from its use in New York), as a warning to the Elisabethville Europeans generally. Unfortunately, as tends to be the fate of warnings delivered on behalf of a group within which there is known to be a division of opinion, it irritated without deterring. These repatriations were, as I have said, from a UN point of view, 'taps on a wedge'. But taps on a wedge are not much use unless followed by hammering, and the Europeans of Elisabethville, vaguely frightened though they were, believed that no hammering from the side of the UN threatened the maintenance of the State of Katanga. The main reason they believed this was that almost all the foreign representatives in Elisabethville were drawn from those countries which opposed any serious implementation of the resolution – representatives who gave the impression, almost without knowing they were doing so, that serious implementation was not within the bounds of possibility. In the British Consul's view – and this was an official, not a personal, view – what I was there to apply was the Security Council resolution *as interpreted in Sir Patrick Dean's reservation*, and the resolution, as so interpreted, boded no harm at all to the Independent State of Katanga. In reality, however, what I was there to apply was the resolution, *as interpreted by the Secretary-General*, and the Secretary-General had very clearly indicated that he would *not* be guided by Sir Patrick Dean's reservation, but by the consensus of those countries, mainly Afro-Asian, participating in the operation.[1]

Our warning taps, with the discreetly negative chorus of the Consular Corps in the background, did not have the effect intended. As a prelude to the implementation of the resolution, *on an interpretation guided by an Afro-Asian consensus*, these repatriations were ominous indeed for the State of Katanga; as a prelude to the implementation of the resolution, *as interpreted by Sir Patrick Dean*, our 'taps' were simply so much clumsy, inconsiderate and irritating noise. And that is how they seemed to the Europeans of Elisabethville, *consulibus Dunnett et Lambroschini*.

In any case, having no choice, we tapped away. Mr Tshombe had agreed, on that trying Muller/Thyssens day, to remove Europeans from the political posts in the Civil Service, and a joint UN-Katangese commission was set up for this purpose under the chairmanship of M Albert Nyembo. M Nyembo, who came from the far north of Katanga, near Kongolo, had been elected to the Congolese Parliament as a Conakat deputy and had been Under-Secretary of State for Defence in the Lumumba Cabinet. On the secession of Katanga he had joined the Katangese Government as Secretary for State for *la Fonction Publique*. This made him nominal head of a civil service which was still, in reality, run by Belgians. '*Les noirs gouvernent*' as *La Libre Belgique* remarked, '*mais n'administrent pas*'.[2] It was certainly true that they did not administer. M Nyembo was a chubby, rather innocent-looking man and he and his colleagues – all, for this unusual occasion, Africans – were quite excited about the subject under discussion. The Europeans in Elisabethville at this time were talking about nothing but lists – *liste ONU, liste*

---

[1] See pp. 61–2.
[2] *La Libre Belgique*, July 8th and 9th, 1961.

Spaak, liste Tombelaine, liste Sendwe – there was even supposed to be a
liste Bomboko. We now found, to our surprise, that there was a *liste
Nyembo*, much longer than any of its competitors. The Belgian picture
of these discussions was that the UN representatives, in their blind
zeal for the proscription of Europeans, were putting pressure on the
Africans to remove Belgians whom these Africans trusted and relied
on. The reality was different.

On the first day we produced our list, mainly *chefs de cabinet* of
the principal Ministers. Victor Tignée was there; so was Carlos
Huyghe of the Ministry of Defence, best known for his mysterious
feud with that much-expelled and ever-recurrent English mercenary,
Captain Browne; the unlikely sounding name of Onckelinckx, of the
Ministry of Commerce, provided a link with the *liste Spaak*; Jean
Bartelous of Tshombe's own 'cabinet', and a few other prominent
people completed the list. On the second day M Nyembo and his
colleagues agreed, with little demur, to these names. Then M
Nyembo asked whether they, the Katangese, had a right to suggest
names? We said that we were interested only in political advisers;
if they informed us that certain foreigners, Belgians or others, were
giving political advice, then we should certainly have to consider
whether paragraph A.2 did not apply. We read them paragraph A.2
– immediate withdrawal and evacuation of all foreign and political
advisers, Belgian or other. M Nyembo and his friends seemed, from
their smiles, to think paragraph A.2 rather well drafted. M Nyembo
himself favoured an inclusive interpretation of this paragraph.
'All Belgians', he said with simplicity, 'are political advisers.' His
colleagues, the nominal heads of the various civil departments,
eagerly corroborated this; each had his own list of Belgians who,
they said, gave them political advice. We noted the names, about
forty in all. M Nyembo went to the door and satisfied himself that
there was no one in the outer office. 'Add', he said as he came back,
'my *chef de cabinet*, M B——. I added M B—— provisionally.

That afternoon I received a letter, signed by M Nyembo, protesting against my arbitrary action in classifying the innocent M B——
as a political adviser; M B—— said the letter, was a Civil Servant of
high ability, integrity and complete political impartiality; he was
absolutely indispensable to the proper working of the Ministry, and
must be removed from the list.

That evening I met M Nyembo at a party. He was anxious to talk
to me. 'Did you get my letter?' he inquired. I said his letter rather
surprised me. 'Listen', said M Nyembo. 'That letter was written by
B—— and of course I had to sign it. What I want you to do now is to

write me back a strong letter, saying you know M B—— is a political
adviser and that he must go. A really *strong* letter please – something
with threats in it.'

All this put us in something of a quandary. On the one hand, the
Nyembo Doctrine contained truth. All Belgians, or almost all, *were*
political advisers. The distinctions which one made in New York
between 'technicians' who were good and might stay, and 'politicians' who were bad and must go, had little relevance here since
almost all the 'politicians' had some technical function and all the
technicians of any importance had also, in this secessionist State,
a political importance. In New York – and Leopoldville – they were
inclined to think that, because they described Katanga in all
official documents as a 'province', and 'recognized' its administration as a 'provincial administration', the province and its administration retained a certain reality, providing a sort of political
vacuum, within which 'non-political' Belgians and others continued
their purely technical work. But the fact which forced itself on you,
when you lived in Elisabethville, was that 'the province of Katanga'
no longer existed except in UN documents. The realities on the spot
were the State of Katanga and those who were fighting it. The
foreign servants – if they could be described as servants – of that
State could therefore never be 'non-political'. The man who
ordered the boots for the gendarmerie, or the paper for the bank-
notes of Katanga, was executing a political act. And the fear which
a Belgian *Chef de Cabinet* could still inspire in the Katangese Secretary
of State told one more about the real nature of the State of Katanga
than one would be likely to learn from reading either *The Times*
editorials or UN documents.

On the other hand, Katanga, like the rest of the Congo, did
desperately need foreign technicians. Teachers and educational
officials, even though they were not 'non-political', even if they were
loading their teaching with political propaganda – under the cover
of morality and anti-communism – were still needed. It was better
that a child should be taught to read the Katangese Declaration of
Independence than that it should not be taught to read at all.
And it might be that, in some cases at least, the people now black-
listed, or white-listed, by M Nyembo and his friends were among
the better and more honest administrators, and had become unpopular by opposing the corrupt practices of this or that Minister.

In the end we decided that, as the list was to be cleared finally
with Tshombe, we would allow all the names, except those of
teachers, to stand provisionally, 'conceding' them later in order to

get his agreement to the names we really wanted, such as Tignée and Huyghe.

So it worked out. Tshombe at the end of July challenged all the names which Nyembo and his friends had put on. Nyembo said that he had pointed out all along that these people were not political advisers. We dropped them one by one, holding on only to the names on our own list. Poor Nyembo's face grew longer with every name abandoned. Finally we reached the name of M B——. Tshombe turned in surprise to Nyembo.

'Your own *chef de cabinet*? Did you agree to putting his name on the joint list?'

M Nyembo had my letter, and a copy of his own letter by him. He quickly established that he had defended M B—— – virtually to the death – and that only the most brutal kind of *force majeure* had overcome his objections.

'We can drop him, of course,' said Tshombe.

I caught M Nyembo's imploring eye.

'I am afraid', I said, 'M B—— must go. We have good reason to know that he is a political adviser.'

This exercise led to the departure of the most obvious advisers, announced at the beginning of August. The most interesting thing we learned from it was that the senior Africans in the Civil Service and the junior members of the Cabinet not only still went in fear of the Belgians, but also went in fear of Tshombe, *and in exactly the same way as they did of Belgians.*

For them, as for the Europeans, and for himself Tshombe had become an honorary white.

The departure of people like Tignée – and Crèvecoeur, who left at the end of July for indefinite 'leave' – was of value only in so far as it might serve to promote the great end of Congolese reunification. The great question at this stage, in the latter half of July, was whether the Conakat deputies – including the equivocal M Nyembo – could be induced to attend the Parliamentary session in Leopoldville, for which the deputies, including those from Stanleyville and Bakwanga, capital of the vaguely independent mining State of South Kasai, were now beginning to gather. With this was linked the question of whether Tshombe would attend a 'summit' in Leopoldville with Kasavubu, Gizenga and (perhaps) the Mulopwe Albert Kalonji. The evolution of Katangan policy on these questions is briefly but accurately set out in the following extracts from reports in *La Libre Belgique*:

'*L.B. July 5th, 1961*: The Katangese deputies will not take part in the parliamentary session, for the security of the parliamentarians could not be guaranteed by the United Nations, which were also present at Coquilhatville. – *Unanimous decision of the National Assembly, sitting on July 4th.*

'L.B. *July 12th, 1961:* As regards the next parliamentary session of July 1st [*sic*] M Kimba ("Foreign Minister" of Katanga) declared that the Katangese Government was not opposed to the sending of its parliamentarians to Leopoldville but that this was entirely a matter for the Katangese Assembly, which is to meet to take a decision in full knowledge of the facts. – *Interview with A. F. P.*

'L.B. *July 13th, 1961:* He (Tshombe) could not take the risk of sending parliamentarians to Leopoldville until the Congolese leaders had met in a summit conference and reached agreement. . . . This meeting must be held outside the Congo, because any new meeting in the Congo, even in Katanga, would be subject to foreign military pressures. – *Press Conference of President Tshombe.*

'L.B. *July 17th, 1961:* "We believe the convocation and the meeting of the Parliament to be illegal." – *Telegram dated July 15th, dispatched by Mr Samalenghe, Minister of Information, to President Kasavubu and the United Nations.*

'L.B. *July 18th, 1961:* "A summit meeting inside the former Belgian Congo is the *sine qua non* condition for Katangese participation in the parliamentary session in Leopoldville."

'That is the definitive reply given on Monday morning by President Tshombe to the representatives of the UN.

'Mr Munongo who, having taken part in the meeting, gave the news to the Press, added: "We are always willing for discussions with the Congolese leaders of the four magnetic poles (Leopoldville, Stanleyville, Bakwanga, Elisabethville). We should prefer Kamina base but we are even ready to go to Stanleyville. I must recall to you that Katanga has always been in agreement on the principle of the meeting of Parliament." ' – *Press Conference by Munongo.*

A signed article, in the same paper which faithfully chronicled these successive and inconsistent positions, made the following comment:

'In this whole matter of the meeting of the Congolese Parliament, Katanga has adopted a realistic position and has adhered to a single line of conduct.'[1]

The comment can hardly, I think, be justified, unless we take it

---

[1] *La Libre Belgique*, August 1st, 1961. Article signed E. M.

that the 'single line of conduct' was not to go to Leopoldville, and not to participate in the election of a Congolese Government, but to give Katanga's numerous and active friends abroad opportunities to hold their favourite line: 'Mr Tshombe is a reasonable man, and not at all opposed to preserving the integrity of the Congo, on some realistic basis. But *either* his opponents refuse to give him the concessions which he reasonably asks, such as a meeting outside the Congo (or inside the Congo) *or* – Katanga is a democracy and the National Assembly has yet to meet and decide the question (which, in any case, it has already decided in the negative).' These reasons were not, of course, presented simultaneously, but any one of them could serve, in some context, the great purposes of gaining time and conceding nothing. In this game, the great art was to make, with much publicity, the most conciliatory offer which you were quite sure would *not* be accepted – thereby making the other fellow look at his most unreasonable. Thus Tshombe had, verbally and in private, agreed, in his talk with Nwokedi and myself at the end of June, that he would be willing to attend a 'summit' at Kamina. Since then he had *publicly* insisted on a meeting outside the Congo. It was only after mid-July, when pressure to compromise was being heavily applied, and when Tshombe and Munongo and their friends were quite sure that there was no longer any danger at all of Kamina being accepted, that the Kamina offer was published, as a new formula. Munongo, for reasons of his own, to which we shall come in a moment, added Stanleyville.

The conversations which produced these meagre and twisted results were long, frequent and exhausting for at least one of the participants. I had been trying, from the beginning, to drive home Katanga's need to be in at the formation of a legal Government. Now Mr Khiary, who was nominally acting Head of UN Civil Operations in the Congo, and in reality the political brains of the operation, came to Elisabethville, on July 17th, as a special emissary of the Secretary-General, to invite Mr Tshombe, most pressingly, to attend a summit at Leopoldville, and to release the Conakat deputies to attend the Parliament in Lovanium.

Khiary presented the case indefatigably over many hours, with immense eloquence and skill. Tshombe, Munongo, Kimba, Kibwe, Kiwele, Samalenghe, sat round in a ring at the Palace, drinking beer or champagne. Khiary drank nothing – like the strict Moslem he is – but he held the room spellbound. His theme was Africa: the need for an African solution. He admitted freely, on my behalf, that I could never understand Africa; he and they were Africans, this was their continent. Mr O'Brien would tell them about the resolutions; that was his affair. He, Khiary, did not attach so much importance to the resolutions in themselves. Nor was he at all opposed to the State of Katanga. Why should there not be a State of Katanga? In any case why should people in Brussels or New York – Europeans, Americans or Russians – concern themselves with what kind of State or States there was, or were, here in Central Africa? That was a matter for Africans. All he wanted them to do was to meet, and reach a settlement – any settlement at all – with their brother Africans. Any settlement reached would be endorsed by African opinion. On the other hand, if they did *not* reach a settlement *entre Africains*, then the mechanisms of world politics would come into play, and when they did, Katanga would be wiped off the face of the earth.

Mr Khiary here clapped his hands with the gesture – very characteristic of him – of a man banging together a pair of invisible cymbals.

The Katangese Ministers, to my utter amazement, started clapping too. Whether they were applauding a rhetorical *tour de force* – Mr Khiary had been building up his effect very skilfully for more than an hour – or whether they were pleased with his great frankness, I cannot say. I think it was the former: certainly Mr Khiary always attracted a larger turn-out of Cabinet Ministers – a better 'house', you might say – than I alone was able to do, with my dry little piece about the resolutions.

Yet, despite the magnetism of Mr Khiary's rhetoric, despite the immense personal impression which he made, the result was entirely negative. Mr Tshombe did not go to any summit and the Conakat deputies did not participate in the meetings of parliament for the election of a Congolese Government.

None of this depressed Mr Khiary in the least. On the contrary, he would smile benignly when, after hours of labouring to persuade Tshombe to go to Leopoldville for a summit, he heard on the radio some new explanation of Tshombe's willingness to meet the other leaders in any place at all, except the only one in which they were willing to meet him. 'A funny President you have here,' he would say. 'Do you think he is quite sincere?' Then his face would become grave and anxious again as the news from Tunisia, then very bad, began to come in.

Since the Thyssens affair, Mr Khiary approved of me, and he had, I think, more confidence in me than he had in most other onusians, which is not saying a great deal. During these visits, he and his confidant-bodyguard, a burly Tunisian named Hatab, used to stay with me in Les Roches. I have a vivid memory of one evening when the three of us came back from an exceptionally long recitation to the Cabinet. Something – a little white spot, it seemed at first – on the dark front step caught his attention. It was a large, pale, ropey-looking spider. Mr Khiary looked carefully at the spider.

'*Tiens!*' he said, '*une tarantelle! Abattez-la, Hatab!*'

Mr Hatab, without haste, liquidated the tarantula. I felt that he would have liquidated me with equal efficiency, although no doubt with more compunction, if what Mr Khiary had said was:

'*Tiens! Un diplomate! Abattez-le, Hatab!*'

The house that evening seemed full of these insects whose bite, according to the Tunisians, was fatal in a few minutes.[1] There was one in a corner of the dining-room and no less than three in the bathroom, one of which was residing in a towel with which I had thought of drying my face. Fortunately, the encounter on the door-step had been of a nature to induce one to be wary about things like towels. Such a visitation of 'tarantulas' was highly unusual, it was said; the cook, Ngoye, said they had been left in 'by the neighbours', but produced no evidence, and, being a member of the Balubakat, was hardly an impartial source. In any case, the little creatures, whether actually deposited by a thoughtful neighbour or not, did rather faithfully reflect the prevailing state of public opinion. As I went to sleep that night – having first checked the sheets with extreme care – I realized more clearly than before that Central Africa was quite a long distance from the Hill of Howth.

It is hard to give an impression of Mr Khiary's enigmatic and formidable personality, without allowing a faint suggestion of the sinister to creep in. And it is true that a touch – the faintest possible touch – of the sinister was actually there: just enough, in reality, to set in relief the charm and unobtrusive kindness of this singular man. When I visited Leopoldville for conversations I stayed in his apartment, and I used to have to leave horribly early in the morning.

---

[1] I gave Professor David Webb of Trinity College, Dublin, a description of these insects and he was kind enough to write me in a letter the following comment: 'The word *tarantula* is much misapplied and the genuine *tarantula*, which is a Mediterranean beast, is not particularly dramatic looking. I am pretty sure that yours was something else, and I think you had better call it a venomous spider. I cannot, of course, say how dangerous this one was, but some spiders have quite dangerous bites; they are not, however, necessarily the most terrifying ones and I suspect yours may have been a bit of a bluffer. Was he a mercenary?'

The ONUC plane for Elisabethville never left before 11 a.m. but it was always supposed to leave at dawn – 6 a.m. – and one had to report at Ndjili airport half an hour before that, in order to spend five hours or more looking at the limited stock of Africana in the airport hall. These arrangements were known as 'movement control' and they were mainly in the hands of Danes who, for this not quite adequate reason, had the distinction of being the most unpopular of all the national contingents engaged in the UN operation in the Congo. For these early departures Mr Khiary, who always worked far into the night, would get up and make the breakfast. When I think of him, two superimposed pictures come into my mind. One is of his closed, watchful face in conference, looking like some impenetrable and resourceful envoy of Genghis Khan. The other is of a tired man in shirt-sleeves, stolidly setting out plates and boiled eggs, looking like an elderly overworked waiter in a Marseilles café.

Overworked, at any rate, he was, driven on by an intense patriotism; he saw his UN work as essentially a patriotic service, the collective defence of the small and vulnerable countries. Success of the UN effort in the Congo justified every effort, for failure, by wrecking the United Nations, could deprive the independence of the new countries of what hard-won reality it had. In his drive for the success of ONUC he had little patience with legalistic detail, with paragraph this of resolution that, and what the Secretary-General had said in August 1960. He had no patience at all with the theory, often asserted in the early days by Hammarskjold, and never explicitly abandoned, that the United Nations must refrain from interfering in the internal affairs of the Congo. 'What are we here for then?' he would ask. '*Il faut faire de la politique!*' And on the word *politique* his brown eyes, usually so disconcertingly blank, would flash.

He and Mr Gardiner did 'make politics', throwing all semblance of non-intervention to the winds, in the precincts of the Lovanium, closed to all the world except to the Congolese Parliamentarians and to them. Ten days before the Government of the Congo was elected, he showed me, written on the back of an envelope, the core of the Government he hoped to see elected: Prime Minister, Adoula; Vice-Premiers, Gizenga, Sendwe, Bolikango. It all came true, except for Bolikango. Bolikango's trouble was that he was convinced that he was going to be President, replacing Kasavubu. 'There is nothing *I* can do about it,' he told Khiary, 'there is nothing *you* can do about it. God has so decided. *C'est Dieu qui l'a voulu.*'

Whatever about God and Bolikango – and people like the Mulopwe Kalonji who thought he *was* God, and had to have his meals at the Lovanium brought up by his disciples on a tray – the emergence of a legal Government from among the chaos of pretenders was a great achievement and a turning-point. If Mr Khiary was less disappointed than one might have imagined at the refusal of Tshombe's supporters to participate, this was because he had feared that Tshombe's participation might simply wreck the *rapprochement* of the other leaders, and push the unhappy country back into anarchy. 'We must try to bring him in', he would say, 'but it will complicate our task.' In these circumstances, I sometimes felt – despite the great resources of persuasion which he tirelessly deployed – that he would have spoken somewhat differently, perhaps less eloquently and with more material arguments, if he had really wanted to succeed. I thought of the instructions Count Sforza is said to have given to the Italian plenipotentiaries on the colonies question: 'Fight to the end, but lose.' *Luttez jusqu'au bout, mais perdez.*

Even so, he came near enough to winning to alarm Munongo and indeed to provoke him into making what was, from Katanga's point of view, a serious mistake. Even Munongo had fallen for a while under Khiary's spell, and had indeed led the applause for his 'African' speech. But he quickly recovered and informed the Press that Khiary was not an African at all 'but an Arab and the descendant of slave-traders'. This was not merely ungracious but ungrateful, for the foundation of the Empire of M'Siri, and the Munongo family fortunes, had been the revenues derived from selling slaves to the Arabs. But Munongo by this time was ruffled by the signs of deterioration in Katanga's position, by the Leopoldville-Stanleyville *rapprochement* and by what he called the 'provocation and blackmail of the UN'. This phrase referred to the action taken, after my return from the north, under the authority of the 'military movements' clause in the February resolution, to bring to an end the punitive activities of the gendarmerie in North Katanga, in so far as such activities were based on centres where both the gendarmerie and UN forces were present.[1] At Nyemba on July 17th, the gendarmerie, in the belief that this prohibition – like some other previous UN decisions – could be safely disregarded, started to remove a UN road block. UN Indian troops, after a warning, opened fire; two gendarmes were killed, and the rest of the party fled into the bush. Mr Munongo then announced, to the alarm of the more prudent supporters of his régime, that he was about to give 'the most important Press conference in the history of Katanga'. Mr Tshombe took to his bed.

---

[1] Chapters VIII and IX.

The Press conference was devoted mainly to a not unexpected attack on the United Nations and Belgium; it contained a fairly accurate, though bitter, account of the America-Afro-Asian 'unspoken bargain'. But the key words of his discourse were the following:

'The Government intends to send, shortly, a Katangese delegation to Stanleyville, to make contacts and lay down a political line capable of conciliating the various Congolese factions.

'Finally, if the future of our country demands it, since the free world does not want to commit itself, and since only the USSR seems capable, at the present time, of helping its friends effectively, we shall not hesitate, together with our Congolese brothers, to seek its effective aid for the organization and future exploitation of the resources (*mise en valeur*) of our young State.

'International opinion must not see in this declaration a piece of facile and perfunctory blackmail (*un chantage facile et sans conviction*)'.[1]

On the whole, informed international opinion thought that that was just what it was. A statesman who is seriously contemplating an appeal to the Soviet Union does not usually, in approaching this theme, refer to the NATO countries as the 'free world', and in fact the announcement was never seriously followed up. There was talk of sending a delegation to – mysteriously enough – Yugoslavia, and to another, unnamed, 'Eastern' country, but, in fact, no delegation went anywhere except to South Africa. Radio Moscow, in referring to the suggestion, used some phrases about 'lackeys', 'murderers', and 'blood-stained hands' which seemed to imply a negative attitude towards a Katanga-Soviet pact. In the West, Mr Munongo's statement was a windfall for politicians who were under fire from the right for betraying the anti-Communist bastion of Katanga; an anti-Communist bastion that seems to be calling in the Russians no longer attracts quite the same degree of sympathy.[2] Even in Belgium, so conservative a politician as M Paul Struye, while paying homage to 'the sense of moderation and political sense which Mr Munongo had always shown' – no doubt a reference to the Press conference on the death of Lumumba – felt that this 'fantastic philippic' must be due to the removal, by the United Nations, of the sagacious and moderate Belgian political advisers.

---

[1] *L. B.* July 21st, 1961.

[2] Thomas Tshombe, Moïse's brother, who was then leading a Katanga mission in the United States, declared on July 29th that Munongo's statement 'should not be taken literally'.

In Elisabethville the posters showing an African with a spear and a map of Katanga and the words: 'Katanga, Shield of Africa against Communism' remained in place. It seemed that a Minister had behaved in a rather foolish and pointless way, but that otherwise life went on as before. This impression was, I believe, misleading. Munongo, who was not, as had been expected, 'disavowed' by Tshombe, had served notice that he would use any threat, and perhaps any means, to prevent the State of Katanga from being reabsorbed into the Congo. The significance of the words 'and future exploitation' in his statement was underlined in Belgium by a report, carried by the Inbel agency, to the effect that 'political and financial circles' in Elisabethville considered Mr Munongo's statement to be 'an ultimatum to the free world'.[1] An ultimatum to the corresponding 'political and financial circles in Belgium', to deter them from trying to liquidate the particular political forms which had hitherto protected their interests, might be a more accurate description.

Tshombe, trembling as so often on the verge of going to Leopoldville, dined with me in Les Roches a few days before the Central Government was elected. He had with him Mr Kiwele and he seemed to be toying with the idea of a change of policy, but wistfully, as if he knew the making of any fundamental change to be beyond his power.[2] He talked again about the old days in Sandoa. Another guest, M Frenkiel, the Rector of the University, showed some of the symptoms described by the Special Correspondent of *The Times* (above, p. 178). He hung on Mr Tshombe's lips as if the history of the former, and now most happily resolved, financial difficulties of a West Katanga ex-grocer was the most enthralling narrative he had ever heard. Mr Kiwele, a more stimulating conversationalist, said that if I called him *macaque* he would jump at my throat. 'Before independence', he said, 'people like him' – indicating M Frenkiel – 'used to call us *macaques* to our faces. Now they don't.' He looked at M Frenkiel with some satisfaction.

Tshombe went, on July 29th, not to Leopoldville, but to Brazzaville. The difference is small geographically, but politically enormous. 'Leopoldville', at this stage, might have meant a serious attempt to come to terms. Brazzaville, on the other hand, was

----

[1] *La Libre Belgique*, July 24th, 1961.

[2] Tshombe was under considerable pressure from the United States at this time to go to Leopoldville to come to terms. (See 'Report dated July 15th of the the Katangese Information Mission in the United States to President Tshombe', in *Congo, 1961*, p. 289.) But apparently this pressure was offset by other pressures.

virtually enemy territory as far as Congolese nationalists were concerned; its radio was hostile to Congolese unity, and it was believed to be a centre for financial-political transactions damaging to the Congo and very helpful to Katanga. Tshombe's journey to Brazzaville was therefore seen not as an attempt to come to terms, but rather as an attempt to detach, away from the Government in process of formation, people like Kasavubu and Mobutu, formerly his partners in 'the spirit of Tananarive'. He somehow failed to make contact with Kasavubu; he subsequently blamed Khiary for this and – although the evidence is confused and the Brazzaville Government's own role is far from clear – he may have been right. At this critical stage, Khiary would not have welcomed interventions in Congolese politics from the right bank of the river, the territory of the politician whom M Hatab – it was his only joke – used to call 'l'Abbé Vulgaire Filou'. M Khiary had delivered his invitation and had honourably stated the case for accepting. Had it been accepted, he would have done his best. Had it been refused, he would not have been disappointed. But he was not a man to put up with the kind of refusal-acceptance which Brazzaville signified. 'Ce n'est pas sérieux, ça!', he would say on such occasions, his voice and eyebrows rising sharply. He usually found ways of discouraging activities which he regarded as 'pas sérieux'. Tshombe returned, disappointed and apprehensive, to Elisabethville on the eve of the day, August 2nd, on which the Adoula Government was formed with Gizenga as one Vice-President and with Jason Sendwe, head of the Balubakat and sponsor of the Province of Lualaba, as another. The situation about which Tshombe had been warned so often had come about: there was now a legal Congolese Government, recognized by the United Nations and without Katangese participation.

On the following day it was announced, but without the fanfare which preceded Munongo's Elisabethville-Moscow axis, that the Vice-Premier of the State of Katanga, Mr Kibwe, and the Minister of Public Works, Mr Kitenge, would visit the Union of South Africa. This visit, unlike the 'rapprochement with the East', which was still being discussed in the papers, actually took place. The pair arrived in Johannesburg on August 3rd and Mr Kibwe on August 8th made a radio statement in favour of 'economic co-operation' between Katanga and South Africa.[1] Mr Daniel Tshombe, another of Moïse's brothers, went to Angola, on a similar mission, on August

---

[1] Congo, 1961, pp. 593–594.

22nd.[1] Despite the quite genuinely 'anti-white' feelings which existed among the Katangese Ministers – and there was, among them, a bitter, as it were a repressed, racism such as was altogether lacking in people like Sendwe and Mwamba Ilunga – they yet knew well that when trouble was impending for their régime, it must seek its friends among the rulers of Angola, the Rhodesias and the Union of South Africa. That fact best describes the 'phenomenon of African nationalism' – to use the language of *The Times* – that the State of Katanga was.

---

[1] *Ibid.*, p. 596.

12

THE ROAD TO RUMPUNCH

'Fly away Peter! Fly away Paul
Come back Peter! Come back Paul'
Nursery rhyme

The Provincial Assembly of Katanga, at its last meeting on July 17th, 1960, declared itself to be, 'henceforward, the House of Representatives of the Republic of Katanga'.[1] In the Constitution of Katanga, however, the word 'Republic' disappears. That constitution, drafted by Professor Clémens and promulgated by Tshombe on August 8th, 1960, is the 'Constitution of the State of Katanga'. The advantage of the word 'State' over the word 'Republic' is that of ambiguity; the advantage of ambiguity, at this stage, was that it enabled Belgian officers to serve in the armed forces of a State which Belgium wanted to support but not to recognize – since the example of recognition, if followed by other 'friendly' States, might detach Katanga and its resources from the Belgian sphere.[2]

For the same reason, the armed forces of the State of Katanga – in which two hundred regular officers of the Belgian Army were still serving in August 1961 – were described not as an Army but as a gendarmerie. Their duties were described as simply 'police duties'; from some of the remarks of Belgian politicians one would have expected to see Colonel Crèvecoeur on point duty in the Avenue

[1] *Dossiers du CRISP*, II, 728. The form in general use – the Independent State of Katanga – echoes the name of Léopold II's 'Independent State of the Congo'. The significance of the word 'independent' is similar in both cases.

[2] Chapter IV, pp. 85–6.

Saio. The real functions of the gendarmerie were, as already indicated, triple: to defend the territory against outside attack, including attack by Central Government forces; to hold down the Baluba of North and Central Katanga by force; and to be ready, if necessary, to crush any rebellion which might start among the tribally-mixed populations of the mining centres.

Belgian regular officers supplied the general staff of this force, and, in August 1961, rather less than half of its officers. The mixed composition of the European element in the gendarmerie reflected Katanga's uneasy political position.

The Belgian authorities, for their part, had never excluded a possible re-integration of Katanga and the rest of the Congo, provided that this could be achieved *à partir d'Elisabethville*, that is to say on terms acceptable to the European interests involved.[1] The trouble was that, by this date, it had become apparent that there were divergencies of opinion as to what such terms might be. 'I'm all right, Jack' tended to be the reaction of the Belgians in Elisabethville when people talked of the need for a settlement which would protect Belgians, and Belgian interests, not only in Katanga, but also in Leopoldville, Orientale, Equateur, Kasai and Kivu provinces. There were exceptions; for example, M Wénès, whose BCK railway was losing heavily by a state of affairs which sent the copper out through Angola, tended to be more broadminded than M Van Roey, the Director of the Bank of Katanga. But by and large the Europeans of Elisabethville, whose views never differed very widely from those of the Union Minière management – which, in one form or another, employed most of them – bitterly resented the policy of 'formal non-recognition' which M Wigny had combined with that of 'effective military aid'; the aid, invaluable as it had been, was now taken for granted, and the Belgians felt themselves 'let down' by Belgium. Worse still, they felt in imminent danger of being further let down, and this fear increased after M Spaak became Belgian Foreign Minister on April 25th, 1961. If even M Wigny had asked the Powers *not* to recognize the 'exercise in self-determination' which he had at the same time backed with his own forces, what might not M Spaak do? And what good would Belgian regular troops be if some Socialist, or otherwise irresponsible, Government in far-off Brussels should decide to sell the pass?

In response to these fears the Katanga Government had recruited mercenaries, to the number of at least three hundred, according to the gendarmerie's own figures, as communicated to Colonel Egge.

[1] Chapter IV, p. 95.

These three hundred or more mercenaries – in addition to the Belgian regular officers, who were not mercenaries but seconded to duty in Katanga by their Government – were all white, and drawn from various parts of the free world. There did exist – among gendarmerie papers captured by UN forces – a curious project for recruiting Zulu warriors from South Africa, with the co-operation of the South African Government, but it does not appear that anything came of this particular 'phenomenon of African nationalism'.

What we knew – as distinct from what we guessed, or were told by Belgians or Baluba – about the mercenaries was gleaned mainly from the interrogation of the thirty mercenaries who were captured by the Ethiopians at Kabalo in April 1961. Of these, sixteen had been South African and ten British. They had been recruited, some at Johannesburg, and some at Bulawayo, Southern Rhodesia. 'Conditions offered', states the relevant UN report, 'included basic pay ranging from £100 to £180 a month, plus a danger allowance, family allowance, insurance and the offer of a free vacation after one year.'[1] This was for white private soldiers in the *Compagnie Internationale*. 'Motives for enlistment given', according to the UN report, 'ranged from financial reasons, domestic troubles and lust for adventure to a desire to serve what they considered a good cause.' My own recollection, from reading the interrogatories in New York, is that, in about twenty-five of the thirty cases, the motives given ranged from financial reasons to financial reasons.

Captain Browne, the British commander of this contingent, told the UN that his own unit 'fired only at military personnel opposing him, when military necessity so required'. He and some of his soldiers were sharply critical of the methods used by 'the Katanga gendarmerie unit' [*sic*] led by Belgians and *les Affreux* whom they accused of burning habitations indiscriminately and firing on people who were not offering resistance. Captain Browne was shocked to learn of the Security Council's February Resolution, which had been kept from him, and he thought that efforts should be made to inform the men under his command 'of their true position and of the advisability to leave Katanga'. 'Leaving Katanga' was a subject on which Captain Browne soon became one of the world's leading authorities. Expelled by the UN on this occasion, he subsequently returned four times, being expelled again each time, either by the UN or by the Katanga Government. The Katanga Government formed the habit of expelling him, not so much out of a laudable

---

[1] S/4790, April 14th, 1961.

deference to the Security Council resolution, as because of a personal difference of opinion which he had with Major (later Colonel) Carlos Huyghe who was, and perhaps still is, in charge of recruitment through Rhodesia.[1]

The capture and the evidence of Captain Browne and his companions made it difficult for the 'friends of Katanga' to maintain their inability to perceive the mercenaries, and the technique now adopted was to send home a few of them – if 'home' was in Rhodesia or South Africa the parting need not be for ever – to redistribute others and to treat the whole matter as a picturesque but closed – well, almost closed – chapter. The following passage from a Belgian right-wing illustrated periodical gives the tone:

'What a lot of talk there has been about that foreign legion, recruited by the Katangese authorities, after Tshombe had proclaimed the independence of Katanga! It is no longer a mystery for anyone: a large number of young Belgians, especially former para-commandos, were recruited for, or joined up in, the Katangese Legion. There, they met with Frenchmen, Englishmen, Dutchmen, lads of every nationality, adventurers like them, if you wish, but like them also, brave. It is at present impossible to say how many Belgians made up these battalions [sic]. The residents of Elisabethville nicknamed these legionaries les affreux, "the frightful ones". They were, as a matter of fact, frightful to look at, with their beards and their disorderly, noisy attitudes: their accoutrements were sometimes unusual. (Translator's note: This is a reference to their habit of going around the bars of Elisabethville, drunk and festooned with knives, revolvers, and grenades.) In Elisabethville people (on) at first were a little afraid of them, but in the end people (on) came to love them and above all people (on) came to recognize their effectiveness in the bush, when the mission of reducing rebel centres of resistance was entrusted to them. (Translator's note: The word on as used here is impersonal, but not colourless.) At the moment, this foreign legion is being broken up. One after another, the men recruited by Katanga for indispensable "cleaning-up" operations are returning to their respective countries. Many Belgians have come home. Some are still in Katanga.'[2]

---

[1] The UN Commission found that 'grave suspicion' rested on Huyghe in connection with Lumumba's murder. Two unnamed English mercenaries testified to the commission that he was guilty of this murder.

[2] Illustrated article, *Vie et mort des affreux au Katanga*, in *Le patriote* (Brussels); July 9th to 16th, 1961.

Some were, indeed. On the admission of the gendarmerie staff – the figures supplied to Colonel Egge – the number of irregular mercenaries, about half of whom were Belgians, continued, up to Operation Rumpunch on August 28th, at the figure, 300, which I have already given. They were, however, no longer called *les affreux: les affreux* had officially gone home, and the mercenaries now did observe rather more discretion in Elisabethville, and clanked less in the bars. It was, after all, possible that the UN might start taking its own resolution seriously: also, even if it continued to have the good taste not to do so, it was preferable not to embarrass it by unnecessary martial displays. None the less, the streets of Elisabethville, as well as those of Jadotville, Kolwezi, Albertville and elsewhere, continued in August to be full of white men in uniform, whose 'immediate repatriation and withdrawal' had been decreed by the Security Council the previous February.

The valuable article from which I have already quoted gives a good idea of the operations and state of mind of the mercenaries, by means of a recorded interview with two young Belgian paracommandos who had just returned. 'Pierre' and 'Paul' had been recruited in the 'rue Marie de Bourgogne' in Brussels; they did not say by whom, nor did *Le Patriote* press them to do so. They had been used for 'indispensable cleaning-up operations' – Pierre in Central Katanga, first at Luena and then at Bukama (areas in which, according to *The Times*, the Tshombe Government 'enjoyed popular support'); Paul in the north around Kongolo. They used to travel, they said, in columns of eight or nine heavily armed jeeps; their 'armament', they said, was 'excellent'. There was usually one white per jeep. The rebels were armed with *pou-pou*, a sort of arquebus, or with bows and arrows.

Pierre and Paul were interesting on the subject of the comparative morale of the rebels and of their own African soldiers. The rebels, said Pierre, were 'extraordinary fighters, fanatical of course, but above all drugged with hemp. They hurled themselves against us, their eyes starting out of their heads, with a courage which can only be explained by their innocence [*sic*] and their state of artificial exaltation. I have seen blacks, hit by several bullets, continue to advance threateningly'.

The emphasis on hemp,[1] constant in all such reports, does not

---

[1] According to a well-informed Belgian observer 'the habit of hemp-smoking does not appear to be a native one' (F. Grévisse in *Bulletin Trimestriel du CEPSI* No. 32). He adds that, in the communities which he studied, 'hemp smokers were rare'.

account for all 'rebel' phenomena described, which include here skilfully organized ambushes and *ruses de guerre* (for example, feigned 'pro-Tshombe' demonstrations, luring the gendarmerie within range of the 'rebels' primitive weapons). By stressing hemp, however, one discredits a bravery which has to be admitted and which might, without the hemp, be ascribed to another motive: something which, in a European or a 'loyal Katangese', would be called patriotism. It may be worth adding that the flag under which these 'hemp-maddened rebels' fight and die is the flag which is universally recognized as being that of their own country – the seven-starred flag of the Republic of the Congo.

The Africans in the gendarmerie for some reason behaved rather differently from the 'rebels'. 'Black soldiers', said Paul, 'panic very quickly, especially when they are not heavily and severely officered (*encadrés*) by Europeans. I have seen black soldiers during an ambush strip themselves of their uniforms, even down to their shoelaces, in order to escape into the bush looking like peaceful black civilians'.

Towards the end of this article – which is illustrated with photographs of, among other things, 'a blazing rebel village', and 'the only person found in Manono:[1] a black woman dying of hunger' – Paul has some general reflections on race relations:

'I must say that of all the blacks we met in Katanga, the only ones I had a feeling of friendship for were our soldiers. Sometimes in the villages we passed through we were met by hostile looks and attitudes. Even in Elisabethville we did not feel loved by the Black. I had always the impression that the White likes the Black better than the Black likes the White.'

However that may be, Pierre made it clear that some Whites like some other Whites. 'The welcome the Europeans of Elisabethville had for us', he said, 'was something fantastic. I was put up by families whom I shall never forget. No really, what they did for me is unforgettable. . . . We were often treated as sons by our European compatriots of Elisabethville, who invited us to go out with them in the evenings, to dine with them, to stay with them, who repaired our equipment, and who demonstrated, by a thousand kindnesses, the gratitude which they were good enough to feel towards us.'

By August 1961, the UN had made it a little more difficult for the successors of 'Pierre' and 'Paul' to earn the gratitude of the Europeans of Elisabethville. Only a little more difficult, however, for as long as this 'police force' of para-commandos remained intact, it would continue pacification by the usual means. Around Kabalo

---

[1] The normal population of Manono is 15,000. See Chapter VIII, pp. 144–6.

and to a less extent in the districts of Kamina, Albertville, Nyunzu, Nyemba and Manono, the presence of the UN force now gave the local African population some protection from being rendered 'pro-governmental' by the gendarmerie's well-tried methods. But everywhere else in the vast areas marked 'pacified' or 'in course of pacification', the gendarmerie, working out of bases where there were no UN forces – Mitwaba, Kabongo, Kongolo, Bukama and many others – continued what would have been called by most of the Press of the free world – if this had not been a European-officered force defending European property and interests – its atrocities and its terror.

These activities, however they are to be described, continued to be directed, from gendarmerie headquarters in Elisabethville, by two distinct groups of European officers. The first was the little group of Belgian officers – the regular staff now effectively headed by Major Mathys – which is referred to in Chapter III. With this group, several of our UN officers had been on friendly terms, but now the Tuesday bridge games had been cancelled and the mutual demeanour of UN and Belgian officers had become, in the language of one of the Irish officers, 'correct with a capital K'.

The Belgian officers at least we knew; about the second group, who were French, we knew very little. M Lambroschini admitted to knowing of five French officers who were in the gendarmerie and of whom he washed his hands. These were: Faulques, Toupé-Thomé, Ege, Labourdonnais, Bousquet. All these had had the rank of Captain or Commandant in the French Army (whether under the same or another name) and had left Algeria, it appeared, after the failure of the April *putsch*. Labourdonnais had worked with Colonel Godard – in charge of the Sûreté in Algiers – or so the Belgians said.[1] Faulques, who also had made a name for himself in the pacification of Algeria, was now in charge of the training centre at Shinkolobwe. About the three other officers we knew virtually nothing except the names; nor did we know how many French officers in all might be involved. M Lambroschini thought perhaps fifteen; we believed there were about thirty, but we had no means of knowing the real total, granted the relative sizes of Katanga and of our forces.

Colonel Egge had an encounter with some of these officers at the cocktail party which M Lambroschini gave on July 14th. Egge was talking to one of them when he felt some hard object being pushed into his back. He turned, as may be imagined, round, and found

---

[1] Cf. *La Libre Belgique*, July 17th, 1961.

himself looking at part of a face, the rest of which had at some time been shot away. Which of the French officers this was, he did not know; he thought either Ege or Toupé-Thomé. The officer, replacing in his pocket whatever it was he used for attracting the attention of UN personnel, said: 'You are betraying the last bastion of the white man in Central Africa. You will get a knife in your back one of these days.'

M Lambroschini, characteristically, wanted *me* to apologize to *him* for 'the incident provoked by the UN on France's National Day'.

This officer's remark reflected the conviction, undoubtedly shared by all these officers, that they were continuing in Katanga the good work they had been doing in Algeria. This conviction was indirectly reflected in the Katanga Government's official propaganda. '*Les Baluba*', states the French text of the Katanga Government's White Book, '*sont des Katangais à part entière*'. This slogan – which is not carried into the English text – is, of course, a simple transplantation of one of the currently popular French formulae about Algeria: '*Les Algériens sont des Français à part entière*'. ('Algerians are one hundred per cent Frenchmen'.) These officers believed – and had imparted their belief to the Katanga Government – that the Baluba were Katangese just as the Algerians were French, and they were trying to convince the Baluba themselves of this by precisely the same methods – including Labourdonnais's 'psychological warfare' – as they had used on the Algerians.

These officers, unlike the discreet Belgians, enjoyed hurling threats in the direction of the UN. Toupé-Thomé had boasted, in the presence of journalists at the Hotel Léopold II, that with twenty kilos of plastic he would take care of the UN. '*L'ONU? Pas de problème! Vingt kilos de plastic et je m'en charge.*'

Feeling that these remarks were not in the best of taste – and also on other grounds – we put pressure on Tshombe to get rid of these people. He gave us the impression that, perhaps for rather similar reasons, he did not care much for some of the French officers either, and he readily agreed to the immediate departure of Labourdonnais, Ege and Toupé-Thomé; Faulques and Bousquet he would keep until he got 'the UN replacements': an embarrassing line because of the awkward implications of 'the Egge plan'.[1]

The three French officers named left at the end of July. Whether they remained outside Katanga is quite another matter. It would have been quite easy for any of them to return to Katanga – from Brazzaville through Angola say – and if Labourdonnais had re-

---

[1] See Chapter V, p. 124.

appeared, under the name of Baron de la Bouffonnerie, as Protocol
Officer to the Union Minière mess at Kolwezi, it would have been
a very long time – for reasons which I have already indicated –
before we got round to apprehending him.

It was becoming plain to us that the piecemeal system, of induc-
ing the Katanga Government to agree to the departure of this or
that officer, could only be a token application of the resolutions: the
kind of token application which would be quite compatible with
the indefinite maintenance, on the old methods, of the State of
Katanga. On the other hand, the 'Egge plan' had the difficulties
already indicated; and I had reported on these. Basically, the difficulty was that it could be implemented only in agreement, not
only with Katanga and Belgium, but also with the Central Government. Whether the last agreement could be obtained, depended on
whether Tshombe would come to terms with what the UN – and
the powers generally – regarded as the legal Government of his
country. If he did not come to terms it was beginning to be clear
that, since methods of persuasion produced only token compliance,
the UN would be obliged, if it insisted on having its resolutions
really applied, to use force.

No one on the UN side was in a hurry to reach this point. We all
still hoped that Tshombe and his backers would come to terms, and
we were encouraged by the fact that – despite the collapse of his
various 'conditions' – he now, after the formation of the Central
Government, sent his Parliamentarians to Leopoldville, headed by
my friend Mr Albert Nyembo. There were those who were inclined
to believe – I was, and so was Khiary – that the purpose of their
journey was to try to split and bring down the Government whose
formation their controllers had failed to prevent – but no one was in
a hurry to conclude that this was the case.

I was so little in a hurry myself that I took home leave on August
5th, returning to Katanga only on the 22nd. I had arranged with
Mr Cordier, before I agreed to join the UN or go to Katanga at all,
that I must be free to keep a commitment already entered into to
act as a Consultant at a Quaker Seminar for Diplomats in Clarens,
Switzerland. Mr Cordier readily agreed – I have an idea he felt
it might save me from the Jesuits – and I now joined the Seminar.
Here I led a discussion on 'The Cold War and some of its Myths'.
I did not discuss Katanga, fruitful in such myths though it was.
Some of my Quaker friends may well have shaken their heads the
following month on reading the Press reports of my bloody deeds.

I felt some compunction about leaving my post at this point, not so much because I believed action to be immediately imminent – if it were, I knew I should be recalled to Elisabethville at once – but because of leaving the already overworked Tombelaine in sole charge of the civil and political affairs of ONUC, Elisabethville. The post was admittedly considered, in some quite august quarters, as a sinecure and a rather bulgy one at that. *The Times*, in that same editorial (July 31st) which displayed so much expertise on 'certain border areas', and found the happy phrase about Mr Tshombe's Government being a 'phenomenon of African nationalism', said some severe things about our official life in Katanga:

'Unfortunately, the creaking civil administration of the UN in Katanga, overstaffed and with too high a proportion of mediocrities engaged in a Parkinsonian paper-chase, does not inspire much confidence.'

What is 'overstaffing', and what constitutes the exactly right proportion of mediocrities, are questions which depend very much on the point of view. We in Elisabethville would have thought *The Times*'s description dead right – and rather well put – if it had been intended for the Hotel Royal in Leopoldville. It is probable that the single UN civilian in Albertville would have said *The Times* had exactly hit off our life in the Avenue Fulbert Youlou. In the rest of Katanga – except for a few technicians in Kamina Base – there were no UN civilians at all, but I always felt that Colonel Alemu, at Kabalo, saw something Parkinsonian about the bloated civil bureaucracy of Albertville. In Elisabethville, the civilian staff numbered about twenty, including typists, and we creaked and chased paper over one office floor which we shared with the military staffs and signals people. Most of us were engaged in mundane tasks, such as finding accommodation, transport, and chaste amusements for the UN troops.[1] We knew we were not equipped to run the Union Minière and we did not hope to 'inspire confidence' in Printing House Square. Our mediocrity was so complete that we had thought it would escape attention, at a distance of more than four thousand miles.

In any case all the 'political and Press' work – there were no 'civil operations' permitted in Katanga – was done by Tombelaine

---

[1] Other amusements were organized by some of the national military contingents. Colonel Egge's attention was caught, in a list of essential equipment of one, French-trained, brigade, by the letters B.M.C. Ever the inquiring Staff Officer, alert for military information, he asked what the letters stood for. He was told that it referred to an item of standard equipment in the Army concerned: *Bordel Mouvant de Campagne*.

and myself and, when I was away, by Tombelaine alone. I returned
to Katanga on August 22nd, to find that all had been quiet during
my absence, but that it was not likely to be quiet much longer. The
Central Government was asking the UN to apply its own resolutions
and expel the foreign officers from Katanga. The UN was about to
accede to this request.

13

RUMPUNCH

*'Quis est hic qui pulsat ad ostium
noctis rumpens somnium?'*
St Peter Damian

The trouble began with the arrest of Mr Bintou.

Up to then there had been, as often before, high hopes of a reconciliation with Leopoldville. Dr Linner, in New York, told the Press
on August 20th, that Tshombe 'would come round'; the talk was all
of reducing the UN forces, and winding up the operation except for
the 'technical aid' side. The 'pretender' Government at Stanleyville
had lowered its flag; the legality of the Leopoldville Government
was uncontested and its head, Mr Cyrille Adoula, was a genuine
moderate, acceptable to Afro-Asian as well as to Western opinion.
The only cloud was the usual one, Katanga; but even there the sun
seemed to be breaking through. The Conakat parliamentarians
had been attending the meetings of the Central Parliament since
August 10th. Mr Samalenghe, Katanga's Minister for Information,
and hitherto one of the most vociferous partisans of Katangan
Independence, told the Press that in Leopoldville 'the atmosphere
was good'. Most people outside the Congo, who took any interest
in the country's affairs, must have assumed at this time that its
troubles, or at least its constitutional troubles, were almost over.

In Elisabethville, things did not look quite as hopeful as that. In
Leopoldville or New York, one could, in a sense, talk the secession
of Katanga out of existence. One referred to the place firmly as 'the
province of Katanga'; one put its 'Minister for Foreign Affairs',
Mr Evariste Kimba, firmly in quotation marks; one was able to deal

206

– but that was a little later – even more firmly with Mr Munongo: 'so-called "Minister of the Interior" '. That took care of these upstarts – in Leopoldville and New York. Unfortunately, in Elisabethville, Mr Munongo continued to be able to put people in prison, and they did not always come out of prison alive. Mr Kimba, who if he was not Minister for Foreign Affairs was not Minister for anything, continued to convene the Consular Corps, who invariably came, for discussions on what can only have been foreign-affairs-in-quotation-marks. It continued to be illegal, and physically dangerous, to fly the flag of the Congo in those parts of 'the province of Katanga' which the secessionist forces controlled. As for the flag of the Independent State of Katanga, that flew on every public building, on many European houses, and – during the Elisabethville International Fair – on the slagheap of the Union Minière.

Finding the outward and visible signs of sovereignty all around me in Elisabethville on my return, I necessarily realized that, although there might now be hope, there had not yet been any fundamental change. The following is an extract from a letter which I wrote to Máire MacEntee on August 22nd, immediately after my return:

'Tignée went quietly, likewise Ugeux and Huyghe (advert in local paper: *Expulsé de l'ONU désire vendre réfrigérateur*). Tshombe is travelling in the north, not having decided himself to go to Leopoldville. I am summoned to Leopoldville tomorrow for conference with Linner, McKeown, Raja, Khiary, re Katsit. *Tant mieux*. Then hope to go to Albertville meet President and try to save his ruddy life.'

This letter includes the sententious and not quite accurate reflection: 'The cause of human dignity and the cause of peace are often not the same, but here they are the same. . . .'

I should have been aware of a certain possible irony in this phrase – I had been thinking, of course, of world peace – for the *tant mieux* used in relation to the civil and military conference indicates an awareness that 'the cause of human dignity' – which I did not, and do not, identify with the cause of the State of Katanga – was about to necessitate at least preparedness for military intervention.

At Leopoldville the conversations – a military conference, which I attended as an observer – and talks with Linner and Khiary, did not lead to any final decision. The interim arrangements were that the UN force in Elisabethville should be strengthened – by bringing in one Indian battalion in addition to the Swedish and Irish battalions already there – and that it should put itself in readiness to start apprehending the foreign officers, using force if necessary, if a last appeal to Tshombe failed.

I flew to Albertville on Friday, August 25th, to make this appeal, but it was already, in every sense, too late. As our plane approached Albertville, the control-tower, then still in Belgian hands, forbade us to land, asserting that it was technically impossible for the runway to take our DC6. Our Canadian pilot said this was nonsense, so we landed, only to find that Tshombe's visit to certain carefully selected portions of north Katanga had been unexpectedly cut short that day and that he had returned to Elisabethville.

Now my thought in trying to reach him in Albertville had been that in that city, where European population and European influence – that is to say, money – were much less than in Elisabethville, and where UN influence was proportionately higher, it might be possible to induce Mr Tshombe to make a real move towards unity. That I was not the only one to whom this thought occurred may be indicated by Tshombe's abrupt departure; a departure which rather spoiled the effect of his carefully built-up north Katanga tour. The tour had been designed to help newspapers like *The Daily Telegraph* to reassure newspapers like *The Times* about those distressing 'border areas'. The local administrator and his Belgian 'adviser', with the assistance of the Belgian-officered gendarmerie command, were able to organize in places like Albertville, demonstrations in which 'Africans and Europeans side by side' displayed their loyalty to the State of Katanga – just as, in Algiers and Oran, 'Moslems and Europeans side by side' used, in the good old days, so touchingly to display their loyalty to *l'Algérie Française*. This particular tour was going very well: Mr Ian Colvin of *The Daily Telegraph* was profoundly, and quite sincerely, moved. The tour would certainly not have been cut short had not something more important than the fate of north Katanga been involved. The 'something more important' was, I believe, the fate of south Katanga. Munongo – then in charge in Elisabethville – had taken a final and unmistakable stand against incorporating this territory, containing most of the Europeans, the mines and the money, into the rest of the Congo.

Two days before Mr Tshombe's hurried return – on August 23rd – Mr Nyembo had been, equally hurriedly, recalled from Leopoldville. Now Mr Nyembo, the senior Conakat parliamentarian attending in Leopoldville, was perhaps the man best capable of acting as a bridge between Tshombe and the Central Government; he had also served briefly in Lumumba's Government, in which his impertinence, as a

Congolese Minister, in giving an order to a Belgian officer, had aroused the wrath of General Janssens.[1] I had noticed myself – *ajoutez mon Chef de Cabinet* – that Mr Nyembo had a certain tendency to emancipate himself from European advice, and it may have been this flaw in his character which now led to his hurried recall. There had been a time – very recently, as time went outside the Congo – when the Europeans of Elisabethville used to proclaim that what the Congo needed was a *solution africaine*, but they had not been thinking of a deal, through Mr Nyembo, between Mr Adoula and Mr Tshombe, African though all these gentlemen are. What they had meant by an African solution was an agreement between responsible African leaders – Tshombe, Kalonji, Ileo, etc. – who were accessible, through channels to which *The Times* has drawn attention,[2] to the advice of moderate Europeans – that is to say Europeans who, by their moderation and other virtues, have amassed considerable property. Any arrangement reached by such leaders under such guidance will be the arrangement which best suits, at the moment, the interests of Europeans who own property in Africa. This is the 'spirit of Tananarive', alias 'the African solution'. Mr Nyembo, who seems to have misunderstood the meaning of *la solution africaine* – possibly because of his *mentalité bantoue* – had to be brought home. Legally, of course, the provincial Government had no right to recall a national deputy (whereas on the alternative 'Katangese' hypothesis, a minister of a sovereign State had no business to attend a foreign Parliament at all). But in Katanga legalities of this kind were relevant only when they embarrassed the Opposition. *Il faut faire de la politique*, as Mr Khiary used to say.

It was not clear whether the 'Government decision' which brought Mr Nyembo home was made by Mr Tshombe, who was in Albertville, or by Mr Munongo, in Elisabethville. The latter is more probable.

The arrest of Mr Bintou seems to have taken place on the same day as the recall of Mr Nyembo. I say 'seems' because Elisabethville was a city where the papers published, with commendable promptitude and edifying commentary, news of the arrest of a European political adviser by the UN, but did not publish news of the arrest of African political offenders unless told to do so by Mr Munongo. This at any rate was the day on which Mr Munongo told the world he had arrested Mr Bintou. On the day following my own return to Elisabethville – August 26th – a small, stout, frightened African

[1] Letter cited in Jules Chomé, *La Crise Congolaise*, p. 94.
[2] See p. 174.

came into my office. He was Mr Bintou's secretary, and he and his
family were the first members of what very soon became a refugee
population of 45,000 people under UN protection in Elisabethville.

Neither the general public nor the UN in Elisabethville appreciated at the time the great political and human significance of
Mr Bintou's arrest. My own first reaction to the news was one of
cynical amusement, for Mr Bintou seemed as unlikely a martyr for
liberty as one could well imagine. In the collection of Congolese
biographies published by the *Dossiers du CRISP*, the relevant entry
reads, in part, as follows:

BINTOU, Raphael:

A leader of the Congolese Socialist Party . . . Participated with
Mr Adoula at the Economic Round table . . . Deputy in the
Katangese Assembly in which he joined the Conakat. Represents
the 'Autonomous State of South Kasai' in Elisabethville. On
September 8th, 1960, delegated by the State of South Kasai
to make contact with official circles in the Union of South Africa
and the financier Oppenheimer.[1]

This moderate socialist, and responsible African nationalist,
seemed so saturated with 'African solution' and 'spirit of Tananarive'
that his arrest was at first hard to understand. Mr Munongo, it is
true, explained it. Bintou, he said, had embezzled 80,000 francs,
and had urged Elisabethville residents, hailing from Kasai, not to
pay back housing loans which they had received, he said, from the
Government of Katanga. (It is more probable that they received
them from the Union Minière, but the slip is a pardonable one.)
Also, certain 'compromising documents of a political character'
had been found in his house. He was – the Belgian agency, Inbel,
gathered – 'engaged in what was considered a suspect political
correspondence with certain authorities of other provinces'.

Whatever else might be said about Mr Munongo's arrests, they
never suffered from paucity of motivation.

I do not know nearly as much about the circumstances leading to
Mr Bintou's arrest as I should like to know, and I can give here only
a general idea of the background which lent to it an ominous significance.

The Mulopwe Albert Kalonji, nominal ruler (with the titles of
King, Emperor and God) of what had been variously called the
'Autonomous State of South Kasai', the 'Mining State' or the
'Federal Kingdom of South Kasai', stood in approximately the same
relation to the diamond corporation, Forminière, as Mr Tshombe

---

[1] *Congo, 1960 . . . Annexes et Biographies*, p. 79.

did to the Union Minière, and, like Mr Tshombe, he was opposed
to Communism and upheld tribal traditions. By setting up, in
August 1960, the 'Autonomous State of South Kasai', based on the
Baluba of Kasai, he manifested his tribalist outlook and he also,
as it happened, kept Lumumba's hands off the mines. His secession
led to a bloody civil and tribal war, the horrors of which were laid
by Western opinion – and to a great extent by the UN also –
exclusively at the door of Lumumba – although it was Kalonji, not
Lumumba, who had been convicted by the Belgians in 1959 of
'incitement to race hatred'.[1]

Readers of the Western Press must have been puzzled, in the
autumn of 1960 and the spring of 1961, by the word Baluba and its
varying significances. The Baluba of Kasai seemed to be decent
people, savagely and unprovokedly attacked by Lumumba's
Lulua; the Baluba of Katanga were themselves the savage and
unprovoked attackers. I should like to proffer, with due diffidence,
a geological and economic solution to this ethnological paradox:

The Baluba of Kasai live in and near areas where there are
valuable mines; a particularist movement among them may,
therefore, help in certain circumstances, to safeguard investments.[2]
The Baluba of Katanga live mainly outside the mining area and
their particularism – especially if combined with an embarrassing
loyalty to the Central Government – is a nuisance and a threat to
investments. That large portion of the Western Press which is
controlled by people who have good reason to sympathize with
the investors, tends, therefore, to be 'pro-Baluba' in Kasai and 'anti-
Baluba' in Katanga. The Baluba in both provinces are of identical
origin, though with dialect variations which impress the mine-
owners as significant.

During most of the lifetime of the State or Kingdom of South
Kasai, Mr Bintou lived happily and comfortably in Elisabethville,
combining a diplomatic existence as representative of Albert 1er, the
Mulopwe, with political activity as a member of the Katanga
Parliament, elected by the Kasai Baluba resident in Katanga. He

---

[1] The news of the murder, in Kalonji's capital of Bakwanga – under similar
circumstances to the death of Lumumba – of five 'Lumumbist' leaders, reached the
Security Council during its February debate and influenced the preparation of the
resolution of February 21st. Bakwanga was known to Congolese nationalists, and
some of their enemies, as 'the slaughterhouse'.

[2] The above account is somewhat simplified: there were times when it suited
the mine-owners better to back the Lulua (who, in any case, appear to be Baluba
under another name). The complications are superficial; the interests are simple
and fundamental.

handled the transmission from Katanga to Kasai of various necessities of independence, such as guns and mercenaries. He was, at
this time, a pet of the local Europeans and one met him at those
receptions at which these Europeans demonstrated the multi-
racial Katangese spirit. He was a solemn 'kasavubulent' man with
one of those watchful and at the same time rapt expressions which
seem to be acquired as a result of exclusive devotion to a single
passion, whether it be the love of God or the love of money.

The horizon had started to cloud for him in the previous April,
when Tshombe was arrested at Coquilhatville. Kalonji was not
arrested (at this time), but drew closer to the Leopoldville group.
Munongo, who was intensely 'Balubaphobe' – and who altogether
failed to notice the profound moral gulf between the Kasai variety
and the Katangan sort which the Western Press had been so prompt
to discern – hinted that not only Spaak but also Kalonji had been
behind Tshombe's arrest. Tshombe himself, however, did not give
countenance to this idea. It seemed possible, indeed, that he might
emulate the Mulopwe's example in drawing closer to Leopoldville.
The test came when, in August, Kalonji quietly jettisoned his
autonomy and also – apparently – his crown, though not his god-
head, and came back into the Congo. Would Tshombe do likewise,
letting the State of Katanga follow the Kingdom of Kasai into
oblivion?

The answer, as so often, was made by Munongo; by arresting
Bintou he shut the door on a 'Kasai solution' and bolted it by
Nyembo's recall.

On the following day, August 24th – whether as a result of
Nyembo's recall and Bintou's arrest or not – the Central Government passed Ordinance No. 70, to 'expel from the territory of the
Republic of the Congo' all the non-Congolese officers and mercenaries etc.[1] This ordinance, in the Secretary-General's view, 'gave
the UN legal rights within the Congo corresponding to the
(February) resolution'.[1] In other words it was taken as legalizing
the use of force, if necessary, by the UN to expel the mercenaries.
When, therefore, I flew to Albertville on August 25th, positions had
so hardened that my attempt at securing an agreed settlement had
an 'eleventh hour' character.

The similarities between the Katanga and Kasai situations are
such as to make it surprising to find Tshombe and Kalonji, hitherto
so harmoniously in step, now sharply diverging. Forminière and the
Union Minière are closely related through the Société Générale –

[1] S/4940 of September 14th.

which has co-operated with Forminière and with other people, including Mr Bintou's friend, Mr Oppenheimer, in founding other companies such as Diamang in nearby Angola. One might expect politicians who have the confidence – as the saying is – of either group to act in the same way. Why did they not do so?

Those who cherish the hypothesis that non-African financial interests do not interfere in African politics may point to the Kalonji-Tshombe divergence as evidence of the truth of their case. For an explanation of the phenomenon, however, they will be likely to fall back on 'Africamanship', the science by which people who have lived a long time in Africa, but have never bothered to learn anything about Africans except as servants or employees, explain 'the African mind' to the new-comer, always as something immensely alien, mysterious and indeed inexplicable (*Je ne commence même pas à les comprendre*). Those who are not satisfied with explanations which confess their inability to explain, are likely to find more mental stimulation in considering the somewhat different positions of the two companies concerned.

The Union Minière's capital is mainly Belgian, partly French and British. Its operations are mainly in Katanga, and appear to be negligible in the rest of the Congo.

Forminière's capital, while also mainly Belgian, includes a substantial American (Ryan-Guggenheim) element (25 per cent).

Its operations are mainly in Kasai, but it also has important interests in other parts of the Congo, including Stanleyville.

The Union Minière operates in an area, remote from the Congolese capital, which has a relatively large proportion of Europeans – not far short of 10 per cent for the mining area Elisabethville-Jadotville-Kolwezi – and is contiguous to another area of similar economic development and relatively dense European population – the Copperbelt of Northern Rhodesia. It has a long and highly permeable border with Northern Rhodesia, where the dominant European population is sympathetic and well-armed and enjoys influence in the capital of a great power, Britain.

Forminière operates in an area, nearer to Leopoldville, which has a very low proportion of Europeans – there were less than 1,000 in Bakwanga, as against 15,000 in Elisabethville – and has a short common border with another foreign country, Angola, of which the Portuguese rulers are certainly well disposed, but also much weaker economically, militarily and diplomatically than the 'superior partners' in Rhodesia.

In the light, as they say at shareholders' meetings, of these

considerations it would have been possible for a prudent man, even
having investments in both areas, and a seat on both boards, to
consider that the arrangements which best suited his interests would
be different in the two areas. Kalonji, in ending his secession, and
Tshombe in maintaining his, both acted in a manner which is
consistent with the hypothesis that they were working in concert
with such prudent men and serving essentially the same interests
in the different ways which fitted different situations.

To this has to be added the important rider that the most significant element in the 'different situation' of Elisabethville was its
high concentration of Europeans, including many who were not
'prudent men' at all and who were often hysterical with fear and
anger, like the Europeans of Algiers. The 'prudent man' therefore
had to take account of the 'imprudent man'. If Mr Tshombe was
the prudent European's favourite African, the imprudent European's
favourite African was undoubtedly Mr Munongo. The presence of
these two in the same Government reflected, and increased, the
uncertainties, tensions and confusions of the Europeans in Elisabethville.

The people who were personally threatened by Mr Bintou's
arrest were Mr Bintou's electors, the Baluba of Kasai, resident in
the mining centres of south Katanga, especially Elisabethville.
I shall have more to say in the next chapter about these unfortunate
people, since their tragedy assumed its full dimensions only in
September, after the UN intervention to remove the foreign officers
and after the Katanga Government's decision, with significant
outside backing, to defy the United Nations and the Central
Government.

I saw Tshombe, in Elisabethville, on Saturday, August 26th, and
conveyed to him Mr Adoula's invitation to go to Leopoldville. I
stressed, as usual, the UN guarantee of his safe return. It was a sad
little conversation. He complained of his health, and did indeed seem
to have some difficulty in breathing. I felt rather sorry for him,
caught as he was between the puzzling, almost inscrutable menace
– as it must have seemed to him – of the UN and the all too scrut-
able menace of Munongo and his friends. I knew in advance that,
when I had missed him in Albertville, hope was virtually at an end,
for I had come by now to regard him, in Elisabethville, as a prisoner
of Europeans and of what Munongo represented.

I told him that General McKeown's plane was standing by, should
he (Mr Tshombe) wish to accept Mr Adoula's invitation. Since he
had pleaded health reasons, I told him that this DC6 – it was the

same which was to crash a few weeks later at Ndola – was comfortably fitted up with bunks, and that he could rest on the journey. I also told him that matters had almost come to a head, and that, should he maintain his present position, resting as it did on foreign mercenaries, whose presence was illegal under a Security Council resolution, some kind of UN intervention was inevitable. He heard me without resentment, but with what I thought of as his 'Don Benito' face – an expression partly harassed, partly apathetic, like a man who knows there is no point in talking since the decisions are already taken. He thanked me for my explanation, and said he would think the matter over and let me know his answer.

The answer came by way of a Ministry of Information bulletin on Radio Katanga – the most powerful station in Central Africa, and a present from the Union Minière to Mr Tshombe's Government. The statement said that I had 'ordered' Mr Tshombe to go to Leopoldville but that he had stood firm. Simultaneously, a good reason for standing firm was indicated by the Minister of the Interior, at a Press conference:

'To the question: "Will the Government put into execution the plans for sabotage of the Union Minière and great companies?" Mr Munongo replied: "I cannot answer you now. You will know tomorrow perhaps." '

La Libre Belgique, which reported that this Press conference took place in the garden of Mr Tshombe's villa on Sunday, August 27th, mentions that the French Consul-General was present. Not only was M Lambroschini present; he actually asked a question, in front of the reporters, thereby going beyond the normal scope of consular activity. The question, perhaps prompted by a sincere desire to elicit information, was, as reported by *La Libre Belgique*:

'whether Katanga would be prepared to issue a radio appeal to the population to come to the aid of foreigners if the position became so critical that the forces of the Government could no longer ensure such protection?'[1]

'Certainly', said Mr Munongo.

That night a contingent of gendarmerie, under the orders of two Belgians, attempted to dig trenches near the runway of Elisabethville airport. This contingent was promptly disarmed by Irish troops and the two Belgians, classified as *adeuxiens*, were expelled. They travelled, philosophically and cheerfully enough, on the DC4 which took Brigadier Raja and myself to Kamina Base on Sunday, August 27th, to confer with Khiary and Fabry who came there from Leopoldville.

---

[1] *L. B.*, August 28th, 1961.

Khiary was not astonished to learn that Tshombe would not be coming. He conveyed authority for the operation for which Raja and his staff had already made plans under the code word 'Rumpunch'. Rumpunch was to be carried out in the early hours of the following morning. Its main element was of course the apprehension of all foreign officers, but there were three 'extras' which I had proposed, in order to diminish the risk of bloodshed. These were the temporary detention of Munongo, and a temporary occupation of the radio and post office. It was clear that Munongo and the radio would be likely to whip up resistance, and endanger the bloodless success of Rumpunch. The point of taking over the post office was, by putting the exchange out of action, to make it more difficult for the opposition to concert its action, and impossible for Munongo to contact, or threaten, anyone.

These plans were now approved. Khiary returned to Leopoldville and Fabry came on with us to Elisabethville.

At four o'clock the following morning the forces under Brigadier Raja's command began apprehending European officers in Elisabethville and in the North Katangan centres, where there were UN garrisons. At the same time, these forces occupied the premises of the post office and radio and set a guard round Mr Munongo's villa. By five o'clock these proceedings had not caused any disturbance, to the provisional relief of Raja and myself, as we walked up and down in the drawing-room of the Villa des Roches. He smoked and walked; I just walked.

At five o'clock I sent off a lively young Swedish officer, Lieutenant Giesler, with a polite note to Tshombe – referring to our previous conversations, informing him of the nature of the present operations, undertaken under the authority of the resolution of February 21st, and inviting his co-operation – and another polite note to Munongo, explaining that, in the interests of public order, we were obliged to put some temporary restrictions on his freedom of movement.

At about 5.20 a.m. we heard the crackle of rifle fire from the direction of Munongo's villa. At about 5.30, Lieutenant Giesler's car came up the drive, at a good rate of speed. When it stopped, we saw that the rear part of the car was riddled with bullets, put there, we all assumed, by Munongo's ferocious Bayeke bodyguard. Lieutenant Giesler was slightly wounded – his back had been grazed by a bullet which had gone through the driver's seat – and it was only gradually, while Verdalee Tombelaine was dressing this wound, that it became clear what had happened. The lieutenant had not had a brush with the Bayeke at all, but with the Irish UN troops, due to a misunderstanding. The Irish, in sealing off Munongo's residence, had established road-blocks and the lieutenant, having delivered his message, had driven rapidly round one of these. He had, he said, waved his hand at the patrol, who all knew him. Unfortunately they could not recognize him, or see him wave, in the dark, so they opened fire.

Raja and I then drove, just after six o'clock and dawn, to the President's Palace. On the way, Avenue Elisabeth, we passed, with much circumspection, through an Irish road-block. At the Palace, the guards were excited and wanted to know what was going on. I told them we were expelling their Belgian officers, news which they received very cheerfully indeed. Laughing, they shook hands with us over the gate. We went on towards the city centre, but soon encountered a cortège of official cars with Tshombe, and most of his cabinet, returning from their tour. They turned back to meet us, and we turned back to meet them, thus creating some confusion. Finally we all managed to get into the Palace. The Ministers were excited and alarmed, but not really angry. Mr Kimba, a tall, handsome and imperturbable man, with a flashing smile, seemed quite amused by it all. They asked us to stop the operations and we said we could not do so. We asked them to co-operate with us in order to avoid incidents. Tshombe said they would have to consider this and discuss the matter together; he promised me an answer by eleven o'clock. I had the impression that the discussions in the interim would not be confined to the Katanga Cabinet.

I then went to the studios of Radio Katanga, which was under the temporary direction of Michel Tombelaine. Its first broadcast that morning – by a happy inspiration of Fabry's – was an apology to telephone subscribers for a temporary interruption of services. The second broadcast, which must have been heard with no little surprise by the Radio Katanga audience, comprised the texts of the Central Government's decree, calling for the removal of the foreign officers, and of a speech by Mr Adoula on the unity of the Congo.

At eleven o'clock, we met the Government and received the answer: Tshombe was willing to give full co-operation, to dismiss all the foreign officers, and to announce on the radio his acquiescence in the UN action. But he asked us, first, to end the 'temporary measures': the occupation of the post office and radio, and the house-arrest of Munongo. Since these measures were ancillary to the action for the removal of the mercenaries I could only agree. Munongo, released, came immediately over to the Palace. As he came in through the french windows, carrying his hat in his left hand, he was smiling, his head held high. He came over and shook my hand. *'Vous m'avez eu'*, he said: 'You fooled me.' He did not add, or have to add, ' . . . this time'.

Tshombe was as good as his word, which was not invariably the case. At one o'clock, from Radio Katanga now back under his control, he broadcast a statement, entirely free from complaint or hostility, in which he said that he bowed to the decision of the United Nations – *je m'incline devant l'ONU* – and that all the foreign officers were dismissed from Katanga service and must leave Katanga.

'A good Simba'[1] – headlined the *Essor du Katanga* next day – 'and back to work!' *La Libre Belgique* said that, that night, they 'swilled champagne' at UN headquarters. Swilled is hardly the *mot juste* – some of the champagne was even sipped by Mr Dunnett, who dropped in to Les Roches that evening, but did not seem in very festive spirits. We were happy at that moment, for we felt that Rumpunch was an unblemished – because a bloodless – success.

---

[1] *Simba La Biére du Lion*, Katanga's national beverage.

14

RUMPUNCH TO MORTHOR

> *'We have scotch'd the snake, not kill'd it.'*
> Macbeth

'We're very happy here', I wrote on the 29th, 'and probably dangerously cocky and euphoric about our *coup* on Monday. . . . Tshombe was a grocer in private life, so the lines apply:

> *And now the sands are running out*
> *From sugar of a sort . . .*

'S.-G. is delighted with operation and I am white-headed boy at present. *"Pourvou que ça doure".* Spaak calls me *l'inqualifiable M O'Brien.'*[1]

As it was claimed in the Belgian and some other right-wing papers that the action of August 28th was a little idea of my own, and as that theory formed the basis of the violent personal attacks on me which began at this time, I think I am justified in quoting what Hammarskjold said. The following is the text of the telegram:

'O'Brien from Linner. Have received following from Secgen: "Congo Club in congress assembled passed unanimous vote of congratulations gratification and sincere respect for an exceedingly sensitive operation carried through with skill and courage. We hope that results will render your task in other aspects easier and increasingly constructive." '[2]

---

[1] This letter to Máire MacEntee is undated but is probably August 29th, and can hardly be later than 30th.

[2] I have also a telegram in similar terms from Linner and McKeown.

The hope was not destined to be fulfilled. Rumpunch was only partially successful. It did get rid of a large number of foreign officers; by September 8th, according to the UN military returns, 273 'non-Congolese personnel in the Katanga gendarmerie' had been repatriated and sixty-five were awaiting repatriation.[1] That was a more significant contribution to the re-unification of the Congo than anything the UN had previously done. It did much to revive the waning confidence of the Afro-Asian countries in the United Nations, and it strengthened the position of the Central Government of the Congo which, shortly thereafter, achieved universal recognition.[2] All that was good in itself, and considerably more effective than peppering Katanga with quotation marks. But the report contained another significant word and figure:

Missing: 104

The missing were ten Belgian regular officers, fifty-four Belgian volunteers, eleven French, four British, one Pole, one Hungarian, one Dane, two Portuguese, one Swede, eight Italians, one South African, one New Zealander, four Dutchmen and five 'others'.

These figures are not necessarily, or even probably, complete. The UN knew what it had caught, but did not know what it had not caught. What it knew – and what the figure '104' faithfully reflects – is the discrepancy between the total 'non-Congolese personnel . . . repatriated or awaiting repatriation' and the total of non-Congolese personnel as supplied by the Belgian command to Colonel Egge. That figure may or may not have been complete as far as the gendarmerie – under Minister of Defence Yav – was concerned. It did not include other military and para-military formations, such as that special force, responsible only to the Minister of the Interior, of whose existence we were shortly to learn from M André Crémer.

Why did the UN not finish the job? The answer to that legitimate question consists of three elements.

The first is that we acceded to the request of the Belgian Consul-General, backed by the other Consuls, and made in the forenoon of August 28th, to stop the arrests. M Créner solemnly undertook to see to the repatriation of the mercenaries – *all* the mercenaries.

---

[1] S/4940/Add 1/Annex III.

[2] Western countries had already indicated that they recognized Mr Adoula's Government. It was only after the Katanga action, however, that Mr Khrushchev sent a telegram of recognition to Mr Adoula. (*Congo, 1961*, p. 599, entry under September 1st, 1961.)

Belgium – it was he who volunteered the thought – owed them something, and had a responsibility towards them. The 'chapter of the mercenaries' was closed. Whatever might be thought of the UN action, Tshombe accepted it, and Belgium would see to the swift repatriation of all the mercenaries. All he asked us to do was to agree to let this be done in an orderly manner. If the arrests continued there was a grave risk of incidents. M Créner's military advisers – the stern Colonel Perrad, and the silky Colonel van de Waelle, called by his admirers, 'the Richelieu of Katanga' – corroborated this. The arrests were an unnecessary humiliation imposed on officers who had orders from their own Government never to fire on UN troops. These officers were willing, indeed anxious, to leave Katanga, but they should be allowed to do so voluntarily. Otherwise anything might happen; if a Belgian officer resisted arrest and was shot by UN forces, the effect on other officers, and on Belgian and local opinion, was incalculable.

These arguments seemed to me to have weight. The great success of Rumpunch, so far, lay in the fact that it was bloodless. If it could be completed bloodlessly, with the co-operation of the Belgian Consulate, that seemed to me so great a gain as to outweigh the danger of partial evasion. Raja took a different view. He thought this was a ruse and that the only effective way of getting rid of the mercenaries was to arrest and eject them. I had subsequently to concede that his point of view was characterized by a certain rugged common sense. We agreed, in any case, to suspend the arrests, and give M Créner an opportunity of doing what he had said he would do. Arrests accordingly were over by 3 p.m. on August 28th. On the following day M Créner told us that he was sorry but that M Spaak had overruled him; he could only accept responsibility for the *Belgian* officers. For the others, the other Consuls must be responsible. Among the Belgians, he distinguished between the regulars who, being under military discipline, were *ordered* to return to Belgium, and the volunteers who could only be *advised* to do so.

Raja said that if all the remaining non-Congolese military personnel had not presented themselves at a UN camp for repatriation by 9 a.m. on August 30th, UN forces would begin the arrests again. This decision was not altogether well received in Belgium (*Trahison de M O'Brien, Duplicité et sottise de l'ONU*, headlined *La Libre Belgique*) but in fact it came too late. The essential thing had been the time for concealment gained by the suspension of arrests. There may have been something in the charge of *sottise de l'ONU*, but as regards *duplicité* the UN was hopelessly outmatched.

The second element that contributed to the entry *missing* was of course our oft-acknowledged lack of intelligence. Our forces, seeing a white man in military uniform, could reach unerringly the conclusion that he fell into the category of 'non-Congolese military personnel' and put him in the bag. But if the same white man – in the time gained by the suspension of arrests – had got into civilian clothes, and acquired from the grateful Katangese authorities antedated civilian identity papers, then the UN lost its old sureness of touch. We could be sure that if we arrested the wrong man, or worse still, the right man, there would be a Press outcry. Similarly if we started an exhaustive check on the Europeans of Katanga we should be accused of mass-persecution of harmless civilians, racialism and disregard of human rights: charges which a national State can take in its stride but which, necessarily and rightly, make the UN falter.

The third element, closely linked with the second, was that throughout large areas of Katanga – including at this time the two important mining centres of Jadotville and Kolwezi, with their sizeable European populations – there were no UN forces at all. Here, the foreign officers could rally, and even organize, with the help of their financial backers, reinforcements through Rhodesia or Angola. The Greek Consul, who visited Jadotville and Kolwezi about this time, in order to reassure the quite large Greek colonies there, told us that the gendarmerie posts in both centres were still openly under the command of European officers. The only change was that these officers, dressed in shorts and bush-shirts – such as any open-air European might wear – no longer bore the distinguishing insignia of the gendarmerie. If UN forces (in adequate number) were to come clanking in along the road from Elisabethville, the officers in question would have been found peacefully painting a fence for the Union Minière. (Indeed one such officer was later discovered painting a fence round one of the Indian camps in Elisabethville.) It is true that, in the centres with UN garrisons, the African soldiers had frequently handed over their own European officers to the UN – a fact which was admitted, and bitterly resented, by the local Belgians – but this was now, at least for a time, less likely to happen. Specifically it was less likely to happen in places where there was no permanent UN garrison, because the soldiers had reason to fear reprisals. The last time they had rebelled, or mutinied, or defended the constitution – the term to be used depends on one's political philosophy – Belgian forces in large numbers had invaded[1]

---

[1] There is no doubt that invasion is the right word. See Chapter IV.

the country and crushed them. They had no guarantee that the same thing – perhaps with Rhodesian forces this time – might not happen again.

But there was a more subtle reason for their continuing to accept what had become, in UN-garrisoned areas, the now necessarily covert authority of their old masters. This was that Rumpunch had produced one unlooked-for result; what might be called the 'mobutification' of the Army. Katanga had now not merely an African President, and an African Government, but also an African Commander. What more do you want?

The new Commander, after August 28th, was Colonel, later General, Muké (or Moké) surnamed, by the Ministry of Information, after the September fighting, 'Muké le Victorieux'.[1] Colonel Muké knew no French, and little Swahili; he was illiterate, or virtually so. He was addicted to shouting and to a complicated gesture – pawing the ground with his left foot, making a butting motion with his head, and swinging his right arm, back-handed, in a wide, downward arc, like the action of a man slashing at the fetlocks of a horse with a tennis-racket. When negotiating with him it was advisable to allow him plenty of elbow-room.

The local Belgians could not refer to Muké without a little snigger of triumph. The UN wanted Africanization? Well, they had it! If they wanted to put the primitive Bantu in charge, they could have what they wanted. Muké was the best of them – and look at Muké! Muké, at least, had one decent quality. He was *honnête;* the others were not even that.

Honnête was another technical term; it meant obedient to Europeans and Muké was certainly that. He was not merely docile; he was touchingly, painfully grateful. 'If there is no God, how can I be a Captain?' asked one of Dostoevski's characters. 'If there are no Belgians', Muké might well have asked, 'how can I be a General?'

There were, in the gendarmerie, a number of intelligent, educated African officers, mainly younger men, but their intelligence and education did not help their advancement; on the contrary. One could not be sure that they were *honnêtes*. Indeed in the technical sense they were not; after September most of them, if not all, left Katanga to join the Central Government's forces. They had, they said, been temporarily deceived by the 'Africanization' of August but in reality things had gone on as before. Tshombe's Katanga was

---

[1] In theory he had been Commander even before August 28th, but the fiction was not seriously maintained. The Ministry of Information did not start to build him up until September.

not something which an African who had both education and self-respect was likely to be happy serving.

In Eisenstein's *Ivan the Terrible* there is a scene in which the boyars hail the Emperor whom, to suit their interests, they have created. He is a half-witted boy, and as he shuffles towards us, vacant-eyed, limply holding the splendid Byzantine insignia of royalty, between the lines of grave and mock-respectful nobles, we hear the words:

Boyarski Tsar – the Nobleman's Emperor!

Poor Muké was a 'Boyarski Tsar' – an African General for Europeans. The insult to human dignity, and to the mentally defenceless, was essentially the same in the two cases.

The worst thing the UN had done on August 28th, according to *La Libre Belgique*, was to break 'the beautiful friendship between black and white' which up to then had prevailed in Katanga. *Cette belle amitié entre blanc et noir*. . . . The sniffles from Brussels were premature. The friendship they referred to – the friendship of Major Mathys and General Muké – flourished as never before, because it was needed as never before.

The remarks – which were to some extent echoed in parts of the British Press – about the UN's having broken the beautiful friendship between black and white, struck us as being silly. In fact they were not silly at all; they covered – with the half-instinctive intelligence of the determined psychological warrior – the need to make a rapid transition from one propaganda line to another. As my education progressed in Katanga, I became less and less inclined to dismiss this or that 'ultra' line or slogan as 'silly', and more inclined to remember Glumov's law:

'There are no such people as fools, only different shades of scoundrels.'[1]

The beautiful, broken friendship, when you had examined it with the aid of Glumov, turned out to mean roughly this:

The 'image of Katanga' hitherto presented to the world, with the devoted aid of people like Ian Colvin, was that of a multi-racial heaven where a wise African Government, enjoying almost universal popular support, relied on Europeans for technical aid and where any sense of differentiation between black and white which may previously have existed was swallowed up in the *belle amitié* of a common sense of Katangese nationhood.

---

[1] Glumov's Law, propounded in Saltykov-Schedrin's *A Contemporary Idyll*, is something to be remembered when people in power show signs of simple-mindedness. When confronted with a sentence like 'The General Motors executive was taken in by Hitler', apply Glumov's Law.

The new image, now hurriedly needed for the sake of interests which remained unchanged, was one of a country in which a handful of whites, deprived of their white military protectors, stood in imminent danger of being torn to pieces by a mob of blacks.

Query: What had happened to all that beautiful friendship?

Answer: The UN had broken it.

How the UN was supposed to have broken it we shall now see. The point is that from August 28th to September 13th, the Katangese gendarmerie were considered, or presented, by the local Europeans and by the Consuls as being on the verge of mutiny and racial massacre. (After September 13th, 'Katangese nationhood' was reinstalled as a necessity of war.) The note had been struck by the French Consul, as his contribution to Mr Munongo's Press conference, even before Rumpunch, and it was now re-echoed in increasing volume at the frequent meetings I had with the Consuls individually, some meetings with the British, French and Belgian Consuls together and one meeting with almost the whole Consular Corps.[1] The burden of their remarks was that if anything happened to any of their citizens they would hold the UN responsible. The interesting thing was that – apart from the Belgian Consul, whose case was rather special – those who were most worried about the fate of their citizens were not those Consuls with the largest colonies – the Greek and the Italian – but those with the largest political and economic interests in Africa, the French and British Consuls. The meeting with the Corps, which was the climax to this onrush of Consular anxiety, took place on the evening of Friday, September 1st, in my office. We did not have enough seats for all the Consuls and some of them, including those who were least worried about the most citizens, stood at the back against the wall. M Créner said he was authorized to speak on behalf of the Consular Corps, of which he was the doyen, in order to inquire what steps the UN proposed to take to protect the lives and property of foreigners, both in Elisabethville and elsewhere, who were in grave danger as a result of the UN's precipitate action.

The telephone on my desk rang. It was Mr Canup, the American Consul, who wished to dissociate himself from the *démarche* of his colleagues. He was not satisfied that it was exclusively Consular in

---

[1] The note had even been struck before the August measures. After the UN prohibited gendarmerie military movements in North Katanga M Créner, as spokesman of the Consular Corps, called on me, on July 21st, to demand a guarantee for the security of Europeans. (See *Congo, 1961,* p. 590.)

character. I thanked Mr Canup for making his position clear. While
I was thanking him I looked round the crowded room. Gratitude
was not the emotion most conspicuous on the faces of the leading
members of the Consular Corps Minus One.

The trouble was, of course, that their citizens had some genuine
grounds for anxiety. The new image – White Colony threatened by
Native Revolt – was much nearer the truth than the old Multiracial
Paradise. A revolt by the gendarmerie or part of the gendarmerie,
with the support of the very large discontented elements in the
mining towns, against the Tshombe régime, was quite possible.
Such a revolt would necessarily take an anti-European turn, and
this for two reasons. First, all those likely to revolt considered that
the Tshombe régime was nothing but a mask for continuing European rule. If they attacked the mask, they would attack the reality
too. Second, the Europeans, who were almost all armed and who
took essentially the same view of the Tshombe régime – as being a
bulwark of their interests – would use force to nip any rebellion in
the bud, and would therefore be victims of, or refugees from, the
rebellion if it succeeded. The general assumption was that the
removal of the European officers was about to precipitate mutiny,
with the horrors that had attended mutiny in the Bas-Congo. This
assumption was open to question, since the mutiny in the Bas-Congo
had been directed against an officer-corps which was then entirely
European. However, this was no time for quibbles. M Créner was
stressing that the UN would be held responsible for any incidents,
involving Europeans, which occurred in Katanga. He and his
colleagues wished to know, without delay, the UN's plans for ensuring the security of foreign lives and property, since the gendarmerie,
by reason of UN action, might not be any longer in a position to
guarantee such protection.

I replied that, in view of the gravity of what they had to say, and
of the unprecedented way in which they had underlined its gravity,
in a joint *démarche* by the whole Consular Corps – or at least by all
the European members of the Consular Corps – I would instantly
inform the Secretary-General of what they had said.

M Lambroschini pushed his chair back against the wall, sucked
in his breath, and opened his yellow eyes very wide. Mr Dunnett
leaned forward in his chair, as if someone had put an additional
weight on his back; additional furrows, as if of pain, appeared upon
his brow. M Créner put into the words the origins of these Anglo-
Gallic symptoms.

This was urgent. European lives might be lost. They wanted to know, now, exactly what security measures the UN was taking.

I told them that, as the meeting had been arranged at short notice, Brigadier Raja was not available, but I would arrange a meeting, between those members of the Consular Corps who were interested in this question, and the civil and military sides of the United Nations as soon as possible. In any case, I understood the situation in Elisabethville itself gave no reason to fear for the safety of the European population.

M Créner indicated that there were other important centres of European population – for example, Jadotville and Kolwezi – and they wanted to know, also, what the UN proposed to do to protect these.

This was a difficult point. The UN, as a result of earlier Consular and diplomatic manifestations of anxiety, had already sent an Irish Company ('B' Company) to Jadotville, but Raja, on military grounds, rightly wanted the Company permanently withdrawn. 'B' Company actually had left Jadotville that day. Its replacement was an open question. ('A' Company replaced it on September 3rd.)

I told the Consuls that the UN would do what it could to protect their citizens but it had also wider responsibilities. The Consuls were worried, very understandably, about their own citizens. The United Nations had responsibilities also for the protection of Africans. Europeans, fortunately, had not yet had to seek UN protection individually in Katanga, but Africans had. There were already 4,000 refugees – refugees from the persecution of Mr Tshombe's police and youth movement – in our camps, and more refugees were arriving every hour at an increasing rate. I asked the Consular Corps to take an interest in this question. The protection of European lives was surely not just a question of military measures – sending a company here or a company there. It was much wider than that. The existence of persecution against Africans by Mr Tshombe's régime created resentment against Europeans, since many Africans – rightly or wrongly – regarded that régime as being sponsored and maintained by Europeans. This kind of resentment was in fact the main source of hatred against Europeans. I asked the Consuls to visit the camps with me, and if they were convinced that persecution was taking place, to use their considerable influence with the Tshombe régime to bring it to an end.

Mr Dunnett looked puzzled, as if I were wandering from the point. M Lambroschini smiled sardonically. M Créner said, on behalf of his colleagues, that they had said what they had come to say and that they awaited the proposed civilian and military

conference. When I rang the Belgian Consulate on the following
day – Saturday – to arrange a meeting that morning, I was told
that M Créner and most of his colleagues were out of town; the
meeting 'would do on Monday'. In my ignorance of Africa, I had
assumed that ravening mobs out for European blood do not take
the week-end off.

My impression of the *démarche* – an impression fortified by
Mr Canup's abstention – was that it was prompted less by humanitarian than by political reasons. It served to indicate – at least it was
so understood in the local context – disapproval of the UN action.
It made the UN responsible for any troubles which occurred in
Katanga. UN 'inability to maintain order' might become a politically relevant factor if an outside power should decide to intervene.[1]

On the day before the Consular *démarche*, the Press had carried
an interesting statement made by Sir Roy Welensky in Salisbury.
Sir Roy said that the high-handed activities of the UN had caused
concern among many Katangese and that he was taking dispositions
to protect the security of the Rhodesian frontiers. 'It is not in the
public interest for me to divulge the exact nature of these dispositions, but they will be adequate'. He added that he had received an
assurance that the British Government 'would not accept an attempt
by the UN to seize Katanga by force'.

Sir Roy's statement was conveyed to Mr Tshombe by the
British and Rhodesian Vice-Consul, Mr David Smith, who was
accompanied by Mr Dunnett, the Consul. Mr Dunnett told me
afterwards that he said nothing, but just sat there while Mr Smith
read Sir Roy's text in French. None the less, Mr Tshombe and his
friends seem to have seen in Mr Dunnett's physical presence, mute
but moving testimony to the truth of Sir Roy's statement about the
assurance he had received from the British Government, and also
to the reality of the British support for Sir Roy's stand. *L'Echo du
Katanga* carried Sir Roy's message prominently on its front page
('Sir Roy Welensky's Encouraging Stand' was the headline) and it
also carried on the back page, above a reassuring communiqué
from the Minister of the Interior ('only suspicious cases will be
arrested') the following:

---

[1] It did not occur to me then, but it has since, that the *effect* of the consular war
of nerves, from Rumpunch on, about their imperilled citizens was to bring about
the dispersal of UN troops, thereby making more unlikely 'illegal' or 'aggressive'
action by the UN – and endangering the success of the UN in any action that did
take place (legal or not). In the event, the only heavy blow inflicted on the UN in
September was the capture of the company at Jadotville.

'*The British Consul conveys his Government's sympathy to the Katangese cause.*

'President Tshombe received the British Consul, accompanied by his Vice-Consul, who came to convey the sympathy of their Government to the Katangese cause. They declared to the Head of State that their Government was following the situation in Katanga with much attention.

'At the same time another delegate from the British Government, coming from Salisbury, arrived in Elisabethville to take stock of the situation after the departure of the European technicians.'[1]

Neither Mr Tshombe nor his advisers are lacking in intelligence, but I doubt if any of them were conscious of certain nuances later established in Whitehall. Her Majesty's Government, we are told, never wavered for an instant in support of the United Nations but I doubt whether Mr Tshombe fully understood this. It may have seemed to him that Rhodesia was on his side and against the UN and that Britain was backing Rhodesia.

This development cannot have failed to weaken the hands of those, in and around the Katanga Government, who felt, following Rumpunch, that a settlement with Leopoldville was urgent; it cannot have failed to strengthen the 'last-ditch' element around Munongo. Mr Munongo must also have been encouraged, and the chances of a peaceful settlement correspondingly diminished, by the activities of Sir Roy in the following week. On September 7th, Sir Roy was in Lusaka, Northern Rhodesia, for talks with the Governor, Sir E. Home, and his own Defence Minister, Mr Caldicott. 'It is understood here', cabled the *Daily Express* correspondent in Salisbury, 'that the talks will lead to proposals to strengthen the border because of the deterioration in Katanga.'[2] On the following day, back in Salisbury, after these talks, Sir Roy pleased his audience at a Gunners' Association dinner by announcing that the Rhodesian Federal Government was to have two field batteries of artillery. 'We cannot', he added, 'regard our armed forces as being concerned only with internal security.'

To appreciate the full impact of such words one needs to know something – and more than I myself knew at this juncture – about the relationship of Katanga and Rhodesia.

The idea that Katanga belongs with Rhodesia goes back to the very beginnings of European presence in Central Africa. Léopold II

---

[1] *L'Echo du Katanga*, Friday September 1st, 1961.
[2] *Daily Express*, September 8th, 1961.

managed to get the area included in the map of the Independent
State of the Congo accepted by the Berlin Congress in 1885, but as
Katanga was the remotest part of the enormous territory thereby
annexed, and as he was busy at the time collecting ivory, he did not
immediately establish a Belgian presence there. Meanwhile, Cecil
Rhodes, the northern borders of whose British South Africa Company's territory were undefined, was pushing in the direction of
Katanga where mineral deposits, of unknown value and character,
were believed to exist. *The Morning Post* – since merged in *The Daily
Telegraph* – discovered that it was immoral to lay claim to an area of
which one was not in actual occupation. For a brief time in 1891 it
seemed as if Belgium and Britain might come into sharp contention
about the territory. The British case was put very well, in retrospect,
by a missionary who lived there at the time:

'The British argument for annexation, if not logical, is at least
geographical, for is not Katanga a true dependency of South
Africa? Moreover the Congo is far too unwieldy and has not
Belgium bitten off more than she can chew?'[1]

Léopold II, however, being a practical man, as well as a good
biter and chewer, saw the desirability of including British capital in
a chartered company, similar to Rhodes's, which would have the
right to whatever of value there might be in Katanga. It was,
therefore, a mixed expedition, led by the Englishman, Captain
'Blue-nose' Stairs, and financed by the mixed (Belgo-English)
Compagnie du Katanga, which in 1891 planted the flag of Léopold's
State on the soil of Katanga.[2] The British (and, it would seem,
Irish) participants in the Stairs expedition were a little sad that it
was not the Union Jack, but they took it philosophically. 'The
civilized States', thought the expedition's doctor, 'would obviously
be pursuing a short-sighted policy, did they forget the duty of
standing firmly together against the Negro.'[3]

The British in Rhodesia and the Belgians in Katanga have not
forgotten this duty. In March 1960, when the Independence of the
Congo was being shaped, Sir Roy Welensky told the *Daily Express*
that the idea of attaching Katanga to the Rhodesian Federation
had been 'suggested' to him. He did not say who had done the
'suggesting', but it seemed, from the context, most likely to be some
of those Europeans who formed, as M Davister has said, the 'cement'

[1] *Thinking Black*, by D. Crawford (1912).

[2] For the early history see René J. Cornet, *Katanga* (Brussels, 1944), and Baron
van Zuylen, *L'Echiquier Congolais* (Brussels, 1959).

[3] *With Captain Stairs to Katanga*, Joseph A. Moloney (1893).

of the Conakat party, of which Mr Tshombe was the standard-bearer. Now Sir Roy, like myself, is a bit of a blurter, and on this occasion he blurted. For the Conakat party was, at this time, fighting an election in which it needed to get a majority of African votes – not a situation with which Sir Roy was familiar – and such votes were, somehow, not available in favour of seeking admission to the great Rhodesian partnership. So the Conakat disavowed Sir Roy, even in rather intemperate language, saying that his idea was 'incompatible with its mentality and its dignity by reason of the racial segregation which still rules in the Rhodesias and in South Africa'.[1]

After the elections, the Conakat was less worried about race relations in Rhodesia. When the Belgian Government, in June 1960, hesitated to give the Conakat the amendment to the Fundamental Law which it needed in order to make itself sole master of Katanga, Mr Kibwe, on June 12th, threatened to enter into negotiations 'openly' with Rhodesia. The Belgian Government gave in, thus opening the way for the secession of Katanga. On July 9th, 1960, Tshombe threatened to appeal for Rhodesian aid, and on July 10th he appealed for British aid, obviously from Rhodesia, although on July 5th he had said (in Leopoldville) that Katanga could not 'associate itself with a neighbouring country which remains under the colonial yoke'.[2]

Mr Macmillan said, in the Commons on July 11th, that such intervention was not possible 'in present circumstances'; this did not seem altogether to exclude the possibility of intervention in some future, unspecified circumstances. As we have seen,[3] M Wigny's hurried Notes of July 11th seemed designed to prevent a too-prompt recognition of the secession of Katanga, which could be followed by an entry of Rhodesian troops 'at the request of the legal Government of Katanga'.

Much had changed since then, but the partnership of what Sir Roy represented with what Mr Tshombe represented remained intact – *cette belle amitié*. Nor did the benefits go all one way. A week before Rumpunch Mr Tshombe had received 'numerous foreign personalities', including 'a delegation' – the pigmentation of which was unspecified – from Rhodesia. The Katangan Government's official communiqué said that the delegation 'thanked Mr Tshombe for the help which he had given to Rhodesia by supporting, during

[1] All this is in *Dossiers du CRISP*, I., p. 235.
[2] See *Dossiers du CRISP*, II, p. 540; 715.
[3] Chapter IV, p. 85.

the electoral campaign preceding the recent referendum, certain moderate leaders'.[1]

Presumably, as things had not fundamentally changed in Rhodesia during the previous year, what he helped them to do was to keep Rhodesia under 'the colonial yoke'.

Against this background, Sir Roy's oratory and armed preparations, and Mr Dunnett's silent sympathy, must have been most heartening to the friends of independent Katanga. 'If things go on', wrote *La Libre Belgique* on September 9th, 'some people consider that Sir Roy Welensky would not hesitate to intervene, with his troops already massed on the Katangan frontier.'

I find it hard to believe that, without such evidence of outside support, the Katangan Government would not, following the expulsion of the mercenaries, have made a real effort to come to terms with the Central Government and the United Nations.[2] What it actually did – once it became clear that help could be expected from across the borders, and that General de Gaulle was right to speak of 'the so-called United Nations' – was quite different.

On the evening of August 30th – the day, as it happened, of Sir Roy's statement – I returned late to Les Roches. It had been a rather busy and disappointing day, mainly taken up with discussions with the Belgian Consulate, whose office corridors were full of large sun-burnt men, all supposed to be awaiting repatriation. Some of the repatriates-designate, it appeared, wanted to take souvenirs with them; one had tried to abstract a document from Colonel Egge's desk. Raja and Egge had doubts about 'voluntary repatriation', feeling that all it involved, in some cases at least, was a trip to Ndola or Brazzaville, followed by return to Kolwezi – where there is an air-strip and no UN presence. I was beginning to realize that, in agreeing to M Créner's proposal, I had accepted bigger risks than I had bargained for.

In the large, badly-lit and sullenly furnished drawing-room at Les Roches there were three Belgians waiting for me. When I came in they stood up, smiling excessively. They introduced themselves, as

---

[1] *La Libre Belgique*, August 21st, 1961.

[2] It must be remembered that, in the brief interval between Rumpunch and the Anglo-Rhodesian encouragement, the tone of the Katangese official statements was by no means one of defiance: 'I consider', said the President, 'that the International Organization slightly exceeded its authority (*a légèrement outrepassé ses droits*). As a matter of fact, the Security Council resolutions never said that the President and the Ministers had to be arrested. Mr Munongo and I were arrested, but Mr O'Brien apologized to me and I forgave him.' (*L'Echo du Katanga*, August 30th, 1961.) This statement was lacking in accuracy but not in moderation.

belonging to the legal side of Mr Tshombe's administration – they each had a long and impressive title with *parquet* or *police judiciaire* somewhere in it. They all looked as if they lived exclusively on sausages and had never been exposed to the light of day. The fattest and palest of the three apologized, too much, for their intrusion. The object of their visit, he said, was very simple. A criminal had escaped from the custody of the Katangan police and had taken refuge in the Indian camp. He was just a common criminal – he had stolen a large number of stamps[1] as a matter of fact – and as such he was not entitled to UN protection. The Indians had refused to hand him back to the police, without clearance from me. If I would kindly give that clearance now, they could go round and collect him, and they need trouble me no more. The man's name was André Crémer, a thief. It was just a matter of routine.

His companions agreed with this. One of them made a little joke about civil servants and red tape.

I pointed out that it was nine o'clock at night. As a civil servant myself, I felt no enthusiasm for red tape after 6 p.m., or for giving clearances on unexamined cases at any time. I could promise them that M Crémer, while in Indian custody, would not go round stealing stamps. Why the hurry? The case could wait until morning.

They were overworked, apprehensive men and they could not think, off-hand, of any good reason why it might be urgent to have their stamp-stealer back. This was rather embarrassing for us all, and I was glad to see them go.

Egge reported that Crémer had an interesting story, which he told me. There was no conclusive proof of what Crémer said, but there was evidence that he was not simply the petty thief which the Katanga *parquet* claimed he was. He carried, for example, a pass from the Ministry of the Interior, guaranteeing him access to all gendarmerie posts. He claimed to have organized, at Mr Munongo's request, an attack on a UN Nigerian jeep near Kamina on July 22nd. Such an attack had actually taken place on that date. This did not prove Crémer had done it but it did show that he was, at least, better informed than the average stamp-stealer – the July 22nd affair had attracted no general attention. Egge said he personally believed Crémer's story, in which close questioning revealed no inconsistencies.

Believing that Crémer's story should be of interest to the Press,

---

[1] He was supposed to have stolen two million francs worth of 'South Kasai stamps' from the commercial offices of the State of South Kasai. These offices were presumably controlled by the Katanga authorities since the arrest of Mr Bintou.

as illustrating some hitherto little publicized, but relevant, aspects of
Tshombe's Katanga, I asked Egge to produce him at my noon
Press conference. André Crémer was a leathery looking, wiry
little man of 36. He replied to the journalists' questions without
hesitation and circumstantially. He said he was a Belgian, who had
served with the French paratroopers and had come to the Congo to
serve, first, with the Katangese forces in South Kasai. He had
arrived in Elisabethville on February 12th and had been com-
missioned by Mr Munongo to organize armed attacks against UN
personnel. For this purpose he had received the little pass, which
was produced. He had gone round gendarmerie posts and had
picked twenty-four men for this work. He had taken care, he said,
to select men straight from the villages; those who had been
'polluted by town life' were no good for this kind of work. The work
of the group he defined as follows – I take the *Libre Belgique* report:

'The group was to kill UN soldiers, blow up ammunition dumps
and intercept convoys. . . . The Baluba would be held responsible
for these actions by the Katanga Government. Finally, Captain
Crémer and his terrorist group were to kidnap or kill M Michel
Tombelaine. . . . Only one of the three actions was partly
successful.

'On July 19th last, Mr Munongo is supposed to have said
(*aurait dit*) to Captain Crémer at his private residence, "I need a
victim" – "*Il me faut une victime.*"'

The date given for this ogreish remark is interesting: it was the day
before Munongo's 'appeal to the Soviet Union' Press conference.
The need for 'a victim' would fit his propaganda line of that time
which was 'Katanga Driven to Despair: UN Creating Anarchy and
Opening Way to Communism'. If Crémer was inventing he picked
his date with a political tact not often found in petty thieves.

'Four [*sic*] days later', the *Libre Belgique* account goes on, 'a
jeep-load of UN Nigerians was fired on (at Kamina) by Crémer and
his picked men. One Nigerian was slightly wounded. Shortly
afterwards Mr Munongo was afraid that Mr Tshombe, who knew
nothing about all this, might learn of the existence of the terrorist
group. He told the Captain to go back to Europe.'

In actual fact, we learned in September from captured Sûreté
documents, what had happened was that Tshombe *had* found out.
On July 24th the Paramount Chief at Kamina, Kasongo Nyembo,
had sent Tshombe a telegram, complaining that a group of
'Munongo's special police', led by a Belgian, had fired on a UN
jeep. Kasongo Nyembo's complaint was that such things should not

be done on *his* territory without notice to him in advance, and without the President's express authorization. Clearly Munongo made the Paramount Chief nervous. Unfortunately, I did not have this element of confirmation of Crémer's story at the time of the Press conference.

Crémer had been ordered, on August 19th, to come back. On his return he had been, he said, framed with the stamp theft. He had certainly escaped from his captors, by a ruse, and reached the Dogra camp.

I believed then, and I believe now, that Crémer was telling the truth. Most of the reporters present had the same impression.[1] I think he was hired by Munongo to do the things he said he was hired to do. He had clearly given as little value for money as a mercenary can well do. He and his unpolluted villagers, it seemed, had been more interested in drawing their pay than in risking acts of violence; I thought this attitude one to be commended. I also thought that other agents, perhaps more zealous and less compromised, might still be at large. Crémer's own excuse for failing to murder Tombelaine was that he had found it impossible to get hold of an African willing to do the job; a European would have been easy, of course, but it had to be an African. Crémer's successors, however, might be able to solve this problem; after all Goering had found an authentic, though mentally defective, Communist for the Reichstag fire.[2]

Considering all this – and other matters, to which I shall come in a moment – I decided to ask Tshombe to suspend Mr Munongo from his functions. This was the day (August 31st) Tshombe had the heart attack, or appeared to have one: he certainly turned grey and seemed to choke. His Belgian doctor gave him an injection and me a reproachful look. Tshombe and I had not, in fact, had a violent scene; he had agreed to look into the charges, and if there was a good prima facie case, to ask the National Assembly to suspend Munongo. It was then he collapsed – from fear, I believe. Nothing

---

[1] What their papers carried is another matter. See Chapter XV.

[2] In fact, though Crémer was in our hands, 'Crémerism' continued. The *Daily Express* correspondent in Katanga, Cyril Ainsley, reported on September 1st, that 'In a bar in town here last night I was told by two European officers of Katanga's army – both carrying revolvers in their pockets – that plastic bombs are being made and that sabotage would begin before the end of the week.' And on the following day the same correspondent reported French officers as 'trying to organize Africans into murder squads to attack UN convoys and personnel'. 'Desperate adventurers with a burning hate of the UN', had, Mr Ainsley stated, 'an assassination list headed by Mr Conor O'Brien.'

came of the National Assembly idea and, in order to keep the pressure up, I told Tshombe, on September 2nd, that it would be impossible to maintain 'normal relations' with a Government which included a man on whom such grave suspicions rested.

There was, of course, an element of bluff in all this. I believed Munongo to be dangerous – and not only, or even primarily, to UN personnel – but I did not think that Tshombe would have the courage to try to sack him. The encouragement which the extremists whom Munongo represented were receiving from Rhodesia, and the silent sympathy from Britain, made the difficult and dangerous feat of dropping the Minister of the Interior even more difficult and dangerous. Nor, of course, could there be any question of 'impartial legal investigation' of the charges; there may be some places where political crimes and conspiracies are investigated impartially, but Katanga was not one of them. Nor was there any point in a UN Commission of Inquiry. Such a Commission, since, found Munongo guilty of the murder of Lumumba. This finding made no difference at all in Elisabethville where he remained Minister of the Interior, wearing his quotation marks with a swagger.

The thing to do with Munongo, in my opinion, was not to investigate him impartially, or to punctuate his titles. The thing to do was to get him behind bars, thus depriving the European die-hards of Elisabethville of 'their' African and their control of the police apparatus. I was now seeking authority, through Leopoldville, from New York to arrest Munongo. The main purpose of my request to Tshombe was to prepare the way, and show the need, for such an arrest. If Tshombe dropped him, well and good; if not, we were justified, by our responsibilities for the maintenance of public order, in arresting him ourselves.

Some people, especially in the Western capitals, considered my behaviour at this point 'swashbuckling'. Those who were dependent on *The Times* and *The Daily Telegraph* for their information on Katanga must certainly have thought so. These newspapers carried, verbatim, a number of things I was saying, and the demands I was making, arising out of Crémer's charges – but did not print one word about Crémer or his statement. The effect on the audience was rather like that which would be made by showing a film of the behaviour of a man who had just overturned a wasp's nest – and omitting any word or image that might suggest the existence of wasps. This fellow, think the audience, is crazy. Can it be that that is what the audience was intended to think?

In any case, even some of those who managed to know of Mr

Crémer's existence thought my reaction to his statement excessive. 'We have been told in the Press', wrote Lord Salisbury to *The Times*, 'that on the evidence of one witness of not at all dependable character' – (Lord Salisbury had not learned of the existence of this witness from the paper to which he confides his thoughts; perhaps when he merely wants information he borrows the *Daily Express* from the butler) – 'who has told a story of an assassination plot by a Katangese Minister – a story not yet it seems corroborated from other sources; the representative of the UN in Katanga, a Mr O'Brien, has declared that he must break off all normal relations with the Katangese Government.' *The Times*, September 8th, 1961.

It all depends, Lord Salisbury, on the point of view. If Hertfordshire were infested with bands of armed men, led by foreign adventurers; if these adventurers boasted in the local taverns of their intention and capacity to blow up Hatfield and murder you; and if, in this general situation, a man with military experience and a criminal record[1] showed you evidence that he had been employed for unspecified special duties by the Chief Constable of Hertfordshire and if he said that these 'special duties' were along the same lines as those of the military adventurers, it is conceivable that you might have asked for the removal, or at least suspension of the Chief Constable. And in Elisabethville, reading whatever the *Echo du Katanga* chose to print about Hertfordshire – say, an account of what you said about the Chief Constable, without any background – I might well have said: 'I say! Poor Salisbury seems to be going off his rocker!' And if, after all, I read afterwards that Hatfield *had* been blown up, with you in it, I should have greeted the news with a ringing 'Tut! Tut!'

The threat which Munongo's name represented was not solely, or even mainly, to Tombelaine and myself. I used to ask myself at this time, what kind of incident would be most helpful to the régime, and the answer is one that haunted my dreams. Not the murder of a senior UN person – I thought (perhaps wrongly) that that would rebound against the régime. It would be the brutal murder of harmless non-political European civilians living in an area where all hitherto had been quiet. I thought of my friends Major and Mrs Geurtz, with their quaint little home and garden,

---

[1] The Belgians produced evidence that Crémer had a criminal record and this, they seemed to feel, showed that he could not be a hired assassin. Crémer, in fact, was a gangster, and that, I believe, is why Munongo hired him. As for Crémer's not being, as Lord Salisbury pointed out, 'a dependable character', Michel Tombelaine, for one, must be rather glad he was not.

'Poet and Peasant', near Jadotville. I considered whether certain people in Katanga had the intelligence to see the propaganda value, at the present juncture, of murder 'by Africans' of people like that, and the ruthlessness to carry out such a plan. I thought of Munongo and the Algerian officers, now in hiding, and I believed the answer to be 'yes' on both counts.[1]

This was a hypothetical consideration in favour of determined preventive action. There was another consideration which had become a reality. This was the incitement to inter-tribal hostility which led to the plight of the Baluba of Kasai.

It is necessary, here, to make a few strictly non-ethnological reflections on tribalism. The newspaper reader has, I think, a picture of the Congo as a place in which the various tribes are constantly at each others' throats, except when the white man is there to separate them. It would be wise, I think, to entertain also another hypothesis: that the tribes may now usually be able to get along well enough, except when it is in someone's financial interest to set them fighting. Tribal conflicts, we are told 'flare up' un-accountably. I used to accept this, without much thought, but now, when I hear of a tribal conflict 'flaring up', I try to find out in whose interest it was to drop a match. Take the case of the Baluba and the Lulua in Kasai. Their antagonism 'flared up', and was considerably more publicized than tribal fights normally are, when it was in the interests of Forminière that these things should happen and be known to happen.[2] When that ceased to be the case, the Lulua and the Baluba seemed to become gradually reconciled. Perhaps it is one of the age-old customs of these tribes to fight each other when there is a Republican Administration in Washington and live in peace when the Democrats are in.

In Katanga, as we have seen, there are two sorts of Baluba, those of Kasai and those of Katanga itself. Fighting between these had

---

[1] 'It is dangerous to leave that gentleman (Munongo) at liberty, as he is,' I wrote on September 5th to Máire MacEntee. 'Dangerous, not for us, but for the unarmed black people in the city who are not Bayeke, and Europeans in the bush.' (Translation).

[2] Michel Merlier takes rather a different view, or views: 'The secession of South Kasai like that of Katanga represents [in the autumn of 1960] an aspect of the new policy of the Société Générale. The new state becomes a bastion of Belgian imperialism. However, financial intrigues play a relatively smaller part in it than violent ethnic conflicts, which seem to affect the majority of the rural population.' (*Le Congo*, etc., p. 317). M. Merlier's last sentence may be right; I have no first-hand knowledge of the Kasai situation. But it is a fact that when Forminière changed its line little more was heard of the tribal conflicts.

'flared up' in Kamina in May 1960. The Katanga Baluba attacked
the Kasai ones with machetes and bows and arrows, the day before
the elections. The police did not intervene and the gendarmerie
were absent. Twenty people were wounded, six killed, including a
child decapitated.[1]

The political background to these disturbances was as follows:
The Baluba of Kasai resident in Katanga, are politically, like most
of the Baluba of Katanga, nationalists ('pro-Sendwe', 'pro-
Lumumba'[2] and now 'pro-Central Government'). However, the
Paramount Chief at Kamina, Kasongo Nyembo, is pro-Conakat;
that is to say he favours the party supported by the Belgians. Most
of the chiefs did, since the Belgians were in the habit of removing
those who did not. Kasongo Nyembo, however, is a very grand chief
indeed, with great spiritual authority, and many of his people,
unlike Baluba elsewhere, supported Conakat, on his advice. The
Baluba of Kasai, who are better educated and more 'advanced'
than the Katanga ones, were less impressed by Kasongo Nyembo and
wished to hear Jason Sendwe, who was prevented by Kasongo
Nyembo's supporters, with police acquiescence, from addressing
an election meeting at Kamina. The attack by Kasongo Nyembo's
supporters on the Kasai Baluba 'flared up' on the night after
Sendwe's visit and before the election. It cannot have been encouraging for electors who were thinking of voting against the Conakat
and their chief, especially since the votes were counted by their
chief's friends.

In this case, therefore, the 'flare up' certainly suited the interests
of the Conakat. The Conakat has been defined by M Davister,
who likes it, as 'an African party which the Europeans had intel-
ligently sponsored at baptism, and whose strings they clearly pulled
in the wings'.[3] 'Certain Europeans', writes the same M Davister,
'did nothing to discourage the gulf between Kasai Baluba and
Katanga Baluba from growing deeper.'[4] He also says that it would
be wrong to say that 'much petrol had to be poured on the flames'
to make the two groups 'tear each other to pieces'.[5] To say that is to
admit that some was poured.

---

[1] *Dossiers du CRISP*, I, p. 242.

[2] This is confusing because of the fight put up by the Baluba in Kasai against
Lumumba's forces. But the 'Lumumbism' of the Kasai Baluba in Katanga is
recognized: See Pierre Davister, *Katanga, Enjeu du Monde*, p. 80.

[3] *Katanga, etc.*, p. 66.

[4] *Katanga, etc.*, p. 79

[5] *Katanga, etc.*, p. 76.

It is not unfair, I think, to take these words as meaning that
'certain Europeans' judged it opportune to arouse inter-tribal or
even intra-tribal, hatred in the pre-election period, thereby diminish-
ing the pull of Congolese nationalism. The antagonisms and archaic
loyalties so revived strengthened the authority of the chiefs and the
obedient chiefs delivered the votes to Conakat. Where the tribal
group concerned was backward and ignorant, like the Lunda, the
chiefly authority was enough in itself. Thus the invaluable M
Davister tells us that 'the Lunda have no political movement of their
own but it is enough for the powerful chief Mwata Yamvo to wave
his hand for his numerous subjects to nod their heads'.[1] (Mwata
Yamvo is Mr Tshombe's father-in-law, and also the particular
current of African nationalism which Mr Tshombe represents.[2])
There is as yet no trouble with the Lunda. It is when a more advanced section, like the Baluba, get political 'ideas' that it is necessary to pour a little, just a little, petrol on tribal fires. The received
version, among the Elisabethville Europeans, of the Kamina episode
was that Sendwe started it, by his impudence in trying to address a
public meeting. The whole thing demonstrated, in their view, the
African's unfitness for self-Government, and refuted the illusions of
well-meaning liberals. And indeed headlines like 'Africans Decapitate Child' have often disconcerted liberals. The headline 'Africans
Instigated by Europeans Decapitate Child' is less snappy, and less
easily assimilated by a European mind but, on this occasion at
least, it would have given a better idea of what actually happened.

After the 1960 elections, the Conakat, which lacked an overall
majority, did a deal with Mr Kalonji, as a result of which Kalonji
threw the Conakat a much needed vote in the Assembly – that of the
MNC-Kalonji representative (our friend Mr Bintou it seems) –
which helped the Conakat to its goal of governing alone and seceding
(this is known as Katanga's right to self-determination). In return
the Conakat guaranteed 'protection' for the Kasaians living in
Katanga. Immemorial tribal antagonisms were thereupon switched
off and so remained until, in August 1961, Mr Munongo decided to
arrest Mr Bintou.[3] Then they began to revive, and early in September they flared up with a vengeance.

---

[1] *Katanga*, p. 40.

[2] He is also a sort of international Uncle Tom, who advised the Lunda in
Northern Rhodesia on their duties as loyal citizens of the Federation. There is a
branch of the Conakat in Lusaka, and it looks as if someone may be toying with the
idea of a Lundaland, taking in all the copper on both sides of the border.

[3] See Chapter XIII, p. 206.

By August 31st, there were 700 refugees in our camps; by September 1st, 4,000; by September 3rd, 10,000; by September 5th, 20,000; by September 9th, 35,000; by September 12th, probably more than 45,000 but in reality we had lost count. These were mainly Baluba of Kasai, with a minority of Baluba of Katanga, Tshokwe and other groups. They included among them the African *élite* of Elisabethville, almost all Kasai Baluba: white-collar workers with good homes, who now came here to squat on the ground round our camps in conditions of the greatest misery and squalor.

Why did they come? It was not entirely because they were terrorized. Among the first arrivals especially there were some who had been beaten, flogged or wounded: many spoke of others who had been killed, but what they said was not necessarily true. Tombelaine and I brought out journalists to see tham at first, but these were rather forlorn little expeditions. If there were atrocities the correspondents were prepared to report them, but there was nothing very much really, just a growing number of Africans, men, women and children, in a smelly camp with emergency sanitation. Where are the atrocities? Nothing very impressive appeared. I remember the refugee leaders pushing forward a young woman who had been kicked. She pulled up her skirt shyly and showed a badly swollen knee. She had been kicked all right, but a kick on the knee is not much of an atrocity anywhere, especially in Africa. One of the correspondents, a South African, grinned. 'Not merely atrocities', he said, 'but cheesecake as well, eh?' The photographers were particularly bored. Someone wanted to show them a man who had been flogged, and whose back was very badly scarred. They were not interested. I asked one of them why and I shall never forget his answer. 'Weals', he said, 'don't show on a black back.'

He was a decent man and he intended this as a purely technical observation; it has, I believe, a wider reference.

Similarly, the campaign against the Kasaians and others by Munongo's police and youth movement, and by their Lunda neighbours, instigated by the radio and by word of mouth, was not exactly a reign of terror, at least not in its visible and audible aspects. 'We are the Jews of Katanga', one of them said,[1] and with some truth – but if so, they were Jews not in Nazi Germany but in some country of more guarded anti-Semitism, like Pétain's France. The people concerned – between a third and a quarter of the African population of Elisabethville – were being told, in effect: 'You are here on sufferance and if you keep a civil tongue in your head, and

---

[1] *Daily Express*, September 4th, 1961.

stay out of politics you will not be molested much, or only occasionally.' The first waves of refugees came in fear for their lives, but the
subsequent and larger waves came, I believe, less in fear than in
protest, indignation and total rejection of what Katanga stood for.

Many of the refugees wanted to leave Katanga altogether and
early on – the date was, I believe, September 3rd or 4th – we had a
train standing by to take away the first contingent to South Kasai.
We were instructed, however, to cancel it and try to arrange the
peaceful return of the refugees to their homes and jobs in Elisabethville – since neither homes nor jobs existed for them in devastated
South Kasai. This was true, but ignored a relevant factor: that only
a revolution could turn Katanga into a place in which these people
would want to live and work.

In any case I took five of the refugee leaders to see Tshombe
(September 2nd). They were grave men in stained, rumpled clothes;
they spoke excellent French and were quite at ease, with all their
wits about them. The man who was not at ease was Tshombe. He
said that 'before independence' he was the only Lunda who could
talk on equal terms with men like them. This, he explained, was
because he had made a million francs. Normally Tshombe spoke to
the point, but he was not happy in the presence of these men and
he began to wander, like Mr Kiwele. The contrast of their squalor
and his wealth gave them the advantage, not him. He had the money
but they had the self-respect. They said they would go back if he
sacked Munongo and got rid of all the Belgians in the police. He did
not, and they did not go back.

Early that month, among the prematurely congratulatory telegrams had been one which began: '*Tous ici applaudissent votre
Rumpunch, mais. . . .*' This was from Khiary (at least we always
took Linner in French to be Khiary) and the *mais* was that the real
object of our endeavours was the reintegration of Katanga in the
Congo and we must now press harder than ever towards this end.
As a beginning, the Central Government wished to assert its
authority in North Katanga, setting up, for example, police stations
and customs posts in towns on the North Katanga frontiers, and
we should co-operate with them in this. There was more to it than
that, but that was the central idea.

I had doubts about this proposition and expressed them. The
centre of the trouble was not in North Katanga, but in the South
Katanga mining towns. In these towns the pseudo-African régime
established in the interest of the mine-owners had hitherto relied,
in part on foreign mercenaries, in part on the excitation of inter-

tribal hatreds, through manipulation of the chiefly power, and in
particular through using the more superstitious and backward part
of the African population in order to terrorize the more advanced
and politically-minded part. After the departure of the mercenaries, the régime had necessarily relied on the second, tribalist,
part of their system, and thus had created the refugee problem. Their
propaganda was now falsely, but not unsuccessfully, accusing the UN
of having started the trouble by 'luring' people into the camps in
order to create anarchy and incite racial strife. Similarly the UN
would be blamed for any acts of inter-tribal violence – very much
in accordance with the pattern whereby such occurrences are
usually laid at the door of 'well-meaning liberals' rather than of
those ill-meaning conservatives who pour the petrol. Furthermore
the most dangerous mercenaries had gone underground. Just as the
period of open Belgian Army intervention had been succeeded by
that of the white-officered gendarmerie, so that period was now
succeeded by one in which an apparently all-African gendarmerie
was being directed, through people like Muké, by the more desperate
foreign elements, encouraged from across the border. The dangerous
situation this created could be aggravated by the proposed action
in North Katanga. It was at the centre, I proposed, that action
should be taken. Munongo was the centre and symbol of the whole
system and by arresting him – or at least removing him from power –
and by taking over the radio to prevent its use for inter-tribal
incitation, we would at least be making clear to those concerned
that their old methods of dividing to rule would no more be tolerated
than their foreign-armed forces. This might induce them, and
Tshombe, to come to terms. I served notice on Tshombe, on September 5th, in writing, that the actions of his Government in provoking
inter-tribal hatred were liable to cause civil war, and could therefore,
if they continued, involve the application of paragraph A.1 of the
resolution of February 21st, which I cited. The point about paragraph A.1. is that it authorizes the 'use of force, if necessary, in the
last resort'. In my opinion, the 'last resort' was almost at hand.

On the same day I conferred, at Kamina Base, with Khiary and
Fabry. It was an inconclusive conference. Khiary agreed with my
view, but had not got clearance from New York. A telegram from
Hammarskjold authorized us to apprehend Munongo if he were
caught *in flagrante* inciting to inter-tribal violence. I felt this was not
likely to happen.

Meanwhile the refugees flocked in, and at an ever-rising tempo.
On September 4th, the Union Minière announced publicly that it

was ready to repatriate European women and children if that became necessary 'as a result of the activities of the UN' and on the following day the first 'spontaneous African' demonstration against the UN took place. Ray Moloney of the UPI described aspects of this campaign:

'I watched the Katanga Government mount a deliberate "hate campaign" against the UN. I saw UN troops being stoned even though they made no attempt to retaliate. The stoning attacks were led by officials of the Katanga Information Service.

'I listened to Katanga Radio while it claimed that UN Indian troops raped and pillaged their way through the African quarters of Elisabethville.'

It should be noted that these activities were not the immediate reaction to the operation of August 28th; they came only after Welensky's message and the Union Minière's pointed reference to the United Nations. The demonstrations were directed against the American Consulate also and its windows were smashed by the youths of the Jenakat. The British and French Consulates were not molested. The untutored and spontaneously indignant natives thereby indicated a surprisingly accurate appreciation of the alignment of the Powers.

On September 9th, Tshombe announced the existence of a plot to arrest him and Munongo and seize the radio; it also involved the disarmament of the gendarmerie, and the bringing in of the Congolese Army. The UN was to do all this, he said, at the request of the Central Government and Parliament. I saw him that day and he told me he had this information from my friend Nyembo, who was then attending the Parliament in Leopoldville, and had heard these measures voted in closed session. Because Nyembo had opposed them he had had to fly for his life – despite the UN guarantee – escaping across the Congo river by night in a canoe to Brazzaville.

Khiary told me, when he came to Elisabethville two days later, that Nyembo's account of the closed session was substantially accurate, with one significant exception. Nyembo and the other Conakat deputies had not voted against the measures; they had voted for them. Remembering the correspondence about the expulsion of M B—— I had no difficulty in believing this.

On Sunday, September 10th, Tombelaine was arrested at the post office, presumably with the intent to use him as a hostage. The following is an extract from a letter written on that day:

'The last week has been one of rock-throwing and abuse carried out mainly by small boys organized by the Security Police and

Belgian hacks in the Ministry of Information. Belgians are also trying to provoke the new African officers of the gendarmerie into fighting the UN. Sir R. Welensky, Lord Salisbury, Senator Dodd, the *Daily Express* and the *N.Y. Tribune* etc., are encouraging Tshombe from the side-lines. The poor man is encouraged by all this into thinking that he can hold out, and even that Rhodesian forces will come to his aid. Operation Mariana. This period of *attente* is a little trying, much palaver with very stupid people, in order to avoid all kinds of silly incidents, and much *glapissement* of Belges and crypto-belges.[1] However we are all pulling well together *tant civils que militaires et tant que vous voudrez mon général*. Khiary's ascendancy in Leopoldville is a help, he being rock of strength, equipped with wisdom of serpent. We now have a battalion of Ghurkas here – Maitra's mongols – so there is no doubt about the military situation. The political and legal situations however are still quite tricky, in New York and Leopoldville as well as here.'

'This letter was interrupted' – it goes on in different ink – 'by news that my assistant Tombelaine had been arrested in the post office and was being held at gun-point (before astonished journalists trying to file copy) by Sûreté, police, gendarmes, paracommandos and godknowswhatall. I careered off downtown with the vikings in a Swedish armoured car, we did some sabre-rattling. I found one sane (African) gendarmerie officer and got Tombelaine out. The man responsible (for the arrest) was a Belgian Sûreté official, so stupid that he actually appeared on the spot. Paragraph A.2 – forty-eight hours. We will now comb out all the Belgians in the Sûreté. Quite a morning. Then a very pleasant lunch with the rescued Tombelaine, Ray Moloney of UPI, Dick Williams of BBC and the vikings.'[2]

---

[1] When I think of my Belgian friends – I have some – and of those few Belgians who, with so much integrity and devotion, attempt the difficult task of enlightening public opinion about the Congo, I am ashamed of having used the word 'Belges' in this context. It was intended as shorthand for the Katanga Belgians and their backers but it should not have been so used.

[2] Letter to Máire MacEntee, September 10th. This was a Sunday afternoon and I went into town with the Swedes, dressed as I was when Ray Moloney rang me from the post office with the news about Tombelaine. I was wearing a striped sports-shirt, and a picture of me so attired, in the Swedish Armoured Personnel Carrier, appeared in many Western newspapers a little later. This lent colour to the growing belief that I was a funny sort of diplomat – 'a striped-shirted Castro' one paper said. – I suppose I should have changed and let Tombelaine look out for himself.

Khiary and Fabry arrived in Elisabethville on September 11th. We met Tshombe on September 12th. He said that he favoured an African solution, based on confederation, in the spirit of the Tananarive Conference. He was ready to meet Adoula, but not in Leopoldville.

Khiary said that, in fact, he was not inviting him to meet Adoula, although no doubt he would do so if he came to Leopoldville. The fact was that the Secretary-General was due in Leopoldville on the following day, and he, Khiary, had been instructed to invite Tshombe to come there to meet him. He felt that this enabled Tshombe to come there without abandoning any principle, and he believed that, with the aid of Mr Hammarskjold, it should be possible for a solution to be worked out. Tshombe thought Mr Hammarskjold should come to Elisabethville. Khiary said he was empowered to convey an invitation, not to negotiate on a venue. Tshombe said he would think it over.

Tshombe then told the Press of his invitation to Hammarskjold to come to Elisabethville. He denied that he had received any invitation from Khiary to meet Hammarskjold in Leopoldville. Kimba announced that 'negotiations with Rhodesia' were under way. We received a report from Jadotville that the Irish company there – sent to protect the European population – was surrounded by the gendarmerie, under the orders of white officers and at the instigation of the local Europeans.

At Les Roches the previous evening Khiary had given us instructions, on the basis of which the military command had prepared plans for which the code word was *Morthor*.

What these plans were, we shall see in the next chapter. These were to be applied in the event of a breakdown of the talks with Tshombe. Khiary and Fabry left Elisabethville on the afternoon of September 12th. Khiary's last words to me were: Above all, no half measures. *Surtout pas de demi-mesures.*

Morthor was set for 4 a.m. the following morning.

Above left, ' "*Nous sommes*," he said, "*la mission d'Albertville*" ' (p. 310). Picture taken in the author's presence of Baluba tribesmen, accompanying Congolese National Army soldiers at Bendera, N. Katanga, November 1961.

Above right, '*I served notice on Tshombe on September 5th, in writing, that the actions of his Government were liable to cause civil war. . . .*' (p. 243). This photograph, taken after the delivery of this message, shows Tshombe with the author and Colonel Bjorn Egge (Norway).

Below, '*Prosper . . . came to Albertville at the risk of his life to take over the administration and prevent reprisals*' (p. 308). Prosper Mwamba Ilunga as President of the Province of Lualaba (i.e. N. Katanga) presents the flag of the Republic of the Congo to the police of Albertville, 13th November 1961.

'. . . many of the Swedes sympathized, in varying degrees, with the local Europeans, and did not altogether approve . . .' (p. 253). A briefing session with Colonel Jonas Waern (Sweden), U.N. Commander, S. Katanga, and his staff.

'. . . being "consulted" rather as the Chinese consult their deceased ancestors' (p. 319). U Thant, General McKeown and the author in the Security Council chamber during the November 1961 debate on the Congo.

15

THE FIRE IN THE GARAGE

'*Man propounds negotiations, Man accepts the compromise,*
Very rarely will he squarely push the logic of a fact
To its ultimate conclusion in unmitigated act.'

Kipling

In the drawing-room of the Villa des Roches, on the afternoon of Monday, September 11th, Fabry opened his brief-case and handed me five individual warrants. He was smiling like a Machiavellian Santa Claus. Khiary looked on benevolently. The documents were *mandats d'amener* – warrants for arrest, in the names of Tshombe, Moïse; Munongo, Godefroid; Kibwe, Jean-Baptiste; Kimba, Evariste; and Mutaka, Charles.[1] The charges were the same in all five cases: '*Tortures et assassinats*'. These *mandats d'amener*[2] were printed forms, with blanks, apparently as used in the former Belgian Congo. There was only a small space for the charge, or *motivation*, and the *mandats* did not say whom these men had tortured or assassinated – presumably Lumumba and his companions, perhaps others also. The document was signed by the head of the Central Government *parquet* – the attorney-general, roughly speaking – in Leopoldville.

I have not preserved copies of the individual warrants, but I have a copy of a collective warrant in the same five names, which

---

[1] I had forgotten the warrant for Mutaka until the acquisition, recently, of some documentary evidence revived my memory. I told Khiary I thought there was very little point in arresting Mutaka and that Samalenghe, Minister of Information, who was completely under the thumb of the ultras, would be a more useful acquisition. Khiary authorized the apprehension of Samalenghe on his own responsibility, but declined to remove Mutaka's name.

[2] I am told that there is some juridical distinction between a *mandat d'amener* and a warrant for arrest, but the physical effect is the same.

accompanied the individual warrants and ran, in translation, as follows:

REPUBLIC OF THE CONGO
Pro Justitia
Mandats d'Amener

Article 15 of the code of penal procedure,

We, de Loof, Adrien, Officier du Ministère Public près la Cour d'Appel de Leopoldville:

On foot of the proceedings instituted against:

Tshombe, Moïse; Munongo, Godefroid; Kimba, Evariste; Kibwe, Jean; Mutaka-wa-Dilomba –

charged with: Sedition, Murder, Arbitrary Arrests and Bodily Torture, crimes envisaged in and punishable under Articles 43, 44, 45, 67, 180, 189, 192, 193 of the Penal Code.

Pursuant to the ministerial decrees of 6 September 1961;

Pursuant to the Parliamentary Resolutions of 8 and 9 September 1961;

As there exists against the aforesaid grave evidence of guilt and as there is reason to fear that they may attempt to evade arrest,

Request and require that the aforesaid be arrested and produced before us,

Request all commanders of the armed forces to assist in the carrying out of the present mandate.

> Leopoldville, 9th September 1961
> *L'Officier du Ministère Public*
> A. de Loof

(Rubber stamp: Republic of the Congo. Parquet General de Leopoldville)

Clipped to this last document (probably in error since it had no direct bearing on the execution of our task) was a copy of a document on the same headed paper, under the same date, signed by the same official, this time in the capacity of Procureur General *ad interim* and reading as follows:

Note to Messrs.....................

– *Procureur d'Etat Torfs*

First Substitute Thirriart

Are requested in conformity with the decision of the Minister of Justice, to place themselves at the disposition of M Khiary,

Agent (*Chargé de Mission*) of the UN at Leopoldville and to obtain all relevant information at the UN Security Office (*Le Royal*).

(Copy for information to H.E. the Minister for Justice).

Khiary explained our instructions to Raja, Waern, Egge and myself. As regards the *mandats d'amener* we were to arrest Munongo, Kibwe, Kimba and Mutaka. We would receive further instructions as to what to do with them.

Colonel Waern pointed out that it was easier to speak of arresting Munongo than actually to do it. On the last occasion, Munongo had been taken by surprise. There was no question of surprise now. The proceedings of the Central Parliament were well known, and everyone expected the UN to act at the request of the Parliament as, in the case of Rumpunch, it had already acted at the request of the Central Government. Munongo expected to be arrested at any moment, and he was no longer living at his villa in the European district but among his henchmen in the *cité*. The UN force was not a police force, and suffered from a deficiency already mentioned. If Munongo's arrest was a condition *sine qua non* of the success of the operation then, in Waern's opinion, it would be better not to go ahead.

I said I thought it should not be a condition *sine qua non*. The essential thing was that the warrant was out for his arrest, and that Tshombe should know it. Khiary agreed.

As regards Tshombe, we were to arrest him only in the last resort. His residence was to be cut off, the entries and exits to it sealed, and then I was to parley with him, making it clear that his only hope lay in co-operating with the United Nations, and in peacefully liquidating the secession of Katanga. Meanwhile UN forces were to secure the post office and the radio studios and transmitters and to raid the offices of the Sûreté and Ministry of Information and remove the files. Europeans and senior African personnel working in these departments were to be apprehended if possible. The flag of the Republic of the Congo should be run up at the earliest appropriate moment on public buildings and on UN buildings: we had a supply of these flags which Michel Tombelaine had recently brought back from Leopoldville. The Central Government would send down a Commissaire d'Etat to take over authority, in co-operation with Tshombe if possible, in co-operation with the United Nations in any case. He could not yet give us the name of the Commissaire; it had proved difficult to find one. Great care should be taken to avoid a clash with the gendarmerie, during these operations.

I pointed out that it might be very difficult to carry out these instructions without bloodshed. It was true that on the day of Rumpunch, and immediately after, relations with the 'Africanized' gendarmerie had been good, but subsequently they had deteriorated, for a number of reasons. One was that the new nominal head of the gendarmerie, Muké, had been hand-picked by Belgian ultras and would do anything they told him. Thus, he had been egged on to try to 're-occupy' the airport – Elisabethville airport, formerly under dual control, had been held by United Nations forces since Rumpunch – and, although the UN had admitted a token Katangese force, in order to avoid a clash, the tension created remained. But much more dangerous than that was the fact that Katanga Radio, and the ultra Ministers, were telling the troops that the Congolese Parliament had voted to disarm the gendarmerie and that the United Nations would do this on behalf of the Parliament, and then bring in Central Government forces. We had denied this, but the situation was complicated by the fact that Katanga Radio had also carried word of other pending action which we had not denied, and which now formed part of our instructions: arrest of Ministers, occupation of post office and radio. The gendarmerie might well regard this – and be encouraged to regard it – as confirmation of the 'disarming' report. As to be disarmed would not only be humiliating but also financially ruinous, there was a distinct possibility that some, at least, of them might fight, even though the junior officers and most of the rank and file, had little enthusiasm for the State of Katanga. It would be pleasant to be able to add that I predicted that the Europeans of Elisabethville would join in, but in fact I did not do so. We all knew, of course, that the mercenaries still at large would be likely to undertake some action, but we did not take this very seriously, because of their small numbers. We did not – at least I did not – appreciate fully the propaganda impact which even action by very small numbers could have.

Khiary asked me whether Tshombe would be likely to co-operate. I told him I thought Tshombe would, if he were sure we meant business, and if he felt the danger of being sent to Leopoldville for trial was greater for the moment than the danger of being murdered by Munongo and his friends. He had 'bowed before the United Nations' on August 28th; he had stopped bowing after Welensky's statement, but he had not been active personally in the anti-UN campaign. He had, indeed, given me the impression of a man who wondered what we were waiting for. If we acted firmly, he would bow again.

As regards the timing, Khiary said that the operation should be carried out either *before* three o'clock on the afternoon of Wednesday, September 13th – the time that Hammarskjold was due to arrive in Leopoldville – or after Hammarskjold's departure, estimated for three days later. Hammarskjold had given authority for these operations, but it would be embarrassing for him if fighting were actually going on in Katanga while he was in Leopoldville.

I said that, since the Katanga authorities knew – because of Mr Nyembo's voyage – of what we were preparing to do, the sooner we could do it the better. What I had chiefly in mind was that the 'disarming' theme would be used to whip up hysteria among some of the gendarmerie, and that mutinous or allegedly mutinous African soldiers would be incited to commit atrocities, perhaps against civilian UN personnel, including women, who were living in hotels in the town, and who had already received some threats.[1] These atrocities would then, in accordance with a well-tried pattern, be used to discredit the United Nations and gain further international support for Tshombe – 'Tshombe's Katanga Menaced by Anarchy of Rest of Congo'. For these reasons I stressed the urgency of the operation.

Khiary asked how long, if fighting did break out, it would take to bring the situation under control. Raja said that the points where there was a danger of resistance were the post office and the radio studio. Even if this were determined resistance, it could be ended in, at most, two hours. In this, Raja's prediction was perfectly correct.

In the light of my insistence on urgency, and Raja's assurance on the duration of possible resistance, Khiary agreed that the operations should be carried out early in the morning of September 13th.

This decision was based on the assumption that Tshombe, *whose movements would be under our control*, would make a radio statement similar to that which he made on August 28th – but more far-reaching – and would order the gendarmerie to co-operate with UN forces. If that had been so, no one doubted that the Africans in the gendarmerie would have obeyed the order – and the gendar-

---

[1] The sort of thing I had in mind is indicated in a dispatch by Peter Younghusband, the *Daily Mail* correspondent in Elisabethville: 'At the city's largest hotel this afternoon (August 30th, 1961) I saw a large group of Katanga secret police arrest four African reception clerks. . . . Shouting hysterically, they dragged the four men through the hotel lobby and into waiting vehicles, hitting them brutally in the faces and about their bodies.' The victims in this case were Kasai Baluba; no one knows what happened to them afterwards. Anyone designated by the régime could become a victim of similar treatment; the régime would simply deny responsibility.

merie in theory was now all African. If so, the remaining mercenaries, and any potential belligerents among the European
population, would have to fight the UN without any semblance of
legality, and without any African screen. We did not think they
would be likely to do so, and if they did we believed they had no
chance of military success or even of propaganda success – since
'the defence of Katanga' must be, for propagandists, an African
affair.

These calculations, based on our general conception of what
'Katanga' meant were, I believe, correct – except that the fundamental assumption as regards Tshombe turned out to have a fatal
flaw.

The general lines of Morthor, and its timing, having been agreed,
the final plans were concerted at a military conference on the evening of the 12th, attended by Raja, Waern, Egge, Lt-Col MacNamee
– commanding the Irish battalion – Colonels Saqbal Singh and
Maitra – commanding the Dogras and the Gurkhas respectively –
and by the staff officers of Headquarters Katanga and of Sector B
(South Katanga); Tombelaine and myself were the only civilians
at this conference. Headquarters Katanga was entirely Indian,
and Sector B was mainly Swedish. I would be departing from the
essential principle of this veracious narrative if I claimed that
relations between the two headquarters were always entirely smooth
and cordial. Some of the Indian officers, who had taken over very
recently – little more than a month before – in what had hitherto
been a Swedo-Irish preserve, did not always succeed in concealing
their consciousness that there was a difference between officers who
had seen active service and officers who had not. Some of the
Swedish officers responded to this by an elaborate and icy formality,
which on the Indian side was sometimes met by a curt reliance on
military hierarchy – Headquarters Katanga being the superior
entity. This rather unhappy state of affairs was much aggravated
by a linguistic factor. English was the lingua franca but for most –
probably for all – of these officers it was a second language. Most of
them were liable to assume that they knew English perfectly, but in
fact, in a university-level examination in oral English, they would
have ranged from 80 per cent down to about 15 per cent. In the
lower ranges this could lead to serious factual misunderstanding; in
the higher ranges to the subtler strains of misplaced emphasis.
People who speak different languages, and know it, can get along
well; it is between people who think they are speaking the same
language, and are not, that trouble starts. The trouble here was no

more than a steady friction, but it involved some loss of efficiency. As often, the linguistic 'fault' fell along a line also of political differences. The Indians were almost all 'anti-Katanga' and felt happy about Rumpunch and Morthor; many of the Swedes sympathized, in varying degrees, with the local Europeans, and did not altogether approve of either operation. This was a difference of emphasis only; both groups of officers loyally executed the instructions they received, but they could not conceal from each other that they felt differently about their instructions. I liked both the Indians and the Swedes (with a small and evenly distributed percentage of exceptions) but I knew that there were some Indians who were suspicious of my friendliness with Sector B, and a rather larger number of Swedes who thought I was 'in the pocket of the Indians'. Such are the troubles of an international force.

Four a.m. on the morning of September 13th found much the same tableau at the Villa des Roches as 4 a.m. on the morning of August 28th. Raja smoked and walked; I walked. Michel Tombelaine was there, preparing material for his new duties as temporary director, 'Radio Congo, Station Elisabethville', formerly Radio Katanga. My secretary, Josie Donzé, was there too; she had moved out of her hotel because she had been warned of a project to kidnap her.

At 4.20 a.m. we heard firing, which became heavier. 'The post office', said Raja. Nobody else spoke.

At 4.30 a.m., while heavy firing continued, the telephone rang. It was Tshombe, very excited. He kept asking 'What does it mean? What does it mean?' I told him what the instructions were, and asked him to order his forces not to resist the United Nations. He said a cease-fire should be ordered on both sides. I said United Nations forces would cease fire if Katanga forces were prepared to do so. The UN forces must, however, take over the objectives assigned to them; my instructions were categorical (*formelles*) and I had no power to depart from them. While we were talking, fighting was going on unnecessarily. I asked him to end it by an unconditional cease-fire order, and then contact me again. He agreed.

At 4.45 a.m. Tshombe rang again. He had sent out an aide, Major Mwamba, to Camp Massart to order the cessation of all resistance to the United Nations. I now asked him to make a statement on the radio declaring the secession of Katanga at an end. He had only one question to ask about this proposition:

'Do you guarantee my personal safety?'

'*Est-ce que vous me garantissez ma sécurité personnelle?*'

I told him that, assuming he agreed to make the statement I suggested, and that he was prepared to co-operate with the Central Government civil representatives who were now on their way, I was empowered to guarantee not only his personal safety but also his retention in office as Provincial President. He said he agreed. *Entendu. D'accord.* I asked him to come over to the Villa des Roches – the distance is about half a mile – to settle the details. He said he was afraid of being shot at on the road and asked for a UN escort.

No escort was immediately available. We sent for one, but, knowing there would be a delay, Michel said he would take his own car and fetch the President. Tshombe agreed to that; he would wait for Michel. I said that I thought his attitude was wise and statesman-like and in the best interests both of Katanga and the Congo. I thanked him for it.

'Not at all,' he said.

'*Pas d'quoi.*'

As I put down the phone, Michel grinned. Both of us felt a lightness of heart such as we were not again to experience for quite a long time. Michel drove off to the Palace.

At 5 a.m. Raja sent the following wireless message to Waern:

'Tshombe has requested all firing to stop. He is ordering own troops to cease fire. If they do so UN troops should stop firing, but they should continue to take objectives with or without firing.'

I dictated to Josie a draft statement for Tshombe to make on the radio. It was a good text, statesmanlike and wise. Before I had finished it, however, Michel was back, without Tshombe. The guard on the gate – excited by the noise of firing still continuing in the distance – had tried to arrest him and as he escaped had shot at his car. But the really grim news he brought was that not a single UN soldier was to be seen in the neighbourhood of the Palace, which we had been assuming to be blockaded as securely as Munongo's villa had been on the morning of August 28th.

Morthor was beginning to go off the rails.

The behaviour of the guards was not necessarily significant. There were smart, well-disciplined units in the gendarmerie, but the Presidential Guard was not among them. Its members had at all times a certain tendency to behave like the Keystone Cops – for example, it was not unusual for the guards on one side of the double gates to open their flap and salute, while the guards on the other side, animated by different tactical or political conceptions, would bolt their flap and hold on to it grimly. My feeling was – though I may have been wrong – that they were picked on the basis of dependability, in the sense of tribal loyalty, and were unpolluted followers of the Mwata Yamvo. This category did not coincide with the intelligensia. The action of the guard, then, was less likely to be the result of a change of front on Tshombe's part, than a simple, panic reflex, of men who were frightened by the noise of firing and thought that they would be personally safer if they had a hostage.

The really grave matter now was the absence of any UN force in the area. I do not know the reason for this absence. I know that Katanga Headquarters and Sector B had different conceptions regarding it; my belief is that the point about encirclement of the Palace got lost in the linguistic and other interstices between the two headquarters. In any case, wherever along the line it had got lost, there was no point in my seeking out the responsible person – and thereby perhaps aggravating certain frictions – because the responsible person was myself. Nobody, so much as myself, appreciated, or could be expected to appreciate, the central and vital *political* importance of isolating Tshombe, and if I had failed to stress this sufficiently, and failed to check exactly what was being done about it – as if it were one among the details of military execution which did not concern me – then I would have to carry the political consequences of these failures. And I did.

We tried to ring Tshombe but the Dogras had just taken the post office, there had been fighting in the building, and the exchange was no longer functioning. Hurriedly we arranged for posts to be placed round the Palace but this could not be done quickly.

Major Mwamba arrived – between 5.30 and 6 a.m. I believe – and confirmed that Tshombe had in fact ordered him to tell the gendarmerie to cease fire. Major Mwamba was the officer who had helped me to rescue Tombelaine on Sunday. He was a young man, intelligent and brave; he had taken a risk on Sunday – as Africans who countermand, in Katanga, orders given by Belgians take a risk – and he was taking a more serious risk now. He wanted a UN officer to go with him to ensure the cease-fire. He and Egge left together for this purpose and then to make contact with Muké. Tombelaine accompanied them, in case it should be possible, through Mwamba and Muké, to resume contact with Tshombe. The most urgent business was necessarily the cease-fire.

Raja learned what had happened at the post office: the Indians had been parleying with the African gendarmerie, explaining to them, as arranged, that there was no intention of disarming them, and were being heard attentively when a sniper opened fire from the roof of the building in which the Belgian Consulate is housed.

An Indian was killed and firing broke out between the Indians and the gendarmerie. The gendarmerie fought bravely but were overcome. At 6 a.m. Katangese armoured cars, handled by mercenaries,[1] counter-attacked the post office.

Meanwhile wireless reports had been coming in from other missions:

0415 Arrest of Mutaka unsuccessful;

0420 Both Sûreté offices taken;

0445 Minister Kibwe taken by Irish battalion;

0515 Arrest of Munongo unsuccessful.

None of this now seemed much to the point: the only point of importance was to resume the contact with Tshombe. For this we pinned our hopes, at this point, on the Egge/Mwamba mission.

About 6.30 a.m. three correspondents arrived at Les Roches, Ray Moloney of United Press, Dick Williams of the BBC, and Gavin Young of *The Observer*. They had witnessed the bloody street-fighting at the post office and all three were considerably shaken, friendly though they were. I told them that we were taking action under paragraph A.1 of the February resolution and that, although there had been fighting, provoked by a sniper, who was probably one of the refractory mercenaries, Tshombe had agreed to a cease-fire. In fact by this time, firing was dying down (by 7.15 a.m. the report was received: 'Situation at the post office is calm'). We had temporarily lost contact with Tshombe but hoped to restore it shortly.

At this time, although I did not know it, Tshombe was at Mr Dunnett's house.

I also told the correspondents, and other journalists later that day, that the secession of Katanga was over. The contrast between this statement, and other statements subsequently made in Leopoldville, became a source of grave embarrassment to the United Nations. I shall comment on this discrepancy later in this chapter.

A tense period of waiting ensued.

The reports in showed that gendarmerie resistance had been

---

[1] There were no Africans in the gendarmerie trained to handle these. M Davister (*Katanga*, p. 150) tells us that for Hammarskjold's arrival in Elisabethville on August 12th, 1960, the Belgians deployed on the tarmac 'the five armoured cars of which Katanga is very proud, having installed in the turret of each of them a black soldier who was told *to touch nothing*'. A year later, in August 1961, one of the Belgian complaints about the dislodgement of the foreign officers was that Katanga would be left defenceless in respect of such weapons.

heavier than expected, in taking over both Radio Katanga studio and the post office. The fighting spirit of the gendarmerie had been generally estimated both by Belgians and by UN officers as low,[1] and this estimate was correct for the bulk of the forces.[2] But the picked para-commandos defending these points fought resolutely, until overcome.

The escort for which Tshombe had asked at 4.45 a.m. came to Les Roches about 7.30 a.m. I left with it in the direction of the palace.

By this time, although I did not know it, Tshombe had left Dunnett's house on his way to Rhodesia.

On the road, outside the abandoned gendarmerie headquarters, not far from the palace, I met Egge and Tombelaine and Mwamba who had discouraging news. Mwamba had communicated the cease-fire order to gendarmerie posts in Elisabethville, but they had been unable to contact Muké. What orders would be given outside Elisabethville – including Jadotville/Shinkolobwe – depended on him; we knew him to be heavily under Belgian influence, and we feared that, under their control, he had left the city to 'continue the war'.

The road blocks around Tshombe's residence were now in place, but too late. We believed that Tshombe had left his residence, but we were not sure of the fact. There were rumours that he had left and then returned. Mwamba, alone, had been in contact with him – apparently between 7 and 8 a.m. – and he said Tshombe was still prepared to meet me. According to Tombelaine's recollection he proposed a meeting at Ndola and I refused. I do not myself recall this, but I am aware that my recollection of the events of that crowded day and fateful morning has gaps and this may be one of them.

In any case, if Mwamba had suggested Ndola, or anywhere else in Rhodesia, I should have refused immediately. What I do remember is that Mwamba thought Tshombe would come to Les Roches if the British Consul, Mr Dunnett, were present there. I agreed to the presence of a Consul, but perhaps unwisely suggested the American Consul, Mr Canup. Mwamba conveyed this to Tshombe – by what channel I do not know – and reported agreement. This was, I believe, about 10.30 a.m. The appointment was for 1 p.m.

After the failure to contact Muké, Egge and Tombelaine had visited the Palace and – with Mwamba's aid – got past the guard.

---

[1] For a typical Belgian report on gendarmerie morale see Chapter XII, page 200.

[2] See Captain Lasimone's evidence (pp. 280–1).

Tshombe was not to be seen, but they found, on a table, a telex message from Brazzaville, dated the previous evening, warning him that a plane with a dozen Congolese was getting ready to leave Leopoldville, with the mission to arrest him. (This was right about the imminent departure of the Congolese; wrong about their mission.) The fear inspired by this message was, no doubt, a principal reason for Tshombe's disappearance.

Mwamba presented himself for the rendezvous with Canup and myself, but Tshombe did not come. Mwamba admitted he had lost all contact with Tshombe; he seemed very apprehensive. He left, shortly before two o'clock, promising to keep in touch. None of us ever saw him again. We learned, after the cease-fire, from a group of young African officers who then left Katangese for Central Government service, that he had been imprisoned 'by order of the Belgians'. They had been told that his hands had been cut off as a warning to others.

In the early afternoon I informed Dr Linner in a telex conversation as follows:

'Tshombe is not under our control. He was to present himself at one o'clock in presence Canup (garbled) cease-fire and surrender statement. He did not present himself and has apparently evaded our forces with Samalenghe. Mwamba believes he genuinely intended surrender and was abducted by Samalenghe perhaps with European aid. Kibwe as Vice-President is senior member Tshombe government now known to be in Eville and is in our hands. Feel statement by him might ease transition if Central Government agree.'[1]

In the afternoon, mixed contingents of gendarmerie and Europeans sniped at the radio studio and the post office.

That was how matters stood, when Hammarskjold landed at Leopoldville.

I shall not attempt here to give any detailed account of the fighting, as I am not qualified to do so, being a total civilian. Ireland, including me, was neutral during the Second World War, and the last time I had heard guns fired in anger was when the forces of order shelled the Four Courts, Dublin, in 1922. I was not present at the places in Elisabethville where there were sharp engagements: the post office, the radio studio; I was even further away from the

---

[1] The copy among my papers of this happens to be only my own side of part of this conversation. Dr Linner's reply apparently concerned the nature of the statement which might be made by Kibwe, as my reply ran: 'Thanks. Have already prepared draft ready Tshombe's use and will emphasize this element.'

THE FIRE IN THE GARAGE

Lufira Bridge and Jadotville. I shall not attempt to reconstruct from hearsay accounts – and even intra-UN eye-witness accounts vary significantly – exactly what happened at these places. I should like, none the less, to make a few remarks, which might be entitled, Observations of a Contemplative Civilian regarding the General Character of the September Hostilities in South Katanga.

The first part of these remarks concerns the Press and Other Atrocities.

I should like to assure my friends among the Press corps in Elisabethville that I do not mean them. Many of the correspondents did an honest job but what came through – by no fault of theirs – was an extremely distorted picture. A correspondent like Ray Maloney, for example, had certainly no prejudice against the UN – so little prejudice against us, indeed, that some of the mercenaries threatened his life – and would be quite incapable of 'slanting' his dispatches against the UN. For an event which he did not witness himself, Ray – or any other conscientious reporter – would file: what the UN said, what the Katanga Government said, and what civilians in Elisabethville said. What the UN said became – for reasons to be considered later – muffled and inconsistent; what the Katanga Government said was war propaganda of unbridled mendacity – 'Fifty-seven Irish killed at Jadotville', when no one at all had been killed; and what Elisabethville civilians – white civilians – said was inevitably and enthusiastically corroborative of what the Katanga Government said. The last was, I think, the decisive factor. The reader in England or the United States or Ireland or Sweden, took the 'eye-witness accounts' of these people at their face value. Statements of 'X., a doctor', 'Y., a priest', 'Z., a Red Cross worker' sounded impartial and reliable, and were always heavily damaging to the United Nations. What the reader did not realize was that all these people were fighting the United Nations – by word of mouth always and often with weapons in their hands as well. Thus, the reader might well be shocked by the testimony of M André van Roey, a particularly observant 'Red Cross worker'. He was a Red Cross worker; he was also Director of the Bank of Katanga, and classified by the United Nations as a political adviser ('with short respite' as a technician).

What the industrious eye-witnesses saw often had some kernel of truth. Thus when they said that the Indians 'turned the Red Cross hospital into a fortress', it was true that there were troops at the hospital and it was also true that there 'had been firing' from there. The troops were there to guard UN wounded, who might otherwise have been taken as hostages by the Katangese. The firing had been a single burst from a sten-gun, fired by an excited soldier (who had just been bringing in wounded) at a gendarmerie jeep (he missed).[1] The local Europeans, with a wealth of detail, turned this incident into a large-scale and deliberately fiendish military operation. They were fighting the United Nations and they knew that atrocity stories were an effective weapon against their cumbrous but sensitive adversary.

The ordinary reader had no idea of this background: he thought of Katanga as an African State which was inexplicably being attacked by the United Nations forces, who – on the testimony of impartial European bystanders – behaved in the most atrocious way. Without being aware of it, the reader – that is, the general public – was a victim of Liebling's Second Law which runs:

> 'the Press association man has neither time nor encouragement to learn or write about the essential nature of the country to which he is assigned. Big news, whether of a revolt in Algeria or of a Guatemalan purchase of Communist arms, always comes as a colossal surprise to the reader (who has never been told that the Algerians are angry or that the Guatemalan Government . . . has been refused permission to buy arms here.)'[2]

Thus, even objective reporting – since the background had not been situated – necessarily turned against the United Nations. And, of course, not all the reporting was objective. A few of the correspondents were working with the Katanga propaganda machine. There was one journalist – I shall call him Mr Copperman – who jumped up and down and shouted at some of my Press conferences. This man informed the world that what he had seen UN forces do was 'worse than anything the Nazis did'. He was an inexhaustible eye-witness: no UN soldier would dream of committing rape or murder without summoning Copperman as a witness to the scene. The trouble was that, while nobody quite believed Copperman, several of his fellow reporters did half believe him, and this coloured their reports. Half-belief was a degree of credence which Copperman by no means deserved. Others of the Press corps were, in varying degrees, 'on the Katanga side'; many of them came from Rhodesia;

---

[1] This was the account given to me when I inquired into the incident, by the Italian head of the hospital, Captain Cipolat, who vouched for it that this was an isolated incident.

[2] A. J. Liebling, *The Press*. This is an excellent book and Mr Liebling is a wise and good man.

many worked for papers whose policy was pro-Katanga.[1] And there was, of course, the Katanga lobby in the Western capitals. This was an active body, but its mysterious powers have perhaps been somewhat exaggerated. All it had to do, in reality, was to feed its handouts – full of impartial testimony by Red Cross workers and disinterested foreigners like Copperman – to a Press much of which was eager to use such handouts, prominently and with copious indignant comment. Katanga benefited in fact from the operation of Liebling's First Law, which runs as follows:

> 'Because of newspaper publishers' wealth they do not have to be slugged over the head by "anti-democratic associations" to force them into using their properties to form public opinion the National Association of Manufacturers approves. The gesture would be as redundant as twisting a nymphomaniac's arm to get her into bed.'[2]

When Katanga is hurt, money screams, and money has powerful lungs. The reaction of 'Press and public opinion' (in the West) to our action was – as the reader is likely to be aware – an ear-splitting and almost universal howl of execration.

This cry now hit Hammarskjold; it continued to ring in his ears throughout the brief remainder of his life. It provided, as it were, the background music to the diplomatic exertions of the British Ambassador, Derek Riches, and Lord Lansdowne – exertions which were, of course, set in motion ultimately by similar forces to those which were producing so much vocal public opinion. Hammarskjold was subjected to the most intense pressure, both psychological and diplomatic, to draw back from what the UN had undertaken – which was in fact the ending of the secession of Katanga by the use of force.

According to statements subsequently made by Dr Linner Hammarskjold did *not* know the plans for Morthor in advance. The

---

[1] I am indebted to Mr Keith Kyle for the following comment, which I accept, on this passage: 'In interpreting the mood of the journalists in Katanga, I think you leave out one element: a vein of idealism among some journalists (*naïveté* if you like; the notion that foreign correspondents are hard-boiled is one of the hoariest of illusions; in my experience they are more likely to be soft-boiled), the idea that UN action must be immaculate. Men who had been in Bizerta, Algiers, Cyprus, etc., would be deeply, genuinely shocked because a perfectly normal accident of war – say a mortar shell falling on a hospital – had been done *by the UN*.' (Letter to the author.)

[2] *The Press.*

operation was undertaken on Dr Linner's own responsibility, in the light of his general instructions and knowledge of Hammarskjold's wishes. Presumably Dr Linner and Khiary informed Hammarskjold, on his arrival, of what had been ordered.[1] Dr Linner has informed inquirers that he was not aware of the transmission to me, by Khiary and Fabry, of the *mandats d'amener* and, if that is so, he (and perhaps also Hammarskjold) was kept in ignorance, by two of his trusted collaborators, of an extremely important fact. In any case, whatever gaps there may have been in Linner's or Hammarskjold's knowledge of the *instructions* given to us, they received an early and clear military report as to the *action* taken on September 13th. The following message was signalled at 7.20 p.m. that evening:

1920 From HQ Katanga Command Eville to ONUC Leopoldville.

Info: HQ Sector A Aville, HQ Sector B Eville, HQ Sector C Kamina.

Sitrep from 121600 Z to 131600 Z

FIRSTLY for OP Morthor plan as follows. Alpha. 1 Dogra Bn Gp with under cmd one coy 3/1 AR. task. seize. one. EVILLE post office and Radio installation in vicinity. two. Radio Katanga studio three. Take in UN custody minister of info SAMALENGHE four. secure air field[2] five custody of arrested personnel. Bravo. 35 Irish battalion Gp. task. seize. one. Radio transmitter at college St Francois. two. take into UN custody Minister of Finance KIBWE three seize and est rd bloc railway tunnel. four secure refugee camp at factory and own line. charlie 12 SWED battalion Gp with one coy of 3/1 AR task to seize. one. radio transmitter en route de Kilobelobe. two take into UN custody Minister interior MUNONGO. officers of sûreté white personnel working and African chiefs. three secure refugee camp. SECONDLY first shot was fired from Belgian Consulate[3] building near post office at 130400 B at DOGRAS. THIRDLY radio Katanga studio and post office captured by DOGRA by 130500 b after heavy stiff

---

[1] My present interpretation, as regards responsibilities in Leopoldville, is different from that in my articles in *The Observer* (December 10th and 17th); it is the result of new information, further thought, and more attentive reading of that remarkable document, S/4940. Written too close to the events they deal with, *The Observer* articles are at variance on a number of points of interpretation, with my considered opinion. The articles placed what I now feel to be an undue emphasis on a single personal factor – Khiary's role.

[2] The airfield was in fact in UN hands; what was involved here was the disarming of a small gendarmerie presence there.

[3] Actually the roof of a building which contained, as well as the Belgian Consulate, a number of commercial offices.

hand to hand fighting. both places counter attacked by gendarmerie with their armd cars led mostly by BELGIANS in civilian
clothes. counter-attack repulsed by DOGRAS and SWEDISH armd
cars. FOURTHLY due heavy mortar fire and automatic fire from
gendarmerie studio completely damaged beyond repairs. FIFTHLY
Irish Bn captured transmitter at College St Francois firmly in
our hands. SIXTHLY Swedish Bn captured radio transmitter
KILOBELOBE. SEVENTHLY. strong and automatic firing and sniping
inside the town continues. EIGHTHLY IRISH COY at JADOTVILLE
attacked by gendarmerie. attack repulsed reinforcement of one
coy and three armd cars sent to JADOTVILLE and coy directed
to remain there until further orders. NINTHLY Kibwe apprehended.
MUNONGO, MUTAKA, SAMALENGHE and KIMBA have disappeared.
Tshombe is not traceable at present. . . .

For Hammarskjold, with this knowledge, there were, it seems to
me, only two possible, consistent courses of action. If he had not
approved, and did not approve, the ending of the secession by force,
he could have gone to Elisabethville, established precisely what
instructions had been given to us, and precisely what action had
been taken, in so far as he may have been in doubt on either point.
He should have taken over personally from me and secured the
quickest possible cease-fire, if necessary on the basis of the *status quo
ante*. He should then have got rid of Linner, Khiary and myself for
having exceeded our instructions.

If, on the other hand, he had approved, or was prepared to cover,
our action, he could have justified it, on the only grounds that could
justify what we had actually done: that UN action had been taken
under the authority of paragraph A.1 of the February resolution,
which authorizes the use of force in civil war situations.[1] He could
have identified the secessionist Government of the State of Katanga
as a fomentor and wager of civil war both inside North and Central
Katanga and between Katanga and the rest of the Congo, and as an
instigator of inter-tribal hate even in the South Katanga towns. He
could have said that, once the force acted under A.1, he, as Secretary-General, under the general authority of the resolutions, was
bound to co-operate with the Central Government in installing its
legitimate authority in the province. It is true that such action is
plainly contrary to the literal meaning of some parts of the resolutions (notably paragraph 4 of the resolution of August 9th). But the

---

[1] I had given Tshombe formal warning on September 5th, that his Government's actions might involve the application of paragraph A.1.

Secretary-General has to interpret the resolutions *as a whole* and could hold that, in the event of apparent conflict between parts of them, the latest and most specific resolution, that of February, was the best guide as to his present mandate.

Either of these courses would have been tenable. The tragedy is that he took a third course, which was not tenable. He allowed the world to be given an official version which was so phrased as to conceal the reality of what had happened, making what had been an active intervention by the United Nations look like a defensive action. These words will make painful reading for Hammarskjold's admirers; I know this because they are words which are painful also to write. I think, however, that there is no escaping their truth. The following is the wording of the relevant section of the UN document (S/4940) issued on September 14th, when Hammarskjold was in Leopoldville:

'*Paragraph 15:* In the early hours of September 13th, the UN forces therefore took security precautions similar to those applied on August 28th[1] and deemed necessary to prevent inflammatory broadcasts or other threats to the maintenance of law and order, while the UN resumed carrying out its task of apprehending and evacuating foreign military and para-military personnel. At this point, an alert was set since arson was discovered at the UN garage. As the UN troops were proceeding towards the garage premises, fire was opened on them from the building where a number of foreign officers are known to be staying. UN troops were subsequently also resisted and fired at as they were deploying towards key points or while they were guarding installations in the city.'

If this is an accurate account of what took place in Elisabethville on the morning of September 13th, my name is Titus Oates.[2] The

---

[1] These precautions, as set out in the document, consisted of 'placing a surveillance on Radio Katanga, on gendarmerie headquarters and on other key points or installations'. This makes Mr Munongo a key point, or installation: true enough.

[2] Mr Ian Colvin of *The Daily Telegraph* (who believes my name *is* Titus Oates), in an article solemnly entitled 'Sifting the Truth about the Congo Operations', attributed the authorship of this report to me. 'Dr O'Brien . . . produced on September 14th last year an official report of the first military operations, a report less than frank. . . . Its contents contrasted markedly with his published reminiscences'. The document is headed "Report of the Officer-in-Charge of the United Nations Operations in the Congo".' I was not the Officer-in-Charge; Dr Linner was. Mr Colvin, dedicated to 'sifting the truth', ought to have noticed these facts.

fighting started in the quite different way set out in this chapter,
and had its origin in Katango-European resistance to a planned
action by the United Nations. The historical inaccuracy of S/4940 –
which, reversing Ridley and Latimer, put out a fire that was never
lit[1] – had very important practical implications. It put the United
Nations, in every sense, in a false position. False, literally, first and
worst of all; false from the point of view of public opinion, false
militarily and false politically. False from the point of view of public
opinion, for it was meeting the Big Lie of Katanga propaganda
with something less than a half-truth. The Big Lie could, I suppose,
be met with another Big Lie; it can also be met effectively with the
truth, as the BBC showed on many occasions during the Second
World War; it cannot be met with evasion, concealment and
ambiguity. Friends of the United Nations could only be puzzled,
and rendered ineffective, by this official version; enemies of the
organization could use it to back their accusations of hypocrisy.
The version was false militarily because the UN forces could not be
given a clear mission. Finally the version was false politically, for
the great political objective of the UN was – and necessarily remained – to end the secession of Katanga, and that objective was
jeopardized, or at least postponed, by an official version which made
it possible for Mr Tshombe at any moment – by simply saying
'I accept a cease-fire' – to come back to Elisabethville and re-
establish his secessionist State.

It is true that the last paragraph of the document contained
indications that the UN action after all did have something to do
with ending secession:

> '*Paragraph 20:* In the afternoon of September 13th, the Central
> Government of the Republic of the Congo dispatched the
> Commissaire d'Etat for Katanga, Mr E. D. Bocheley, to assist the
> provincial authorities in the restoration of law and order. The UN
> dispatched a team of technical experts to help in the restoration
> of essential utilities and public services.'

Both the delegation and the team were dispatched, though the
report does not say so, in the same UN plane. Nor does the report

---

[1] I have no idea what the source for the 'arson' statement may be. No such fire
was ever reported by me, or to me, or ever referred to in my presence. Nor is there
any reference to such a phenomenon in the military 'situation report' quoted above.
Some days before, an empty UN vehicle was upset and damaged by the 'spontaneous demonstrators' outside a garage in the town (properly speaking there was
no 'UN garage'). This incident, the nearest known to me to the 'arson alarm', was
no longer present to our minds on the morning of September 13th.

mention the decisions of the Central Parliament. Mr Bocheley-Davidson, and his Government, thought that his mission was to end the secession. The UN action had been designed solely towards that end, and from that end it was now beginning, murkily and ir-resolutely, to recede.

I did not see S/4940 until the fighting was over, and I did not imagine that our action would, or could, be explained to the public in anything like this way. My instructions taken as a whole, had the unmistakeable meaning of ending the secession of Katanga, following the application of A.1 (preventing civil war). I saw no point in attempting to pretend that our action had any other character, and I declared that the secession of Katanga was at an end. In my opinion, if the UN had not tried to disguise its own action, but had firmly followed it up, the secession then could have been ended. I do not believe that the military command was of a different opinion. But, in view of the very different decision, or indecision, represented by S/4940, my remarks, and similar remarks on Radio Tombelaine, sounded very bad in Leopoldville. We were severely rebuked. As we had not read S/4940 we could not understand what was now happen-ing, since we did not know what was supposed to have happened already.

I must make it clear that the account of the origin of the fighting given in S/4940 was not based on reports from me. My reports, on the morning of September 13th, said nothing about arson in garages. They said we had caught Kibwe, but Tshombe had got away. 'Mr Kibwe', said document S/4940 (paragraph 19), 'is reported to be in a UN camp.' I have already quoted the military situation report for the day in question.

Security Council document S/4940 is technically a Report of the Officer-in-Charge of the United Nations Operation in the Congo to the Secretary-General. The Secretary-General was, however, in Leopoldville on September 14th, the date the document carries, and no one who knows the United Nations will doubt that a report released at such a time would be gone over, word by word, by Hammarskjold himself. And whatever high-level agnosticism now prevails about what we had been instructed to do – and, as I found later in Leopoldville and New York, there is a veritable 'Cloud of Unknowing' surrounding the whole subject – it is hard to see how he and Dr Linner can altogether have escaped knowing the essentials of what Khiary and Fabry knew, especially since the military command knew the military aspects of Operation Morthor. *Morthor* is a Hindi word. It does not mean 'Sound the alarm; there is arson in the garage' or 'Let us now assist the provincial authorities to maintain order'. It means 'Smash'.[1]

Some readers will, I think, feel that I am making rather heavy weather about Security Council document S/4940. Ambiguities are, after all, a constant in diplomacy. The reference to the arson alarm, on a similar view, was no doubt the result of a misunderstanding and is, in any case, rather a side-issue.

I cannot agree with this view. Ambiguities are, indeed, often necessary but there are times when they should be eliminated as far as humanly possible. One of these times is the outbreak of fighting. UN soldiers were risking death in Elisabethville. They had a right to know, in plain language, what it was all about. This statement not only did not tell them; it prevented them from being given any clear aim. The combination, in this statement, of a factual inaccuracy on an important point – the origin of the fighting – with misleading or opaque language on so much else, put the UN operation on a wrong, and ultimately indefensible, footing.[2]

There were, of course, powerful arguments, as there often are, in favour of not inquiring very closely into what had happened, and of not presenting very clearly what was unavoidably known. These arguments were practical, humane, diplomatic, and concerned with public opinion: they were also, less scrutably, psychological.

Practically, Morthor had gone wrong. Rumpunch, having been – as far as it went – successful, could be acknowledged. Morthor could not now be pushed through without grave difficulty and it might be in the interests of the United Nations to disavow it in whole or part.

---

[1] This interpretation, is once more, radically different from that in *The Observer* articles. In *The Observer* interpretation, I went wrong for two reasons. First, I accepted uncritically certain accounts later given me in Leopoldville and New York; I no longer accept them without reservation. Second – and first in importance – I shrank from facing what was to me a painful truth about Hammarskjold's last decisions.

[2] There has been, and still is, some difference of opinion as to exactly who knew exactly what in Leopoldville. There is not much point in my pursuing this, I think. The information about the Elisabethville action was fully there on the Sixth Floor of the Hotel Royal, and anyone who managed not to know what had happened, must have been strangely lacking in curiosity. Even if Khiary and Fabry did not spontaneously report the instructions they had given to us, they could hardly have refrained from answering questions if Hammarskjold or Linner had interrogated them at all closely about their obviously crucial pre-Morthor journey to Elisabethville. For one thing, all concerned must have assumed that Hammarskjold would see Raja and myself quite soon, so that concealment would be impossible.

Humanely, Morthor involved bloodshed, loss of UN and other lives. To Hammarskjold's honour, this sickened him more than it would most men, and it must have been a powerful motive for seeking any kind of peace. S/4940, by adulterating the content of the UN action, lowered the price of peace.

Diplomatically, the British reaction had to be considered. Hammarskjold had lost the confidence of two of the four effective Permanent Members of the Security Council (France and the USSR). There was some question now whether he could afford to lose the confidence of a third Permanent Member – Britain – and become dependent exclusively on American support.

Mr Arthur Gavshon, in his valuable book *The Mysterious Death of Dag Hammarskjold* (Walker & Co, New York, 1962), has given a detailed account, clearly based on conversations with eye-witnesses, of Hammarskjold's last days in Leopoldville. Amid much else of interest, he records the crucially important *démarche*, made on the evening of September 13th, by the British Ambassador, Derek Riches, to Hammarskjold, on instructions from Lord Home:

'The Ambassador began to read with care a compelling passage in his instructions, Hammarskjold's aides leant forward to listen more intently. The sense of what they heard amounted to just this:

'Her Majesty's Government was serving notice, with the greatest emphasis at its command, that Britain would have to consider withdrawing *all* support from ONUC's missions unless:

'1. Hammarskjold could provide an acceptable explanation for what had happened in Katanga; or

'2. Hammarskjold could provide an assurance that the fighting would swiftly be ended.' (Gavshon, page 130.)

That night, after discussions, following the departure of Ambassador Riches, between Hammarskjold and his senior advisers – discussions in which McKeown, Khiary and Fabry favoured reinforcement and a firm line, but were overruled – 'Hammarskjold, Linner, Khiary, Fabry and some of the others turned to the precise terms of the official report that had to be sent early next day to New York'.

The official report, Document S/4940, contained, in paragraph 15, an attempt to find the 'acceptable explanation', so insistently demanded by Lord Home. Later, after Lord Lansdowne had travelled to Leopoldville (on September 15th) to lend extra weight to the representations of Ambassador Riches, Hammarskjold made a spectacular effort, through his Ndola mission, to give satisfaction to the British Government on Riches' second point also: 'assurance that the fighting would swiftly be ended'.[1]

Hammarskjold must have seen, in the British reaction, a threat to the whole conception of the Secretary-General's office, as he had established it. He could, of course, have answered British objections by suggesting that challenges to his interpretation would best be made before the Security Council. He would be on quite safe ground here, because the Security Council is, for structural reasons (the veto), most unlikely to overrule any interpretation by the Secretary-General, unless he acts in such a way as to affront, simultaneously, all the Permanent Members. This ratchet-mechanism gives the Secretary-General considerable freedom of interpretation. None the less a Permanent Member, if it withdraws its confidence, can, later and on another ground, hamper the effectiveness of the Secretary-General. Inherently, there was a strong temptation to bring Morthor within hailing distance of paragraph 4 of the resolution of August 9th and of Sir Patrick Dean's reservation – the British Government's sacred texts. This accommodation could not be made without straining the facts.

Public opinion affected every plane. Practically, the Press outcry and campaign made Morthor less likely to succeed. Humanly it made Morthor sound much more bloody than it actually was (the final official reckoning of dead on both sides was eleven UN and fifty gendarmerie).[2] Diplomatically it created, even within the only important country – the United States – which was giving Hammarskjold support, a powerful and angry current against him. The Democratic Administration stood by him loyally but they would hardly have been human if they had not given some indication of a hope that he would not provide too much ammunition for their Republican adversaries. And even the most fanatical Republican could hardly condemn the UN for trying to put out a fire in its own garage.

Psychologically, one can only hazard a few guesses. Hammarskjold

---

[1] In my *Observer* articles (December 10th and 17th) I attributed, as I now realize, excessive importance to Lord Lansdowne. The real damage was done by Riches, on his Government's instructions, on September 13th. From the time of the issue of S/4940, following Riches' *démarche*, the UN's posture was defensive and untenable.

[2] The Katangese figures are subject to caution. Their casualty statistics fluctuated according to their propaganda needs, and in the 'victory' atmosphere after the cease-fire, high casualty figures would have been embarrassing. Also the mercenaries killed could not be acknowledged.

was a very proud man, who had been under intense strain and subjected to violent personal vituperation. He had taken this, from the Soviet side, unflinchingly but I believe that some of the Western attacks must have hurt more deeply, because they struck a responsive chord in himself. For him, determined action in Katanga, of the Rumpunch-Morthor character, was warranted by international necessities, but I suspect that he may have felt some sense of guilt at the need to disturb the order which reigned there. He was affected, in any case, by the fact of his own past reluctance to disturb that order, and by words which he himself had spoken, a year before, about not interfering in internal affairs, and not using the UN force to influence the outcome of constitutional disputes.

He was involved, here, in a concealed contradiction. An essential element of his policy, in the early days, was *not* to use the UN force to end the secession – which was the object for which the Congo Government had invited the force in. The Afro-Asian Governments had criticized this severely, and ultimately carried the February resolution which, as they interpreted it, provided a means, in effect, of using the force to end the secession. And Hammarskjold had bound himself to seek their guidance on how to apply the resolution. This contradiction may have led him to seek consistency with previous words at the expense of consistency with present action. This might have cost him less of a struggle than it would have cost anyone who delighted less in ambiguity. The successful wielder of ambiguity has a certain high imperiousness in his attitude to facts and inclines to a magician-like confidence in the overmastering power of language. This confidence is unfortunately contagious.

Here endeth speculation. The only whiff I got of the reality of Hammarskjold's ambiance in Leopoldville came when General Seán McKeown arrived in Elisabethville on September 17th. The fact that he came was characteristic of him; he was the only one who did during that week. I was shocked by his appearance; his eyes were swollen and red-rimmed. He told me he had been up every night until 4 a.m. while Hammarskjold examined and re-examined the situation; the discussions, I gathered, were circular and extremely exhausting. General McKeown, by comparison, obviously found our life in Elisabethville very attractive. We were housed by this time in a house called Clair Manoir, in the grounds of the Indian camp. Civilians and Indian officers together, we were living on Indian box-rations and sleeping, crowded together, on the concrete floor of the basement; it was a good basement with fine solid walls, and we were sleeping in it because the Katangese were in the habit of hitting the upper floors with mortar-fire. General McKeown went to sleep. At 9.45 a.m. on the following morning we woke him up. He sat up, rubbing his eyes luxuriously. 'That', he said, 'is the first decent sleep I've had in five days.'

Throughout the period from the beginning of hostilities up to Hammarskjold's decision to go to Ndola, my principal concern was to try to re-establish the contact with Tshombe which had been lost on Wednesday morning.

The first rumours of where he might be reached Egge – perhaps through Baluba sources, I am not sure – on Wednesday afternoon. I reported to Leopoldville that Tshombe was believed to be in the British Consulate. I asked permission to search the Consulate. This was a silly idea in itself and, of course, in the context of S/4940, it must have sounded alarming in the extreme. The emphatically negative reply included the words 'without prior repeat prior authorization', giving us our first hint that our actions might not be fully covered. It may reasonably be asked why, instead of making so drastic a proposition, I did not go and see Dunnett myself. Part of the answer is that I believed that, if Tshombe had indeed gone to Mr Dunnett's house, and if Mr Dunnett had made no attempt to contact me, then Mr Dunnett did not intend to co-operate with the United Nations in this matter. If he did not intend to co-operate, then a search-party would be a more effective method of resuming the contact than a personal appeal. This reasoning is not entirely sound, and the cause of this is that, at the time, I was sore. The reader may say that I ought not to have been sore and that, even if I were sore, I should not have allowed this to govern my actions. This is true; the only consideration I would offer in mitigation is that I did not allow it to govern my positive actions; I allowed it to affect my abstentions and recommendations. I was angry, but I was not an angry young man; I was an angry middle-aged civil servant.

We tried another method. We released Mr Kibwe on Thursday, September 14th. The Vice-President, since his apprehension, had co-operated with us very cheerfully and had made a very nice broadcast statement, drafted by Michel Tombelaine, ordering the gendarmerie – in his capacity as Vice-President of Katanga – to cease resistance.[1] This was not made under any other duress than that implied by confinement. We proposed it to him as a draft; we thought it would be helpful, but he did not have to make it; also he could make any amendments he liked. Mr Kibwe thought the statement was fine, and added that fighting was silly. He seemed to enjoy

---

[1] S/4940/Add 2. Paragraph 8.

recording his piece. I felt no doubt at all that President Tshombe, in the same position, would have behaved in the same way as his Vice-President.

I went out to the camp, near the airport where Mr Kibwe was 'staying'. I found him prone on his back. He seemed glad to see me and said the Indians were very nice to him, and kept bringing him cups of tea. He had never really had much tea before, but he rather liked it, he thought. Could I ask the Indians – who knew no French – to put a little less sugar in it? (There, from experience at Clair Manoir, I sympathized with him.)

He readily agreed to help me to resume contact with Tshombe. He did not know, of course, exactly where Tshombe was, but the Consulate would know. I asked him, what Consulate? He seemed a little surprised at the question. 'The British Consulate', he said, 'Mr Dunnett'.

Why Mr Dunnett was likely to know, Mr Kibwe was unable to say. 'It's the only way I can think of', he said finally.

Before going to the Consulate, Egge and I took Mr Kibwe home. Mr Kibwe's villa was a splendid one, with an Anglo-Belgian garden, full of rocks and statues. Mr Kibwe rang the front door bell. For some time there was no answer. Then, round the side of the house came a procession of Africans, men and women, about forty in number, and ranging from crippled elders to toddlers. All embraced Mr Kibwe as if he had risen from the dead. Mr Kibwe took leave of them, with tears in his eyes, and we went to Mr Dunnett.

I had not seen Mr Dunnett since hostilities broke out. His manner, though polite, was stiff and rather guarded. Mr Kibwe said he was looking for Mr Tshombe, and hoped Mr Dunnett would be able to help him.

Egge asked whether Tshombe was in the Consulate.

Mr Dunnett looked surprised and said Tshombe was not.

Egge asked when Tshombe had left.

Mr Dunnett paused.

'I think I ought to tell you', he remarked finally, 'that President Tshombe came here yesterday morning. It was six o'clock. He was . . . distressed. There was mud on his coat. He had climbed over a wall. He sat here for an hour. My wife gave him a cup of coffee. Then he left – at seven. He did not say where he was going.'[1]

I asked whether any discussion had taken place.

'We did not discuss politics', said Mr Dunnett.

---

[1] I cannot guarantee that this is absolutely verbatim, but it is very nearly so. Mr Dunnett's prose style is lapidary, and the content of his remarks was memorable.

After thinking that over, I said it was a pity Mr Dunnett had not contacted me; we could have arranged a cease-fire then and there.

Mr Dunnett, after reflection, said he supposed it was a pity, but the telephone had not been working.

The distance from Mr Dunnett's residence to mine was less than five minutes by car; there was firing at the time, but not in our suburb.

Mr Kibwe may have realized by now that our presence might be having an inhibiting effect on the conversation. He said he would 'go on trying' to contact Tshombe.[1]

He succeeded somehow, by the following morning (September 15th). Tshombe, he said, agreed to meet me at the British Consulate at 7 p.m.

I went to the Consulate accordingly at 7 p.m. By about 8 p.m. Tshombe had not yet appeared. Mr Dunnett kindly proposed dinner and I readily accepted. It was a very good dinner and the wine was welcome, even to a palate blistered by vegetable curry. We talked about subjects like modern painting – on which Mrs Dunnett is very well informed – and the Senate speeches of W. B. Yeats. (I believe I gave Mr Dunnett an inscribed copy of these; at least I intended to.) Tshombe did not come: we heard from Kibwe that 'those around him' – presumably Munongo's friends – had persuaded him that this was a trap. He was said to be about two hours' drive away down the Sakania road, near the Rhodesian border. It must have been after 11 p.m. when I left. I fear I enjoyed the evening more than the Dunnetts. They had not been living on Indian box-rations and sweet cups of tea.

During this period I had another interesting encounter with Mr Dunnett, which, unfortunately, I cannot accurately date. It was, I think, on September 15th or 16th that he came to me in Clair Manoir, in a state of considerable, though controlled excitement. His face was a little flushed, his jaw set. A missionary had reported to him that three British subjects driving along the Sakania road – the main road to Rhodesia – had been dragged from their car and savagely beaten by Africans. They were reported to be on the point of death, perhaps already dead. Mr Dunnett asked whether the United Nations could ensure security along this road, which he described as the lifeline for British subjects in Katanga. I told him we were not in a position to patrol the road; we were very short of

---

[1] He wrote a 'thank-you' letter to Tombelaine, beginning 'Cher Michel' and signed 'Jean-Baptiste'. You might say what you liked about the Katangese Ministers, but their manners, on being released from arrest, were unexceptionable.

transport, even for our own immediate military needs. Mr Dunnett said he was asking the Katangese Government to patrol the road but he feared that 'as a result of UN action' they might not be in a position to do so. In that case, the situation might be a very grave one. The Rhodesian Government might have to consider what steps were open to them to protect lives along this road. I said I would report his remarks to ONUC, Leopoldville, and I did. I saw Mr Dunnett again on the following day, and he was much more relaxed. The British subjects were all right; they had been badly beaten – they had been mistaken for UN personnel, as a matter of fact – and they were in hospital, but they were in no danger. As for the road, the Katanga police could look after it.[1]

None the less, the Rhodesian authorities continued to take an active interest in Katanga. An African informant, himself from Rhodesia, wrote to me on September 23rd a letter containing the following paragraphs:

'On September 14th, I went with a friend to Kipushi, our intention was to go through the border into Northern Rhodesia, we found white Rhodesian Army camping there, surprising enough they were not only camping on the Rhodesian side of the border but also on this side of the border. They had all sorts of fighting equipment, among them I saw twenty-one armed cars. I saw them being painted in Katanga colour. I also saw a few Katangese soldiers there. I got the information that Tshombe and some of his ministers were kept there heavily guarded by Rhodesian troops. The temporary transmitter and telephone were erected and I understood that through these the communication between Tshombe and Rhodesian Government authorities conveyed.

'At about 6 p.m. we left coming back to EVILLE as we could not be allowed through into N. Rhodesia. After driving for minutes we stopped on the road, and after some 15 minutes or so, we saw a convoy of trucks coming from Kipushi direction – I cannot specify what type these were as by then it was growing dark – Eventually, they reached us and stopped. Four white soldiers came out from the leading jeep, they were in Katanga gendarme uniform, they walked towards us on the side of the road where we parked our car, it was my friend's car, a Katangaise. They talked my friend in English but he could not understand them, then they came to me. They started asking several questions. Later, a good number of them surrounded us,

---

[1] There sprang to my mind, no doubt irrelevantly, a line from the film 'Drame de Shanghai': *Les deux matelots d'une puissance amie ne sont pas encore assassinés.*

they tried to collect any information from me about EVILLE and the places in which United Nations troops could be found that night. I told them I knew nothing of EVILLE as I was a stranger from Rhodesia and that I was only two days in the town. They inquired of my identity card and a travelling pass from Rhodesia to Congo. Those I showed them. I gathered they were suspicious of me, nevertheless, they found I had all the necessary documents with me. Reaching the African locations we went through the round way led by a Katanga jeep which we met near the town.

'The following day, as all Katangese soldiers shifted from their camp into another camp right in the centre of African civilian location – as I was anxious to see what was going on. I saw over 150 of these white Rhodesian soldiers gathering into this emergent camp all dressed in Katangese gendarme uniform. After sometime they came out now dressed in civilian clothes got into private cars and made for town. I asked one of the Katangese soldiers to tell me how they fought, when he found out that I was from Rhodesia he was not afraid of telling me how the position was. He admired the Rhodesian Government which sent in plenty of their soldiers, arms and ammunition. He told me that they were advised not to fight during the day time, but by night because then they can have the full use of Rhodesian white soldiers, these, he said manned all heavy guns and armed cars. He added that they were the ones who did most of the fighting during night time. I proved this to be so when in the afternoon I saw plenty of these whites coming back to the camp for dressing.'[1]

Whatever the extent and character of Rhodesian intervention – and I believe that while my informant may have exaggerated as to numbers, notably of armoured cars, his information was substantially correct – it is certainly true that the fighting, with the exception of aerial bombardment, soon became almost exclusively a nocturnal affair. UN forces held their positions and unknown persons fired on these, rather at random, during the night. The firing did little harm to UN forces – as the casualty figures show – but it hit what it was intended to hit; the front page of every Western newspaper. Tshombe's Katanga was Fighting on against Overwhelming Odds.

In a sense – if one leaves aside the question of Rhodesian aid – the odds *were* against them. If the gendarmerie had all fought, numbers would have been against us, but the gendarmerie, normally, fought only if it was convinced that a UN contingent was

[1] I am withholding this informant's name for obvious reasons.

attempting, or about to attempt, to disarm it. Most of the fighting –
or, more precisely, firing – seemed to be done by Europeans, local
people with a stiffening of mercenaries and probably of Rhodesian
volunteers – totalling probably much less than our four battalions –
using the weapons of the gendarmerie and perhaps Rhodesian Army
weapons also. From Mr Tshombe's references to 'our pangas
and our bows and arrows' some readers in Europe may have
imagined that Katangese tribesmen were fighting the United
Nations. One American magazine – before the December fighting –
even printed a picture of 'Mr Tshombe's tribal levies': I recognized
the picture because I had met the picturesque originals, on the
occasion when the picture was taken.[1] Far from being supporters of
Mr Tshombe, they were a mixed group of Congolese National Army
from Stanleyville, with Baluba Jeunesse. The people who were now
fighting the UN were not tribesmen, and seldom Africans, and they
were not using bows and arrows. Their armament was often, I
believe, superior to that of the UN forces. For example, they had the
Belgian NATO model FN rifle, whereas the Indian rifles were 1918
style. They had modern Mercedes armoured cars, where the Irish
had 1940 makeshift models, made in Carlow. And there was also the
sole military plane in the Katanga skies, the Belgian-piloted Fouga,
noted for its punctuality at Press conferences.

The UN forces suffered from the great lack of any clear concept
of what they were now supposed to do. This was inevitable, once the
divergence between the instructions on which we had acted, and the
version of our action given in Leopoldville, began to make itself felt.
We had taken action to end the secession, under the authority, as
we thought, of the 'civil war' proviso, but it soon became clear that
that was not what we were supposed to be doing. We were supposed
to be defending ourselves; so we defended ourselves.[2]

In these circumstances, what to do with Mr Bocheley-Davidson?[3]

The Commissaire d'Etat, a large courtly man with a carved stick,
arrived at Elisabethville airport on the night of September 13th,

---

[1] Chapter XVI.

[2] Early on – on September 14th I believe – I had asked for provisional authority
– conditional on Raja's assessment of military possibilities at any given moment –
to consolidate the UN's control of Elisabethville by taking over the CSK building, the gendarmerie's Camp Massart and the President's Palace. This authority
was refused.

[3] The official British Central Office of Information publication, *Factel* (No. 279)
says that Bocheley returned to Elisabethville after only a few hours (on September
15th). This is not correct.

with a considerable following – I suppose about fifteen people. My friend, Walter Fulcheri, from ONUC Leopoldville, was there shepherding them, and there were UN technicians to keep the radio and the telephone exchange running. I met them at the airport. There was a fair amount of shooting going on in town. The Congolese said they would like to take over public buildings as soon as possible. I suggested – I do not know whether wisely or not – that it might be better to wait until the firing stopped, or the situation became clearer. They agreed, and in fact their stay in Elisabethville was confined to the airport; after several uncomfortable and dangerous days there, the Congolese party went sadly back to Leopoldville. Mr Bocheley-Davidson was supposed, in Elisabethville and other parts of the free world, to be a particularly ruthless Communist. Perhaps he was. He struck me as a gentle, rather ineffectual person. I think a Communist would have come on into town 'to assist the provincial authorities in the restoration of law and order'. All Mr Bocheley-Davidson wanted to know about the provincial authorities was how many of them we had caught. I told him one, and he seemed disappointed. It was not to be his only disappointment, or mine, that week.

Yet even in that week – with its long, grim, waiting times, its good news that proved false, its bad news that proved true, and the incredible catastrophe of its end – there were moments of brightness. Josie above all. Josie Donzé was the heroine of the Siege of Clair Manoir. She is Franco-German-American, a sort of one-woman Free World and if the rest of the free world were like her it would be all right. Josie, who normally dresses with the care of a Frenchwoman, plus some American top-spin, wore for the 'siege' khaki shorts and shirt borrowed from Canadian Signals. Horn-rimmed spectacles, a voice like an alarm-clock and a heart like a house were the rest of her equipment. She went everywhere at the double, like Colonel Alemu's Ethiopians, but her version of the double showed a trace of Marxist influence – Grouchist-Marxist. She regarded Katanga as preposterous, and the UN as inexplicable. Her view of Africans might be called maternalist; she considered the local Europeans as having in some way gone native; she thought I was a little crazy, but she liked my English dictation. There was, inevitably, some little tension at this time between civilian and soldier, Swede and Indian. One thing united us all: everybody loved Josie. When she would fly out of the door of Clair Manoir in the evening, bound on some errand of mercy or just retribution, I often heard a spontaneous and affectionate cheer go up from the men. I have sometimes thought that, if Josie had not stayed – when most of the civilian staff and almost all the women were evacuated – things might have gone much more sour as Morthor went wrong. Inside our eucalyptus-tree stockade, we tried to live up to Josie.

Outside the stockade too, life had its brighter moments. From the papers you might have thought of the street-fighting in Elisabethville at that time as being something like Warsaw. It was not at all like that. Most of the time, by day, the straight, broad avenues were deserted and unharmed. Some UN officials used to drive around without escort in 'soft-skinned vehicles', like Pierce Fitzgerald, our Finance officer, in his Volkswagen. I was more prudent; my face was fairly well known in town (although later in September the Brussels telephone exchange refused to accept a personal call for me on the grounds that I was 'unknown in Elisabethville') and also I had my critics, some of whom were in a position to make their point in a convincing way. I therefore preferred, by day – except when I was with Mr Dunnett under the protection of the Union Jack – to travel in armoured vehicles. This often meant very long waits; one of our chief military handicaps was a shortage of vehicles. One had the choice, or rather the chance of drawing, an Irish armoured car or a Swedish Armoured Personnel Carrier (APC). The armoured cars were cramped, and unsafe as the enemy had weapons which could easily destroy these products of County Carlow's Ruhr. This thought, combined with the fact that our drivers seldom knew their way, and kept backing and turning in the cul-de-sacs of Elisabethville, made one prefer the Swedish APC. These were large vehicles, rather like Corporation refuse removers; they were heavily armoured at the side but open on top. This seemed odd to the civilian mind: well and good if the enemy stuck to honourable warfare and peppered the sides of the thing with rifle fire, but how if the despicable fellows stooped to the ruse of lobbing some explosive object *into* the APC? A Swede explained to me that the vehicle would remain undamaged, once it had been washed out.

The fact was that these journeys contained a real, but slight, element of risk. This is an admirably tonic proportion for getting your mind off the hard day at the office. Best of all were the night journeys. I remember one night coming back from the airport, lying in the back of an open goods-truck, looking up at the sparse, not yet familiar, Southern stars. It had been, of course, another bad day: the operation was going all wrong, I knew my own share of responsibility, but I felt for the moment altogether happy. I thought, as I looked up, of Tolstoy's Prince Andrey on the field of

Austerlitz. This was not Austerlitz, and I was not exactly Prince Andrey, or Tolstoy, but no matter. I knew what the old man meant.

Whatever about Austerlitz, things were going badly at Jadotville.

The Irish ('A') Company which had gone there on September 3rd had already been cut off before the fighting started by much larger forces of gendarmerie, from the main base at Shinkolobwe. At 4.50 p.m. on September 13th, it reported that it was under heavy fire and required reinforcements immediately. An attempt to relieve it was made by a single Irish company on that day, but this was stopped at the Lufira bridge, a fortified position on a ravine. 'A' Company reported, on September 14th, 'water cut off and food getting scarce', and that their position was bombed and strafed by the Fouga, probably from a base in Kolwezi. On September 15th they reported themselves 'very short of water and food'. On September 16th a helicopter got through to them with 'limited supplies of food and water'. At 12 noon on that day they reported themselves 'under ever-increasing pressure' but that afternoon there was a most unexpected change:

1430 Cease-fire in Jadotville requested by the Lord Mayor of Jadotville[1] to Commandant Quinlan (O.C. 'A' Company)

1715 Cease-fire agreed to by Commandant Quinlan on the following conditions:

    (1) That the water would be turned on for them.

    (2) That food would be made available.

    (3) That the Fouga jet would also be grounded.

    (4) That Lufira Bridge garrison also observe cease-fire.

By early the following morning, we were feeling very happy about Jadotville. I indeed was so elated that Dr Linner – very wisely, as it happened – advised me over telex to keep my hair on. I was pleased not only because the news at this point was good in itself but also because I thought it meant that the Africans in the gendarmerie were no longer willing to fight, or even act as a screen, for the European enterprise of mystification which the State of Katanga, in my eyes, represented. But even Commandant Hugh McNamee, the able and tough commander of the Irish battalion, who had no political preconceptions, was happy about the position. He reported to Mr Aiken – who had come to Leopoldville mainly because of

---

[1] An African named Amisi.

Irish concern about the wildly exaggerated Press reports of 'A'
Company's losses – as follows, on the basis of the reports then to
hand:

> '*Situation well under control in Jadotville. No serious casualties. Five
> other ranks slightly wounded, some of them with shell shock. A truce was
> asked for last (sc. afternoon) by Lord Mayor. Conditions very acceptable to
> Irish. Company Commander invited by Chief of Police to tour the town
> today.*'

That was on Sunday morning, September 17th, at 6.30 a.m.
Already, though Commandant McNamee, in Clair Manoir, could
not yet know it, the situation seems to have deteriorated:

> *0500 hours 'A' Company completely surrounded at Jadotville, estimated
> enemy at 2,000. Running short of food and water.*[1]

At 11.30 a.m. on the same day the log notes:

> '*Report that Mr Hammarskjold is to fly from Leopoldville to Ndola for
> cease-fire talks with Mr Tshombe who is reported to be already in Ndola
> for the purpose.*'

(Hammarskjold, when he decided to go to Ndola, probably did
not know either of the improvement in the situation or of the
subsequent deterioration. Anxiety about the fate of the Company
was undoubtedly a factor in his decision.)

> *1340 'A' Company position very acute. Despite promises still no water
> made available. Very severe pressure being exerted on them.*

And at 7.35 on Sunday evening, word was received that 'A'
Company had surrendered to Munongo.

What had happened on the Saturday afternoon, and how had it
been reversed during Saturday night?

Captain Lasimone, about a month later, gave me a large part of
the answer. Lasimone was a subordinate, and enemy, of Faulques.
He was a Frenchman, but had been in Chad, not Algeria, and for
this reason he did not rate socially with the other French officers,
whom he called *Les Fascistes*, but that may have been just to please
me. We had learned about him from a young Polish LRP (locally
recruited personnel) of the UN, Terry Infeld, who was his girl and
whom, about September 8th or 9th, he had beaten up, apparently
because Faulques felt she was not very good at filching relevant UN

---

[1] The promised supplies do not seem to have been delivered, except for some
small quantities.

documentation.[1] She was very pretty, even with a black eye, and Egge, who interrogated her, felt that she would not be safe in Elisabethville, nor would we. So she was sent to Leopoldville, and that was why Lasimone – on, it must have been, about October 10th – came to see me in Les Roches. He had repented his impulsiveness; he now realized that the Polish girl meant everything to him and he wanted to join her in Leopoldville. Furthermore, Faulques was a scoundrel and a sadist. Lasimone was prepared to work for the Central Government, or the UN, and tell everything he knew, provided he was allowed to join his Terry in Leopoldville. He was a thin, tense, romantic young man, and I believe he was quite sincere. When I showed some degree of sympathy with his plight, and agreed to pass on a letter (open and checked) to Terry, he became quite talkative on the subject of Jadotville.[2]

He had been G.3 in charge of operations, under Faulques, at Jadotville. The only troops that they could rely on were the Europeans: all the white male able-bodied residents of Jadotville, with three exceptions, were under arms and the exceptions – including my elderly friend Major Geurtz – were in jail. It was impossible to get the Africans to fight. The most they would do was to encircle the Irish. It was he, Lasimone, who had cut off the water – a stratagem, he seemed to feel, that would never have occurred to the civilian mind – and that had done the trick. But there had been some bad moments, especially when, on the Saturday, there had been a decay of morale (*pourrissement*) and 'black politicians' in Jadotville had induced the African troops to fraternize with the Irish. However, Munongo and Faulques had rushed in 'fresh troops', the ringleaders among the 'mutineers' had been shot, the 'politicians' had been jailed, and by morning the situation had been restored.

Lasimone's account was, I think, substantially true, but there was an additional important element in the situation. Faulques and Munongo would not, I believe, have found it so easy to deal with the 'mutiny' if the UN had been getting across to the potential

---

[1] Her information with regard to Faulques's intentions towards us, made the UN shift its headquarters from the Avenue Fulbert Youlou to the less accessible Clair Manoir.

[2] There may be some unworthy readers who are more anxious to know what became of Lasimone and Terry than to consider the political implications of September 16th, in Jadotville. I am afraid I have no happy ending for these readers. I recommended that the Central Government should hire Lasimone, and extract all the information he had. ONUC Leopoldville turned this down, mainly on the grounds that 'he only wanted to go to Leopoldville to join his girl friend'. As that is exactly what he said himself, I could not see the point.

'mutineers' – those Africans, that is, who rejected the authority of foreign officers illegally present in Katanga – the word that the UN was on their side. We had the proof, after the events, that there were many, including officers, in the gendarmerie who wanted to see the State of Katanga brought to an end. In the beginning, September 14th, Radio Congo, Elisabethville Station, stressed the theme: the secession is over, arrest the white officers. It is true that, on the first day, our Swahili translator – a refugee – fell into the unfortunate habit of saying 'the whites' instead of the white officers, but Mrs Mumford put a stop to that. Mrs Margery Mumford, like Josie, helped to keep our hearts up in those days. She was a rare phenomenon, a European who had lived in Kenya throughout the Mau Mau time without losing her generosity, her human solidarity or her sense of humour. She was a niece of Miss Margery Perham, the great, but not wildly radical, authority on Africa. I don't know what Miss Perham thought of her niece, directing the Swahili broadcasts of Radio Tombelaine, in September, in Elisabethville. In any case, the broadcasts now came out with 'white officers' instead of 'whites' which was an improvement.

The improvement did not satisfy ONUC Leopoldville. We received, on September 15th, a stinging rebuke for our 'propaganda' and an order to confine ourselves, in future, to 'objective news bulletins'. It is hard to know what constituted, in Leopoldville's eyes, an objective news bulletin, but it was clear that our exhortations had to stop. The events of Jadotville show, I believe, that these exhortations were not falling on deaf ears. But at the very moment when it was beginning to have effect, the voice of the UN in Katanga faltered and died. This matter of the use of the radio was not a side-issue; it was absolutely central, both politically and militarily. The rulers of Katanga fought, as they ruled, behind an African screen. As long as they were able to do so, it would be hard for the UN to win, and impossible for them to win without killing a lot of Africans who were not, in reality, enemies. Many, if not most or even all, of the Africans who formed the screen did so because they were hopelessly confused – and small wonder! – about what the UN was trying to do. We felt that the only way of removing the screen, and therefore the only way of bringing Morthor now to a successful conclusion, was to use the radio to tell the Africans not to fight against the unity of the Congo, and not to obey their white officers. This was entirely in the logic of the only Morthor we knew, which was aimed at ending secession. It was, of course, entirely alien to the version now proclaimed in Leopoldville, and, since S/4940 had issued, our radio was bound to be gagged, as far as any effective use of it was concerned.

It is true of course that our use of the radio had revolutionary implications in the Katanga context. So had the February resolution. So had the Americo-Afro-Asian bargain. So, above all, had the prevailing Afro-Asian interpretation of the February resolution, and it is by that interpretation that Hammarskjold had said he would be guided. The messages reaching us from Leopoldville were not noticeably affected by the spirit of the Afro-Asian interpretation. They were noticeably affected by the spirit of Sir Patrick Dean's reservation. I have already speculated as to some of the reasons – and they were powerful ones – for that.

The divergence between Morthor in Elisabethville and the pseudo-Morthor of Leopoldville made itself felt in wider ways even than through the radio. Officers and men in the UN force were confused, and some of them partly discouraged, by effective hostile propaganda; no one was gagging the Katangese 'clandestine' radios and everyone was listening to them. On the UN side we neither made, nor could suggest, any effective answer. I could no longer give the military any political guidance because, by September 15th, I knew I was no longer in tune with Hammarskjold in Leopoldville. And there was no point in giving them the Leopoldville version – even if I had been aware of what it was – because they would have known it to be untrue.

After the surrender of the Jadotville Company – who, I firmly believe, need never have surrendered had it not been for the UN's confusion of purposes – it is possible to argue that the sooner Morthor was put out of its misery the better. The only argument against that is that it might have been better to await the arrival of the Ethiopian jets – for the passage of which the Uganda authorities were refusing clearance on technical grounds – before coming to terms with Tshombe. The terms then would, I think, have been better. If the Uganda authorities, and the British Government, had been made aware that the UN would not agree to a cease-fire before it had its jets, the technical difficulties at Entebbe might not have proved insoluble for long.

It has been argued retrospectively that an immediate cease-fire was necessitated by the military situation. That has been argued by civilians. It was not, I believe, the view of the UN Command.[1] The

---

[1] In some of our dispatches from Elisabethville we did paint the military situation in sombre colours, as a means of putting on pressure for the jets. This was a mistaken tactic, but General McKeown knew the situation in Elisabethville at first hand and was not, I believe, unduly alarmed.

reasons which caused the operations to end in stalemate were fundamentally not military; they were political.

From the very outset, of course, we had been looking for a cease-fire, but the word cease-fire took on different meanings with the passage of time. At 4.45 a.m. on September 13th it would have meant unconditional surrender by Tshombe – if his house had been sealed off. A little later that morning, if Mr Dunnett had been good enough to contact me, it could have meant a satisfactory settlement. But now, with Tshombe in Rhodesia, and after S/4940 and all it implied (and later the capture of the Irish Company) the word 'cease-fire' was more likely to mean at best stalemate and a return to the *status quo*.

At midnight on September 16th Mr Dunnett told me that Tshombe was prepared to meet me at Bancroft, N. Rhodesia.[1] I cabled to Leopoldville for instructions, adding a recommendation that I should not go to Rhodesia, since to do so might be tantamount to accepting something resembling the arbitration of Sir Roy Welensky. I had already made it clear to Tshombe, through Mr Dunnett, that I was prepared to meet him without escort anywhere in Katanga.

I may perhaps make the comment here that I have been rather surprised at the ease with which public opinion in the West accepted Tshombe's odd relation to Rhodesia. Tshombe was, in international law, a rebel against his own Government, and also a person whose illegally-officered army – illegally-officered in relation to a resolution for which Britain had herself voted – was waging war against the United Nations. Northern Rhodesia is a territory for which the British Colonial Office is responsible, and the British Government is, normally, punctilious both about forms of legality and being seen to discharge its duties to the United Nations. Yet here it allowed its territory to be used by Tshombe, as a secure base for his action against the UN.[2]

I got back a lengthy message from Hammarskjold for Tshombe: a message which must have been exceedingly satisfactory for the recipient. Amid much that cannot have been altogether clear to him, certain phrases must have stood out:

---

[1] This was just after the *pourrissement* – from Tshombe's point of view – of the Jadotville situation, reports of which may conceivably have prompted his request.

[2] Technically his headquarters were supposed to be near the Rhodesian border. In practice in a place like Kipushi, partly in Rhodesia and partly in Katanga, there is no clearly defined border (see p. 274). When Tshombe and his 'military advisers' were on or near the border they were effectively under Rhodesian protection; that is why they were there.

(3) 'A principle of the United Nations which is absolutely binding upon all is the maintenance of peace and, to that end in order to protect human life they (UN) are bound to cease all hostilities and to seek solutions to the conflict by means of negotiation, mediation and conciliation.'

(7) 'I have been informed of the message received by Mr O'Brien from Mr Dunnett, the British Consul, inviting him to meet you tomorrow at 11.30 at Bancroft in Northern Rhodesia. I suggest that I should try to meet you personally, so that together we can try to find peaceful methods of resolving the present conflict, thus opening the way to a solution of the Katanga problem within the framework of the Congo'.[1]

I requested permission, if Hammarskjold was going to Ndola, to join his party at Kamina Base, as I felt it very desirable to report to him on the situation at Elisabethville, both past and present. I also meant to try to dissuade him from going to Rhodesia at all; anything I knew of Tshombe – and I had by now more experience of dealing with him than any Onusian then in the Congo – suggested that he was something of a chameleon. In Leopoldville, the previous year, Rhodesia had been, for him, a 'territory under the colonial yoke'[2] with which he could have nothing to do; it was likely that, in Rhodesia, he would be equally difficult about Leopoldville.

Hammarskjold rejected my proposal, saying that he wished to negotiate with Tshombe 'outside the framework of ONUC'.

Tshombe's reply was transmitted to me, by the inevitable Mr Dunnett,[3] at 10 a.m. on the morning of September 17th. Tshombe agreed on 'the principle of an immediate cease-fire'.[4] He requested that UN troops be confined to their camps, and that troop movements be stopped. He agreed to go to Ndola: his delegation would be Kibwe, Kimba and 'the Secretary of State for the Common Market, Mr Mwenda-Odilon'.

There was, it will be noted, an interesting absentee: Mr Munongo, who was just then in Jadotville, about to accept the surrender of 'A' Company.

Hammarskjold at first sent a sharp reply to Tshombe's message:

---

[1] The full text of this is in S/4940/Add. 4 (September 17th).

[2] See p. 231.

[3] I do not of course mean to criticize Mr Dunnett for helping to bring about a cease-fire at this point. On the contrary, his activity on September 17th shows a distinct improvement over September 13th.

[4] The words 'the principle' in this mean that in practice the firing went on.

'Kindly inform Tshombe that the Secretary-General finds it impossible to accept the conditions for a cease-fire and a meeting which have been conveyed to him.'

None the less he took off from Leopoldville at 1700 hours on September 17th for Ndola, where Tshombe, Kimba and Lord Alport, British High Commissioner in Rhodesia, awaited him.

In Elisabethville I do not think there was anyone who believed that his death was an accident. This of course proves nothing, but it may help to situate the event in a political context. About the technical circumstances surrounding his death my opinion is, obviously, of no value. In so far, however, as the Katanga political context may have been relevant to his death, it may perhaps be useful to say something about it.

The Rhodesian Commission of Enquiry into the crash of the DC6 made the following observation:

'No reason was suggested, and we can think of none why anyone should have wanted to attack it as it carried Mr Hammarskjold on the mission he was then undertaking.'

I can think of some reasons and now suggest them.

Let us assume that he *was* murdered. Who would, or could, have murdered him?

Tshombe himself may be excluded to start with. Tshombe had no more reason to murder Hammarskjold on the way to Ndola than Hitler had to murder Chamberlain on the way to Munich. (The personalities and situations are very different in many respects, but they have some points in common; including this one.)

For similar reasons any suspicions that Tshombe's more respectable backers, like Sir Roy Welensky, could have had any complicity in the commission of such a crime, may be discarded. It was simply not in their interests.

I may add that I do not believe either Tshombe or Sir Roy Welensky, or even Mr Macmillan, to be murderous by disposition. But that is a less telling argument in favour of their innocence than the fact that such a crime was not in their interests.

It was not, however, Tshombe who was waging war in Katanga. Tshombe had always one foot, and often two, in the Rhodesian sanctuary. The warrior was Munongo. Munongo's was the one group in Katanga which would have been capable of such an act, and would have regarded it as being in accordance, not so much with its interests as with its conception of the good. The men principally concerned were the OAS officers – Lasimone's 'fascists'. They were, and are, fascists, and they had scores other than the

Congo to settle with Hammarskjold: Algeria, Suez, Tunisia. There is no doubt that they had eyes and ears and hands in Brazzaville and Leopoldville, as well as control over the air-strip at Kolwezi: they almost certainly also had friends at Ndola. There is no doubt that they were experienced in political assassination and that they would have regarded the murder of Hammarskjold as a virtuous act.[1]

Melodramatic speculation? It is, and can only be, speculation. Melodrama was a constant element of existence in Katanga, as it is in many other parts of the world.

At mid-morning on September 18th, Lieutenant Delin came over Clair Manoir with his Fouga. Captain Nanda of Raja's staff waved to me. The Captain was standing beside a hole in the ground. His idea seemed to be that I should come quickly and sit in this hole. I came and so, though a little less quickly, did a *Life* reporter, a well-built gentleman, who sat on me. A *Life* photographer stood up on a mound of earth – the corollary of our hole – and took a picture of this scene. This proves nothing, except perhaps that diplomats are fleeter of foot than reporters, and that photographers are braver than either.

That afternoon I had word from Tshombe: an unsolicited assurance that he had ordered the Fouga to be grounded 'temporarily' (*provisoirement*).[2] The same afternoon we received confirmation that the wreckage of Hammarskjold's plane had been found.

Tshombe's message does not prove that the Fouga shot down Hammarskjold's plane. What it does indicate, I think, is that

---

[1] In addition to the hypothesis of murder, that of a last-minute change of plan has been considered: 'How', asks Arthur Gavshon, 'would Hammarskjold have reacted if at the last moment he had learnt from Fabry – Khiary's collaborator – just how the UN action in Katanga had come to be ordered? Is it conceivable that the Secretary-General may have felt a need to talk to O'Brien – who had asked to be taken along to Ndola – before seeing Tshombe?' (*The Mysterious Death of Dag Hammarskjold*, p. 238.) It remains conceivable, certainly; if I no longer feel it to be probable – as I should have done at the time of writing *The Observer* article – it is because I have been reluctantly driven to the conclusion that Hammarskjold knew as much as he wanted to know about what had happened in Elisabethville. Nothing that Fabry could have said would have lessened the force of the Riches-Lansdowne representations: the diplomatic propellant towards Ndola.

[2] The British Foreign Office announced on September 19th that, through Mr Dunnett, it had requested Mr Tshombe to ground the Fouga. This was a kindly thought, although perhaps a shade belated. It appears that Lansdowne, at his last interview with Hammarskjold, had offered to 'try to persuade' Tshombe to ground the Fouga. This offer, at this time, appears to have been part of a proposed bargain, rejected by Hammarskjold, under which the UN was asked not to bring any jets to Katanga (Gavshon, *op. cit.*, page 179).

Tshombe and his friends thought it might have done so. Indeed, in a suitable context, he was not above making use of the thought. A resident of Jadotville informed Irish officers about a fortnight later that Tshombe, speaking in Swahili to Africans of that town on Sunday, boasted that the mighty forces of Katanga had not merely compelled the Secretary-General of the United Nations to sue for peace, but had actually struck him down while he was doing so. I have little doubt that he did say this – it sounds very much what I would expect him to say, in Swahili, in Jadotville. I have no doubt either that he had nothing at all to do with Hammarskjold's death. He may, however, have learned something about it, after his return to Katanga, from the Minister of the Interior, and this may have inspired him at Jadotville.

On September 20th at Ndola, Khiary signed a provisional cease-fire agreement, ending the operation which his instructions of September 11th had begun. Tshombe and Munongo returned to Elisabethville. The secession was maintained; officially, no one had even tried to end it.

16

A FLAG FOR ALBERTVILLE

'The answer is in the back of the book
but the page is gone
And grandma told you to tell the truth
but she is dead.'

Robert Penn Warren

Sacha Guitry in his film on Napoleon plays the part of Talleyrand telling his friends, under the restoration, the great story. Having told of the victories of 1805, Ulm and Austerlitz, he is moving on to 1806, when one of his listeners interrupts him. 'Eighteen hundred and five?' she asks, 'Was not that also the year of Trafalgar?'

'Trafalgar?' says Talleyrand. 'Trafalgar? Let the English talk of that; not us. *Que les Anglais en parlent – pas nous!*'

In a similar spirit I shall leave Moïse (or his ghost) to tell, in his autobiography, the detailed story of the return of his régime to Elisabethville. This was his apotheosis. In his newspapers and on his radio, his Minister for Information, Samalenghe, compared him to Jesus Christ, crucified and risen again. He was hailed as 'Tshombe the Magnanimous' with, at his side, 'Muké the Victorious'. The epithet 'magnanimous' seems odd, but in fact it had a propaganda function similar to that, at an earlier stage, of the theory that the United Nations had broken the beautiful friendship between black and white.[1] The difficulty and its solution may be expressed in dialectical form.

Thesis: Tshombe's forces defeated the forces of the United Nations.
Antithesis: But the forces of the United Nations are still in Katanga.
Synthesis: How magnanimous Tshombe is!
Militarily, of course, the operation had been a stalemate – indeed,

---

[1] Chapter 14, pp. 224–5.

as will be seen in a moment, much nearer a defeat for Tshombe's forces than for the UN – but politically, granted the relative importance of the UN and of Tshombe, it was certainly a victory for what Tshombe represented. Tshombe himself, indeed, had done little or nothing to earn that victory; he had run away to Rhodesia and, from beneath Sir Roy's protection, had hurled defiance at the United Nations. Poor 'Muké the Victorious' was visibly incapable of doing more than letting himself be trundled around by the European officers who directed the fighting. The only African on the Katanga side who had played a serious part in the campaign was Munongo. Munongo had appeared at Jadotville, at the moment of crisis – both for Katanga and the United Nations – and had swung the trembling balance to the side of Katanga. M'Siri's grandson was an adversary who compelled respect. His standards were the bad standards of a cruel and archaic world but at least he held to them bravely. One thought of him as the Franks in the Song of Roland thought of one of the great Moslem warriors:

> *God what a Baron, had he had Christianity!*
> *Deus quel Baron s' oüst Chrestientet!*

The essential elements in the cease-fire agreement were that the prisoners should be exchanged and that the public buildings held by the UN should be handed back to the Katangese.[1] The tacit understanding was that the apparatus of the State of Katanga could be set up again, while the United Nations would continue to refer to the province of Katanga and bring quotation marks ruthlessly to bear. Nobody mentioned a Commissaire d'Etat any more. I still had, in the drawer of my bedroom in Les Roches, the *mandats d'amener* which poor Fabry had given me, and my instructions to apply them had never been officially countermanded. But I realized – although I am not always quick on the uptake in such matters – that I was no longer supposed to do anything about them.

The first attempt at implementing the agreement was unsuccessful, because the Katangese tried to collect their public buildings without

---

[1] There were other provisions, e.g. that the radio was not to be used for hostile propaganda against the United Nations. The station's first broadcast, after its return to the Katangese, was devoted to hysterical denunciation of the UN forces. There was a more important provision for inspection by mixed commissions of military centres in Katanga. The Katangese participated in such inspection of UN centres (Albertville etc.), but refused to allow inspection of any of their own centres (Kolwezi etc.). This did not deter Sir Patrick Dean from informing the Security Council in November that, so far as his Government knew, Mr Tshombe had respected the cease-fire agreement.

handing over the prisoners – the arrival of the Jadotville Company was delayed by a 'hitch in transportation'. Raja and I said, in effect, 'no prisoners, no buildings'. Tshombe – who had, I think, by this time convinced himself that he had won a real victory – was much put out by this. My new deputy,[1] Al Succar, of Syria, a gentle and worldly young man, was in charge at the radio transmitter, with instructions to relinquish it only on receiving word that the Irish prisoners had arrived at the 'old airfield', the place appointed for the exchange. When Tshombe arrived at the transmitter, and no prisoners had arrived at the airport, Al Succar, with the exquisite combination of oriental and occidental courtesy which is all his own, informed Tshombe that it would be for him, Succar, both an honour and a pleasure to take part in the ceremony of handing over the transmitter – as pledge of mutual confidence of the United Nations and of Katanga – simultaneously with the equally touching and reassuring ceremony of the exchange of prisoners at the airport. Tshombe, when he had assimilated this, flew into a Hitlerian frenzy, quite unlike the mildly depressive behaviour to which I had been accustomed on his part in the pre-Morthor days. He flopped down on his knees, raised both arms above his head in his well-known king-sized V-sign, and in this awkward posture perambulated the station calling down God's vengeance on 'the little Lebanese'.

But when he finally understood that he could not have his buildings without handing over the prisoners, he handed over the prisoners.

These days of the aftermath of Morthor were bitter enough to live through for the United Nations people in Katanga, including myself. They must have been far more bitter for those Africans – virtually all the politically-conscious Africans in the province – who were oppressed by the State of Katanga, and for whom Morthor had seemed to mean the coming of freedom. The period from the arrest of Bintou through Rumpunch and Morthor had been one of revolutionary ferment. That ferment, and the counter-revolutionary action against it, had produced the refugee camp with its population of 45,000 men, women and children – more than a quarter of the African inhabitants of Elisabethville.

The revolutionary crisis had passed, abortively; the camp was still with us.

What you called the camp was a test of where you stood politically. Good UN people always spoke of 'the refugee camp'. Local Europeans – and the Consular Corps – always referred to 'the Baluba

---

[1] Tombelaine had been due for a transfer to New York at the end of August, voluntarily stayed on for September and returned to New York after 'the events'.

camp.' Neither term was quite accurate; they were not just refugees
and they were not just Baluba.

If the word 'refugee' implies a passive victim of persecution, then
it is the wrong word for some of the inhabitants of the camp. They
included among them – as well as a majority of women, children
and more or less quiet males – a number of ferocious fighters,
mostly members of the Jeunesse Balubakat. These people, armed
with sticks or bits of packing-case, with the nails in, were capable
of attacking a jeep-load of gendarmerie armed with light automatic
weapons, and cutting the gendarmes, quite literally, to pieces.
Europeans and gendarmes were in the habit of sniping at the camp,
and the Jeunesse regarded any 'Belgian' as an enemy to be killed on
sight. This situation where a minority among a vast population
which had sought UN protection, tried to wage terrorist war
against European rule (for that is how they saw it) created appalling
problems for the Swedish Camp Commander, Major Arne Forslund,
and his men. Their task, of protecting the refugees from some of the
Europeans, and the Europeans from some of the refugees, was almost
impossible. It drew them into conflict, particularly with the refugees,
many of whom regarded the UN forces as having inexplicably taken
the side of their persecutors. After October 5th when a Swedish
soldier was badly injured by members of the Jeunesse and the Swedes
opened fire, killing a number of refugees, relations between the UN
and those under their protection settled into mutual suspicion and
aversion.

The Europeans and their Consuls said 'the Baluba camp' but in
fact in addition to the Baluba of Kasai (40 per cent of the refugee
population) and the Baluba of Katanga (25 per cent) there were
16,000 non-Baluba in the camp, coming from virtually every other
province of the Congo. 'The Congolese camp' would have been a
more accurate description, but the word Baluba was undoubtedly
better from a Katangese point of view. It underlined the tribal
element involved, and avoided the political implications. Also the
word Baluba had acquired, from the publicity about the atrocities
in the north, a certain horrifying resonance, reaching indeed far
outside Katanga.[1] It is true that the Baluba who had acquired a bad

---

[1] In Ireland, as a result of the tragic death of nine Irish soldiers ambushed by
Baluba at Nyemba, the word 'Baluba' has passed pejoratively into popular
language. 'He jumped on to the platform', a bus conductor will say, 'behaving like
a bloody Baluba'. The word 'Baluba' is, of course, a plural and bus conductors
should say 'a bloody Muluba', but I have not heard the singular in use. I hope
any bus conductor who may read this book will practise in future a more correct
Swahili.

name were those of Katanga, whereas those of Kasai – best known for Lumumba's 'genocide' against them, which those I met did not seem to resent[1] – were the most advanced and peaceable elements in the community, and also the largest group in the camp. However, the distinction between 'those of Kasai' and 'those of Katanga' – an ethnological gulf in some other political contexts – became almost invisible to European eyes when those concerned had passed into the UN camp.

It must be said that the horror which the camp inspired in Europeans, and which was perceptible in a little shudder produced by the words 'the Baluba camp', was not altogether unfounded. It was not safe for a European to stray into the vicinity of the camp. If he had the bad luck to encounter certain groups of the Baluba Jeunesse he would be likely to be killed and he might also be eaten. In the world of the camp, side by side with modern men and women, were people from parts of Katanga – parts lacking mineral resources – where life remained much as it had been under M'Siri and ritual cannibalism was not extinct.[2] Some of these people were cannibals, and under the influence of sorcerers. A sorcerer named Mantefu, an elusive but influential character in the camp, did a lucrative trade in hemp and possessed a cauldron said to contain an abominable stew.

It is necessary here to say a few words about cannibalism, from a political and economic point of view. The continued existence of the phenomenon in places like the Belgian Congo comes as a surprise to new-comers – it certainly did to me – because both the main currents of European thought tend to conceal it. The liberal's whole cast of mind makes him incurious about the subject; the conservative, in Europe, likes to point to the disappearance of cannibalism as among the benefits conferred by European civilization: 'When the Belgians came, these people were cannibals.' The fact that many of them were still cannibals after the Belgians, in theory, left, is a fact that seems to suit nobody. In reality it does suit some people very well. Colonialism, like so many other cults, has its public and esoteric doctrines. The public doctrine is: We have civilized them. The esoteric doctrine is: They are incapable of being civilized. The public doctrine is proclaimed in Europe. The esoteric doctrine is main-

---

[1] The Kasai Baluba resident in the Katanga towns were Lumumbists, as P. Davister admits.

[2] F. Grévisse, writing about the population of the mining towns, says: 'Certain natives affiliated to sects flourishing in the regions in question (Bayembe etc.), were necrophagous. . . . These customs have apparently disappeared, although one would not swear to anything.' (*Bulletin Trimestriel du CEPSI*, Mars, 1155, p. 137.)

tained, in undertones, among Europeans in places like Katanga.
Cannibalism, in this context, has the importance of establishing
virtually a qualitative distinction between 'them' and 'us'. The
colonial European forgets – if he ever knew – that his own ancestors,
not really so very long ago, were cannibals, and he easily fastens on
the survival of cannibalism as the mark of the inherently, incurably,
degraded nature of the African. This obviously has useful political
and economic corollaries, but there is a little more to it than that.
I used to notice, among some Europeans in Katanga – not always
Belgians – a curious undercurrent of furtive pleasure beneath the
horror with which they discussed this subject. They were rather like
puritans denouncing sexual immorality; of course the subjects are
interconnected, by reason of the highly selective dietary practices of
many religious cannibals. Perhaps there is a suppressed cannibal in
us all. In any case, he who exploits may well find pleasure, as well as
justification, in dwelling on the degradation of those whom he
exploits. The partial survival of cannibalism, as well as its partial
extinction, were of course results of the manner in which the resources of Katanga had been exploited. The continuance, virtually
untouched, of the traditional society – *le milieu coutumier* – supplied
the Union Minière and its allies with a pool of reserve labour. If
cannibalism was among the customs which survived in the pool, that
did not really matter very much – provided they only ate each
other. This was not of course the point of view of the missionaries,
but the impact of the Union Minière on Katanga is more readily
discernible than that of the missionaries.

Besides cannibalism, another tendency said to exist in the camp
was Communism. It is true that among the street-names of the
camp – for the camp was in reality a vast shanty-town divided into
'avenues' with shops, bars and restaurants – was not only an 'Avenue
Lumumba' but also an 'Avenue Khrushchev'. The fact is by no
means without significance, but it did not mean that the people in the
camp were Communists, yet. Few of them can have known much
about Communism, and I think they only knew two things about
Mr Khrushchev. One was that he had supported Lumumba, whom
they regarded as a hero and a martyr, when the Western countries
and even the UN had hounded him to his death. (I do not say that
this is a fair picture; it is the picture accepted by many, perhaps
most, Congolese nationalists.) The other thing they knew about
Mr Khrushchev was that he was a Communist, which was the term
applied, in Katanga, to anyone who supported a party not sponsored
by the Union Minière. There are certain kinds of anti-Communist

propaganda which have a pro-Communist effect – Hitler's, McCarthy's and Verwoerd's are examples. On the refugees and many others in Africa, Tshombe's anti-Communism produces the same effect.

The camp was a secondary effect of policies pursued by the Union Minière: the policies, symbolized by the Conakat, of encouragement of tribal hostilities and of annexation through secession. It was a result of these policies, but it was a result which had not been intended. The Kasai Baluba in particular were a valuable element in the economic life of Elisabethville, and the Union Minière did its best to get them to go back to their work – which some of them did for a while – and to their homes, which hardly any of them did. Tshombe, at the instance of Union Minière, tried to help to bring this about. He appointed a Commissioner for the refugees – Mr Alidor Beia, a portly and circumspect Muluba from Kolwezi – and he announced a number of excellent measures: disarming of the Garde Nationale (a sort of Conakat militia), dissolution of the Jenakat youth movement, setting up of mixed committees, with heavy refugee and even UN participation, for the reintegration of the refugees into their communities. Unfortunately none of these measures was ever carried out: the Garde Nationale continued to be armed – and indeed killed a number of Baluba in Kipushi shortly after Tshombe's announcement – the Jenakat continued its approved and organized hooliganism and Munongo scrapped the committees. The refugees, who were not at all surprised by the contrast between Tshombe's words and Munongo's acts, stayed where they were.

There were in reality only two ways of clearing up the camp. One was through revolutionary change in Katanga; that had misfired with Morthor. The other possible solution was repatriation to their places of origin. ONUC and the Central Government at this date were still unwilling to co-operate in mass repatriation. The following extract from a report by the principal UN civilian worker in the camp, a devoted and capable young Dutchman named Kuitenbrouwer, shows the position of ONUC and that of the refugees:

'It was when Mr Mahmoud Khiary arrived at the end of September, that ONUC's and the Central Government's policy became clear and it was explained to the tribal and political representatives of the refugees by Mr Khiary, in his meeting with them at the Swedish camp on September 29th. His words were in substance the following: "The Central Government and ONUC are not considering – and cannot consider – organizing any large-scale evacuation of refugees. If after the situation in Katanga quiets down again, there are among you persons who want to leave Katanga, they are of course free to do so on their own resources just as any Congolese has the right to free circulation. Each Congolese has the right to live and work in any part of the territory of the Congolese Nation, including Katanga. If you leave Katanga, where you have built your lives, you give evidence to Tshombe that you consider yourselves as foreigners who have less right to live and work in Katanga which should be reserved for 'real Katangese'. If you leave, you destroy your own cause and rights and you are traitors to your own cause and the interests of your country. Katanga is for all Congolese. As soon as conditions permit, you should integrate yourselves again into the communities of which you have, up to recently, been part. For the moment, you can be assured of ONUC's protection which will last as long as this is necessary to assure your safety. I beg you to exercise patience for the moment. The United Nations and the Central Government will do all possible to clear up the situation as soon as possible."

'After Mr Khiary's words, two speakers replied, the leader of the Balubas of Kasai in the refugee camp, and the leader of the Balubas of Katanga. The first one declared: "Your way of thinking and your proposals are inacceptable for us. We do not want to stay here. We prefer to die (*Nous préférons mourir debout que de vivre à genoux*)". The leader of the Balubas of Katanga, to explain his stand, resorted to a legend of his people and declared: "In the beginning of the world, there were many animals. Most were small and innocent but there was one dangerous lion. He devoured many of the small animals and wounded others. All those which remained alive fled away to the borders of the world. Gradually, the lion began to feel lonely and sad and felt he would like to live again with the small animals. He took off his claws and went to them and with gentle voice and manners flattered them and told them that he wanted to be a good friend of all of them and that they should forgive his sins of the past. The small animals, however, recalling how bad and cruel the lion had been with the deceased members of their families and their friends, did not believe a thing of what the lion said and told him that they would never return as long as the lion would live." Thus the leader of the Balubas of Katanga made his position clear and leaving his metaphoric language behind, accused Tshombe and his Government of being totally unreliable and untrustworthy and said they could never accept such a Government as representative of Katanga.'[1]

Thus the camp continued in being, an oppressive reminder of a stalemate. Had it not been for Belgian intervention, first open, then disguised, the most advanced elements in the African community, who were now, along with others, in the camp, would be likely to be in charge in the city. Had it not been for the presence of the UN most of them would be living in their homes, sometimes beaten, liable to arbitrary arrest, but living what many people – though clearly not the refugees themselves – would regard as a more normal life than their life in the camp. The UN had provided what was for some of these people a refuge, for others a means of venting a protest, but that was all it had been able to do.

For me, at this time, the refugees formed a sombre background to thoughts which were in themselves none too rosy. I had thought, towards the end of Morthor, after Hammarskjold's death, that I was about to be promptly replaced, in circumstances which would have amounted to disgrace. My predecessor in Katanga, M Georges Dumontet, was dispatched to the Congo and the Press reported, generally with satisfaction, that he was about to replace me. This was bitter, not only personally – to be replaced by one's predecessor has unflattering implications – but also politically. M Dumontet was known for having 'got on well' with the Katangese and particularly with Mr Munongo whom he regarded as being at heart a moderate. His relations with the Katangese had, no doubt, been appropriate in their time but to reappoint him now would have been pushing the appeasement of Tshombe to the farthest point yet reached. Some people in Leopoldville – notably Mr Khiary and Mr Adoula – felt in the same way, and in the event M Dumontet got no further than that city.

There were in any case some difficulties in the way of removing me. My tenure in Katanga had won me, as well as condemnation in Western Europe, a considerable degree of approval in Afro-Asian countries. This had been symbolized by a message of good wishes and concern for my safety sent by Dr Nkrumah, whom I did not then know, to the UN during the fighting in Elisabethville. It would have been difficult to drop me immediately without giving further offence to Afro-Asian opinion, already incensed by the way in which the

[1] 'Report on the Refugee Camp at Elisabethville, Katanga', by Joost B. W. Kuitenbrouwer (February 20th, 1962). The report is marked restricted but I have released these two paragraphs.

UN seemed to draw back from what it seemed to have undertaken.

Yet there were two powerful and interconnected reasons why I should be dropped.

The first reason was that my version of the nature and purpose of Morthor, as given to the Press at the time, was at variance with the UN's official version, as presented in S/4940.

The second reason was that the British Government infinitely preferred Morthor in its official version to Morthor in its raw state of brute fact, as all too faithfully portrayed by me.

The official version had represented a kind of shrinking back from the realities of Morthor in the direction of the resolution of August 9th, 1960, and Sir Patrick Dean's reservation. The British Government wanted the shrinking to go all the way; and it wanted to commit the UN to the doctrine that it was unthinkable to try to end the secession by force. The British Government may have had a shrewd suspicion that my indiscreet remarks in Elisabethville were nearer the truth than the Leopoldville version, but that was all the more reason for taking the Leopoldville version very seriously indeed and for getting me repudiated and removed. This was what Lord Lansdowne had meant when, in Leopoldville, he 'expressed concern' to Hammarskjold 'at certain statements attributed to UN personnel in charge of Katanga operations'.[1] Hammarskjold did not disavow me but he could not, in the light of S/4940 and what it represented, altogether avow me either.

After Hammarskjold's death, the pressure continued with persistence. It was logical that it should do so for I was in Elisabethville still, the incarnate negation of Sir Patrick Dean's reservation. And of course the British Government was pressing on what was for the UN a very sensitive nerve. My statement about ending secession was not only contrary to what Sir Patrick had said; it was also contrary to what the UN itself had said it had done. This put any British representative discussing me with any UN official in rather a strong position. The dialogue might be imagined as running something like this:

UK: The UN position is much better understood now of course. What still gives us a lot of trouble though are those extraordinary statements of O'Brien's about ending the secession, and arresting Ministers, and so on. Did you ever get to the bottom of that?

UN: Well, you know, a lot of reports coming out of Katanga at that time were pretty garbled. . . .

---

[1] *Factel*, No. 279 (September 16th to 17th).

UK: There's not much doubt about these ones I'm afraid. Some of the worst of them are recorded. . . . By the way, I suppose I am right in taking it that there's nothing in what the fellow said? I mean there was no question of using the UN forces to arrest the Government – the provincial Government – and end the secession, as he called it?

UN: No, of course not. It was just completing the August 28th operation really – you've seen the report.

UK: I entirely accept that, naturally. I should have thought, though, that from the point of view of bringing the UN operation to a successful conclusion – which is what we all want – it's hardly wise to leave O'Brien in such a delicate post. After all he not only has been gravely indiscreet but he seems to have wildly exceeded his instructions. He certainly arrested Vice-President Kibwe – Dunnett is quite clear on that. I don't mind telling you that people in Britain would feel much happier about the UN Katanga operation if it were in other hands.

UN: We've told him to be more careful about what he says to the Press. . . .

As a result, no doubt, of some such conversations, I received – in, I think, late September or early October – two telegrams from New York stressing the embarrassment which reports of my verbal ending of the secession were still causing the UN. One of them mentioned a Foreign Office official who had referred to quote that dreadful statement unquote. UN headquarters in New York wanted to know, it said, what I had really said.

I now knew the official version of what had happened and I took it, perhaps wrongly, that New York was animated, not by a dispassionate intellectual need to know exactly what I had really said, but by a desire to have from me, in order to strengthen its own diplomatic hand, an account of my words which would not be entirely irreconcilable with the official version.

As well as being sick at heart with the failure of Morthor and haunted by the social and political implications of the refugee camp, I was bewildered and depressed by the way in which, from the beginning of Morthor, I had lost the rapport with headquarters which I had believed myself to possess up to then. I was rather childishly anxious to reinstate myself in their good graces; a feat the impossibility of which should have been clear to my mind, had the lucidity of analysis not been rendered turbid by hope.

In this situation and condition I committed the only actions of my Katanga time of which I am ashamed. First of all I referred headquarters to statements which I had indeed made during the fighting, but in the later days of it, when it had already been impressed on me, by the telegrams from Leopoldville, that talk about ending secession was frowned on. These statements were naturally more guarded and *nuancé* than my first statements. They were not really much use to New York, however, as they still based the action on paragraph A.1 (prevention of civil war) and not on paragraph A.2 (mercenaries) which was the basis given in the official version of the officer-in-charge. I also referred them to an interview I had given Keith Kyle, for the BBC. Khiary, who was in Elisabethville at the time, asked whether it was an 'orthodox' interview. *C'est catholique, au moins, cet interview-là?* And smiled the smile of a man who knows that all official versions are, have been from the beginning of time, and will for ever be, worded to deceive the enemy and appease the clamour of the ignorant.

Khiary was also there at a Press conference when someone raised the question of what I had said on September 13th. I gave an answer based on what I had said, but with some rather fine-spun legalistic qualifications. They were very felicitous and balanced qualifications. They had only one little defect: I did not make them at the time.

Khiary smiled.

Conscience at this moment, to my surprise, assumed the voice and shape of Mr John Latz. Mr Latz had a large nose, an RAF moustache and small close-set eyes. He kept a laundry in Elisabethville, and was part-time correspondent for the Associated Press. He was a friend of Captain Browne, the mercenary, and had been his host during some of the Captain's frequent but brief visits to Katanga. He was, of course, hostile to the UN. We were short of chairs at our Press conference and Mr Latz was sitting on the floor, on my right hand, with his back to the window.

He had been at my earliest Press conferences during the fighting – as most of those present had not – and when I had finished this rather carefully-worded exposition, he shook his head.

'That', said he, 'is not what you said.'

He spoke very quietly, not much above a whisper and in a tone even of some sympathy. That was the worst of it. I found myself unable to reply. Mr Latz had over me at that moment the immense moral authority of the man who is telling the truth over the man who is dodging it. That is why I shall remember all my life exactly where he was sitting on this occasion, and how he looked. As for me, I was sitting tilted back in a swivel chair and feeling as if I could do with a good cleaning in Mr Latz's laundry.

At this moment I began, dimly and reluctantly, to see the truth; that I could not recover or preserve my self respect unless I could rip myself away from the sticky clutches of the official version of what had happened on September 13th. In fact, as it turned out, the UN saved me the trouble by doing most of the ripping for me. It would not have done so, I think, however, if I had been prepared to take a hint and my reluctance to take a hint had something to do with unwillingness, following six words from Mr Latz, to accommodate myself any more to the necessities imposed by the discrepancy between the official version and the historical reality.

The hint took the form of a letter from a friend in Dublin, written about mid-October. This friend had been informed by a prominent UN personality, who had been in contact with Dr Bunche, that Dr Bunche felt that I might be wise to apply for a transfer from Katanga. I had inevitably lost the confidence of Tshombe – through no fault of my own – and that obviously curtailed my usefulness.

It is unwise – how unwise I was soon to find – for an official to disregard a hint of this kind: a hint which is tantamount to a semi-official request. I disregarded this hint, for reasons which were on several levels.

First of all I knew whose confidence I had lost. When Dayal had 'lost the confidence of President Kasavubu' what he had in fact lost was the confidence of the State Department. Similarly, in my case, for 'Tshombe' read 'the Foreign Office'. Tshombe did not in fact dislike or distrust me; he just thought I was rather naïve. ('He's not a bad fellow – only he doesn't know Africa', he said to Khiary about this time). It is true that he had ostentatiously proclaimed his unwillingness to have anything to do with me (or indeed with Khiary, with whom he then negotiated the cease-fire agreement), but in fact he or Kimba got in touch with me when they needed to do so. Thus, on, I think, October 16th, Tshombe rang me about 11 p.m. This was a day when the Katanga Government had published an ultimatum, which was due to expire at midnight, to the effect that if the UN had not cleared out the refugee camp by that time, the gendarmerie would move in and clear it out themselves. I had replied that if the gendarmerie attempted to do so the UN forces would resist. Tshombe now wanted to know whether it was true that UN forces were going to attack at midnight. I reminded him that what was due to expire at midnight was his own ultimatum, not one of ours. Tshombe indicated that his ultimatum was not really as ultimate as all that. I told him in that case he need have no fear. He was very relieved; for a man who never ceased to pro-

claim that I was a liar he derived a remarkable amount of reassurance from my simple word. 'I can sleep in peace' he said,
'Thank you! Thank you!' 'Not at all' said I nostalgically. '*Pas
d'quoi*'.

The talk of losing Tshombe's confidence was, as Khiary would
say, *pas sérieux*. What was *sérieux* was the Foreign Office and I did
not feel inclined, either politically or personally, to apply for a
transfer just because the Foreign Office wanted to get rid of me.

I could not be sure, either, of exactly what Bunche had said. I
trusted completely my informant in Dublin but I thought that the
information reaching him from New York might itself be affected by
the Foreign Office viewpoint as expounded by Sir Patrick Dean.
There was a game sometimes played in the Delegates' Lounge which
we used to call 'Sastroamojojo', from a taciturn Indonesian diplomat
often cited in connection with it. The object of the game was to get
your Government to do what a great power – say Great Britain –
wanted it to do. The obstacle to be overcome was the reluctance of
members of your Government to be used merely in the interests of
the great power in question. To play the game you had to get hold
of a neutral diplomat, particularly one of a non-argumentative
disposition, and recite to him, in as persuasive language as possible,
the case supported by the great power. During the conversation the
neutral delegate, if well chosen, will be likely, while sipping his
coffee and munching his cream bun, to make some positive replies,
which can form the basis of a not untruthful telegram beginning:
'I understand from Ambassador Sastroamojojo that there appears
to be some feeling even within the Afro-Asian group in favour of
X.', X. equalling the course of action favoured by the great power.
I thought 'Sastroamojojo' might have a hand in this: as a matter of
fact he was not needed.

I felt, in any case, that if the Secretariat wanted to shift me it
could do so, making it clear where it was shifting me to. If one is
transferred 'at one's own request', one can find oneself editing
pamphlets or compiling the first draft of the definitive official history.
I knew, of course, why it was desired that the request should come
from me. The Afro-Asian countries, aware of British pressure, and
suspicious of it, would be likely to criticize my transfer as a surrender
to the Foreign Office view. The effective answer to this was to
produce my own request for a transfer – or, as it eventually turned
out, my Government's request for my return.[1]

---

[1] My Government's request was made in agreement with me in circumstances
set out later.

To Dr Linner who, in the course of one of my visits to Leopoldville, had asked whether I would like a transfer from Elisabethville,
either to Leopoldville (taking over Khiary's political work) or to
New York (possibly as successor to Wieschhoff), I wrote as follows
on November 8th:

'As I understand it, there are two questions to be decided:
how long I should stay in Katanga and where I am to go then.

'As regards the first question, the important thing seems to be
that my departure should not take place at a time or in a way
which would give Mr Tshombe and his friends the impression
that they had scored a victory or that they had some sort of say,
or veto, on how the UN should be represented here. Such an
impression could only tend to increase their obstinacy and multi-
ply their evasions thus making the UN's task all the more
difficult and prolonged.

'I take it as axiomatic that Tshombe will not negotiate seriously
until he, and above all his friends, are convinced that the balance
of forces is shifting against them. That moment has not yet
arrived and Tshombe has therefore no intention at present of
negotiating seriously. When the balance does shift – and this
moment may now be fairly near – it may be that a fresh representative here might be able to take better advantage of the
changed situation. I may add that even on this point I am not
altogether convinced as I think that when Tshombe feels that he
needs our help as intermediaries with the Central Government
he will not be fussy about the personality with whom he may have
to deal. In spite of the Press campaign, he knows quite well that
there was no element of personal enmity in my dealings with him
and I don't believe he feels any personal enmity towards me.
The "O'Brien must go" idea is mainly a British one and, whereas
it may be expedient and useful to the UN to yield or appear to
yield to their pressure on this matter at the right time, it will be
well in my view to wait before doing so for some real proof of the
goodwill which they profess in relation to Katanga. I have little
doubt that if they wished to apply the necessary pressure they
could get Tshombe to go to Leopoldville. The day after they do
so would be an opportune moment to transfer me from here.

'So much for the timing. As regards the place I would, on consideration, like to go to Leo as political adviser to you (or whatever the title might be, assuming this to be the general idea). This
would be on the understanding that Mr Khiary wishes to devote
much more of his time to his duties as Chief of Civil Operations,

although I know and am very glad of the fact that his great experience and skill will be still available in the political field also.

'As regards New York, if the possibility you mentioned is offered to me I shall take it. I would not, however, wish to go straight from here to New York without a specific assignment nor, in the light of the considerations in the first part of this letter, do I think it desirable that I should be asked to do so.'

I felt there was still work for me to do in Katanga. It is true that, from the point of view of those who relied on persuasion and argument to induce Tshombe to 'see reason',[1] I was no longer, if I ever had been, the ideal man for the post. But I had become convinced that persuasion and argument, in themselves, would never bring the secession to an end. More than ever, at the present moment, the Magnanimous flanked by the Victorious was unlikely to agree to anything beyond 'the spirit of Tananarive'. Any progress he would be willing to make would be a function, not of a UN representative's powers of verbal persuasion, but of a weakening of the objective basis of the secession. And in the situation in North Katanga – to which we shall come in a moment – I saw the best opening now remaining for progress on this method.

It was not of course entirely a matter of cold and abstract calculation. As I was not an IBM machine, personal factors also came in, in the shape of two of the Seven Deadly Sins: Pride and Anger. Pride forbade me to apply for a transfer because that would be accepting defeat. And Anger urged me to carry on the fight against the Independent State of Katanga by any means to hand. Pride and Anger are of course good partners who reinforce each other's arguments. And their arguments are not necessarily always unsound.

The anger was directed not against President Tshombe, or General Muké, but against their backers, and specifically against the British Government, which I saw as principally responsible for the survival of the State of Katanga, with all it represented.

In that view of the British Government's role, there were both subjective and objective factors. Let us face the subjective ones first.

First of all, I knew the British Government was out for my blood. They had no personal feelings about this, but I had. It was my blood. Second, the Anglo-Irish relation is an ambivalent one; a situation like this does not bring to the top the 'love' element in a 'love-hate' attitude. Third – the third is more complex and concerns Hammarskjold.

In these days immediately after Hammarskjold's death, I felt,

[1] As regards 'seeing reason' refer to Glumov's Law (p. 224).

not personal grief but an obscure sense of misunderstanding mingled with, not exactly guilt but uneasiness. I knew that my pressing for renewed action in Elisabethville – following up Rumpunch – my emphasis on urgency, leading to the timing of the action for the morning of his arrival in the Congo, and my failure to avert certain errors in execution, were among the links in the chain that led to his death. Among the other links were two puzzling factors: 'the official version' and the decision to go to Rhodesia. In interpreting the latter, I attributed, I now believe, probably too much import-ance to Lord Lansdowne. British diplomatic pressure, exerted relentlessly, more through Riches than through Lansdowne, was as I have said in the previous chapter, decisive in extorting from Hammarskjold, first the evasive 'official version' and then the decision to fly to meet Tshombe in the land of Tshombe's friends. But such pressure, even reinforced by the ululations of a large part of the British Press, could hardly have had its decisive effect if Hammarskjold himself, with part of his mind and conscience, had not shared the feelings and ideas of those who, in Britain and else-where, were indignant about the action in Katanga. The divergence between what the UN was saying in Elisabethville, and what it was saying in Leopoldville during the early days of Morthor – the diver-gence that produced the stalemate – reflected a divergence on a deeper level. Ultimately this divergence concerned the answer to be given to the question referred to near the beginning of this book: 'Which is preferable, revolution in South Africa or the indefinite continuance of servitude?' The policy which Hammarskjold was pledged to apply – and which, knowing what he was doing, he picked me to apply – implied revolutionary change in Katanga (and Katanga, fundamentally, is South Africa with a thin but expensive black screen). But, when it came to the point Hammarskjold shrank back.

That said, and the subjective factors laid aside, the objective facts of Anglo-Rhodesian interference for the protection of the State of Katanga remain. Welensky's encouragement after Rumpunch, his veiled threats of military intervention, the association of the British Consul in Elisabethville with Welensky's message, the nerve-war of the Consular Corps – with British but without American participa-tion – Dunnett's failure to contact me on the morning of Morthor. Riches's menacing diplomacy in Leopoldville, Kibwe's automatic assumption that the way to resume contact with Tshombe was through the British Consulate, the open toleration and unofficial encouragement given to Tshombe to fly the flag of Katangan independence from the safety of Rhodesian soil, the refusal, under the pretext of a technicality, to permit the transit, through Uganda, of the jet fighters needed by the UN – all this forms, unmistakably, a pattern of political interference by the British Government in support of Tshombe against the United Nations. The British position was not unlike that of Belgium more than a year before – formal refusal to recognize the secession, combined with active local support for it.

For many reasons, then, both good and bad, I stayed on in Katanga until such time as the UN should see fit to recall or transfer me, which I knew it would find a little difficult to do. In view of Afro-Asian attitudes it would be difficult to recall me to New York (or transfer me to Leopoldville) except for an important political post – and an important political post was just what those who most wanted to see the last of me in Katanga did not want to see me fill in New York.

On October 31st, two important visitors joined me at Les Roches.

The first was George Ivan Smith. The 'Ivan' is an Australian remnant of Sullivan and that has always formed a bond. I like Australians generally and this Australian in particular and his arrival at this time was a ray of light. George was a very old UN hand, who had known Hammarskjold well, and was the principal UN expert in Press relations. It was in that capacity he had come, I believe, to see that I made no more 'dreadful statements'. He did this effectively and so nicely that one hardly noticed him doing it. George is tough and wily, with a face like a sunset over a sheep farm; he was a friend of James Stephens, loves poetry both good and bad and recites it with a strange plangency; he has an exuberant sense of humour, both personal and catholic, and he is apt to break, on suitable occasions, into a solo dance of his own design: a sort of shuffling saraband with both hands clasped over his head.

'I'm glad', said my daughter Kathleen to me once when I relented after being cross with her, 'that you finally got over that old seriousness.' A certain amount of old seriousness was in the air in the days after the cease-fire, and George was the man to blow it away.

October 31st was a good day.

My second visitor that day was Máire MacEntee. So great is the impact of the confluence of the political and the personal life that several million people now know that Máire and I loved each other (we still do as a matter of fact) and it was for that reason that I asked her to spend her holidays in Elisabethville and that she had come. Some people have told me since that this was indiscreet on our part and there is no doubt at all that it was. What impressed me about some of the people who most emphasized the indiscretion, however, was the complacency with which they accepted the implication, regarding themselves, that they had never cared enough about anybody or anything to do something indiscreet for the sake of him, her or it.

Máire shares my views and interests, only more so – rather like Mrs Dunnett and Dunnett – and these views and interests were at this moment concerned with Albertville, which George and Máire and myself visited frequently in the first half of November.

The situation in Albertville, and throughout UN garrisoned North Katanga, was a strange one in the days after Morthor. In all these centres the UN had effectively got rid of the foreign officers during Rumpunch and had established complete military predominance during Morthor. In Manono, the gendarmerie had capitulated without firing a shot; in Nyunzu they had fled into the bush, and then fled back again, for fear of the Baluba; finally they had placed themselves under UN protection. Only in Albertville, where there is a sizeable European population, was there fighting. There, on September 17th, a mixed force of gendarmes and Europeans opened fire from the buildings on the hillocks round the UN camp – the hospital, in particular, was turned, Major Padda told us, into 'a pukka fortress'. Sharp fighting followed in which Major Padda, a hawk-nosed Indian cavalryman distinguished himself, capturing with, as he liked to say, his 'lo-onely armoured car', a great number of gendarmerie positions. The gendarmerie then fled and the European population, deprived of any screen, subsided.

Under the cease-fire agreement, the gendarmerie in these places were released from captivity – exchange of prisoners – and got their weapons back. The gendarmerie in Nyunzu, however, did not want their weapons back; they wanted to go home, so we let them go. The inhabitants immediately set up a Balubakat administration, which co-operated very well with the UN (Irish) forces. The flag of the Congo now flew over Nyunzu as well as over Kabalo, and in many smaller places all along the CFL railway line from Kabalo eastwards towards Lake Tanganyika.

In Albertville itself the situation was complicated. The gendarmerie, or some of them, had returned but they and the police were encouraged by Mr Jerkovic – the UN civilian representative, who had succeeded M Béraud, the friend of the railroad – and by Major Padda, to refrain from participation or interference in the political life of the town. The European population were encouraged to do likewise, and they responded positively to this, after a few *adeuxiens* ('bad heads' as Jerkovic used to call them) had been invited to leave. The result of this was that the Balubakat organization, hitherto in practice suppressed, emerged openly. Jerkovic's problem – the solution of which required allowing a little more dust to gather on the resolution of August 9th, 1960 – was to induce the local Conakat to co-operate with the Balubakat in a mixed municipal adminstration which would rally to the Central Government. Jerkovic, a Jugoslav of tremendous presence and persuasiveness, with a head like an idealized Roman Caesar, succeeded in this with the aid of Prosper Mwamba Ilunga. I had gone to Kabalo, where Prosper was, and had asked him to come to Albertville, then still nominally under Katangese control. Gendarmerie and armed police, paid from Tshombe's treasury, were still in Albertville and recently Belgian mercenaries[1] had been there, and had instigated riots in which three members of the Balubakat had been killed. Prosper without hesitation came to Albertville, at the risk of his life, to take over the administration and prevent reprisals.

A letter of Máire's to my son gives a fresher account of the change in Albertville than I could now give. It is dated Tuesday, November 14th:

'My last predicted that before long the Central Government flag would fly over Albertville – it does so now as from yesterday. Manono will be the next and that will leave only Kongolo under the Katangan flag in the North Katanga – I beg its pardon – the loyal province of Lualaba[2]. . . . Everything so far has gone swimmingly but one false step could mean disaster, not to the ultimate outcome, which is certain, but to the morale of the Balubakat and the credit of the UN.[3] To take up where we left off last time – after we left Kabalo, Mwamba Ilunga, as good as his word, flew to Albertville and did a magnificent job of work, rallying the Balubakat, 75 per cent of the population' –

I do not know what the proportion really was. The Belgians said that the Baluba were a minority; Jerkovic said the Cartel, which no doubt comprised other tribes beside Baluba, were about 65 per cent of the population. What was clear enough was that the Balubakat

---

[1] One of these was captured and I visited him in his cell. He was a peaceful farmer in a bush shirt who, when I came in, stood to attention, saluting smartly.

[2] This is not quite correct – Kongolo was the northernmost garrison, but there were still others in north central Katanga.

[3] Máire's order.

here were the only active and enthusiastic political movement in sight among the Africans.

'– and persuading them to abandon hostilities, to trust the UN and the local administration and to work with their Conakat brothers for the good of the community within a united Congo. . . . The truce has been maintained and there is now in Albertville a joint Balubakat-Conakat administration, loyal to the Central Government, while Albertville itself awaits only the arrival of Sendwe from Leopoldville to be instituted the provisional capital of Lualaba.'

Máire goes on to speak of the funeral of the Balubakat members killed in the riots:

'Our connection with the funeral began when Conor, Jerkovic and George, with myself tagging along and expecting to be sent home any minute set out for the native township to try to ensure that there would be no hostile demonstrations in revenge for the lynchings. Halfway up the steep mud road to the houses we met a truck coming down loaded with as ragged and anxious-looking bunch of Africans as I had ever seen. To my astounded amazement these were the party leaders. Jerkovic was out of the car in a flash, shaking hands, throwing his arms round their shoulders, introducing us. "Courage, patience, dignité, mes amis, pas de vengeance." You could feel the cloud of grief and panic and hate dissipating as he spoke. They had in fact been coming to look for him to ask for Indian protection for the funeral. The famous Major Padda of the armoured cars is whistled up and standing there on the muddy road it is arranged. The ragged men with the moth-eaten leopard-skin badges are Monsieur le Président du Cartel, Monsieur le Secrétaire, etc., etc. It is all very friendly and formal and everyone is presented punctiliously to me. . . . I am reminded of political meetings in Dunquin and Dingle (Co. Kerry) after the civil war, with the Blasket Islanders in for the day: same poverty, same strong sense of tradition, same class angle, same language difficulty; someone like Daddy or Ernest Blythe in a city suit explaining that the war is over, no more enmity etc., etc., and the local party bosses and clan chieftains constituting an uneasy liaison between two worlds. . . .

'That afternoon we watched the funeral, intolerably pathetic, file on file of ragged people singing Lumumbist songs and giving the Cartel salute. . . . It was a Catholic service and there were no inflammatory speeches. The Indian officers stood to attention as the truck – the one we had met that morning – trundled past with the bodies, relatives, mostly women, crouched over them in the back. . . .

'On Sunday (November 12th) Mwamba Ilunga (now acting District Commissioner) addressed a meeting of several thousand people on his constant theme, work, co-operation, no reprisals, united Congo. As you know he is a superb figure and he wore his leopard-skin kepi insignia like a field-marshal. The meeting was enthusiastic and orderly, distinguished among other things by a body of women *militantes* marching carrying green branches for all the world like Palm Sunday. . . . I had been learning a little Swahili and could follow some of Mwamba Ilunga's speech which was forceful, simple and repetitive. . . .'

Among the things he repeated most often, I noticed to my surprise, were the words *Roi Baudouin*, which seemed to be greeted with approbation. I had heard, with some scepticism, of the King's popularity among the Africans; a popularity which had been gained, I gathered, by some 'no-colour-bar' displays on earlier visits to the Congo. The popularity gained by this had apparently not been altogether forfeited by the icy and patronizing speech which the same monarch had made on Independence Day. It showed, I thought, that it was not very hard to win the affection and trust of ordinary Congolese, and that it was rather hard altogether to lose these. None the less many Belgians had succeeded in the latter feat by turning to the Congo, on behalf of Europe, faces marked by greed, cunning and contempt.

'Afterwards', the letter goes on, 'the crowd dispersed in good order and went straight home to their villages as they had been instructed and the European community opened their shops again and breathed a sigh of relief.'

The flag of the Republic of the Congo had been hoisted over Albertville.

'The first shadow fell that evening with a report that the ANC (Congolese National Army) advance contingents had taken Bendera, the power-station about fifty miles from Albertville near the Kivu border, vital of course to the town. Conor and Smith with the Commander (Colonel Sathe) fly up at the crack of dawn with the Beaver[1] and one Gurkha bodyguard to investigate.'

Captain Mika of the ANC introduced himself superbly, and in excellent French, when we landed on the little airstrip at Bendera. '*Nous sommes*', he said, '*la mission d'Albertville*'. Part of the mission was crowded around him, a prey, it seemed, to conflicting views as to

---

[1] The four-seater aircraft, not the millionaire Christologist.

how we should most appropriately be received. All of these had strings of hand grenades round their necks and seemed to model themselves, quite successfully, on *les affreux*. George, while I was talking to Captain Mika, located another part of the mission in the bushes on the edge of the airstrip. These were tribal warriors, wearing very elaborate hats – enormous ones and, in some cases, of Parisian elegance, made out of various kinds of skins – and, what was more to the point, they all had arrows trained on us. George, using all his charm, coaxed these birds out of their bushes and got them to pose for their photograph. This was the photograph which afterwards appeared in an American news magazine as 'Mr Tshombe's Tribal levies'.

After Captain Mika had produced his credentials, I told him that the UN could not prevent him coming into Albertville, but that, if they were disorderly when they came in, they would be disarmed. I explained that Albertville had already rallied to the Central Government[1] and that the UN was co-operating with the civil representative of the Government in maintaining order – which included the putting down of looting and other forms of brigandage. Captain Mika agreed with all this, but it was clear that *la mission d'Albertville* was in the nature of an armed democracy and he had relatively little influence over its proceedings. There was a young white man there, a Swiss, very pale and tense, who spoke to me rapidly in English. He and his companion, an Italian, had been beaten the previous night when Mika's troops arrived. They were supervising technicians in the power-station and their lives had been saved by their Congolese assistants, who had produced their own Cartel cards, to back their testimony that the two whites were 'not bad, not Belgians'. The Italian was suffering from shock, the Swiss said he was seriously wounded but fortunately he turned out not to be. They wanted to be flown out.

None of us, I think, was sorry to leave Bendera. I was obliged, though, to ask the Danish civilian pilot to go back there to pick up the Swiss and the Italian – we had no room on this flight. The Dane agreed without hesitation. This was just two days after the murder, at Kindu, in Kasai province, of eleven Italian airmen at the hands of an ANC grouping similar to *la mission d'Albertville*.

---

[1] The Central Office of Information publication *Factel* (No. 279) under November 14th, makes the entry of ANC into Albertville precede the setting up of a Balubakat administration. The truth is the reverse. A left-wing Belgian writer, M Merlier, falls into a similar error: 'The soldiers of Stanleyville preceded by an enormous peasant army took Albertville on November 1st'. (*Le Congo* etc., p. 350.)

After returning to Elisabethville I received a telegram from Colonel Sathe to say that *la mission* had arrived and had started looting. The last instruction I gave, in Katanga, jointly with Raja, on November 15th, was for the disarming and punishment of offenders. As for poor Mika, a well-intentioned man (who had intervened to protect the whites in Bendera and get them medical attention), he later had to seek UN protection from his own men.

When UN forces first came to the Congo in July 1960, to bring their undefined military assistance, General Alexander of Ghana urged that the Congolese armed forces, their discipline having broken down, should be disarmed and retrained. The Congolese National Army – the old *Force Publique*, which had been used by the Belgians in various parts of the Congo for work similar to that of Tshombe's gendarmerie in North Katanga – had been officered entirely by Belgians and its commander, General Janssens, apparently had felt that it would serve to continue the realities of the old Belgian Congo, within a Republic of the Congo whose independence, as a Belgian Catholic writer had said, had never been intended to be anything but 'purely fictitious and nominal'.[1] This is what the General meant by his celebrated equation: 'Before Independence = After Independence'.

Lumumba, understandably enough, resisted this concept. Mutinies – some of which may have been artifically stimulated by those in Elisabethville, Bakwanga and elsewhere who stood to gain by them – broke out in a few places and General Janssens and his officers departed with remarkable celerity. The Army, now entirely deprived of trained officers, became an anarchic force, torn between factions, a helpless prey to demagogues and *agents provocateurs* of all stripes, backed by foreign and financial intrigue. Some of its groupings went unpaid, and lived by looting, others became the legionaries of whatever military adventurer could raise the money – inevitably from abroad – to pay them. These were the forces which General Alexander proposed to disarm. Subsequent developments suggest that General Alexander was right. His advice, however, was not taken and the UN and the unfortunate Congolese had at this time the worst of both worlds. The UN seemed at this point (November) to have accepted the doctrines that it could not itself allow its forces to be used to end the secession of Katanga by force, but that it could not prevent the forces of the Central Government from doing so. This meant that sizeable and undisciplined Congolese forces, owing nominal allegiance to the

[1] M Staelens in *La Relève*, August 27th, 1960.

Central Government, were drifting around the Katangese borders, in Kasai and Kivu, nominally carrying on a great patriotic war, and actually pillaging. The standing pretext for the existence of the disorderly troops was the secession of Katanga, and, conversely, the standing pretext for the secession of Katanga was the existence of the disorderly troops. 'Save us from the disorder of the rest of the Congo' was the cry of the people who, by setting up the State of Katanga, provided an unfailing spring of disorder in the rest of the Congo. The mere existence of the State of Katanga had a tendency to do this, but elements in the State also actively fomented trouble beyond their border. Radio Katanga's broadcasts, diplomatic mischief-making through Brazzaville, and the régime's equivocal relations with General Mobutu all had this effect.

In this situation the UN, perhaps inevitably, had been hesitant. The West was saying, in diplomatic language, 'Hands off Tshombe' and many Afro-Asians were saying: 'If you won't take action against Tshombe yourself, at least don't prevent the Central Government from doing so.' To obey both these injunctions is an excellent recipe for permanent anarchy in the Congo. In my opinion the right course and ultimately the most tenable both inside the Congo and diplomatically, is a firm hand *both* in ending the secession of Katanga *and* in preventing the entry to it of undisciplined Congolese units. This policy would make possible a 'retraining' programme under which most members of these absurd and dangerous forces – both gendarmerie and ANC – would be paid off, necessarily on generous terms, and a small, well-disciplined force loyal to the Central Government would be built out of the better elements now under arms. This is not likely to be done while the secession of Katanga, and the tensions which it creates, continue.

That is my opinion. The point had now been reached, however, though I did not know it, where my opinion had ceased to have any practical importance in Katanga.

'When we arrived back', Máire's letter goes on, 'Conor was summoned to New York with McKeown for the Security Council debate. He is very pleased as it means he will get a hearing at the highest level.'

Yes, indeed.

There is a good novel, in an Orwellian vein, by David Karp, called *One*. It is set in the remote future, when universal peace has been firmly established, on a psychological basis. Scientists have studied those elements in human character which can lead to subversion, dissension, rebellion and war. There is a great organization devoted to the surveillance of humanity, and to the eradication of such characteristics. The central character is one of the millions employed by the organization to furnish reports on his fellows. The opening of the book finds him setting out for the seat of the organization, having been officially summoned there. He is a cocky fellow and he is confident that he is going to be given some kind of medal for his brilliant reports. In fact his superiors have found, in the tone and language of these reports, the very characteristics – bumptiousness, individualism – against which they are pledged to hold the ramparts of society. The only thing they are in doubt about is whether to liquidate him or give him 'a new personality'. Finally they decide on the latter course. By various horrifying methods, they eradicate his memory and build up a new one in his brain, with a different name, a different job, a different home-town, a different family. He is still required to furnish reports but on new colleagues. At the organization they read the reports very carefully. The first few seem all right but – there it is again! – in the latest report, a touch of the old bumptiousness, conceit about phrase and judgement. There is no doubt about it now: this time he will be liquidated. He is summoned to headquarters. The last scene of the book finds him in the train, content in the conviction that he is about to be awarded some kind of medal.[1]

He is about, you might say, to get a hearing at the highest level.

---

[1] *One*, though grim reading, is basically, unlike *1984*, an optimistic book, for its theme is the indestructibility of human personality.

17

WHO IS MISS MACANDREW?

' "*Jackuse!*" cried *Zola from the
dure. An' they thrun him out.*'
Mr Dooley

A prominent UN personality, a close and longstanding acquaintance of mine, hereinafter called Punp, invited General McKeown to dinner on the night of our arrival, for a discussion of the Congo situation. The other guests were Sir Patrick Dean, Permanent Representative of Great Britain, Mr Charles Ritchie, Permanent Representative of Canada, and Dr Bunche.

'I hope you won't mind my not asking Conor', said Punp to General McKeown, 'but he's not quite the right colour.'

François Mauriac, writing about the deceitful glosses of Parisian society, says that there is only one sure index of one's rating at any given moment and that is the place assigned to one at table. *Seule, la place à table ne trompe pas.*

By this index it appeared that in Punp's opinion I did not rate at all. This was bad, because Punp's opinion was a sound one. As Tshombe was apt to reflect the balance of forces in Elisabethville, so Punp recorded the prevailing wind on the East River. And the wind was blowing from a point somewhere between Mr Charles Ritchie and Sir Patrick Dean.[1]

I turned up my collar.

In the Security Council chamber I sat behind the Secretary-General. Mr Thant had greeted me politely and without comment.

---

[1] Perhaps not necessarily the prevailing wind, but certainly the wind to which I was most exposed.

Dr Bunche's greeting had been friendly but absent-minded. Mr
Narasimhan had told me what a strain he had been under in
September.

M Spaak was addressing the Security Council. M Spaak, in the
flesh, which he is, looks like M Spaak in the photographs, only more
so. I looked at M Spaak and thought of M Muller and M Thyssens
and even of MM de Vos and Michel. I also thought of our well-fed
cat at Les Roches which Francis Nwokedi had christened Spaak
and which used to give us so much innocent pleasure: 'Down, Spaak,
down!' '*Bas les pattes, Spaak!*'

M Spaak, for his part, seemed, at this moment, to have little
feeling for the days when he and I had been, as you might say,
fellow-workers in the same field, making our parallel and over-
lapping collections of *conseillers occultes*. He was talking about me,
but without any touch of nostalgic affection.

M Spaak's speech fell into two parts, easily recognizable by anyone
who has ever had anything to do with speeches. There was the
statesmanlike bit, for the *New York Times* and the 'Life of Spaak',
and there was the bit for the home papers. The bit for the home
papers was about me. There had been a time when M Spaak had
despaired at the task of finding an appropriate epithet for me: I was
l'inqualifiable M O'Brien. His spirits had recovered a little, however,
and he was now fumbling for the *mot juste*.

What interested me about this was not M Spaak's invective,
which I thought rather provincial in style, but what the Secretary-
General was going to say in reply.

The Delegate for Ceylon, a scholarly-looking man whom I took
to be a lama, spoke up in my defence. I thought this very decent of
him. I thought it even more decent when I had had a look at the
text of the Secretary-General's draft reply.

The draft, which Dr Bunche had written and which he showed me,
said nothing specific about me. It said that the Secretary-General
was not going to make any defence of the Secretariat because he
thought it needed none. The Secretariat did make mistakes, it
added, but these mistakes were not caused by a spirit of discrimina-
tion against a particular country (Belgium).

This might, perhaps, I thought, be called a vindication, but it
could hardly be called a ringing vindication. Having brooded over
it for a while, I passed a note to Dr Bunche. The note said that Spaak
had attacked me personally, with the clear implication that I had
exceeded my instructions. By not replying specifically on this point,
the Secretary-General would seem to confirm this. I set down, lest

there be any doubt about it, the instructions which I had received from Khiary.

The note, I thought, rather worried Dr Bunche. He made some changes in the draft, but I could not grasp their purport. In all essentials the draft remained as it had been. At the end of the debate Mr Thant read it out.

Someone – General Rikhye, I believe, but I am not sure – said to me at this time: 'Spaak saved you, you know.' What I had been saved from was not clear. The appropriate comment was made by the Herald in *Murder in the Cathedral*:

> '*There are several opinions as to what he meant*
> *But nobody considers it a happy prognostic.*'

There were other prognostics. One day, as we stood behind the Secretary-General's chair, while interpretation was going on, Dr Bunche asked me, with concern:

'What have you done to Mrs Punp?'

I said I had done nothing to Mrs Punp.

'She is saying some frightful things about you', said Dr Bunche, 'I don't think Punp feels that way.'

I heard some of the 'frightful things' from another source. At a cocktail party, Mrs Punp had expressed the opinion that I was 'a —— crook'. The adjective she chose was one which plays a crucial part in the vocabulary of Mr Brendan Behan, but Brendan uses it in the spirit of broad humanity and charity which distinguishes him, but does not distinguish Mrs Punp.

Mrs Punp's language is of no intrinsic importance. Her significance is solely as a tabloid version of the thought of Punp. If she was, as it were, dancing on my corpse, then Punp must consider I was not looking in very good health. And he is an excellent diagnostician.

I was not looking very well, as a matter of fact, even physically. Whether as a result of the change of climate, from the tropics to winter in New York, or for psychosomatic reasons, I had developed an unsightly sore on my upper lip, which added to my internal absence of hilarity. I felt as I moved through the corridors and in the Delegates Lounge as if someone should be ahead of me ringing a bell, 'Unclean!' 'Unclean!' This would have been to some extent superfluous, for most Western delegates acted as if they had already heard the bell. There were exceptions. My friends on the Netherlands delegation, for example, did not allow political differences to affect social relations. And once, from her seat behind Sir Patrick Dean, at the Security Council, Miss Ann Warburton smiled at me, across the havoc of war. It was a wan little smile, but a real one. Thank you, Ann.

The Security Council passed, on November 24th, its resolution calling for the end of 'secessionist activities illegally carried out by the provincial administration of Katanga' and authorizing the use of force to apprehend mercenaries. This retrospectively validated our Rumpunch action of three months before. Sir Patrick Dean abstained, along with M Bérard of France. On a paragraph-by-paragraph vote, M Bérard alone recorded an abstention on a section deploring violence to UN personnel. As he did this he looked around the room, smiling broadly. Sir Patrick Dean, however, voted for this paragraph, I was glad to see.

I had come out, nominally, for consultations in connection with the Security Council proceedings. I had not been told that I was being replaced in Elisabethville, although I knew that this was, or had been, under consideration. Now that the Council meeting was over I had my passage booked back to Elisabethville and sent on a cable to George Ivan Smith to tell him of my impending arrival. Among the inward cables from the Congo, of which copies came to me on the following day (either November 25th or 26th), was one from Linner to Bunche referring to this cable and expressing incomprehension. I gathered that Dr Linner had not been expecting me back.

Dr Bunche did not clarify the position at this stage, but he did ask me not to leave just yet as I was needed for further consultations about the refugee camp. What I had to say about the camp, in reality, was short and simple. If further action was imminent in Katanga, which would be followed by revolutionary changes, then the refugees should stay, in order to return to their homes after the end of the secession. If no such action or changes were likely in the near future then it would be better to transfer the refugees: the Balubakat to North Katanga, the Kasaians to Bakwanga, the rest to Leopoldville. I spelled out these concepts in detail, at various meetings of the Congo Club – now presided over by Dr Bunche, without the participation of Mr Thant – over the next few days. There were also other discussions, of a political and military character, and while these were important, I did not feel that they were the reason why I was being retained in New York.

Mr Dayal had been recalled for conversations, had been kept on ice, and then left the Secretariat. I was now being kept on ice. I was about to leave the Secretariat.

In a murder, they say, the difficulty is not how to kill the victim but how to dispose of the body.

Administratively I had already been killed. My successor, Brian

Urquhart, whom I knew well and liked, was already in Leopoldville, and went to Elisabethville, and to a most memorable reception, soon to be recorded, on November 28th. But the body, the physical remains of the administratively defunct O'Brien, was still shuffling zombie-like up and down the long corridor of the 38th floor, being 'consulted', rather as the Chinese consult their deceased ancestors.

Fortunately, the problem of the disposal of the body was about to solve itself in a rather dramatic way.

It was, I believe, on the morning of November 27th (it may have been the 28th) that Dr Bunche, after the ceremonies of consultation, called me into his office.

Dr Bunche always looks a little rueful; his face is humorous but harassed. On this occasion he looked a bit more than rueful: he looked sad. The name that flashed across my mind was that of a character in Damon Runyan – Regret, the Horse-player. I like Dr Bunche, as everybody does, and I had the feeling that he did not much care for what, at this point, he had to do.

'Who,' he said, 'is Miss MacAndrew?'

I set him right about the name, which had become garbled in transmission. (Englishmen often have trouble with Irish names.) I told him that I had taken the first steps for a divorce, that Máire and I intended to get married as soon as the divorce was through, and that Máire had come to spend her holiday in Elisabethville on my invitation. When I left Elisabethville, I had thought I should be returning in a few days, and she had stayed to await my return. Since the consultations had become protracted, I had sent her word not to wait for me but to go on home. I did not know whether she had yet left Elisabethville.

Dr Bunche spoke mildly, but somehow definitively:

'I think', he said, 'that you have made a mistake.'

That, for a very short time-being, was all.

It was not until the evening of November 29th that word of 'Senator Dodd's party' reached New York.

We were sitting round the conference table – Dr Bunche, General Rikhye, Mr Gardiner, myself and one or two others. Mr Narasimhan came in with a very long sheet of paper – a telex report.

'This is very bad news,' he said.

He passed the message to Dr Bunche who, as he read it, kept saying 'My God'. Obviously stricken, he passed the report to me.

The report was from Elisabethville. It began by saying that Brian Urquhart, George Ivan Smith and Máire MacEntee of the Irish Foreign Service had set out from Les Roches. . . .

The print did not, as people say it does, swim before my eyes. But there seemed suddenly to be an immense amount of print, almost impassable, and holding somewhere in its core some fact which would have to be found and faced, perhaps death.

It was not as bad as that and – since the news was of injury inflicted on two of my friends – I can only hope they will forgive me, in the circumstances, when I say that my first feeling, on finishing the message was one of overpowering relief.

What had actually happened is best told in Máire's own words:

'After Conor had gone to New York I stayed on in the Villa des Roches expecting him back from day to day; Josie and Paddy (Conor's driver, Private Patrick Wall) were there too. George Ivan Smith, who was acting as Conor's deputy, travelled to and fro between Elisabethville and Leopoldville and brought me news of him. In the afternoon of Tuesday, November 28th, a little after three o'clock – I had just left Les Roches in the car for Mr Kuitenbrouwer's house, on the edge of the refugee camp, where I took Swahili lessons – a UN car piled with luggage passed us on the road from the airport. I thought it was Conor, and Paddy turned back. It was George Ivan Smith and Brian Urquhart. They brought a message from Conor for me to go to Dublin. There had been strong rumours that Brian was to succeed Conor and I was uneasy and depressed. I arranged to take the first plane next morning.

'I had been invited that evening to a cocktail party at the American Consulate "in honour of Senator and Mrs Dodd". I liked the Hoffackers very much and I had accepted. I thought it might be a slightly sticky occasion and that by going I could be of some help to Mrs Hoffacker, who had arrived in Katanga only a few days before. I felt now that I would rather stay at home and pack for the journey. George and Brian persuaded me to change my mind and come with them.

'It was an exceedingly good party. The drawing-rooms of the American Consulate look out on a courtyard shaded with tall trees and while the guests, very elegant and *mondains*, moved about inside under the bright lights, the "Apostles" from the President's Palace up the road gathered in the dark of the courtyard outside to put on a show for the Senator. They danced and sang, swaying and stamping in and out of the shadows, the women wearing their lovely African dresses – richly coloured cottons, elaborately draped – and complicated, knotted turbans. Watching them were the Senator's motor-cycle escort in the bravura uniform of Tshombe's guard. As the evening moved on, guests drifted out to the dancing and

"Apostles" began to infiltrate towards the buffet through the french windows.

'Most of the UN people I knew were at the party as well as everyone else, practically, who played any avowably important part in the life of Elisabethville – some of the less avowably important too. Tshombe and several of his Ministers were pointed out to me and I was introduced to Mr Kimba, "the Minister of Foreign Affairs", who had great charm.

'The UN officers were not in uniform. I imagine that like myself they came to the party solely out of affection and respect for Lew Hoffacker and did not want to make things more difficult for him by the risk of provoking "an incident". Tshombe had made his murderous speech[1] on the Sunday before, just after the news of the Security Council resolution, and there was considerable tension in town. As I was talking to General Raja, a young Indian officer joined us, looking harassed. "You shouldn't have come, Sir; you're being marked". Raja was clearly not pleased. I thought the Indians were rather overplaying the military melodrama and put the whole thing out of my mind.

'We left early. George had another party for the Senator to attend, a dinner this time, given by the Mobiloil representative in Elisabethville. (In fact, as we found out later, this gentleman had to go to Leopoldville on business and a cousin of his wife's was acting host.) I was going to eat in town with Brian Urquhart and Fitzhugh Greene of the US Information Service, who was covering the Senator's tour. We all got into a UN car, driven by Paddy Wall, intending to drop George first.

'The Mobiloil house is only a few doors away from the suburban residence of General Muké, Commander of the Katangese forces. Paddy knew this was not a healthy area for UN personnel, but his opinion wasn't asked and he didn't volunteer it. As we turned into the avenue, we saw a military truck parked at the side of the road with some soldiers in it and heard them shout, 'ONU! ONU!' We drew up at the gate of the Mobiloil house a few yards farther on and were immediately surrounded by a sullen, aggressive crowd of Africans in camouflage uniforms, very heavily armed. Someone said they were "paras".

'They asked for documents. Through the window of the car Paddy handed his UN pass. The man who took it flung it down in the roadway and stamped on it. I heard George Ivan Smith say,

---

[1] This was the speech in which he threatened to resist implementation of the new Security Council resolution, using pangas and bows and arrows.

"Easy, Paddy" and saw Paddy visibly control himself. Then he got quietly out of the car, picked up his pass, put it in his pocket and stood still in the middle of the road with the "paras" all round him.

'Meanwhile the Senator's hosts had heard the commotion and three or four gentlemen came out of the house. One of them, a big man, had short reddish hair, almost a crew cut, and a bow tie; I had seen him at the American party. They expostulated with the "paras", who were, it appeared, General Muké's guard. They explained about the dinner-party, that Senator Dodd was "the friend of Katanga", that even President Tshombe might turn up. The "paras" were not impressed, but, reasonable according to their lights, they agreed that their NCO would go with us into the house and telephone Minister Kimba for confirmation that we were there in good faith. At first they wanted to hold Paddy as a hostage but finally gave way on that and let him come with us.

'As I remember it, the house had a fairly large hall opening into a very large room with french windows, the two rooms forming an L so that not all the drawing-room could be seen from the hall. Perhaps a dozen people were already there, among whom I recognized Mr Dunnett. The Hoffackers and the Senator had not yet arrived. The telephone was on a low table to the left of the hall door; people busied themselves getting Kimba. George went on into the drawing-room as an invited guest and Fitzhugh Greene – as a good USIS-man alert for copy? – did likewise. Brian stayed with the group at the telephone and sat, I think, on a low chair near the table. Myself and Paddy sat on a bench opposite the door, feeling a little awkward. The lady of the house came very kindly and offered us drinks.

'The telephoners contacted Kimba and handed the phone to the "para" corporal (?) who was actually in conversation with him when the action, so to speak, suddenly speeded up. The hall door burst open and six or eight "paras" exploded into the room, fantastically over-excited and brandishing lethal weapons, sub-machine-guns, I think, which they seemed to be constantly loading and unloading, as if to make it quite clear that they really had ammunition. Someone tried to explain about Kimba. The first man in screamed "*Je me fous de Kimba*" and snatching the phone from his fellow-soldier, dashed it to the floor. I think at the same time a similar group had come through the french windows in the drawing-room, out of sight of the hall, and gone for George Ivan Smith.

'By now Paddy and I were on our feet. I could see Brian Urquhart, his face unrecognizable, covered with blood. In the confusion, I had moments of not being sure even that it was Brian and thought, irrationally, that it might be Fitzhugh Greene, although I knew him to be in the other room. Paddy had seen the blow; the "para" had got Brian on the nose with his skull as he got up from the chair. He seemed to stand swaying as we moved across to him and then to collapse back again. He was saying firmly and politely, "*Il y a erreur, Messieurs, il y a erreur*". I stood in front of him; the telephoners had been dispersed. I have never spoken French in my life with such an urgency of conviction as I did to those "paras". I called them "*mes enfants*"; I even touched one boy on the cheek. I said this was not the way to treat a visitor, that they had hurt the poor gentleman and that soldiers should be ashamed to behave like this. I said, "*Soyez gentils*" – "Be nice". I had the impression that under their bluster they were frightened and disconcerted. I was certain that if I could only keep on talking I could win. They weren't used to breaking into Belgian houses; they *were* used to doing as they were told by French-speaking ladies. They were like children, who, having begun to stone a cat, are unable to stop and yet half hoping to be prevented. Paddy stood beside me and held them off; he put aside the barrels of the sten-guns with his arm as they came at us and they didn't persist. I seemed to be thinking on several different levels simultaneously: "Perhaps I am only making things worse" – the classical argument against interference, especially by women – but I knew I wasn't; "Here goes our hope of a quiet divorce" – and I knew that that was for sure; "I don't think I could bear it if they smashed my face with one of those things" and I was so frightened that fear was a new dimension, but I kept on talking. Brian's head had fallen forward against my hip from behind and the back of my right arm, all the way down, was covered with blood.

'And in the moment I thought that I might have persuaded them, the worst happened. A third wave crashed in, older and somehow darker men with faces carved in deep wrinkles like gashes, grim, tough and experienced – not at all children. One of them hit me across the face. Paddy and I were simply thrown bodily aside, poor Brian was yanked from his chair and, as he was thrust out the door, George Ivan Smith, heels dug in and fighting every inch, was forced past us from the drawing-room with another battered figure through the door into the garden on a wave of "paras". I saw Fitzhugh Greene, volubly protesting, but unharmed, swept out with them – and that was strange because in some way I had thought at intervals that he was the man behind me.

'Someone shut the door and stood against it. A terrible despair, such as I hope never to feel again, flooded over me. I was quite certain I would never see George and Brian alive any more. They would be killed in spite of my trying so hard, perhaps because of it, and I was so desperately tired. My friend with the crew-cut said, "This is your fault; they were trying to protect you." Indignation flared in me. I can't remember exactly what I said, but I got my own back. I held out the white skirt of my dress: the front was clean, the back heavily stained with blood, where Brian's head had been. I indicated with some force that what protecting there had been, had been done by me. Mr Dunnett was standing in the entrance to the drawing-room. Paddy was insisting on being allowed to use the phone to call headquarters. Someone said, "If your Indian friends get here we'll all be killed." I heard Paddy saying, "If they don't Mr Smith will be killed." Someone reported that the "para" truck had driven off, accompanied by a big car at high speed. Paddy got Indian headquarters and gave the alarm. I also spoke to them. We both had the same impression: the Indians thought it was a joke – in poor taste. It would be hard to blame them.

'The lady of the house was having hysterics, "I will not sleep another night here with those savages loose. *Franchement je préfère l'ONU!*" Paddy said, "It's no good waiting here. I'll try to get to the civilian mess and come back with an armoured car." He went out over the back-garden wall and did just that – only he didn't wait for the armoured car, but came back immediately with a civilian driver and a machine-gun in a Volkswagen, having run the whole distance to the civilian mess where they thought at first he was drunk. Meanwhile the dinner guests were telephoning broadcast: the police – "they would come if we sent a car"; Muké – "if the animal could talk any known language".

'A neighbour came in through the garden. He had the strange detachment of people who are no longer shocked by violence. His wife would take the children, it might be safer. All was quiet now outside, he reported; the UN car had been driven off by a white man, *"un blanc"*. A frightened teenager and a sleepy little girl, wrapped in a blanket, were brought downstairs and handed over. *"Proteste pas, mais fous-le-camp, que je te dis."* We sat and looked at each other. There was a phone-call for Mr Dunnett. Rather grudgingly he told us that George and the Belgian banker, the second captive I had seen carried out, were safe in the US Consulate. There was no news of Brian. Mr Dunnett did not say at the time that it was George himself on the phone asking for me –

perhaps it did not seem important. The front door opened; it was Paddy and the UN driver. I have never been so glad to see anyone in my life.

'The story of George's rescue has been told elsewhere, but I would like to set it down here now as I heard it from him in the small hours of that morning. It is a heart-warming story to tell.

'The "paras" had got the three men on to the truck and had ordered them to lie down. Brian and the Belgian banker did so and were savagely bludgeoned. Perhaps it was some atavistic stubbornness which made George an enemy to lying down to be beaten, perhaps it was his Australian upbringing. He got his back against the cab of the truck and fought them off with his feet. A glare of headlights and a roar of motor-cycle engines and the US Consulate car with its superb escort of Katangese Keystone Cops swept up behind them. Mrs Dodd was heard to exclaim, "Why, if it isn't that nice Mr Smith!" and Hoffacker was out of the car hurling "paras" left and right and shouting "Consul Américain!" – I should add that he is a thin, rather lightly-built young man. He got George Ivan Smith off that truck and went back for the banker. He was going back for the third time when the "paras" realized what had hit them and drove off. Crouched on the floor of the big, luxurious car the Senatorial party with its rescued got the hell out of there. So quickly was it all over, that in the house we did not know it had happened. All we knew was that an unidentified car had driven rapidly away. I never heard what became of the escort.

'At about four o'clock that morning, Brian was released from Camp Massart where he had been held. The negotiations and operations which led up to this are a matter of record and I will not try to re-tell them. Nor will I attempt any interpretation of the night's happenings. I will only add a picture of George Ivan Smith with his face swollen and holding his cracked ribs together with both hands, directing, advising, restraining, imperturbably at the centre of everything until the very moment he fell asleep exhausted, and of Brian being brought into Indian HQ and saying wryly, "A pity it wasn't some other fellow – if they'd killed me what a magnificent *casus belli!*"

'When we got back to Les Roches I couldn't sleep. It was about six in the morning and I sat on the verandah listening to the Ghurka guard going about their breakfast. Banza, one of the Baluba servants, who arrived on his bicycle imperturbably every morning, came up to me. "Mademoiselle," he said, "there is a dead Indian on the road near Tshombe's Palace." Quite cheerfully he went back with the Gurkhas to show them where. When they got there the body was gone, but there is little doubt that it was the murdered Gurkha driver.

'Later that day I flew in a UN plane to Leopoldville. The Cuban pilot landed too steeply and snapped the blade of the propellor sharp across. It seemed quite an everyday occurrence to me by this time.'

When I had finished reading the dispatch, which Dr Bunche had passed to me, I got off a telegram to Máire to tell her to get out of Katanga immediately.

At the end of the meeting Dr Bunche took me aside and asked me to see to it that Máire left Katanga without delay.

I told him of the telegram I had sent, and added that I had sent it because of concern for her personal safety.

Dr Bunche seemed a little surprised about the 'personal safety' but quickly agreed. He is by nature a humane man and it is symptomatic of the rather thin air on the 38th floor that the personal impact which such a dispatch might be presumed to make on me does not seem, at first, to have occurred to him. When it did he was, as one would expect, sympathetic.

On the following day – with the Elisabethville story now in the papers – he called me into his office again. Mr Thant had been talking to him about 'this business'. He seemed upset. Dr Bunche did not know just how upset. He would have known with Dag. Dag would have gone through the roof. But with this new man it was hard to tell.

That was all, for the moment.

Very shortly after this – not more than an hour I believe – Mr Aiken, who was in New York for the Assembly session, asked me to come and see him in his room at the San Carlos Hotel.

Mr Thant, he said, had been in touch with him, through Dr Bunche, about Máire's presence in Elisabethville. Mr Thant had asked him to recall me to the Irish Foreign Service. Mr Thant had indicated that, if Mr Aiken did not do so, he, Mr Thant, would call for my resignation. The reason given was that I had now shown myself to be so indiscreet as to be unsuitable for further service with the United Nations.

Here perhaps I may insert some reflections on the subject of indiscretion from one who is now considered an authority on the subject. I say 'now' because one who, like myself, has worked for twenty years in the Civil Service of a small country, to the rather apathetic satisfaction of his superior officers, can hardly be considered to have been born indiscreet. Some people have indiscretion thrust on them.

The fact is that indiscretion is a function of public attention and public attention, in my case, was a function of politics. Let us assume that my colleagues in ONUC, without exception, possessed the austerity of a Savonarola and the discretion of a Coolidge. But if, *per impossibile*, one of them had committed such an enormity as I had committed, no one would have given a tinker's damn. They would not have rated four lines in the *News of the World*. My case was different. The spotlight was on me and a section of the British Press, in particular, would, on a signal or even without one, give me the full treatment. The mud which they would offer in such profusion would splash over on the United Nations. And any British representative, concerned for the Organization's good name, would be justified in giving warning of this danger. . . .

I found myself in the jaws of a pincer-movement. Sir Patrick Dean's disciplined divisions had long been doggedly pressing on my right flank and now, on the left, over the brow of the hill, I could hear the noisy vanguard of Lord Beaverbrook's uncouth but formidable columns.

What to do?

I had often quoted with approval Joseph Biggar's pithy saying: 'Never resign, Misther, get yerself fired!' Reluctantly I realized that this was not the moment for a rugged Biggar stand. I had failed to take a hint before – that of applying for a transfer – and it had now come to much more than a hint. Something told me that if I tried, at this moment, to make a stand, people might start getting rough. The thing to do now was to extricate myself with all speed, and with the honours of war, from the Dean-Beaverbrook convergence. That meant pulling out of the United Nations, quickly, and coming to rest, at least for a time, on the firm and friendly ground of my own country's service. Operation Antaeus.

I said that in that case, Mr Aiken, if he agreed, had better ask for me back. Mr Aiken was very upset. His attitude towards Máire and myself is paternal – that is to say, affectionate and a shade testy – and, in his undemonstrative and sincere way, he wanted to help. I gave him a letter asking him to ask for my return, and he sent off one, as requested, to Mr Thant. Both letters were, as is usual on these occasions, distinguished for their decorum rather than for their candour. Mr Thant, replying in the same spirit, agreed to my release. He also said some kind words about the devotion, ability and courage with which I had served the UN in Katanga. The honours of war, at any rate, were safe.

I saw Dr Bunche, to say good-bye, shortly after Mr Thant's *congé*. Dr Bunche was friendly and more relaxed than he had been before. He seemed to be sorry about the way the break had come, but indicated that my position had become, in any case, untenable, as a result of the uncompromising British attitude towards me.

What had happened to me fell, I think, under the head of what is known as expendability. This is quite a rational doctrine. It asserts that what is sacred are the principles and purposes of the organization; the men who serve it are expendable. Thus, in my case, the objectives of the UN regarding Katanga remained the same. In attempting to reach these objectives I had aroused the hostility of one major power, Britain, whose co-operation was very desirable for the attainment of these same objectives in the future. It became therefore necessary to get me out of the way. As I failed to take a gentle hint, the hint had to be repeated, less gently.

Il faut faire de la politique, as Mahmoud used to say.

Whatever about the logic of expendability, whose beauty is less clear to the expended than to the expender, I remained strongly in favour of the objectives of the United Nations and especially of ending the 'secessionist activities illegally carried out by the provincial administration of Katanga . . . aided by foreign resources and mercenaries'. (Resolution of November 24th.)

I remained unconvinced by the theory that this end was most likely to be achieved by patiently seeking the co-operation of the British Government, and quietly sand-bagging such officials as were indiscreet enough to incur its displeasure. To me it seemed that a more promising line to explore would be that of publicly exposing the British Government's support for Tshombe. I knew that they would deny that they supported him, but I felt that, in the course of my accusations and their denials, 'support for Tshombe' would come to seem a little more heinous, and therefore a little more difficult, than it had been up to now.

This, I thought, would be objectively a useful activity, and it was also subjectively a congenial one. Those old *conseillers occultes*, Pride and Anger, had a share in my decision and I do not, in retrospect, feel that they gave me bad advice.

One cannot, as a member of the foreign service of a small and friendly country, go round publicly denouncing the British Government. To permit oneself that luxury one has to become a private citizen. This I now determined to do.

I rang up Máire on the evening of December 1st in Dublin to tell her that the news of my recall, which had just then reached Dublin, would soon be followed by the news of my resignation. I had prepared a resignation statement.

'That's fine,' said Máire, 'I resigned this morning.'

Máire, on her return, had learned from her father that the Secretariat had officially raised the question of her presence in Elisabethville. Being a woman of spirit she promptly resigned. At the moment of her resignation, she did not know of my recall.

On the morning of the following day, which was a Saturday, I sent Mr Aiken my resignation. I expressed my profound and sincere regret for this break in a long and happy association; I told him that I was making the step irrevocable – he would not, I knew, have been likely to accept my resignation otherwise – by sending at the same time a statement, of a political and controversial character, to the Press. I gave the *New York Times* my statement on Saturday morning, December 2nd.[1]

At London Airport, on his way back to the Congo, General McKeown endorsed my statement. So did Mr Nehru in the Indian Parliament.

The line of official British comment on my departure was that I had been an obstacle to conciliation and negotiation and that the way now lay open for a peaceful settlement. Three days later, on December 5th, the second round of fighting between UN and Katangan forces started in Elisabethville. On December 8th the British Government announced 'conditional agreement' to supply 'a small number' of bombs for use by UN aircraft. On December 10th, Sir Roy Welensky attacked the decision about the bombs, and on the following day the British Government returned to what was for me a more familiar posture by expressing 'concern at the UN attacks on non-military targets and at certain reported statements by UN officials in the Congo about the objectives of the UN operation'. It added that it was not, after all, providing the bombs, pending 'clarification'. On December 13th, it made a 'formal request to the UN for cease-fire in Katanga in order to bring to an end the fighting [*sic*] and thereby create the conditions in which, as a united Congo, a peaceful and just basis for co-operation might be negotiated'. On December 14th, the cease-fire took place and Mr Tshombe flew to Kitona with the US Ambassador to meet Mr Adoula.

My 'UN case history' is now over and I leave the reader to draw

---

[1] The text of this statement is in Appendix III. It appeared in the *New York Times* and also – slightly garbled in cabling – in *The Observer* on December 3rd, 1961.

his own conclusions from it. As I write, the Congo crisis is not yet finished, and I shall make no predictions about its evolution. See Chapter VI: 'A Turn for the Better'.

Máire and I were married in New York on January 9th. After our honeymoon in Trinidad I settled down to write this book.

I shall leave the last word with Dr Luce. I had the pleasure and the privilege, shortly after the events here narrated, of sitting beside Dr Luce at a term dinner in Trinity College, Dublin. He is the great authority on Berkeley's philosophy, and a highly respected senior figure in Trinity.

'What shall we talk about', he asked me kindly, 'and what shall we not talk about?'

We talked about the Venerable Bede, and then about the Albigensian Crusade. We did not talk about contemporary politics.

Dr Luce asked me whether I was writing a book.

I said I was.

What would the book be about? asked Dr Luce.

I said well, the Congo, mainly.

Dr Luce sipped his claret. I could see that he was trying to place the Congo in the perspective of the history of human thought.

He turned on me the benevolent but disconcerting scrutiny of his pale, luminous eyes.

'The Congo?' he said. 'Is there a book in that, do you think?'

APPENDIX I

RESOLUTIONS ON THE CONGO ADOPTED
BY THE SECURITY COUNCIL AND GENERAL ASSEMBLY

1. RESOLUTION ADOPTED BY THE SECURITY COUNCIL ON JULY 14TH (S/4387)

The Security Council,

Considering the report of the Secretary-General on a request for United Nations action in relation to the Republic of the Congo,

Considering the request for military assistance addressed to the Secretary-General by the President and the Prime Minister of the Republic of the Congo (document S/4382),

1. *Calls upon* the Government of Belgium to withdraw their troops from the territory of the Republic of the Congo;

2. *Decides* to authorize the Secretary-General to take the necessary steps, in consultation with the Government of the Republic of the Congo, to provide the Government with such military assistance, as may be necessary, until, through the efforts of the Congolese Government with the technical assistance of the United Nations, the national security forces may be able, in the opinion of the Government, to meet fully their tasks;

3. *Requests* the Secretary-General to report to the Security Council as appropriate.

This resolution was adopted by eight votes (Argentina, Ceylon, Ecuador, Italy, Poland, Tunisia, USSR, and United States) to nil, with three abstentions (China, France and the United Kingdom).

2. RESOLUTION ADOPTED BY THE SECURITY COUNCIL ON JULY 22ND (S/4405)

The Security Council,

Having considered the first report by the Secretary-General on the implementation of Security Council resolution S/4387 of July 14th, 1960 (document S/4389),

Appreciating the work of the Secretary-General and the support so readily and so speedily given to him by all Member States invited by him to give assistance,

Noting that as stated by the Secretary-General the arrival of the troops of the United Nations force in Leopoldville has already had a salutary effect,

Recognizing that an urgent need still exists to continue and to increase such efforts,

Considering that the complete restoration of law and order in the Republic of the Congo would effectively contribute to the maintenance of international peace and security,

Recognizing that the Security Council recommended the admission of the Republic of the Congo to membership in the United Nations as a unit,

1. *Calls upon* the Government of Belgium to implement speedily the Security Council resolution of July 14th, 1960, on the withdrawal of their troops and authorizes the Secretary-General to take all necessary action to this effect;

2. *Requests* all States to refrain from any action which might tend to impede the restoration of law and order and the exercise by the Government of Congo of its authority and also to refrain from any action which might undermine the territorial integrity and the political independence of the Republic of the Congo;

3. *Commends* the Secretary-General for the prompt action he has taken to carry out resolution S/4387 of the Security Council and his first report;

4. *Invites* the specialized agencies of the United Nations to render to the Secretary-General such assistance as he may require:

5. *Requests* the Secretary-General to report further to the Security Council as appropriate.

This resolution was adopted unanimously.

3. RESOLUTION ADOPTED BY THE SECURITY COUNCIL ON AUGUST 9TH (S/4426)

The Security Council,

Recalling its resolution of July 22nd, 1960 (S/4405) *inter alia*, calling upon the Government of Belgium to implement speedily the Security Council resolution of July 14th (S/4387) on the withdrawal of their troops and authorizing the Secretary-General to take all necessary action to this effect,

Having noted the second report by the Secretary-General on the implementation of the aforesaid two resolutions and his statement before the Council,

Having considered the statements made by the representatives of Belgium and the Republic of the Congo to this Council at this meeting,

Noting with satisfaction the progress made by the United Nations in carrying out the Security Council resolutions in respect of the territory of the Republic of the Congo other than the Province of Katanga,

Noting however that the United Nations had been prevented from implementing the aforesaid resolutions in the Province of Katanga although it was ready, and in fact attempted, to do so.

Recognizing that the withdrawal of Belgian troops from the Province of Katanga will be a positive contribution to and essential for the proper implementation of the Security Council resolutions,

1. *Confirms* the authority given to the Secretary-General by the Security Council resolutions of July 14th, and July 22nd, 1960, and requests him to

continue to carry out the responsibility placed on him thereby;

2. *Calls upon* the Government of Belgium to withdraw immediately its troops from the Province of Katanga under speedy modalities determined by the Secretary-General and to assist in every possible way the implementation of the Council's resolutions;

3. *Declares* that the entry of the United Nations force into the Province of Katanga is necessary for the full implementation of this resolution;

4. *Reaffirms* that the United Nations force in the Congo, will not be a party to or in any way intervene in or be used to influence the outcome of any internal conflict, constitutional or otherwise;

5. *Calls upon* all Member States, in accordance with Articles 25 and 49 of the Charter, to accept and carry out the decisions of the Security Council and to afford mutual assistance in carrying out measures decided upon by the Security Council;

6. *Requests* the Secretary-General to implement this resolution and to report further to the Security Council as appropriate.

This resolution was adopted by nine votes to nil, with two abstentions (France and Italy).

4. RESOLUTION ADOPTED BY THE SECURITY COUNCIL ON SEPTEMBER 17TH (S/4526)

The Security Council,

Having considered the item on its agenda as contained in document S/Agenda 906,

Taking into account that the lack of unanimity of its permanent members at the 906th meeting of the Security Council has prevented it from exercising its primary responsibility for the maintenance of international peace and security,

Decides to call an emergency special session of the General Assembly as provided in General Assembly resolution 377 A(V) of November 3rd, 1950, in order to make appropriate recommendations.

This resolution was adopted by eight votes to two (Poland, USSR), with one abstention (France).

5. RESOLUTION ADOPTED BY THE FOURTH EMERGENCY SESSION OF THE GENERAL ASSEMBLY ON SEPTEMBER 20TH (A/RES/1474/REV.1. (ES-IV)

The General Assembly,

Having considered the situation in the Republic of the Congo,

Taking note of the resolutions of July 14th and 22nd, and of August 9th, 1960 of the Security Council,

Taking into account the unsatisfactory economic and political conditions that continue in the Republic of the Congo,

Considering that, with a view to preserving the unity, territorial integrity and political independence of the Congo, to protecting and advancing the welfare of its people, and to safeguarding international peace, it is essential for the United Nations to continue to assist the Central Government of the Congo,

1. *Fully supports* the resolutions of July 14th and 22nd, and of August 9th of the Security Council,

2. *Requests* the Secretary-General to continue to take vigorous action in accordance with the terms of the aforesaid resolutions and to assist the Central Government of the Congo in the restoration and maintenance of law and order throughout the territory of the Republic of the Congo and to safeguard its unity, territorial integrity and political independence in the interests of international peace and security;

3. *Appeals* to all Congolese within the Republic of the Congo to seek a speedy solution by peaceful means of all their internal conflicts for the unity and integrity of the Congo, with the assistance, as appropriate, of Asian and African representatives appointed by the Advisory Committee on the Congo, in consultation with the Secretary-General, for the purpose of conciliation;

4. *Appeals* to all Member Governments for urgent voluntary contributions to a United Nations Fund for the Congo to be used under United Nations control and in consultation with the Central Government for the purpose of rendering the fullest possible assistance to achieve the objective mentioned in the preamble;

(5) *Requests*

(*a*) All States to refrain from any action which might tend to impede the restoration of law and order and the exercise by the Government of the Republic of the Congo of its authority and also to refrain from any action which might undermine the unity, territorial integrity and the political independence of the Republic of the Congo;

(*b*) All Member States, in accordance with Articles 25 and 49 of the Charter, to accept and carry out the decisions of the Security Council and to afford mutual assistance in carrying out measures decided upon by the Security Council;

6. Without prejudice to the sovereign rights of the Republic of the Congo, *calls upon* all States to refrain from the direct and indirect provision of arms or other material of war and military personnel and other assistance for military purposes in the Congo during the temporary period of military assistance through the United Nations, except upon the request of the United Nations through the Secretary-General for carrying out the purposes of this resolution and of the resolutions of July 14th and 22nd and of August 9th, 1960, of the Security Council.

This resolution was adopted by seventy votes to nil, with eleven abstentions (Albania, Bulgaria, Byelorussia, Czechoslovakia, France, Hungary, Poland, Romania, the Ukraine, Union of South Africa and the USSR). Bolivia was absent.

6. Resolution Adopted by the General Assembly (without reference to a Committee) (1592 (XV) on December 20th, 1960)

The General Assembly,

Having considered the item entitled 'The situation in the Republic of the Congo',

Noting that the previous resolutions of the Security Council and the General Assembly on this subject are still in effect,

Decides to keep this item on the agenda of its resumed fifteenth session.

This resolution was adopted unanimously.

7. Resolution Adopted by the General Assembly (on the Report of the Fifth Committee (A/4676) 1583 (XV) on December 20th, 1960)

The General Assembly,

Recalling the Security Council resolutions of July 14th, 1960, [1] of July 22nd, 1960,[2] of August 9th, 1960,[3] and General Assembly resolution 1474 (ES-IV) of September 20th, 1960,

Having considered the report of the Secretary-General on the estimated cost of the United Nations operations in the Congo from July 14th to December 31st, 1960,[4] and the report of the Advisory Committee on Administrative and Budgetary Questions thereon.[5]

Recognizing that the expenses involved in the United Nations operations in the Congo for 1960 constitute 'expenses of the Organization' within the meaning of Article 17, paragraph 2, of the United Nations Charter and that the assessment thereof against Member States creates binding legal obligations on such States to pay their assessed shares,

Recognizing that, in addition to the expenses for the regular and continuing activities of the Organization, the extraordinary expenses arising from the United Nations operations in the Congo will place a severe strain on the limited financial resources of a number of Member States,

Noting with appreciation the willingness of certain Members not to request reimbursement for the cost of air-transport facilities they have provided to move troops and supplies to the Congo,

Noting also with appreciation, that additional financial assistance in a substantial amount has already been pledged voluntarily and will enable a reduction to be made in the level of assessment of those Members having least capacity to pay,

1. *Decides* to establish an *ad hoc* account for the expenses of the United Nations in the Congo;

2. *Approves* the recommendation of the Advisory Committee on Administrative and Budgetary Questions contained in paragraph 18 of its report;

3. *Notes* that the waiver of airlift costs announced by certain Governments

---

[1] S/4387.   [4] A/C, 5/836.
[2] S/4405.   [5] A/4580.
[3] S/4426.

will reduce the level of expenses from the amount of $60 million recommended by the Advisory Committee on Administrative and Budgetary Questions to the amount of $48,500,000;

4. *Decides* that the amount of $48,500,000 shall be apportioned among the Member States on the basis of the regular scale of assessment, subject to the provisions of paragraph 5 below;

5. *Decides further* that the voluntary contributions already announced, in addition to those referred to in paragraph 3 above, shall be applied, at a request of the Member State concerned made prior to March 31st, 1961, to reduce by up to 50 per cent;

(*a*) The assessment that the Member States admitted during the fifteenth session of the General Assembly are required to pay for the financial year 1960 in accordance with Assembly resolution 1552 (XV) of December 18th, 1960:

(*b*) The assessment of all other Member States receiving assistance during 1960 under the Expanded Programme of Technical Assistance, commencing with those States assessed at the minimum percentage of 0·04 per cent and then including, in order, those States assessed at the next highest percentages until the total amount of the voluntary contributions has been fully applied;

6. *Calls upon* the former administering Power of the Republic of the Congo (Leopoldville) to make a substantial contribution, such a contribution to be applied to reduce further proportionally the assessment of Member States affected by the provisions of paragraph 5, sub-paragraphs (*a*) and (*b*) above.

This resolution was adopted by forty-six votes to seventeen with twenty-four abstentions.

8. RESOLUTION ADOPTED BY THE SECURITY COUNCIL ON FEBRUARY 21ST, 1961

A.

The Security Council,

Having considered the situation in the Congo,

Having learned with deep regret the announcement of the killing of the Congolese leaders, Mr Patrice Lumumba, Mr Maurice Mpolo and Mr Joseph Okito,

Deeply concerned at the grave repercussions of these crimes and the danger of widespread civil war and bloodshed in the Congo and the threat to international peace and security,

Noting the report of the Secretary-General's Special Representative (S/4691) dated February 12th, 1961, bringing to light the development of a serious civil war situation and preparations therefor

1. *Urges* that the United Nations take immediately all appropriate measures to prevent the occurrence of civil war in the Congo, including

arrangements for cease-fires, the halting of all military operations, the prevention of clashes and the use of force, if necessary, in the last resort;

2. *Urges* that measures be taken for the immediate withdrawal and evacuation from the Congo of all Belgian and other foreign military and para-military personnel and political advisers not under United Nations command, and mercenaries;

3. *Calls upon* all States to take immediate and energetic measures to prevent the departure of such personnel for the Congo from their territories, and for the denial of transit and other facilities to them;

4. *Decides* that an immediate and impartial investigation be held in order to ascertain the circumstances of the death of. Mr Lumumba and his colleagues and that the perpetrators of these crimes be punished;

5. *Reaffirms* the Security Council resolutions of July 14th, July 22nd and August 9th, 1960, and the General Assembly resolution 1474 (ES-IV) of September 20th, 1960, and reminds all States of their obligation under these resolutions.

B.

The Security Council,

Gravely concerned at the continuing deterioration in the Congo, and the prevalence of conditions which seriously imperil peace and order, and the unity and territorial integrity of the Congo, and threaten international peace and security.

Noting with deep regret and concern the systematic violations of human rights and fundamental freedoms and the general absence of rule of law in the Congo.

Recognizing the imperative necessity of the restoration of parliamentary institutions in the Congo in accordance with the fundamental law of the country, so that the will of the people should be reflected through the freely elected parliament,

Convinced that the solution of the problem of the Congo lies in the hands of the Congolese people themselves without any interference from outside and that there can be no solution without conciliation,

Convinced further that the imposition of any solution, including the formation of any Government not based on genuine conciliation would, far from settling any issues greatly enhance the dangers of conflict within the Congo and threat to international peace and security;

1. *Urges* the convening of the parliament and the taking of necessary protective measures in that connection;

2. *Urges* that Congolese armed units and personnel should be recognized and brought under discipline and control, and arrangements be made on impartial and equitable bases to that end and with a view to the elimination of any possibility of interference by such units and personnel in the political life of the Congo;

3. *Calls upon* all States to extend their full co-operation and assistance and

take such measures as may be necessary on their part, for the implementation of this resolution.

This resolution (S/4722) was adopted by nine votes to nil, with two abstentions (France, USSR).

9. RESOLUTION ADOPTED BY THE SECURITY COUNCIL ON NOVEMBER 24TH, 1961 (S/5002)

The Security Council,

Recalling its resolutions S/4387, S/4405, S/4426 and S/4741,

Recalling further General Assembly resolutions 1474 (ES-IV), 1592 (XV), 1599 (XV), 1600 (XV) and 1601 (XV),

Reaffirming the policies and purposes of the United Nations with respect to the Congo (Leopoldville) as set out in the aforesaid resolutions, namely:

(a) To maintain the territorial integrity and the political independence of the Republic of the Congo;

(b) To assist the Central Government of the Congo in the restoration and maintenance of law and order;

(c) To prevent the occurrence of civil war in the Congo;

(d) To secure the immediate withdrawal and evacuation from the Congo of all foreign military, para-military and advisory personnel not under the United Nations Command, and all mercenaries; and

(e) To render technical assistance,

Welcoming the restoration of the national Parliament of the Congo in accordance with the *Loi fondamentale* and the consequent formation of a Central Government on August 2nd, 1961,

Deploring all armed action in opposition to the authority of the Government of the Republic of the Congo, specifically secessionist activities and armed action now being carried on by the Provincial Administration of Katanga with the aid of external resources and foreign mercenaries, and completely rejecting the claim that Katanga is a 'sovereign independent nation',

Noting with deep regret the recent and past actions of violence against United Nations personnel,

Recognizing the Government of the Republic of the Congo as exclusively responsible for the conduct of the external affairs of the Congo,

Bearing in mind the imperative necessity of speedy and effective action to implement fully the policies and purposes of the United Nations in the Congo to end the unfortunate plight of the Congolese people, necessary both in the interests of world peace and international co-operation, and stability and progress of Africa as a whole.

1. *Strongly deprecates* the secessionist activities illegally carried out by the provincial administration of Katanga, with the aid of external resources and manned by foreign mercenaries;

2. *Further deprecates* the armed action against United Nations forces and personnel in the pursuit of such activities;

3. *Insists* that such activities shall cease forthwith, and *calls* upon all concerned to desist therefrom;

4. *Authorizes* the Secretary-General to take vigorous action, including the use of requisite measure of force, if necessary, for the immediate apprehension, detention pending legal action and/or deportation of all foreign military and para-military personnel and political advisers not under the United Nations Command, and mercenaries as laid down in paragraph A.2 of the Security Council resolution of February 21st, 1961.

5. *Further requests* the Secretary-General to take all necessary measures to prevent the entry or return of such elements under whatever guise and also of arms, equipment or other material in support of such activities;

6. *Requests* all States to refrain from the supply of arms, equipment or other material which could be used for warlike purposes, and to take the necessary measures to prevent their nationals from doing the same, and also to deny transportation and transit facilities for such supplies across their territories, except in accordance with the decisions, policies and purposes of the United Nations;

7. *Calls upon* all Member States to refrain from promoting, condoning, or giving support by acts of omission or commission, directly or indirectly, to activities against the United Nations often resulting in armed hostilities against the United Nations forces and personnel;

8. *Declares* that all secessionist activities against the Republic of the Congo are contrary to the *Loi fondamentale* and Security Council decisions and specifically *demands* that such activities which are now taking place in Katanga shall cease forthwith;

9. *Declares* full and firm support for the Central Government of the Congo, and the determination to assist that Government in accordance with the decisions of the United Nations to maintain law and order and national integrity, to provide technical assistance and to implement those decisions;

10. *Urges* all Member States to lend their support, according to their national procedures, to the Central Government of the Republic of the Congo, in conformity with the Charter and the decisions of the United Nations;

11. *Requests* all Member States to refrain from any action which may directly or indirectly impede the policies and purposes of the United Nations in the Congo and is contrary to its decisions and the general purpose of the Charter.

This resolution was adopted by nine votes to nil, with two abstentions (France, United Kingdom).

APPENDIX II

REPORT OF THE OFFICER-IN-CHARGE OF THE UNITED
NATIONS OPERATION IN THE CONGO TO THE SECRETARY-
GENERAL RELATING TO THE IMPLEMENTATION OF PARA-
GRAPH A.2 OF THE SECURITY COUNCIL RESOLUTION OF
FEBRUARY 21st, 1961

1. Paragraph A.2 of the resolution adopted by the Security Council on
February 21st, 1961:

'*Urges* that measures be taken for the immediate withdrawal and
evacuation from the Congo of all Belgian and other foreign military and
para-military personnel and political advisers not under the United
Nations Command, and mercenaries.'

By far the largest concentration of such personnel, about 500, was to be
found in the Katangese armed forces. Efforts to implement the above
provision, which had to be pursued by way of negotiations in view of the
lack at this stage of legal authority for the UN to take other steps for implementation of the resolution within the Congo, remained for several
months without appreciable results.

2. On August 24th, 1961, the President of the Republic of the Congo,
upon the advice of the Government, enacted Ordonnance No. 70, providing
for the expulsion of all non-Congolese officers and mercenaries serving in
the Katangese forces, not under a contract with the Central Government.
The Prime Minister of the Republic of the Congo requested UN assistance
in the execution of this Ordonnance and in ensuring the evacuation of the
personnel falling under the expulsion decree.[1] These actions gave the UN
legal rights within the Congo corresponding to the terms of the afore-
mentioned resolution.

3. On August 26th, Mr Munongo, Minister of the Interior of the Katanga
provincial Government, announced that the United Nations was planning
to disarm the Katangese armed forces and that 1,500 ANC soldiers in
United Nations planes were on their way to Elisabethville to occupy
Katanga. This announcement and similar false rumours created an atmosphere of tension notwithstanding the fact that they were immediately denied
by the United Nations. The UN was therefore compelled to take security

---

[1] See Annex I.

340

precautions when, on the morning of August 28th, it proceeded to take measures for evacuating foreign military personnel and mercenaries. It placed a surveillance on Radio Katanga, on gendarmerie headquarters and on other key points and installations in the city of Elisabethville. During the few hours that this surveillance lasted, the radio continued to broadcast normally, with the sole exception that no statements of an inflammatory nature, likely to lead to an incitement to civil or tribal disturbances in violation of paragraph A.1 of the Security Council resolution of February 21st, were permitted. Moreover an appeal was made to the Katangese gendarmerie to co-operate and to the Katangese population to maintain calm and proceed with their normal occupations. No resistance was encountered from the Katangese armed forces or police in the execution of the evacuation measures, and life continued normally throughout Katanga.

4. Mr Tshombe was informed by the UN representative of the objectives of the United Nations action. At noon of August 28th, Mr Tshombe stated in a broadcast that his Government had approved of the evacuation of foreign military personnel and had terminated the services of all foreigners in the Katangese armed forces effective that day.[1]

5. In the morning and again in the afternoon of August 28th, UN representatives met with the Elisabethville Consular Corps at their request to discuss repatriation procedures. The Belgian Consul, who presided over these meetings, stated that by arrangement with his colleagues he would undertake the responsibility for ensuring the surrender and repatriation and travel of all personnel required to be evacuated, irrespective of their nationality. He introduced two senior officers who had served in the Katanga gendarmerie and who were to assist the United Nations in arranging an orderly withdrawal of all foreign personnel who served in the Katangese armed forces. The United Nations agreed to this evacuation procedure on condition that the evacuation would not thereby be delayed and that the United Nations retained the exclusive authority to decide who should be evacuated and when. On this understanding the United Nations refrained from continuing to search for and apprehend foreign military personnel, and permitted about seventy Belgian officers to stay in the Belgian Consulate building in Elisabethville until transport for them became available.

6. Unfortunately, these arrangements were not scrupulously observed. Only the officers already stationed in the Belgian Consulate building and officers of the Belgian Army placed at the disposal of Katanga by the Belgian Government were dealt with under this procedure, and even in the case of these officers delays or administrative exemptions were proposed. The foreign officers and mercenaries, profiting from this relaxation of evacuation measures, re-infiltrated into the gendarmerie, and there were indications that they began distributing arms to certain political or ethnic groupings. The foreign elements also began exercising pressure on some Katangese ministers to dissuade them from moving towards political

[1] See Annex II, S/4940/Add. 1, to be distributed shortly.

reconciliation to the authority of the Central Government. Finally, the foreign military personnel, together with the so-called 'ultras' among the non-African residents, exercised an adverse influence on the Katangese Government, inciting them to terroristic actions and violations of fundamental liberties.

7. Thus, the actions of the political police (Sûreté) which must be regarded as falling under paragraph A.2 of the resolution and which is an instrument of Mr Munongo largely directed by foreign officers, combined with the inflammatory propaganda broadcast on Radio Katanga and spreading of rumours, caused panic among the Baluba population, who began to throng into UN camps, asking for protection. The influx of Baluba refugees, who constitute the economically and educationally most advanced part of the African population of Elisabethville, began on August 24th, following the arrest of their spokesman, Mr Bintou, and a few other leaders. By September 9th, the number of refugees had reached 35,000 and created not only a very serious problem for the United Nations which had to protect, feed, shelter and care for them, but also a situation likely to lead to tribal and civil war.

8. Information obtained by the United Nations from various sources established that Mr Munongo and his Sûreté officials had conspired, or were attempting, to carry out attacks on United Nations personnel, military as well as civilian. These reports were to some extent confirmed by the occurrence of inspired demonstrations against the United Nations in the first week of September, which resulted in considerable material loss to the UN and in injury to a number of United Nations personnel.

9. Of a much more dangerous character, however, was the menace to the security of the United Nations personnel and property constituted by the terroristic conspiracies and activities of some of the foreign officers in the Katangese armed forces who had thus escaped evacuation measures. Most prominent among them were a group of officers of French nationality, some of whom were unable to return to their own country because of their implication in the recent revolt by French military elements in Algeria. Another group consisted of soldiers of fortune, while a third group were the so-called 'volunteers' recruited from amongst foreign settlers in the Congo. Information received to the effect that one such group planned to introduce plastic bombs into the building in which the UN offices in Elisabethville were located compelled the United Nations on September 6th, to move its headquarters to one of the military camps. There was also evidence that these officers were organizing a guerilla group among the gendarmerie personnel, that they were maintaining their hold over certain units of the gendarmerie preventing them from co-operating with the UN, and that they organized the attack on the UN garage and the burning of UN vehicles.

10. The day of September 9th was set as the time-limit as of which all foreign military personnel had to report to a United Nations unit for evacuation. By that date, however, only 273 foreign officers and mercenaries

had been repatriated and sixty-five were awaiting repatriation. At least 104 foreign personnel were known to have failed to report or to give any account of themselves.[1] The United Nations representative thereupon called once more on the consuls, asking them to ensure the immediate departure of their nationals, failing which the United Nations would have to resume action for implementing the February 21st resolution by all means at its disposal.

11. On the morning of September 11th, the deputy United Nations representative in Elisabethville was arrested on orders given by a non-Congolese officer of the political police (Sûreté). This was the culmination of a long series of wrongful acts by these officers, including the organization of attacks on the United Nations, repeated threats, and incitements to violence. Moreover, it was impossible to persuade the Baluba refugees to return from the UN camp to their homes as long as they were exposed to threats and arbitrary arrests by, or at the direction of, Sûreté officials. The United Nations therefore requested that all the non-Congolese officers of the Sûreté be evacuated within forty-eight hours.

12. At the instigation of the remaining foreign officers, as well as of the local extremists, heavily armed patrols and guard posts began to be maintained by the gendarmerie at all public buildings and other installations in Elisabethville. The police was reinforced by 300 members of Mr Munongo's Bayake tribe. Arms were also being distributed to individuals and groups who were not properly trained and disciplined to handle them.

13. On September 12th, the 'Foreign Minister of the Katanga Government', Mr Kimba, announced that negotiations had been opened for reinforcing Katangese units with personnel and equipment from Rhodesia.

14. Also on September 12th, UN representatives met with Mr Tshombe and members of his Government in an attempt to obtain a lessening of the tension, a withdrawal or at least reduction of the military elements from the streets in Elisabethville, an end to the inflammatory propaganda, redress of refugee grievances which would permit their return to their homes, and assurance that the evacuation of all personnel falling under paragraph A.2 of the February 21st Security Council resolution would proceed promptly. UN representatives also attempted to persuade the Katanga Government to reconcile their political differences with the Central Government by constitutional means and gave assurances concerning Mr Tshombe's safety if he wished to travel to Leopoldville for discussions. On all these points the answer of the Katangese Government was a negative one; they refused emphatically to permit the evacuation of the foreign officers serving in the Katangese Sûreté.

15. In the early hours of September 13th, the UN forces therefore took security precautions similar to those applied on August 28th, and deemed necessary to prevent inflammatory broadcasts or other threats to the main-

[1] See Annex III, S/4940/Add. 1, to be distributed shortly.

tenance of law and order while the UN resumed carrying out its task of apprehending and evacuating foreign military and para-military personnel. At this point an alert was set since arson was discovered at the UN garage. As the UN troops were proceeding towards the garage premises, fire was opened on them from the building where a number of foreign officers are known to be staying. UN troops were subsequently also resisted and fired at as they were deploying towards key points or while they were guarding installations in the city. UN troops returned fire.

16. While it is yet too early to reconstruct from the incomplete reports the whole story of the events of the day, a report transmitted at noon on September 13th, by the Commander of UN forces in Katanga, Brigadier S. K. Raja, states that the radio station and post office guarded by UN troops were attacked several times and that extensive sniping fire was directed against UN troops and the residence of the UN representative from houses occupied by non-African residents of the city. Non-Congolese officers and mercenaries were observed leading the attacks, directing fire and handling the weapons. On the other hand there is no evidence of any spontaneous or large-scale actions having been taken against the UN by the Congolese personnel of the gendarmerie.

17. Sporadic sniping and occasional bursts from heavier weapons were reported throughout the day and up to the time of writing this report, the Katanga Radio Station was reported substantially damaged by mortar fire directed at it when the UN sought to use it to appeal for calm and cessation of fire. Casualties so far ascertained include one Indian soldier and one Swedish officer killed, six Indian, three Swedish, four Irish and one Norwegian personnel wounded.

18. The UN representative contacted Mr Tshombe and attempted to obtain a cessation of the hostilities as soon as possible. A cease-fire was in fact issued by Mr Tshombe, but was disregarded by the mercenaries involved in the fighting. Throughout the incident, the adjutant of the President, Major Mwamba, assisted the UN headquarters in their efforts to contact responsible authorities who could have used their influence to restore calm.

19. To this end, a meeting was arranged between the UN representative, the United States Consul, Mr Tshombe and other political and military leaders to take place at noon. Mr Tshombe and the Congolese leaders did not come to that meeting, however, and contact between them and the UN representative was not re-established up to the time when this report was being drafted. Mr Kibwe is reported to be in a UN camp.

20. In the afternoon of September 13th, the Central Government of the Republic of the Congo dispatched to Elisabethville a delegation headed by the Commissaire d'Etat for Katanga, Mr E. D. Bocheley, to assist the provincial authorities in the restoration of law and order. The UN dispatched a team of technical experts to help in the restoration of essential utilities and public services.

ANNEX I

Letter dated August 24th, 1961, to the United Nations
Chargé de Mission in the Congo from the Prime Minister
of the Republic of the Congo transmitting the text of
Ordinance No. 70 of the President of the Republic.

I have the honour to refer to my letter No. 001148 of August 22nd, 1961,
by which my Government requested the assistance of the United Nations
in putting an end to the aggressive activities of the Katanga gendarmerie
and in securing the evacuation of the foreign officers and mercenaries serving
in the armed forces of Katanga.

I am taking the liberty of bringing to your attention the text of Ordinance
No. 70-1961 issued today by the Head of the State on the advice of my
Government and ordering the immediate expulsion from the territory of
the Republic of the Congo of all non-Congolese officers and mercenaries
serving in the Katanga forces who have not entered into a contractual
engagement with the Central Government of the Republic of the Congo.

The Government of the Republic of the Congo requests the assistance of
the United Nations in implementing this Ordinance and in securing, in
conformity with paragraph A.2 of the resolution adopted by the Security
Council on February 21st, 1961, and with due respect for considerations of
security, the evacuation of the individuals affected by this expulsion order.

I have the honour to be, etc.

(Signed)
CYRILLE ADOULA.

Ordinance No. 70 of August 24th, 1961, relating to the
expulsion of non-Congolese officers and mercenaries serv-
ing in the Katanga Force.

THE PRESIDENT OF THE REPUBLIC,

Considering the Fundamental Law of May 19th, 1960, in particular its
articles 2, 27 and 219;

Considering the decree of June 4th, 1956, concerning expulsion, local
banishment and prescribed residence;

Considering paragraph A.2 of the resolution adopted by the Security
Council of the United Nations on February 21st, 1961, requesting that
measures should be taken for the withdrawal and immediate evacuation
from the Congo of all military and para-military personnel of Belgian and
other nationalities not forming part of the United Nations Command as well
as of the mercenaries;

Considering the Agreement of Principle dated April 17th, 1961, concerning the implementation of that resolution and concerning the assistance to be rendered by the United Nations in that regard;

Considering that it is necessary and urgent to put an end to the aggressive actions of the Katanga gendarmerie, which are a source of constant suffering to the people and impede the economic rehabilitation of the country;

Considering that these aggressive actions are exclusively attributable to the non-Congolese officers and mercenaries who are commanding and serving in units of the Katanga Forces;

On the proposal of the Ministers of the Interior, of Foreign Affairs and of National Defence;

ORDERS:

Article 1

All non-Congolese officers and mercenaries serving in the Katanga forces who have not entered into a contractual engagement with the Central Government of the Republic of the Congo shall be considered as undesirable aliens who by their presence and their conduct are jeopardizing tranquility and public order in the country.

Article 2

All the non-Congolese officers and mercenaries serving in the Katanga forces who have not entered into a contractual engagement with the Central Government of the Republic of the Congo are expelled from the territory of the Republic of the Congo and must leave Congolese territory forthwith.

Article 3

The Minister of the Interior and the Minister of National Defence shall be responsible for the fulfilment of this ordinance.

LEOPOLDVILLE, *August 24th, 1961.*

By the President of the Republic
JOSEPH KASA-VUBU
CYRILLE ADOULA, *Minister of National Defence*
J. BOMBOKO, *Minister of Foreign Affairs,*
CH. GBENYE, *Minister of the Interior.*

APPENDIX III

The author issued the following statement on December 2nd, 1961, on his departure from the UN and from the Irish Foreign Service.

On December 1st, the acting Secretary-General of the UN acceded to the request of Mr Frank Aiken, the Irish Foreign Minister, to release me from the service of UN in order to return to the Irish Foreign Service, from which I was seconded at the invitation of the late Secretary-General, six months ago. Mr Aiken's move was made at my request.

I had explained to him that, since I was regarded in some quarters as an obstacle to conciliation and negotiation in Katanga, my continued service with the UN would not be helpful to the Organization.

I have now sent to Mr Aiken my resignation from the Irish Foreign Service.

I have done so in order to recover my freedom of speech and action. It is, therefore, now possible for me to be more explicit about the quarters which have come to regard me as an obstacle of conciliation in Katanga; about their reasons for holding that point of view, and about their methods of expressing it.

I went to Katanga in June of this year, my mission being to see to the implementation of the resolution of the Security Council, and specifically of the resolution of February 21st, which called for the immediate withdrawal and evacuation of all foreign military and para-military personnel, including mercenaries and foreign political advisers.

This resolution, though passed in February, had remained a dead letter.

There were more than 500 foreigners serving in the Katanga gendarmerie, including 200 officers of the Belgian regular army. All the key advisory posts in the Katanga service were held by Belgians.

Months of negotiation had failed to modify this situation. My instructions from the late Secretary-General were to effect a break-through and end the situation in which a Security Council resolution was being openly flouted.

When I got down to this task I found myself increasingly exposed, both inside and outside the Organization, to mounting criticism. This criticism

347

came not only from Belgium but from two permanent members of the Security Council, Britain and France.

If either of these countries had frankly opposed the resolution it could not have carried. They did not oppose its passage, but they did most bitterly oppose its implementation.

One form their opposition took, especially after August 28th – the date on which a large number of mercenaries were apprehended and expelled – was a demand for my removal.

After September 13th, when the UN was obliged to take counter-measures against a hate campaign launched by Tshombe with the more or less open support of these same members of the Security Council, the demand for my removal turned into active and heavy pressure.

The British delegation at the UN was particularly active in this respect and not unduly fastidious about the methods it employed.

The immediate end pursued and eventually obtained was to make my continued presence in the Organization a burden both to the Secretariat and to myself. The remoter end was to bring home to all servants of the Organization that, whatever resolutions of the Security Council may say, it is unwise to apply them if these Powers do not wish them to be applied.

The point of principle involved here is exceedingly important for the Organization.

The Soviet Union has been accused of excessive use of the veto, that is, of voting against resolutions it does not like.

There is no doubt that excessive use of the veto power by a permanent member of the Security Council is a danger to the Organization, but a danger not less great and much less known is failure by a permanent member to vote against – and thereby veto – resolutions which it is, in fact, radically opposed to. In this way the Organization becomes committed to tasks the fulfilment of which is obstructed by very powerful members of the Organization.

Servants of the Organization trying to carry out these tasks on behalf of the Security Council are squeezed out by members of the Council itself. I am not the first and I am very far from being the most distinguished victim of this process.[1]

My predecessors have usually kept silent, no doubt because they judged silence to be in the best interests of the UN.

I cannot share this view but feel on the contrary that the UN can only

[1] The above statement appeared simultaneously in the *New York Times* and in *The Observer* (London) on December 3rd, 1961. Unfortunately, the version which appeared in *The Observer* was somewhat garbled in transatlantic transmission and the word 'plot', which was not used by me, appeared (p. 115) instead of the word 'process' (which I had used and which was carried by the *New York Times*).

gain by having public attention brought to bear on the real source of many of its present troubles in the Congo.

This is not the place for a detailed narration or discussion, but one point is worth making. On November 24th, the Security Council passed a resolution which was even stronger than that of February as regards Katanga. Britain and France once more[1] abstained.

If my resignation and consequent publicity make it even a little harder for these members of the Council to obstruct the implementation of the Council's new resolution also, thereby wrecking the UN operation in the Congo, then my resignation will have been worth while.

In conclusion, as M Spaak has said some hard things about me, I have pleasure in saying something nice about M Spaak. M Spaak's country openly opposed the resolution and M Spaak openly attacked me at the Security Council for applying it. M Spaak, therefore, has the distinction of having acted in this matter with candour, consistency and honour.

---

[1] I was wrong in assuming that the British Delegation had merely abstained in February. It had actually voted 'in favour'.

BOOKS CONSULTED

TO KATANGA AND BACK is a 'case history', not a treatise based on reading. Such relevant reading as I have done has been part of an effort to situate my own experience in a wider context. Since my reading was neither extensive nor profound, I was in some doubt about including a bibliography at all. The main reason why I decided to do so was that the Belgian literature about the Congo – especially the unofficial Belgian literature – does not seem to be as widely known in English-speaking countries as it deserves to be.

The standard work on the early period of European exploitation of the resources of Katanga is René J. Cornet's *Katanga* (Brussels, 1944). The works of the admirable English missionaries to M'Siri's court – notably Daniel Crawford's *Thinking Black* (1912) and F. S. Arnot's *Bihé and Garanganze* (1893) – supplement Cornet's work usefully. Joseph A. Moloney's *With Captain Stairs to Katanga* (1893) crisply expresses the outlook of the early prospector-explorers. Comte Louis de Lichtervelde's *Leopold II* (Brussels, 1935), a deferential but informative biography of the most repulsive European monarch of the nineteenth century, is essential for background, although it contains little specific about Katanga. Ruth Slade's *King Leopold's Congo* (1962) – published while this book was going to press – carries an extensive bibliography for this early period.

Baron Pierre van Zuylen's *L'Echiquier Congolais* (Brussels, 1959), a diplomatic history of the Congo question, contains an account (Chapter XIV) of the Anglo-Belgian rivalry over Katanga in 1891. It also contains (Chapter XXIX) a fully-documented account of the Chamberlain Government's March 1938 offer to Hitler of a colony 'in the Congo basin'.

For Belgian policy in the Congo (including Katanga) between the wars, an important source-book is *Etapes et Jalons* (Brussels, 1946), the collected speeches of Governor-General Pierre Ryckmans. These speeches, by one who was regarded as a 'liberal' Governor-General, constitute a classic of Belgian paternalism.

For the period immediately preceding independence, the two-volume *Belgian Congo* (Inforcongo, Brussels, 1959–60) is a useful, though far from candid, presentation in English of the official Belgian theses; the second volume contains valuable basic statistics.

Gaston Derkinderen's *Atlas du Congo Belge et du Ruanda-Urundi* (Brussels, 1955) – a lavishly-illustrated album, rather than an atlas in our usual sense – presents similar theses, with some additional documentation. In a somewhat different category, D. P. Dugauquier's *Congo Cauldron* (London, 1961), is a bitter and – not always consciously – revealing statement of the experience and outlook of a European settler (an English woman married to a Belgian).

For the crucial ten-day period from the Congo's Independence Day to the Belgian invasion, we are fortunate in having a detailed, well-documented and candid study; Jules Chomé's *La Crise Congolaise* (Brussels, 1960) which ought, but does not seem, to be required reading for all who write about the problems of the Congo today. Colin Legum's *Congo Disaster* (1961) is a well-balanced and clear account of the sequence of events up to, and a little beyond, the fall of Lumumba. A very recent book, Michel Merlier's *Le Congo de la Colonisation Belge a l'Indépendance* (Paris, 1962) takes the story up, not merely beyond independence (despite its title), but beyond the Katanga-U.N. fighting of December 1961. This book is, however, more interesting on the general background, which the author seems to have studied carefully, than on the recent events with which he is – understandably enough – imperfectly acquainted.

For the 'Independent State of Katanga' and its early struggles, Pierre Davister's *Katanga Enjeu du Monde* (Brussels, 1960) is of great value. Davister belongs to a category rather better represented on the Continent than in Britain: that of candid Conservative writers. This book is a collection of dispatches sent by him from Katanga to the Belgian weekly *Pourquoi Pas*. His point of view is friendly to the Europeans of Katanga and he takes pleasure in their triumphs in maintaining their rule, even against such novel threats as the Republic of the Congo and the United Nations. His second book (with P. Toussaint) *Croisettes et Casques Bleus* (1962) seemed to me less interesting, possibly because the background to the events considered – the Katanga-U.N. encounters of 1961 – was, in part at least, better known to me than to Davister.

As regards one highly important element in the Congo-Katanga situation – the financial background – *Les Trusts au Congo* (Brussels, 1961), by Pierre Joye and Rosine Lewin, is of considerable interest. It is written from a left-wing point of view; I have not been fortunate enough to discover any comparable survey written from a right-wing point of view. The various companies concerned, including the Union Minière, have, however, all produced sumptuous commemorative volumes about those parts of their history on which they like to dwell.

I have already acknowledged, in the introduction, my heavy debt to the Dossiers du CRISP for the *Congo, 1960* and *Congo, 1961*. U.N. documents and newspaper sources which I have used are cited in the footnotes to the text.

As regards the United Nations, I have not relied on any of the many – sometimes excellent – theoretical works about the organization. This was not because I have any inclination to depreciate the value of such works, but because my purpose was to supplement them with a book of a quite different kind: a case history. Two books bearing on the United Nations were, however, of use to me: *Dag Hammarskjold*, by Joseph P. Lash (London, 1962) and *The Mysterious Death of Dag Hammarskjold*, by Arthur Gavshon (New York, 1962). The second book has not (as I write this) yet been published in England. Mr Gavshon is diplomatic correspondent of one of the major news agencies. His detailed day-to-day account of Hammarskjold's last days in Leopoldville is of the greatest interest and importance for students of the United Nations and of the Congo problem.

INDEX

353